Net Neutrality Compendium

Luca Belli • Primavera De Filippi

Editors

Net Neutrality Compendium

Human Rights, Free Competition
and the Future of the Internet

 Springer

Editors
Luca Belli
Center for Technology & Society
Fundação Getúlio Vargas
Rio de Janeiro, Rio de Janeiro, Brazil

Primavera De Filippi
e-Gouv
CERSA / CNRS / Université Paris II
Paris, France

ISBN 978-3-319-26424-0   ISBN 978-3-319-26425-7   (eBook)
DOI 10.1007/978-3-319-26425-7

Library of Congress Control Number: 2015953442

Springer Cham Heidelberg New York Dordrecht London

Printed on acid-free paper

Springer International Publishing AG Switzerland is part of Springer Science+Business Media (www.springer.com)

Preface

Net neutrality is a term that has taken on many apparent meanings and has served to provoke many debates over the past several years. The issues that invoke the use of the term vary depending on geography, economic and business conditions and regulatory environment. A consequence is that the arguments for or against net neutrality may be inconsistent when compared side by side. This year's meeting of the Dynamic Coalition on Network Neutrality is an opportunity to compare notes and observations on the ongoing debate.

In the USA, there is limited competition for provision of broadband Internet access. Historically, the dial-up Internet had many providers (some reports estimated more than 8000 ISPs), but broadband technology tended to be associated with coaxial cable television networks, hybrid fibre/coax, digital subscriber loops on copper (DSL, ADSL, etc.) and fibre to the home (FTTH). The usual providers of these broadband services were traditional telephone companies and television cable companies. Residential subscribers might have a choice of two broadband providers (a telco and a cableco), or perhaps only one of them or, especially in rural areas, no broadband service choice at all.

Alternative access methods including Wireless Internet Service and satellite tended to have limits either with regard to speeds or latency or both. In all cases, the residential services tended to be asymmetric, providing higher speeds in the download direction. In the recent past, some providers, notably Google, have been offering very high capacity in the gigabit per second range in both directions.

After lengthy debates, the American Federal Communications Commission decided to reclassify Internet service as a Title II Telecommunications Service, while forbearing to apply most of the regulations found in that title to the providers of Internet service. This was a controversial decision but understandable, given that court cases disputing the FCC's jurisdiction in the space turned on the earlier decision by the FCC to declare the Internet a vertical information service. The new classification appears to give the FCC authority to respond to potential anticompetitive behaviours by Internet service providers. A risk is that the forbearance might be reverse and a more elaborate regulatory practice might be adopted. Perhaps the most practical outcome would be a new title in an amendment to the Telecommunications Act that would be specific to Internet and suitably constrained.

In other jurisdictions, while the same term, *net neutrality,* is used, the local regulatory conditions may be different. In some countries, broadband services are provided on a wholesale basis to any party that wishes to use the infrastructure to provide residential customers with access to Internet. In the UK, Australia, the Netherlands and New Zealand, variations on this theme have been undertaken with varying results.

There are also debates about quality of service, fueled by the belief that the Internet should be sensitive to application requirements and provide low latency or high bandwidth, depending on the need. Some take the position that there is no need for special controls for quality of service if the absolute capacity of the access is high enough. Others think that users and application providers should be able to obtain the appropriate quality of service needed for specific applications. It is common, however, to argue that the broadband access providers should not be in a position to selectively extract additional rents from the application and content providers, effectively controlling which application can be used or content providers can be reached and used satisfactorily by users—essentially dictating user choice.

It seems important to preserve the notion that the Internet should support what is sometimes called "permissionless innovation"—that is, that innovators of new applications and services should *not* be forced to conclude some kind of contractual agreement *with every Internet access provider in the world* before a service can be offered. One must accept, however, that some services may work poorly or not at all if adequate capacity is not available to support them.

The conundrum in the net neutrality debate is to fashion incentives for access providers to continue to invest in and upgrade service capacity while preserving user choice and provide incentives for new applications to be brought to the Internet and made accessible to all access subscribers without inhibiting new entrants into the marketplace of Internet services by erecting barriers to their entry.

Vinton G. Cerf
Google
Mountain View, California, USA

About the Authors

René Arnold has studied business administration at Heilbronn University and holds a Ph.D. in Consumer Behaviour from the University of Edinburgh. He is head of the Department "Markets and Perspectives" and a frequent invited speaker at various European universities and industry events. With his team, René focuses on demand side issues of electronic communication and Internet-enabled markets. His main research areas include net neutrality, over-the-top (OTT) services, economic platforms and business model analysis. He has been leading projects for both public and private clients. Before he joined WIK-Consult, René was a research analyst with IW Consult, a subsidiary of the Cologne Institute for Economic Research. His main area of investigation was ICT and Internet where he was responsible for various projects from private as well as public contractors.

Luca Belli, Ph.D., is a full researcher at the Center for Technology and Society (CTS) of Fundação Getulio Vargas Law School, Rio de Janeiro, where he leads the Internet Governance Architectures project. Before joining CTS, Luca worked for the Council of Europe Internet Governance Unit, served as a Network Neutrality Expert for the Council of Europe, worked as a consultant for the Internet Society and completed his Ph.D. in public law at Université Panthéon Assas (Paris II). His monograph *"De la gouvernance à la régulation de l'Internet"* is published by Berger-Levrault, Paris. Luca is also the founder and co-chair of the Dynamic Coalition on Network Neutrality of the United Nations Internet Governance Forum (IGF) as well as co-founder and co-chair of the IGF Dynamic Coalition on Platform Responsibility.

Vinton G. Cerf is a computer scientist and widely recognised as one of the "Fathers of the Internet." He was one of the inventors of the Internet architecture and co-designer of the basic protocols (TCP/IP) along with Robert Kahn. He serves as vice president and chief Internet evangelist for Google and his primary responsibility is to identify new enabling technologies to support the development of advanced Internet-based products and services for the company. He is also currently involved in the Interplanetary Internet Project.

Angela Daly is a Postdoctoral Research Fellow in the Swinburne Institute for Social Research (Australia), affiliate of the Swinburne Law School and a research associate (adjunct) at the Tilburg Institute for Law, Technology and Society (Netherlands). Her specialties lie in the interaction between law and new technologies, encompassing a range of areas including privacy, free expression, data protection, intellectual property, and competition and regulation. In March 2016, she will join Queensland University of Technology's Law Faculty as Vice-Chancellor's Research Fellow.

Primavera De Filippi, Ph.D., is a permanent researcher at the CERSA/CNRS/ Université Paris II. She is a faculty associate at the Berkman Center for Internet & Society at Harvard, where she is investigating the concept of governance by design as it relates to distributed online architectures, such as Bitcoin, Ethereum, etc. Primavera holds a Ph.D. from the European University Institute in Florence. She is a member of the Global Agenda Council on the Future of Software & IT Services at the World Economic Forum, as well as the co-chair of the Internet Governance Forum's Dynamic Coalition on Network Neutrality and Platform Responsibility. In addition to her academic research, Primavera acts as a legal expert for Creative Commons and the P2P Foundation.

Benoît Felten is CEO and co-founder of Diffraction Analysis. Benoît Felten is a recognised expert on issues related to next-generation access (NGA). Felten has been the director of Access Network Research at Yankee Group, where he led the company's research efforts in the NGA field. Prior to that, Felten worked for Arcome and for Belgacom France, where he was responsible for their fibre to the office offers.

Maryant Fernández Pérez is the advocacy manager at European Digital Rights, where she focuses on network neutrality, Internet governance and trade and investment agreements.

Nathalia Foditsch is a licenced Brazilian attorney focused on communications policy and regulation. She has worked for the Center of Technology and Society at Getulio Vargas Foundation, for the Communications and Society Programa at the Aspen Institute and for the Broadband Special Programme at the Inter-American Development Bank. Her interest in communications policy and regulation started when she worked for the Brazilian Antitrust Authority (CADE). Foditsch holds a master's in law and a master's in public policy and is currently co-presenter for the course 'Comparative US Brazil Legal and Judicial Systems' at the Washington College of Law (WCL), American University. She is currently a Ph.D. student in Communications at American University, supported by the Google Research Award and advised by Professor Laura DeNardis.

Leonidas Kanellos is a law professor and an attorney at law, practising for more than 25 years regulation of electronic communications and competition law and policy. In 2013 he served as chair of the Body of European Regulators for Electronic Communications (BEREC) and as vice chair in 2011 and 2012. From 2009 to 2013, he served as president of EETT, the independent regulatory authority for the telecom and postal sectors in Greece. Dr. Kanellos has served as a legal expert in numerous international and national committees, such as the Legal Advisory Board of the EU Directorate-General for Information Society and the European Committee for Standardization. He is currently teaching legal and business aspects of the electronic communications market at the University of Piraeus and he has previously taught at the University of the Aegean. He has authored numerous monographs, articles and contribution to books and studies related to the Information Society. He is a graduate of the National and Kapodistrian University of Athens and the University of Montpellier, France.

Roslyn Layton is visiting fellow at AEI's Center for Internet, Communications, and Technology Policy, and studies Internet economics at the Center for Communication, Media, and Information Technologies (CMI) at Aalborg University in Copenhagen, Denmark. Layton has a background in the information technology (IT) industry, having worked with a variety of companies offering digital-marketing software, Web analytics platforms, disruptive technologies, outsourcing, health care and biotechnology IT and Eeb development services. She wrote key performance indicators for 'Search Engine Marketing' (McGraw-Hill, 2009) and managed a digital advertising agency. She has been employed in California, India, Holland and Denmark. Layton has been active in the start-up, nonprofit and educational sectors, advising entrepreneurs, mentoring students and providing business expertise. She has served in various leadership roles for educational, health, and community organisations.

Maria Löblich (Ph.D., communication sciences) is an assistant professor at the Department of Communication Science and Media Research, Ludwig-Maximilians-Universität München. She was part of the fellowship class at the Berkman Center for Internet & Society at Harvard University in the 2012–2013 academic year. Her research focuses on Internet policy with a particular interest in political processes and actor-structure interactions.

J. Scott Marcus is an independent consultant dealing with policy and regulatory issues related to electronic communications. He is best known as an economist, but his academic training is as a political scientist (with a specialty in public administration) and as an engineer. Current and past private consulting clients have included the European Parliament; the Electronic Frontier Foundation (EFF); the International Telecommunications Union (ITU); national regulatory authorities of Bahrain, Jamaica, and Namibia; and various market players. From July 2005 to August 2015, he served as a director for WIK-Consult GmbH. He continues to conduct individual projects for WIK. From 2001 to 2005, he served as senior advisor for Internet Technology for the United States Federal Communications Commission (FCC), a position equivalent in rank to the chief economist or chief technologist.

Christopher T. Marsden is professor of Media Law at the University of Sussex, since April 2013. He is author of four monographs on Internet law: 'Regulating Code' (2013, MIT Press with Dr. Ian Brown), 'Net Neutrality: Towards a Co-regulatory Solution' (2010, Bloomsbury), 'Internet Co-regulation: European

Law, Regulatory Governance and Legitimacy in Cyberspace' (2011, Cambridge) and 'Codifying Cyberspace' (Routledge/Cavendish 2007 with Dr. D. Tambini, D. Leonardi). He was formerly senior lecturer (2008–2012) and then professor of Law (2012–2013) at Essex, having previously taught and researched at Warwick (1997–2000), Oxford (2004–2005) and LSE (1995–1997).

Andrew McDiarmid is a senior policy analyst at CDT's Washington, DC, office. He works on policy issues related to digital copyright, free expression and Internet neutrality. Prior to joining CDT, Andrew was a research assistant at the Samuelson Law, Technology, and Public Policy Clinic at the UC-Berkeley School of Law, where he researched a range of issues including electronic surveillance and licencing solutions for peer-to-peer networks. He has a master's from Berkeley's School of Information and a bachelor's in art history from Washington University in St. Louis.

Joe McNamee is the director of European Digital Rights, an association of digital civil rights associations from 20 European countries. He holds master's degrees in international law and in European politics. Prior to joining EDRi, he worked for a consultancy, primarily on Internet regulation issues. He also was responsible for three studies for the European Commission—on local loop unbundling, convergence of telecoms and Internet networks and communications markets and regulation in eight former Soviet states. He has a strong interest in industry self-regulation issues, particularly with regard to privatised law enforcement.

Bastian Morasch studied business administration at the University of Cologne, majoring in marketing and market research. He graduated in 2009. He has been working at YouGov since 2001–2010, as senior consultant since 2004–2014 with a focus on research in the fields of telecommunications and technology. He has conducted and managed numerous research and consulting projects in the areas of product, pricing and branding research as well as consumer insights and behaviour (offline, online and panel research). His work includes optimising product portfolio and pricing strategies; identifying, segmenting and profiling consumer target groups and their behaviour; and analysing brand awareness and image including brand strengths and weaknesses. His activities regularly involve complex statistical analyses such as conjoint, cluster and regression analysis. He has extensive experience in conducting and managing international research projects and in working among multinational project teams.

Francesca Musiani, Ph.D., is a researcher at the Institute for Communication Sciences (ISCC) of the French National Centre for Scientific Research (CNRS), Paris-Sorbonne and University Pierre and Marie Curie, and an associate researcher at the Centre for the Sociology of Innovation of MINES ParisTech-PSL. Francesca's research focuses on Internet governance, in an interdisciplinary perspective, blending information and communication sciences with Science and Technology Studies (STS). She is the recipient of the Prix Informatique et Libertés 2013 awarded by the French Privacy and Data Protection Commission, and a member of the Commission to study rights and liberties in the digital age established by the French National

Assembly in June 2014. She is a former author and current academic editor, Internet governance area, for the Internet Policy Review.

Alejandro Pisanty is a professor at Facultad de Quimica, Universidad Nacional Autonoma de Mexico (UNAM). He has been Director of Academic Computing Services and held other technology leadership positions in that institution; there, he directed the growth of important Internet services, founded the National Research and Education Network CUDI, created a virtual reality services, expanded super-computing, and other technology services oriented to as enablers for community empowerment. He has also been a member of the Boards of ICANN and the Internet Society and is Chair of Internet Society (ISOC) Mexico. He has published on technology in education, e-learning, m-learning, network neutrality, and Internet governance as well as his original field of research in Theoretical Chemistry. In 2009 he co-led the #InternetNecesario campaign that established Internet-related policy in the legislative and policy environment of Mexico.

Louis Pouzin is the inventor of the datagram and designed an early packet communications network, CYCLADES, that influenced the development of TCP/IP used by the Internet. He is considered one of the fathers of the Internet and is currently a consultant, giving seminars on Internet evolution. He is an active participant in the UN Internet Governance Forum and contributes to several non-profit organisations, EUROLINC (native languages in Internet), MAAYA (federation for cultural and linguistic diversity) and ATENA (high-level seminars). He has created a company, Savoir-Faire, for selling new top-level domains (Open Root).

Frieder Schmid holds a M.Sc. in psychology. He joined YouGov more than 3 years ago and has been working on various subjects in telecommunications and Internet. His methodological focus is on quantitative methods addressing B2B and B2C target groups. He is specialised in research topics such as pricing, product development and consumer attitudes and conducted a variety of studies on consumer preferences towards innovative products, customer satisfaction, brand perception, media usage behaviour and consumer attitudes. He has great experience in conducting and managing international research projects and in working among project teams.

Anna Schneider is a senior consultant at YouGov, Germany. Here, she oversees qualitative research across all sectors and heads the German hub for the development and implementation of future qualitative methods. She holds a Ph.D. in psychology from the University of Bonn. She has more than 12 years of experience in market research and consulting covering a wealth of methodological approaches both qualitative and quantitative. She has great expertise in online, panel and offline research methods (*e.g.* in-depth interviews, focus groups, workshops, online chats, bulletin boards, usability, user experience, etc.). She has been involved in a broad variety of projects for different sectors that combined qualitative and quantitative research with a strong and growing focus on telecommunications.

Matthew Shears leads the Center for Democracy and Technology's Global Internet Policy and Human Rights (GIPHR) activities. A UK national, Matthew has extensive experience in Internet and telecommunications policy and governance in the nonprofit, public and private sectors. Most recently he assisted CDT's Internet governance and policy work at the World Conference on International Telecommunications (WCIT), the UNESCO World Summit on the Information Society (WSIS) review and the World Telecommunication/ICT Policy Forum (WTPF). From 2005 through 2009, Matthew was the Internet Society's Public Policy Director, responsible for building the global policy team and representing the organisation during the Tunis phase of the WSIS, at ITU Telecom World and at the Internet Governance Forum. From 2006 to 2008, he was a member of the UN Secretary General's Advisory Group on Internet governance.

Frode Sørensen is a Senior Adviser at the Norwegian Communications Authority (Nkom) and he holds a Master of Science degree from the University of Oslo. He has been leading the development of the Norwegian net neutrality policy at Nkom since 2007, and he has been an architect behind the Norwegian guidelines for net neutrality published in 2009. Frode has been chair of BEREC Net Neutrality Expert Working Group since it was established in 2010. He has more than twenty years of experience in telecommunications and has previously worked at Agder University, Telenor and Ericsson and he is the author of several books on Internet technology.

Konstantinos Stylianou is a lecturer in Competition Law and Regulation at the University of Leeds in the UK. Before joining Leeds he was a fellow at the Center for Technology and Society at FGV Direito Rio (Brazil). Previously, he worked and/or interned at the Council of Europe, the US Federal Communications Commission, the Berkman Center at Harvard and the European Platform for Regulatory Authorities, and he has advised numerous Internet startup companies. Konstantinos holds an S.J.D. from the University of Pennsylvania (US), an LL.M. from Harvard (US) and a bachelor's and master's from the Aristotle University of Thessaloniki (Greece). He has also been a visiting scholar at the Centre for Socio-legal Studies, University of Oxford (UK). His main research focus is on EU/US competition law, telecommunications law and policy, regulation and regulatory economics.

Félix Tréguer is Ph.D. candidate in political science at the School for Advanced Studies in Social Sciences (CRH/EHESS) in Paris, researching on the consequences of the Internet for free speech and citizen empowerment in democratic regimes. He is also a legal analyst and founding member of La Quadrature du Net, an advocacy group promoting fundamental rights on the Internet

Matthijs van Bergen works as a legal advisor at ICTRecht and is simultaneously developing his PhD thesis concerning net neutrality and the protection of freedom of speech and privacy in information societies at Leiden University. Matthijs has advised the Dutch NGO Bits of Freedom concerning net neutrality from 2010 to 2012, on an entirely voluntary ('pro bono') basis. Currently Matthijs is serving as a network neutrality expert for the Council of Europe.

Patricia A. Vargas-Leon is currently a Ph.D. candidate in the School of Information Studies. Her research interests focus on the area of information policies and Internet governance, taking into account considerations about national security, civil liberties (in particular, freedom of expression and privacy), government attempts and legislative proposals to 'shut down' the Internet and the implementation of policies to monitor social networks. Patricia was a consultant for the Division of Ocean Affairs and Law of the Sea (DOALOS) of the United Nations and got a law degree by the Pontifical Catholic University of Peru with specialisation in International Law and Law of the Sea and a master's degree in Library and Information Sciences with focus on legal research from Syracuse University. Her legal thesis addresses the problem of sea boundaries between Peru and Chile, currently a case in the International Court of Justice (ICJ).

Martin Waldburger works as a senior consultant in the Markets and Perspectives Department at WIK-Consult. His area of expertise covers the analysis and assessment of technological, business and legal dimensions emerging from electronic communication services, the Internet and ICT. He focuses in particular on the digital and data-driven economy, on smart services/infrastructure and on how consumers perceive and use the Internet. He has been contributing significant research on these topics in various projects performed for the European Commission, BEREC/National Regulatory Agencies, the German Federal Ministry for Economic Affairs and Energy as well as for the private sector. He was also involved in standardisation in the ITU-T, where he was a co-author of Recommendation Y.3013 (socio-economic assessment of future networks by tussle analysis).

Michał Andrzej Woźniak is network security, privacy and media education expert and activist, advocating free software and open standards in education, public institutions and business. Between 2006 and 2012, he was the systems administrator, then CTO of Mobile Technologies Laboratory BRAMA at the Warsaw University of Technology and vice president since 2011 and afterwards president (2012–2014) of the Board of the Free and Open Source Software Foundation. He was a participant to a number of public consultations and public debates, both in Poland and on international level, centred around new technologies, privacy, Internet censorship, data retention, public data reuse, access to public information, Internet governance and copyright reform. Between June 2014 and March 2015, he became a member of the Council for Digitization at the Polish Ministry of Administration and Digitization and co-author of the Media Competences Catalogue and media education materials, in collaboration with Modern Poland Foundation and Panoptykon Foundation.

Acknowledgements

This book reflects many of the ideas discussed by the members of the Dynamic Coalition on Network Neutrality (DCNN) of the United Nations Internet Governance Forum, between 2013 and 2015. The editors would like to express their gratitude to all the DCNN members for their inputs.

Furthermore, the editors would like to thank the Fundação Getulio Vargas Law School, which has provided support and guidance, stimulating this research effort.

The editors would also like to thank the Council of Europe for the organisation of the Multi-Stakeholder Dialogue on Network Neutrality and Human Rights, an event that played a pivotal role in advancing the discussion on network neutrality, providing the inputs and stimuli necessary for the establishment of the DCNN.

Lastly, this book is published thanks to the precious editorial help of Luã Fergus and Marion Jahan.

Contents

Chapter 1
General Introduction: Towards a Multistakeholder Approach to Network Neutrality

Luca Belli and Primavera De Filippi

This book is the result of a collective work aimed at providing deeper insight into what is network neutrality, how does it relates to human rights and free competition and how to properly frame this key issue through sustainable policies and regulations. The Net Neutrality Compendium stems from 3 years of discussions nurtured by the members of the Dynamic Coalition on Network Neutrality (DCNN), an open and multi-stakeholder group, established under the aegis of the United Nations Internet Governance Forum (IGF). The creation of the DCNN was proposed by one of the co-editors of this book, Luca Belli, during the Council of Europe's Multi-Stakeholder Dialogue on Network Neutrality and Human Rights (MSDNN), in order to foster a cooperative analysis of the net neutrality debate and promote the elaboration of policy suggestions for the protection of network neutrality. Many of the stakeholders involved in the Council of Europe MSDNN manifested their interest in the initiative, and the establishment of the DCNN was officially approved by the IGF Secretariat in July 2013.

Along with its annual workshops, the dynamic coalitions represent the structural elements of the IGF. Both workshops and coalitions have a multistakeholder composition and are aimed at the discussion of "public policy issues related to key elements of Internet governance", as foreseen by the IGF mandate. (Tunis Agenda for the Information Society, para. 72.a) While the IGF workshops are designed for various stakeholders to debate specific topics at a specific point in time, the dynamic coalitions are meant to guarantee continuity over the years, offering an exceptional opportunity to generate an enduring policy-shaping effort. Most importantly, the

L. Belli (✉)
Center for Technology & Society, Fundação Getúlio Vargas, Rio de Janeiro, Brazil
e-mail: luca.belli@fgv.br

P. De Filippi
e-Gouv, CERSA/CNRS/Université Paris II, Paris, France
e-mail: pdefilippi@gmail.com

© Springer International Publishing Switzerland 2016
L. Belli, P. De Filippi (eds.), *Net Neutrality Compendium*,
DOI 10.1007/978-3-319-26425-7_1

long-term nature of dynamic coalitions is particularly suited to elaborate the material necessary to fulfil one of the most important (and often forgotten) missions defined by the IGF mandate, according to which the Forum shall "[i]dentify emerging issues, bring them to the attention of the relevant bodies and the general public, and, where appropriate, make recommendations" (Tunis Agenda, para. 72.g).

The purpose of the dynamic coalitions is to allow long-term multistakeholder cooperation to produce concrete outputs. Although the opinions expressed in this book are the sole responsibility of the authors, rather than an official position of the DCNN, this book is a tangible example of what issue-specific multistakeholder cooperation has the potential to produce. Particularly, the DCNN has been created to provide a discussion arena, allowing all interested stakeholders to jointly scrutinise the various nuances of the network-neutrality debate, ultimately contributing to the circulation of best practices through continuous online interactions. The DCNN has been established with the purpose of being proactive, fostering the elaboration of concrete outcomes. Since its inception, the coalition has produced a Model Framework on Network Neutrality, it has facilitated the elaboration of several annual reports, and it has guided the drafting of a Policy Statement on Network Neutrality that may be used as supporting material for policy-making and (self) regulatory efforts. In particular, the Model Framework on Network Neutrality has been delivered to the Council of Europe to provide guidance on how to frame net neutrality and it has been subsequently used it as background material for the elaboration of a Recommendation on Network Neutrality.

The DCNN can be regarded as a true Internet Governance experiment, transposing the working methods used by the technical community to enable the elaboration of policy documents. In this regard, the elaboration process of both the Model Framework and the Policy Statement was based on the open and participatory *modus operandi* of the IETF (Internet Engineering Task Force) working groups. Over the first 3 year of existence, the DCNN has triggered debate on three essential issues: the role of the non-discriminatory traffic management in facilitating the full enjoyment of fundamental rights; the analysis and comparison of existing net neutrality frameworks; and the implementation of net neutrality rules in order to frame emerging challenges. Such debates are reflected in the three parts of this book. We provide below a brief overview of the tripartite structure of the Net Neutrality Compendium.

1.1 Network Neutrality: A Human Rights Enabler

Network neutrality prescribes that Internet traffic shall be treated in a non-discriminatory fashion so that Internet users can freely choose online content, applications, services and devices without being influenced by discriminatory delivery of Internet traffic. Such freedom of choice is allowed by the original architectural choices that made the Internet an open and general-purpose network fostering end-users' creativity and innovation while preserving individuals' freedom of expression. The concept of network neutrality refers to the policy and regulatory choices that should be made to frame network management practices so that Internet openness and full respect for human rights can be safeguarded. Indeed, some traffic management techniques have the potential to limit end-users' freedom to seek, impart and receive information and ideas or to compromise the privacy of end-users' communications. In this regard, network neutrality policies aim at safeguarding individuals' capability to access and use lawful online content, applications, services and devices, without having to request the authorization of any operators. Most importantly, net neutrality supports the full enjoyment of end-users' rights by defining the legitimate purposes for the achievement of which discriminatory traffic management techniques need to be used, rather than to leave the utilisation of such techniques to exclusive market criteria. As such, net neutrality corroborates the decentralised and open architecture of the Internet, deflating entry barriers to the 'free market of ideas', and thus setting a level playing field for any user to participate in the development of the Internet ecosystem.

The limitations of discriminatory traffic management techniques, promoted by net neutrality advocates, seem instrumental to ensure that all content (and not only commercially profitable content) is transmitted with sufficient quality and that all data packets can count on a 'best-effort' delivery. Such non-discriminatory treatment guarantees that Internet users maintain the ability to choose freely how to utilise their own Internet connection, without undue interferences from public or private entities. In the current information society, the ability to freely receive and impart ideas and information, as well as the right to fully participate in democratic life is truly reliant on the nature of one's Internet connection. As such, net neutrality enables self-determination, by directly contributing to the effective enjoyment of a range of fundamental rights as well as to the promotion of a diverse and pluralistic media landscape, while unleashing a virtuous cycle of permissionless innovation.

The success of the Internet is dependent on its open end-to-end structure that ascribes to individual users the responsibility of managing their electronic communications, thereby avoiding that operators act as Internet chokepoints. The first part of this book aims at demonstrating that net neutrality maintains the open and decentralised nature of the Internet thus safeguarding a user-centric system for global connectivity that is immune to the forces of centralisation and control. Indeed, this open architecture has become essential to enjoying fundamental rights in the context of a permanently interconnected society and, for this reason, deserve protection. Several regulatory strategies have been chosen to implement concretely net neutrality principles, involving a more or less ample spectrum of stakeholders both within the elaboration and the implementation of the various frameworks. Part II explores such regulatory strategies.

1.2 Regulatory Approaches to Network Neutrality

Depending on the characteristics of their juridical systems, different states have adopted a different regulatory approach to Network Neutrality. While the network neutrality principle is clear in that all traffic should be treated in a non-discriminatory fashion, regardless of content, application, service, device, sources or recipients, the actual implementation of this principle into law is much more discretionary. In particular, regulatory approaches to Network Neutrality may greatly vary depending on the characteristics of the national telecommunications market as well as the degree of infrastructure development. The main motivation of a net neutrality framework may be to preserve or establish a competitive telecommunications market but also to protect the fundamental rights of individuals, as abusive and discriminatory practices might undermine the free flow of information.

For many years, the European Union has been struggling to reach a compromise concerning the establishment of a shared set of rules on Network Neutrality. The diverse legal and cultural backgrounds of European Member States constitute a challenge when it comes to elaborate a single and harmonised regulatory solution ensuring openness and non-discrimination in the telecommunication sector. Yet, to the extent that network neutrality is regarded as an essential requisite to promote innovation and foster competition within the common market, it becomes crucial to enact common rules at the pan-European level that would effectively uphold the Network Neutrality principles. The first European country to enshrine network neutrality into law was Norway, which introduced, as early as 2009, a set of guiding principles preventing the blocking and throttling of applications, while fostering a co-regulatory approach involving the telecom regulatory authority, online operators and consumers associations. The Norwegian example was followed by both the Netherlands and Slovenia, which both included specific Network Neutrality provisions within their Telecommunications framework not only in order to boost competition but also to protect fundamental rights and consumers rights of Internet users.

In 2012, a joint investigation by the European Commission and the Body of European Regulator for Electronic Communications demonstrated that European users were affected by a wide range of traffic management restrictions. To cope with such situation, the European Commission proposed a new regulation that triggered intense debate and was substantially amended by the European Parliament's first reading, in 2014. Recently, a political compromise on network neutrality regulation was presented by the European Commission, the Parliament and the Council of the European Union, but such political agreement still needs to be officially adopted and implemented. Meanwhile, the 47 members of the Council of Europe have been working on a Recommendation of the Committee of Ministers on Network Neutrality, whose draft took inspiration from the Model Framework on Network Neutrality elaborated by the IGF Dynamic Coalition on Network Neutrality. However, after almost 2 years of debate, the Council of Europe Recommendation has not been adopted yet.

In the U.S., while network neutrality has always been a very controversial issue, the Federal Communications Commission (FCC) has finally taken a strong stance in favour of non-discriminatory traffic management. There had been, for many years, heated debates as to whether or not to impose network neutrality regulation on Internet Service Providers (ISP). On the one hand, network neutrality has often been criticised as an unnecessary attempt to regulate the Internet. It was believed that transparency requirements (mostly concerning the terms of use of telecommunication and other internet operators) would be sufficient to foster consumer choice, by enabling fair competition on the market for telecommunications. On the other hand, network neutrality advocates have intensively lobbied for the prohibition against discriminatory traffic management techniques due to the risks that some of these techniques s may impose both on Internet users' fundamental rights and on content and applications providers' capability to freely compete in the market. On this ground, the FCC has recently adopted net neutrality rules preventing all operators from blocking and throttling specific traffic or enacting pay-for-priority schemes. Importantly, the FCC reclassified both fixed and mobile broadband as a telecommunications service, now regulated as common carriers under Title II of the Communications Act.

Latin American countries have been particularly active in promoting network neutrality via specific net neutrality laws (such as Chile) or including net neutrality protections within broader telecommunications or Internet frameworks (such as Brazil, Colombia, Peru and Mexico). Although Latin American approaches present many differences, they converge concerning the need for banning arbitrary blocking, interference or discrimination of legal content, applications or services through the Internet. The motivation underpinning the establishment of net neutrality regulation are also quite similar, principally aiming at strengthening competition and fostering a sustainable expansion of the telecommunications market, while trying to avoid possible—or proven—abusive traffic management practices. Furthermore, the regulatory frameworks of most Latin American countries converge as regards the need to implement net neutrality provisions through administrative means, although some frameworks, such as the Brazilian one, do not specifically identify the administration(s) to which implementation is delegated, thus leaving to the executive branch the possibility to define an appropriate system.

1.3 Net Neutrality Implementation in an Evolving Internet Ecosystem

Many countries around the world are progressively leaning towards some network neutrality regime presenting some common features. This compendium provides two distinct contributions (as the conclusion of Part I and Part III) offering concrete policy recommendations, based on a series of best practices developed at the national level. Yet, many issues are still open, most notably with regard to the definition of precise characteristics of the so-called "specialised services", which represent an exception to net neutrality rules, as well as the application of the network neutrality principle to cases that may be categorised as "positive discrimination" such as zero-rating practices.

Over the past years, specialised services have been a highly controversial issue in the context of network neutrality. Any service provided by telecommunication operators which relies on enhanced functionalities—such as guaranteed quality or security—and, therefore, does not qualify as an Internet access service (*e.g.* IPTV, guaranteed quality online gaming, *etc.*) are not contemplated within the scope of network neutrality regulations. However, many mobile operators are increasingly providing specialised services, often at the expenses of traditional Internet access service. Therefore, there may be an inherent conflict of interest in having operators providing both Internet access and specialised services on the same network. In fact, due to the limited bandwidth that is available to telecom operators—with particular regard to mobile networks—the provision of specialised services (which are often more profitable than the provision of open Internet access) might actually undermine the viability of Internet access services. Indeed, operators may prefer to allocate most of their bandwidth to most profitable specialised services. Besides, reducing the quality of Internet access might ultimately make specialised services more appealing to consumers, thus creating a negative feedback loop that might lead to the progressive degradation of open Internet access services.

Hence, as more and more operators start developing their specialised services on top of their networks, specialised service may *de facto* compete for bandwidth with Internet access services. In 2014, the European Parliament tried to address the issue by requesting that specialised services be offered only when the network capacity is sufficient to provide them in addition to Internet access services, so that the provision of the former is not to the detriment of the availability or quality of the latter. However, the tension between the need to provide open Internet service and the willingness of operators to promote their specialised services does not seem to be a resolved issue.

Simultaneously, as mobile operators introduce new zero-rating practices, based on the provision of sponsored applications provided by their commercial partners, users choice is increasingly oriented towards the platform provided by their mobile operators, because it may otherwise be too expensive or extremely slow to rely on other services. As such, many claim that network neutrality is not exclusively related to the technical discrimination of packets (*e.g.* blocking, throttling, and other forms of packets discrimination), but also to the economic or price discrimination of applications and services (*i.e.* sponsored data plans). The price of open Internet access becomes, therefore, a key factor in determining whether or not the principles of network neutrality have been properly accounted for. In the context of mobile communications, in particular, more and more online operators are entering into agreements with telecom operators to sponsor the data consumption of their services thus encouraging the use by consumers. While this does not apply in countries where users have access to unlimited Internet access at a flat-rate or to very large data caps, in other countries where mobile Internet prices are very high, or where mobile internet access is subject to limited data caps, zero-rating practices may be very appealing and lead to a situation where mobile users increasingly find themselves interacting exclusively with vertically integrated online environments, rather than within the (full) Internet. For this reason, some observers have considered zero-rating as an anti-competitive practice insofar as it puts competing services (which cannot afford to pay for their traffic) at a competitive disadvantage. Moreover, some people claim that the practice of zero-rating might encourage mobile operators to set artificially up low volume caps, to profit from sponsored data. Finally, it has been argued that zero-rating reduces the ability for consumers to choose amongst a variety of competing services, which are longer be judged according to their inherent quality, but rather according of their market price.

Accordingly, although price discrimination was not originally regarded as falling within the scope of network neutrality, it might have a significant impact on the ability for users to access Internet service. In particular, given that a large portion of Internet access is increasingly done through mobile networks and devices, cases of positive price discrimination will soon become a crucial factor to deal with in order to uphold network neutrality principles in practice. Current implementations of Network Neutrality principles, however, provide for very heterogeneous approaches to zero-rating or other forms of price discrimination. For instance, while the FCC's rules prohibit paid prioritisation of an operator's own traffic or a third-party's internet traffic, they do not precludes the implementation of zero-rated services which should be evaluated on a case by case basis. Similarly, in Europe, the proposal put forth by a few Member States to ban harmful price discrimination practices such as zero-rating is currently facing strong opposition from other EU Member States and the larger incumbents in the telecommunication market.

This leads to yet another important issue concerning network neutrality, which is linked to the question of spectrum allocation. This issue acquires particular relevance concerning mobile network operators that need to decide whether to allocate the licensed public radio spectrum to specialised services or Internet access services. Moreover, the issue of spectrum allocation has significant implications for the deployment of wireless community networks (WCNs), which rely on the availability of unlicensed radio spectrum in order to provide flexible and affordable Internet connections to underserved communities. Given their grassroots approach and non-commercial nature, WCNs generally cannot afford to pay for the licensing fees required to broadcast radio signals on the licensed spectrum. In the U.S., the FCC has already undertaken an effort of expanding the unlicensed national radio spectrum by opening the so-called "white spaces" left by the obsolescence of analogue television. In Europe, instead, although the EU Parliament began assessing the need for and the feasibility of opening more of the radio spectrum to unlicensed uses in 2012, the EU Commission never took any concrete action to expand unlicensed uses of the radio spectrum. Hence, while the potential of WCNs to foster access to the open Internet has been recognised, still a lot of regulatory work needs to be done to ensure the viability and long-term sustainability of these networks.

Part I
Framing the Network Neutrality Debate: Net Neutrality, Human Rights and Openness

Network Neutrality (NN) refers to the principle whereby all electronic communications should be treated in a non-discriminatory way, regardless of their type, content, origin or destination. Although only a few countries have decided to establish net neutrality frameworks, so far, the preservation of an open and neutral Internet has been increasingly considered as instrumental to facilitate a virtuous circle of innovation while fostering the full enjoyment of human rights.

In his paper on "End-to-end, Net Neutrality and Human Rights", Luca Belli reflects on the value of network neutrality in order to maintain an open and decentralised Internet architecture and facilitate the full enjoyment of Internet users' freedom of expression and other fundamental rights. After analysing the role played by the original end-to-end system design, along with the best-effort delivery to promote a user-centric Internet, the author categorises various traffic management techniques, based on their purposes. While acknowledging that application-specific techniques may be used for reasonable traffic management, the author highlights that such practices may have potentially negative consequences for Internet users' rights when used in an unnecessary and disproportionate fashion. Indeed, although traffic management should not be considered as something negative *per se*, certain techniques are explicitly aimed at discriminating against specific content, applications and services, thus allowing operators to act as Internet chokepoints with negative implications on end-users' capability to freely seek, impart and receive information.

The Internet design, based on the end-to-end principle, has played a pivotal role in unleashing end-users' fundamental rights—including, but not limited to freedom of expression, access to knowledge and democratic participation—enabling individuals to freely choose (and run) applications and services of their choice, as well as to connect the devices that they consider the most appropriate to their needs. Yet, as illustrated by Andrew McDiarmid and Matthew Shears in "The Importance of Internet Neutrality to Protecting Human Rights Online", Internet's full potential can only be unleashed insofar as the network stays compatible with the net neutrality principle. To preserve users' fundamental rights, the Internet must remain *global* (allowing for communications to be distributed worldwide), *user-controlled* (as opposed to being controlled by the content or access provider), *decentralised* (with most services and applications run at the networks endpoints), *open and competitive* (with relatively low barriers to entry). The authors argue that, given the growing role that the Internet plays concerning various facets of individuals' life, states have the duty to intervene so as to ensure that the network design remains such as to promote the exercise of human rights. Indeed, the non-discriminatory treatment of Internet traffic mandated by net neutrality principles may be regarded as a true precondition for users to fully enjoy their fundamental "right to freedom of opinion and expression [that] includes freedom to hold opinions without interference and to seek, receive and impart information and ideas through any media and regardless of frontiers", as affirmed by the Universal Declaration of Human Rights.

In order to stress the impact of net neutrality on individuals' capability to freely communicate, Francesca Musiani and Maria Löblich analyse the potential of Internet traffic management to control and restrict democratic participation and interaction in the public sphere. In their paper on "Net Neutrality from a Public Sphere Perspective", the authors apply Peter Dahlgren's three-dimensional framework of the public sphere to examine the relationship between net neutrality issues and the degree of fairness, pluralism of views, agenda setting, ideological biases, and other evaluation criteria for media content. Particularly, Dahlgren's framework distinguishes between the *structural dimension* of public sphere, referring to the various media available for the public to communicate, the *representational dimension*, referring to the output of such communication, and the *interactional dimension*, referring to the ways in which users interact with these media. The authors use this framework as an entry point to examine specific net neutrality issues that relates to each of these three dimensions: the structural dimension serves as a basis to investigate the issues related to actual access to the Internet infrastructure; the representational dimensions is used as a means to investigate how net neutrality relates to content, concerning diversity, control, and censorship; and, finally, the interactional dimension is used to describe how new forms of communication that are emerging online could be affected by a derogation to the net neutrality principle. They conclude that NN has become today an important precondition for achieving a properly functioning public sphere, fuelled by a variety of information, ideas and opinions.

Yet, given the technical implications of managing Internet traffic without discrimination of content, ports, protocols, origin, or destination, it seems beneficial to evaluate traffic management techniques according to their context, their justifications, as well as the effective impact they might have on human rights. In this regard, Alejandro Pisanty analyses "Network Neutrality under the lens of Risk Management", by providing an valuable framework to assess the likelihood of net neutrality violations, along with suggestions on how to best deal with such violations. Particularly, the framework proposed by Pisanty can be used by different parties in varied environments for dealing with preventive as well as reactive actions in the face of net neutrality violations by Internet Service Providers and other infringing parties. The framework includes an identification of the forms of network neutrality violations, their weighting by likelihood and impact, and actions for risk avoidance, detection, mitigation, business continuity, contingency planning, and prevention. The actions are shown in a graduated-response order so that scaling up towards the resolution of conflict or controversy around network neutrality violations can be appropriately planned and executed.

In his paper on "There's no Economic Imperative to Reconsider an Open Internet", Benoît Felten clearly presents the different implementations and recurring costs of various Internet traffic management models to subsequently describe different solutions to solve traffic management problems without relying on traffic discrimination. The author points out that the Internet's success can be attributed to a few simple network management principles, most of which are based on the adoption of open standards such as the Internet Protocol. Such principles delineate an online environment where no single player—public or private—can exert control over who is entitled to access the Internet while no blocking or degrading of lawful Internet traffic is allowed. This open environment significantly empowers end-users, providing them greater choice and control over their online activities. Furthermore, while highlighting that discriminatory traffic management may be used as a lever for commercial negotiations, the author notes that such discrimination may ultimately lead to fragmentation of the Internet ecosystem.

Benoît Felten continues by providing an overview of how Internet traffic crosses operators' networks allowing Internet users to access content, applications and services offered by multiple online service providers (OSPs). Particularly, the author analyses the dynamics of different traffic management solutions—such as transit, peering and content delivery networks—in order to clarify the investments and costs that must be incurred by both ISP and OSPs. Based on this analysis, the author underlines the fallacy of the argument according to which OSPs can be considered as "free riders" on the ISPs networks, by highlighting the OSPs' role concerning investing and financing international, regional and national transport networks. Finally, the author examines the debate regarding network capacity and growing transit, with particular regard to the French market, highlighting that costs related to external traffic management concern less than 0.3 % of the main operators' average revenue.

The open and decentralised architecture originally established by the end-to-end principle ascribes an active role to Internet users, trying to avoid interferences that may potentially limit their ability to receive and impart information, at the network layer. Such individual empowerment, confirmed by the delegation to users of the responsibility to manage communications, may be seen as one of the most significant galvaniser of freedom of expression in recent history. However, the user-based of the Internet is nowadays composed of less technically-erudite users compared to the original community of Internet pioneers and, as highlighted by Louis Pouzin in his paper on "Net Neutrality and Quality of Service," a large majority of Internet users are not (interested in becoming) network experts. The rise of cyber-crime and the growing threats to network integrity and security have stimulated the development of "trust-to-trust" models, where private entities (such as ISPs, CAPs or DNS operators) undertake some forms of "network-patrolling" in order to provide a more trustworthy network. It is, therefore, the democratization of the Internet that spurred the establishment of various types of intermediations to ensure the provision of secure Internet communication—thus transforming the Internet into an increasingly centralised network structure. These elements add further complexity to the meaning and implementation of the net neutrality debate. Pouzin explores the various standpoints and interpretations of different actors, including network operators, content providers and end-users, arguing that content providers and operators are reluctant to invest in network upgrades, generating suspicion and frustration among users. Lastly, the author argues that an important element of the open Internet debate is the degree of openness of the Domain Name System, which is considerably limited by the existing monopoly exercised by the Internet Corporation for Assigned Names and Numbers.

To conclude, Luca Belli, Matthijs van Bergen and Michał Andrzej Woźniak explore the nuances of the network neutrality concept and analyse the process that led to the elaboration of a Model Framework on Network Neutrality by the IGF Dynamic Coalition on Network Neutrality (DCNN), as well as the application of that model. The authors argue that, since the early 2000s, the need for net neutrality policies and regulations has emerged as a result of the discriminatory treatment of Internet traffic, put in place by several operators. Hence, the elaboration of a Model Framework has been deemed as instrumental to foster a scalable approach to net neutrality, in compliance with international human-rights standards. In their paper on "A Discourse-Principle Approach to Network Neutrality Policymaking", Belli et al. describe the conceptual framework that led to the elaboration of a net neutrality policy-blueprint, along with the participatory process put in place by the DCNN in order to craft the Model Framework. The paper analyses the result of such process providing guidance with regard to the interpretation and implementation of the various provisions contained in the Model Framework.

Chapter 2
End-to-End, Net Neutrality and Human Rights

Luca Belli

2.1 Introduction

The network neutrality (NN) debate focuses on the effects that Internet Traffic Management (ITM) practices, implemented by network operators, may deploy on Internet users' rights and, particularly, on their capability to freely seek, receive and impart information and ideas. Certain ITM techniques are indeed aimed at discriminating against specific content, applications and services and, therefore, have the potential to substantially interfere with the end-user's Internet experience. Over the past 15 years,[1] NN discussions have been scrutinising the extent to which ITM techniques may be deemed as reasonable, trying to find a delicate balance between the interests of the operators, which have the technical possibility to manage Internet traffic; the interests of the Content and Application Providers (CAPs) that rely on non-discriminatory Internet connectivity in order compete on a level playing field; and the interests of Internet users, who rely on non-discriminatory Internet connectivity in order to fully enjoy their fundamental rights while, as customers, have a legitimate expectations to enjoy the quality levels for which they pay.

As I will briefly argue in this paper, the very design of the original Internet architecture was not only instrumental to allow thousands of heterogeneous networks to interoperate, but played also a key role allowing end-users to fully enjoy freedom of expression and innovation. Indeed, in the online environment, freedom to receive and impart information and ideas is directly reflected on users' capability to freely access and share content, applications and services, using the device of their choice, without being unduly influenced by discriminatory delivery of Internet traffic.

---

[1] Even before the creation of the expression "network neutrality", by Wu (2003), the substance of the debate had already been explored by several scholars starting from the late 1990s. See *e.g.* Marsden (1999), Cooper (2000), Lemley and Lessig (2000).

L. Belli (✉)
Fundação Getúlio Vargas Law School, Rio de Janeiro, Brazil
e-mail: luca.belli@fgv.br

© Springer International Publishing Switzerland 2016
L. Belli, P. De Filippi (eds.), *Net Neutrality Compendium*,
DOI 10.1007/978-3-319-26425-7_2

Such user capability has been unleashed by the originally open design of the Internet, which substantially differed from the traditionally closed and centralised architecture of telecommunications networks. Differently from previous communication systems, which were based on the operators' capability to define the networks' purpose, the Internet has been designed as a decentralised, general-purpose network. This open and decentralised architecture did not allow operators to discriminate against specific applications, services or content. The Internet has been conceived as an agnostic platform with regard to the content that may be conveyed and the purpose for which it can be used, thus allowing end-users to freely decide how to utilise their applications. Such fundamental features have empowered individuals with the capability to freely communicate and innovate, thus realising the promise of the Universal Declaration of Human Rights: "Everyone shall have the right to freedom of expression; this right shall include the freedom to seek, receive and impart information and ideas of all kinds, regardless of frontiers and without interference."

In this paper, I argue that the safeguard of the NN principle plays an instrumental role in maintaining the aforementioned open and decentralised architecture. NN is commonly referred as the principle according to which all electronic communication networks shall carry data in a non-discriminatory fashion regardless of their content, the type of application, the identity of their sender and recipient or the type of device used.[2] Hence, this paper stresses that NN policies are key to facilitate the full enjoyment of Internet users' freedom of expression, as well as other fundamental rights. Simultaneously, this paper highlights that ITM practices consisting in blocking, filtering, throttling or prioritising specific data flows, are in contrast with the NN principle and have the potential to unduly interfere with end-users' enjoyment of their fundamental rights as well as to jeopardise the Internet's fundamentally open architecture. It is important to note that, as freedom of expression, NN is not an absolute principle and limitations should be foreseen. However, in light of the instrumental role played by NN to safeguard Internet users' rights, limitations to this principle should be allowed only when necessary and proportionate to the achievement of a legitimate aim.

After providing a brief overview of the Internet's end-to-end architecture (Sect. 2.2), the article will categorise some commonly used ITM techniques, stressing the impact that such techniques may have on Internet users' fundamental rights (Sect. 2.3). Lastly, the article will analyse the emergence of NN policies and regulations protecting the NN principle (Sect. 2.4), and will provide some policy suggestions aimed at fostering a human rights approach to this all-important topic.

2.2 From End-to-End to Centralisation

The original Internet architecture was grounded on the end-to-end (E2E) design principle (Saltzer et al. 1984; Carpenter 1996). The E2E principle essentially affirmed that the various functions for which the Internet might be used "*can*

---

[2] See United Nations (UN) Special Rapporteur on Freedom of Opinion and Expression, the Organization for Security and Co-operation in Europe (OSCE) Representative on Freedom of the Media, the Organization of American States (OAS) Special Rapporteur on Freedom of Expression and the African Commission on Human and Peoples' Rights (ACHPR) Special Rapporteur on Freedom of Expression and Access to Information 2011, para. 5; DCNN Model Framework on Network Neutrality, para 1.

completely and correctly be implemented only with the knowledge and help of the application standing at the end points of the communication system. Therefore, providing that questioned function as a feature of the communication system itself is not possible" (Saltzer et al. 1984). The E2E system design established an open, non-discriminatory and general-purpose network, decentralising the definition and implementation of the network functions—*i.e.* the Internet's "intelligence"—at the end-user level. Although this design choice was made for efficiency purposes, its collateral effect has been to unbridle end-users' freedom of expression and innovation in an unprecedented way.

The E2E principle may be considered as one of the underlying arguments in favour of NN. Indeed, the E2E argument ascribes to users the "responsibility for the integrity of communication",[3] assuming that operators manage internet traffic in an essentially non-discriminatory fashion and delegating the detection and resolution of potential data-delivery problems to the applications run at the edges of the communication network. As such, according to the E2E principle, end-users play an active role, running and creating applications at the "endpoints" of the network whilst the communications network are considered as passive infrastructure, tasked with the mere transportation of data packets[4] on a best-effort[5] basis.

Decentralised End-to-End Structure

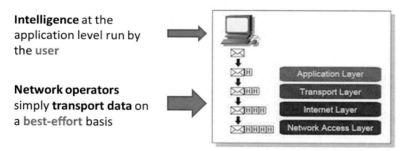

Source: Belli 2015a

As famously stated by the Internet Engineering Task Force, "*the goal* [of the Internet] *is connectivity, the tool is the Internet Protocol, and the intelligence is end*

---

[3] According to the Request for Comments 1958, "[…] certain required end-to-end functions can only be performed correctly by the end-systems themselves. A specific case is that any network, however carefully designed, will be subject to failures of transmission at some statistically determined rate. The best way to cope with this is to accept it, and give responsibility for the integrity of communication to the end systems". See Carpenter (1996).

[4] In an electronic communications network, information is fragmented into so-called data packets. The data packet is the basic a unit of digital information that travels along a given network path on 'packet-switched' networks.

[5] The concept of "best effort delivery […] refers to the way in which data is conveyed over the Internet – namely operators transmitting data streams to convey them from their point of departure to their destination, with no guarantee on performance but only an obligation of best endeavor". See ARCEP (2012), p. 16.

to end rather than hidden in the network" (Carpenter 1996). Conspicuously, by requiring that functionalities be implemented at the network's endpoints, when possible, and at the network level only when necessary, the E2E principle places the end-users, rather than the operator, in control of their Internet experience. Such decentralised system has proven to be essential to foster and maintain Internet openness, removing discriminatory barriers that may hinder the free flow of information and innovation. However, since the early 2000s, the Internet ecosystem has started to manifest some early sign of centralisation, triggered by the increasing use of discriminatory ITM techniques. In this regard, discussions regarding the need for NN policies have been sparked by the fear that network operators' ITM capabilities may allow them to act as chokepoints (Cooper 2000). Indeed, operators may be tempted to use discriminatory ITM measures to block or downgrade the content, applications and services that compete with their own offerings—or with the offerings of their commercial partners—thus hampering competition, jeopardising end-users' freedom of expression and, ultimately, "putting an end" to the end-to-end architecture (Lemley and Lessig 2000). On the contrary, the limitation of network operators' capacity to discriminate against specific content, applications and services to what is necessary and proportionate to the achievement of a legitimate aim, has been considered as essential to minimise possible side effects of ITM practices, thus preserving an open and user-empowering Internet (FCC 2010; BEREC 2012c).

NN has been first conceptualised as a "network design principle" whereby a maximally useful public information network aspires to treat all content, sites, and platforms equally, thus granting to all Internet users universal access to all online resources (Wu 2003). However, NN has rapidly evolved into a policy principle or even a "policy priority",[6] due to the increasing realisation of the impact that ITM techniques may have on free competition as well as on end-users rights (BEREC 2012a; FCC 2015). NN policies are aimed at preserving an open and decentralised Internet architecture, avoiding possible negative impacts of ITM practices on the free flow of information. Indeed, non-discriminatory traffic management is supposed to facilitate a virtuous cycle of innovation (FCC 2010; Williamson et al. 2011), reinvigorating end-users' freedom of expression and unleashing their capacity to share new applications and services (Lee and Wu 2009; BEREC 2012a; Belli and Van Bergen 2013). However, it is important to note that, although ITM measures are expression of the operators' power to act as centralised Internet points of control, the use of ITM techniques should not be considered as something illegitimate *per se*. On the contrary, although extensive use of ITM favours the centralisation of network control in the hands of operators, it must be noted that some forms of traffic management are essential to preserving well-functioning networks. As an instance, the use of ITM techniques to block the expansion of malware

---

[6] See BEREC (2012b). Furthermore, since 2010, the Council of Europe members have explicitly declared their intention to preserve "the interoperability of the Internet as well as its end-to-end nature" arguing that "[t]hese principles should guide all stakeholders in their decisions related to Internet governance. [and t]here should be no unreasonable barriers to entry for new users or legitimate uses of the Internet, or unnecessary burdens which could affect the potential for innovation in respect of technologies and services". See Council of Europe (2010).

clearly serves the legitimate interests of the end-users, preserving the integrity and security of the networks. On the other hand, some ITM techniques may be used for purposes that can harm end-users rights. For instance, blocking or throttling applications provided by the operators' competitors is undeniably an unreasonable and illegitimate practice, because the only rationale of such discriminatory treatment is to avoid free competition. The section below provides some further elements aimed at categorising the purposes of existing ITM practices and clarifying their possible effects on Internet users' rights.

2.3 Internet Traffic Management and Mismanagement

As noted above the original Internet architecture was based on the "best effort delivery" model for transmission of data packets, whereby operators convey Internet traffic in a non-discriminatory fashion without any guarantee of quality or obligation over the result. The non-discriminatory traffic management enabled by the best effort model has proved to be particularly beneficial, "defining low barriers to entry on the open platform of the Internet, which has provided particularly fertile ground for new content and applications to develop" (BEREC 2012a). However, it must be noted that, even within a best-effort paradigm, Internet traffic is continuously processed both by the end-users' terminal machines and by the network genitive operators equipment. On the one hand, end-users' machines constantly perform congestion control, increasing or decreasing the data transmission rate, depending on network congestion.[7] On the other hand, operators commonly implement ITM practices to mitigate the effect of network congestion, protect networks' security and integrity and optimise available network resources. To do so, operators monitor their networks to understand the traffic behaviour and implement technical means that target the traffic sent or received by end users. The ITM techniques implemented by operators may be protocol-agnostic or protocol-specific. The former do not discriminate against specific classes of applications while the latter do. As an instance, "First-in, first-out" (FIFO) routing technique is fully protocol-agnostic while blocking or prioritising Voice over IP (VoIP) applications like Skype is quintessentially protocol-specific. Furthermore, ITM practice may also be application-specific thus targeting specific content or a particular application or service, rather than a class of applications.

Application-specific techniques may raise net neutrality concerns because they explicitly aim at managing Internet traffic in a discriminatory fashion, by blocking, filtering, throttling or prioritising specific data flows, thus impeding the end-user from having full control of his/her Internet experience. As such, application-specific mea-

---

[7] It is important to note that "there are two types of congestion that generally present themselves in a network. The first general type of congestion is regularly occurring and is the result of gradually increasing traffic levels up to a point where typical usage peaks cause congestion on a regular basis. [...]The second general type of congestion is unpredictable congestion, which can occur for a wide range of reasons. One example may be due to current events, where users may be all rushing to access specific content at the exact same time [...]." See Bastian et al. (2010).

sures may result in restrictions to access legitimate content and/or applications and may be exploited by operators to favour the CAPs with which they vertically integrate or disfavour their competitors (BEREC 2012a; FCC 2015). At the European level, for instance, an investigation led in 2012 by BEREC (the Body of European Regulators of Electronic Communications) and the European Commission highlighted the existence of a wide array of traffic management practices resulting in undue restrictions (BEREC 2012a). Therefore, applications specific measures should be considered as contrary to net neutrality when they are not necessary and proportional to the achievement of a legitimate purpose (BEREC 2012c; Belli and van Bergen 2013).

It is important to note that network operators may implement ITM techniques at different levels of their infrastructure (*e.g.* access lines, transit lines, switching nodes, etc.) and protocol-specific or application-specific ITM may have different purposes. Particularly they may be aimed at:

- Blocking access to specific content, applications and services. Such practice may be put in place in order to comply with national legislation, may be used for security purposes *e.g.* blocking ports to prevent spam or other harmful traffic, but may be also implemented to inhibit competing services. To this latter extent, some network operators have been inhibiting protocols exploited by competing services, such as VoIP, in order to preserve their business model. Blocking practices prevent communications without inspecting data packets, whereas filtering techniques imply that the content of communications must be inspected before being blocked.
- Filtering specific data packets. This practice aims at granularly analysing Internet traffic to identify specific content and apply a particular treatment, such as blocking, throttling or prioritisation. Hence, this technique requires installing content inspection equipment so that Internet traffic is analysed when passing through the filtering equipment. This technique can be used to preserve network security and integrity, for instance filtering out spam or limiting the effect of malicious attacks, but may also be used for censorship purposes and has the potential to jeopardise the privacy of end-users' communications.
- Bandwidth throttling. In this case, the operator downgrades specific type of Internet traffic (*e.g.* all video traffic) or specific bandwidth-greedy applications (*e.g.* peer-to-peer) in order to limit the congestion they generate. However, bandwidth throttling may be also exploited to reduce the quality of competing applications. Such technique may be applied temporary and exceptionally but can be also applied on a general basis, to discriminate against a specific type of traffic or applications, despite the existence of congestion.
- Traffic prioritisation. Differently from bandwidth throttling, this kind of technique gives, preferential treatment to specific types of traffic *e.g.* by prioritising time-sensitive applications, such as VoIP, or to guarantee quality of service of specific services. This latter case may happen when operators implement pay-for-priority schemes, allowing specific CAPs to purchase preferential treatment, or when operators deploy specialised services (such as IPTV or e-health services) with no separation from Internet access services. It is important to note that the quality of the non-prioritised applications—or of the general Internet

access service, in case of non-separated specialised services—may be degraded, due to sharing resources.

As stated above, protocol-specific and application-specific ITMs can be considered as legitimate exceptions to the NN principle only when necessary, proportional to a legitimate purpose. Although blocking practices have been criticised for their negative side-effects (SSAC 2012; BITAG 2013), such techniques may be justified by court orders aimed at impeding access to material deemed as illegal by national legislations, in conformity with human rights norms and international law. However, blocking may be also used to impede access to specific applications, such as instant messaging, VoIP or Video on Demand (VoD), that may compete with traditional services offered by the operators, such as text messaging, voice calls or TV (BEREC 2012a; BITAG 2013). Therefore, operators may have a concrete incentive to block access to competing services, particularly when operators vertically integrate with CAPs offering analogue services. Likewise, operators may temporarily and exceptionally throttle bandwidth-greedy applications—or prioritise time-sensitive applications—in order to handle congestion but the same measures may be used in order to downgrade competing services or prioritise the applications provided by commercial partners (BEREC 2012a; FCC 2015). For instance, in 2005 the U.S. Federal Communication Commission (FCC) found the Internet access provider Madison River Communications unduly blocking the Voice over IP (VoIP) service Vonage (FCC 2005a) whilst, in 2008, the FCC found the operator Comcast unduly throttling the peer-to-peer application BitTorrent (FCC 2008).

As it has been noted above, besides undermining free competition, the unrestricted use of such application-specific techniques may jeopardise the effective exercise of fundamental rights and freedoms such as freedom of expression or privacy. On the one hand, by blocking or downgrading legitimate applications and services, operators exercise an undue interference in users' freedom to seek, receive and impart information and ideas. It is important to stress that such risks are not merely theoretical or confined to authoritarian regimes. As an example, in 2012, four British operators blocked access to the TOR-project website, a website offering privacy-enhancing technologies (TOR Project 2012), while another mobile operator blocked access to the website of the advocacy group La Quadrature du Net (Cappuccini and Craggs 2012). Both cases highlight the very tangible threats that unregulated blocking may determine on freedom of communication and information. On the other hand, it must be noted that the use of pervasive inspection techniques—such as Deep Packet Inspection (DPI)—for filtering purposes may determine nefarious consequences on users' fundamental right to privacy (EDPS 2011, 2013). DPI technologies are indeed able to examine the content of the data packets conveyed through an electronic network and, based on the result of the analysis, can apply a discriminatory treatment defined by the operator. DPI technologies are commonly used to monitor and manage both fixed and wireless networks for many purposes, amongst which the prevention of online pornography and copyright infringement. In the UK, for example, DPI technology Clean Feed has already been imposed on internet access providers to block access to child abuse material and alleged copyright infringements.[8] However, due to the processing of high quantity of personal data, the unnecessary and disproportioned use of such invasive techniques may severely compromise the privacy of Internet users' electronic communications (EDPS 2011, 2013).

In light of the above considerations, it seems essential to stress that ITM measures should not be considered as a mere technical issue and the potential implications of such practices on Internet users' rights should be carefully assessed. On the one hand, the implementation of protocol specific—or application-specific— ITM techniques must be legitimate, proportional and necessary[9] while, on the other hand, the use of non-discriminatory ITM promoted by the NN principle should be preferred and fostered due to the social benefits that it can determine (Van Schewick 2010; BEREC 2012a).

2.4   From End-to-End to the Rule of Law

After having been suggested by several U.S. academics (*e.g.* Cooper 2000; Lemley and Lessig 2000; Wu 2003), the risks of ITM practices have been concretely demonstrated by a number of cases around the world. Some violations may be patent and clearly identifiable, as the abovementioned Madison River case (FCC 2005a), in which the American ISP Madison River Communications was found guilty of using port blocking to prevent its subscribers from using VoIP services offered by Vonage, in order to protect its telephone service business. Madison River deliberately impeded access to a VoIP service perceived as competing, disregarding end-users' freedom to choose a perfectly legal VoIP application as well as their freedom to communicate with such perfectly legal service. However, not all violations may have such a clear-cut nature and may be difficult to identify or prove in the lack of an appropriate framework. Due to the negative effects that certain ITM measures may have on the free market as well as to the full enjoyment of Internet users' rights, many regulators and policy-makers consider the protection of the NN principle as a true policy priority (BEREC 2012b). In this regard, several national systems already protect NN by means of legislation or through self/co/regulatory frameworks.

The first regulatory approach to NN was adopted by the U.S. Federal Communications Commission through Policy Statement (FCC 2005b), establishing four basic principles, according to which Internet users should be entitled to:

• access the lawful Internet content of their choice;

---

[8] See UNESCO (2012).

[9] These criteria have been elucidated by the jurisprudence of the European Court of Human Rights in order to delineate "margin of appreciation" of Council of Europe members with regard to the application of the ECHR. The term "margin of appreciation" is a common notion in administrative law systems and the ECtHR utilises it to refer to the space for manoeuvre granted to national authorities, in fulfilling their obligations under the ECHR.

- run applications and use services of their choice, subject to the needs of law enforcement;
- connect their choice of legal devices that do not harm the network;
- competition among network providers, application and service providers, and content providers.

This approach to NN nurtured the European policy-making efforts, both at the EU level, during the 2009 revision of the Telecoms Package, and at the Council of Europe level, with the adoption of the Committee of Ministers' Declaration on Network Neutrality, in 2010. On the one hand, the Universal Service Directive affirmed that European end-users "*should be able to decide what content they want to send and receive, and which services, applications, hard ware and software they want to use for such purposes, without prejudice to the need to preserve the integrity and security of networks and services*" while leaving to market competition the task to "*provide users with a wide choice of content, applications and services*" and delegating to national regulators the task to "*promote users' ability to access and distribute information and to run applications and services of their choice.*"[10] On the other hand, recognising the possibility that "*users' right to access and distribute information online and the development of new tools and services might be adversely affected by non-transparent traffic management*" and the instrumental role played by NN in order to foster the full enjoyment of fundamental rights, the Council of Europe's Committee of Ministers declared "*its commitment to the principle of network neutrality*".[11] further specifying that "*Internet users should have the greatest possible access to Internet-based content, applications and services of their choice, whether or not they are offered free of charge, using suitable devices of their choice*".[12]

Both the original FCC and EU approaches were grounded on competition and no-blocking rules, to which EU policymakers added transparency obligations[13]— taking inspiration from the Norwegian Principles on Internet Neutrality[14]—as well as the national regulators' power to impose "*minimum quality of service requirements*".[15] On both sides of the Atlantic, the rationale was to avoid hard regulation on ITM practices and delegate to free competition and informed consumer choice the task to avoid discriminatory treatments. However, it should be noted that, in order to be both market efficient and human-right-efficient, competition law principles and transparency obligations presuppose an ideal situation. In such ideal situation, competition would guarantee that all information and ideas can be freely conveyed without discrimination, while rational consumers have both the time and the technical skills necessary to analyse the ITM information contained in Internet-access-service contracts and, subsequently, "vote with their feet", abandoning

---

[10] See Directive 2009/136/EC, recital 28.

[11] See Council of Europe (2010), para. 9.

[12] See *ibid.*, para. 4.

[13] See Directive 2009/136/EC, recital 23.

[14] See Annex 1.

[15] See Directive 2009/136/EC, recital 34 and art 22(3).

those network operators that unduly discriminate against specific content, applications. Such scenario seems overconfident for several reasons.

On the one hand, the aforementioned scenario relies on the assumption that all end-users have the technical background necessary to understand that eventual problems to access or use a given application may be due to the implementation of discriminatory ITM techniques rather than supposing the malfunctioning of the application (*i.e.* the so-called "the-application-doesn't-work situation"). Furthermore, the competition-based approach overestimates the market capability to distribute efficiently speech. Indeed, not all information has the same value. Due to the profitability of content, services and applications, network operators that vertically integrate with CAPs have a considerable incentive to "*use the architecture of the Internet to nudge their customers into planned communities of consumerist experience, to shelter end users into a world that combines everyday activities of communication seamlessly with consumption and entertainment* [eventually pushing] *consumers back into their pre-Internet roles as relatively passive recipients of mass media content*" (Balkin 2004). It is important to note that some information and ideas may be more profitable than other and, therefore, if information flows were to be determined primarily—or even solely—by profit maximisation criteria, there could be a serious risk that inconvenient and non-profitable information would be *de facto* excluded (Belli and van Bergen 2013).

On the other hand such assumption underestimate the fact that, even in a competitive market, the majority of the operators—or, potentially, all operators—may discriminate against specific content, applications and services, thus making it irrelevant to switch from one operator to the other. In this regard, it seems important to mention that the joint investigation led by BEREC and the European Commission found that in Europe—which is usually considered as a quite competitive market—at least 36 % of mobile Internet users and 25 % of all European Internet users were affected by some type of restrictions, particularly involving blocking and throttling practices (BEREC 2012a). Lastly, the competition-based approach fails to consider the fact that, the Internet ecosystem is composed of an interconnection of networks and, therefore, discriminatory practices implemented by network operator A—*e.g.* blocking a specific application—may also affect the capability of other operators' customers to freely communicate. Indeed, the customers of network B or C would be unable to communicate with the users of network A, *e.g.* using the blocked application, even if traffic restrictions are implemented only within network A. Hence, in light of the abovementioned considerations, it is important to stress that although competition and transparency are essential in order to guarantee NN, they are not sufficient *per se*.

2.5 Conclusion: Towards a Human Rights Approach

As highlighted above, NN focuses on preserving a distributed and user-empowering Internet architecture, allowing individuals to fully enjoy their freedom of expression, imparting and receiving any lawful content, services or application, using any legal device. NN aims at strengthening the fundamental features of the original

Internet environment, such as end-to-end architecture and best-effort delivery, in order to safeguard the Internet's user-empowering capacity. As such, the non-discriminatory treatment mandated by the NN principle seems to be instrumental not only to facilitate the full enjoyment of fundamental rights but also to safeguard the "openness and fairness" as well as the "decentralized control, edge-user empowerment and sharing of resources" that represent the very "scope of the Internet," as recognised by the Internet technical community itself (Alvestrand 2004).

In order to preserve an open and user-centric Internet, the implementation of ITM techniques capable of shifting the control of the Internet experience from the user to the operator should be allowed exclusively when necessary and proportionate to the achievement of a legitimate aim. Particularly, the use of such measures should be justified on grounds of verifiable technical necessity or to address transient network management problems which cannot otherwise be addressed, or should be required by court orders and national laws in conformity with international human rights norms and legislation. As argued above, discriminatory ITM practices have the potential to jeopardise end-users fundamental rights such as privacy and freedom of expression. Authoritative jurisprudence has stressed that freedom of expression "*applies not only to the content of information but also to the means of dissemination since any restriction imposed to the [means] necessarily interfere with the right to receive and impart information*" (ECtHR 1990). Indeed, from a European perspective, discriminatory traffic management can be seen as an interference with freedom of expression, which "*applies not only to the content of information but also to the means of dissemination*" (ECtHR 2012). Likewise, the Inter-American Court of Human Rights (IACHR) has explicitly argued that "*equity must regulate the flow of information*", establishing the state obligation to "*extend equity rules, to the greatest possible extent, to the participation in the public debate of different types of information, fostering informative pluralism*" (IACHR 2008, 2011).

It is important to note that, in the absence of any policies or regulations aimed at promoting NN and avoiding the possible negative impact of ITM techniques, the only entities able to define the contours of ITM are the operators themselves. Such entities frequently integrate with CAPs, thus having a substantial economic incentive not to be neutral, thus favouring commercial partners and disfavouring competitors. Hence, it seems necessary to foster the definition of "rules of the road" for operators, aimed at guaranteeing the full enjoyment of end-users' rights while avoiding the potentially nefarious effects of discriminatory traffic management. However, it seems important to note that, as freedom of expression, the NN principle should not be considered as absolute and exceptions to the NN should be allowed and clearly defined, in order to allow so-called "reasonable traffic management", while fostering legal certainty. To this latter extent, policymakers should promote the elaboration of regulatory approaches—or co-regulatory approaches, where the definition and implementation of NN principles or codes of conduct is overseen by regulators—aimed at clearly defining the limits of ITM practices, so that end-users rights are fully respected.

2.6   Annex 1: Norwegian Principles on Internet Neutrality

1. Internet users are entitled to an Internet connection with a predefined capacity and quality.
2. Internet users are entitled to an Internet connection that enables them to (a) send and receive content of their choice; (b) use services and run applications of their choice; (c) connect hardware and use software of their choice that do not harm the network.
3. Internet users are entitled to an Internet connection that is free of discrimination with regard to type of application, service or content or based on sender or receiver address.

Principle 1 states that the characteristics of the Internet connection are to be contracted in advance, also with a view to cases where Internet access is provided together with other services on the same physical connection. Principle 2 states qualitatively that the Internet connection must be able to be used as the user wants. And Principle 3 states that traffic over the Internet connection is to be transferred in a non-discriminatory manner.[16]

2.7   Annex 2: Dutch Legal Provision on Network Neutrality

Article 7.4a, Telecommunications Act (unofficial translation[17])

1. Providers of public electronic communication networks which deliver internet access services and providers of internet access services do not hinder or slow down applications and services on the internet, unless and to the extent that the measure in question with which applications or services are being hindered or slowed down is necessary:

   a) to minimize the effects of congestion, whereby equal types of traffic should be treated equally;
   b) to preserve the integrity and security of the network and service of the provider in question or the terminal of the end-user;
   c) to restrict the transmission to an end-user of unsolicited communication as referred to in Article 11.7, first paragraph, provided that the end-user has given its prior consent;
   d) to give effect to a legislative provision or court order.

---

[16] See Norwegian Post and Telecommunications Authority, *Network neutrality Guidelines for Internet neutrality*, Version 1.0, 24 February 2009, available http://www.legi-internet.ro/fileadmin/editor_folder/pdf/Guidelines_for_network_neutrality_-_Norway.pdf.

[17] See Daphne van der Kroft, "Net Neutrality in the Netherlands: State of Play", in *Bits of Freedom*, 15 June 2011, available at https://www.bof.nl/2011/06/15/net-neutrality-in-the-netherlands-state-of-play/.

2. If an infraction on the integrity or security of the network or the service or the terminal of an end-user, referred to in the first paragraph sub b, is being caused by traffic coming from the terminal of an end-user, the provider, prior to the taking of the measure which hinders or slows down the traffic, notifies the end-user in question, in order to allow the end-user to terminate the infraction. Where this, as a result of the required urgency, is not possible prior to the taking of the measure, the provider provides a notification of the measure as soon as possible. Where this concerns an end-user of a different provider, the first sentence does not apply.

3. Providers of internet access services do not make the price of the rates for internet access services dependent on the services and applications which are offered or used via these services.

4. Further regulations with regard to the provisions in the first to the third paragraph may be provided by way of an administrative order. A draft order provided under this paragraph will not be adopted before it is submitted to both chambers of the Parliament.

5. In order to prevent the degradation of service and the hindering or slowing down of traffic over public electronic communication networks, minimum requirements regarding the quality of service of public electronic communication services may be imposed on undertakings providing public communications networks.

2.8 Annex 3: Slovenian Legal Provisions on Network Neutrality

Article 203, Electronic Communications Act (unofficial translation[18])

(1) The Agency encourages the preservation of the open and neutral character of the internet and the access to and dissemination of information or the use of applications and services of their choice of end users.

(2) The Agency goals in the previous paragraph must be carefully considered in the exercise of its jurisdiction under Articles 3 and 4 the second paragraph of the 132nd of this Act, and the third and fourth paragraphs of the 133rd of this Act and their responsibilities in relation to the implementation of the second of the first paragraph of Article 129 Article by the network operator and provider of Internet access services.

(3) Network operators and Internet access providers shall make every effort to preserve the open and neutral character of the internet, thus it may not restrict, delay or slowing Internet traffic at the level of individual services or applications, or implement measures for their evaluation, except in case of:

---

[18] See Slovenian Electronic Communications Act, available at http://www.uradni-list.si/_pdf/2012/Ur/u2012109.pdf#!/u2012109-pdf.

1. necessary technical measures to ensure the smooth operation of networks and services (*e.g.* to avoid traffic congestion);
2. necessary steps to preserve the integrity and security of networks and services (*e.g.* elimination of unfair seizure of over a transmission medium—channel);
3. emergency measures for limiting unsolicited communications in accordance with the 158th of this Act;
4. decisions of the court.

(4) The measures provided for in Articles 1, 2 and 3 of the preceding paragraph shall be proportionate, non-discriminatory, limited in time and to the extent that this is necessary.
(5) Network operators' and Internet service providers' services shall not be based on services or applications, which are provided or used via internet access services.
(6) The Agency can issue a general act to implement the provisions of the third, fourth and fifth paragraphs of this Article.

2.9 Annex 4: Brazilian Legal Provisions on Network Neutrality

Article 9, Law No. 12 .965, 23 April 2014 (unofficial translation[19])

The party responsible for the transmission, switching or routing has the duty to process, on an isonomic basis, any data packages, regardless of content, origin and destination, service, terminal or application.

§1° The discrimination or degradation of traffic shall be regulated in accordance with the private attributions granted to the President by means of Item IV of art. 84 of the Federal Constitution, aimed at the full application of this Law, upon consultation with the Internet Steering Committee and the National Telecommunications Agency, and can only result from:

I—technical requirements essential to the adequate provision of services and applications;
and II—prioritization of emergency services.

§2° In the happening of discrimination or degradation of traffic provided in §1°, the responsible entity mentioned in Art. 9 o must:

I—abstain from causing damages to users, as set forth in art. 927 of Law n° 10.406, January 10th, 2002 the Civil Code;
II—act with proportionality, transparency and isonomy;

---

[19] See Lei N° 12.965, de 23 de abril de 2014, also known as Marco Civil da Internet no Brasil. http://www.planalto.gov.br/ccivil_03/_ato2011-2014/2014/lei/l12965.htm.

III—provide, in an advanced notice, in a transparent, clear and sufficiently descriptive manner, to its users, the traffic management and mitigation practices adopted, including those related to network security;

and IV—offer services in non-discriminatory commercial conditions and refrain from anti-competition practices.

§3° When providing internet connectivity, free or at a cost, as well as, in the transmission, switching or routing, it is prohibited to block, monitor, filter or analyze the content of data packets, in compliance with this article.

References

Alvestrand, H. T. (2004, October). A Mission Statement for the IETF. Request for Comments: 3935. BCP: 95. https://www.ietf.org/rfc/rfc3935.txt

ARCEP. (2012, September). *Report to Parliament and the Government on Net Neutrality*. http://www.arcep.fr/uploads/tx_gspublication/rapport-parlement-net-neutrality-sept2012-ENG.pdf

Balkin, J. M. (2004). Digital speech and democratic culture: A theory of freedom of expression for the information society. *New York University Law Review, 79*(1).

Bastian, C., Klieber, T., Livingood, J., Mills, J., & Woundy, R. (2010, December). *An ISP Congestion Management System. RFC 6057.* https://tools.ietf.org/html/rfc6057#page-9

Belli, L. (2015, June 8) *From Internet Standards to Regulatory Standards? A Net Neutrality Experiment.* Presented to Conferência Internacional sobre a Elaboração de Regras de Neutralidade de Rede, FGV Rio de Janeiro. https://www.youtube.com/watch?v=_W_jV14Xc-4

Belli, L., & van Bergen, M. (2013). *Protecting Human Rights through Network Neutrality: Furthering Internet Users' Interest, Modernising Human Rights and Safeguarding the Open Internet.* Council of Europe. CDMSI(2013)Misc19.

BEREC. (2012a, May 29). *A view of traffic management and other practices resulting in restrictions to the open Internet in Europe*, Findings from BEREC's and the European Commission's joint investigation. BoR (12) 30. https://ec.europa.eu/digital-agenda/sites/digital-agenda/files/Traffic%20Management%20Investigation%20BEREC_2.pdf

BEREC. (2012b, November 27). *Overview of BEREC's approach to net neutrality*. BoR (12) 140 http://berec.europa.eu/files/document_register_store/2012/12/BoR_%2812%29_140_Overview+of+BEREC+approach+to+NN_2012.11.27.pdf

BEREC. (2012c, December 3). *Summary of BEREC positions on net neutrality*. BoR (12) 146. http://berec.europa.eu/files/document_register_store/2012/12/BoR_%2812%29_146_Summary_of_BEREC_positions_on_net_neutrality2.pdf

BITAG. (2013, August). *Port Blocking. A Broadband Internet Technical Advisory Group Technical Working Group Report.* http://www.bitag.org/documents/Port-Blocking.pdf

Cappuccini, A., & Craggs, G. (2012, February 15). Orange UK blocking La Quadrature du Net. Open Rights Group. https://www.openrightsgroup.org/blog/2012/orange-uk-blocking-la-quadrature-du-net

Carpenter, B. (1996). *Architectural Principles of the Internet. Request for Comments: 1958.* https://www.ietf.org/rfc/rfc1958.txt

Cooper, M. (2000). *Open Access to the Broadband Internet: Technical and Economic Discrimination in Closed, Proprietary Networks*, 71 U. Colo. L. Rev. 1011.

Council of Europe. (2010). *Declaration of the Committee of Ministers on Network Neutrality.* Adopted by the Committee of Ministers on 29 September 2010 at the 1094th meeting of the Ministers' Deputies. https://wcd.coe.int/ViewDoc.jsp?id=1678287&Site=CM&BackColorInternet=C3C3C3&BackColorIntranet=EDB021&BackColorLogged=F5D383.

DCNN. (2013). *Model Framework on Network Neutrality*. Presented at meeting of the Dynamic Coalition on Network Neutrality held during the 8th Internet Governance Forum. Bali 2013. http://www.networkneutrality.info/sources.html

Directive 2009/136/EC of the European Parliament and of the Council of 25 November 2009.

ECtHR. (1990, May 22). Autronic AG v. Switzerland, 22 May 1990. Application no. 12726/87. http://hudoc.echr.coe.int/eng?i=001-57630

ECtHR. (2012, December 18). Case of Ahmet Yıldırım v. Turkey. Application no. 3111/10. http://hudoc.echr.coe.int/fre?i=001-115705

EDPS. (2011, October 7). *Opinion of the European Data Protection Supervisor on net neutrality, traffic management and the protection of privacy and personal data*. http://ec.europa.eu/bepa/european-group-ethics/docs/activities/peter_hustinx_presentation_(1)_15_rt_2011.pdf

EDPS. (2013, November 14). *Opinion of the Europe on Data Protection Supervisor on the Proposal for a Regulation of the Europe on Parliament and of the Council laying down measures concerning the Europe an single market for electronic communications and to achieve a Connected Continent*.

FCC. (2005a). Madison River Communications, LLC and affiliated companies, Acct. No. FRN: 0004334082. https://transition.fcc.gov/eb/Orders/2005/DA-05-543A2.html

FCC. (2005b). Policy Statement. 20 FCC Rcd 14986, 14987–88. Retrieved from https://apps.fcc.gov/edocs_public/attachmatch/FCC-05-151A1.pdf

FCC. (2008, August 1). *Commission Orders Comcast to End Discriminatory Network Management Practices*. News Media Information 202/418-0500. https://apps.fcc.gov/edocs_public/attachmatch/DOC-284286A1.pdf

FCC. (2010). *Preserving the Open Internet*, GN Docket No. 09-191, WC Docket No. 07-52, Report and Order, 25 FCC Rcd 17905, 17911.

FCC. (2015). *Report and Order on Remand, Declaratory Ruling, and Order on the Matter of Protecting and Promoting the Open Internet*. GN Docket No. 14-28.

IACHR. (2008). *Case of Kimel v. Argentina. Merits, Reparations and Costs*. Judgment of May 2, 2008. Series C No. 177. Para. 57.

IACHR. (2011). *Case of Fontevecchia y D'Amico v. Argentina. Merits, Reparations and Costs*. Judgment of November 29, 2011. Series C No. 238. Para. 45.

Lee, R. S., & Wu, T. (2009). Subsidizing creativity through network design: zero pricing and net neutrality. *Journal of Economic Perspectives, 23*(3).

Lemley, M., & Lessig, L. (2000, October 1). The end of end-to-end: preserving the architecture of the Internet in the broadband era. *UCLA Law Review, 48*, 925, 2001, available at: http://ssrn.com/abstract=247737

Marsden, C. (1999). *Pluralism in the multi-channel market. Suggestions for regulatory scrutiny*. Council of Europe MM-S-PL(1999)012 http://www.coe.int/t/dghl/standardsetting/media/Doc/MM-S-PL(1999)012_en.asp

Saltzer, J. H., Reed, D. P., & Clark, D. D. (1984). End-to-end arguments in system design. *ACM Transactions on Computer Systems*, (2). http://web.mit.edu/saltzer/www/publications/endto-end/endtoend.pdf

SSAC. (2012, October 9). *SSAC Advisory on Impacts of Content Blocking via the Domain Name System*. SAC 056. https://www.icann.org/en/system/files/files/sac-056-en.pdf

Tor Project. (2012, January 17). *A tale of new censors – Vodafone UK, T-Mobile UK, O2 UK, and T-Mobile USA*. https://blog.torproject.org/blog/tale-new-censors-vodafone-uk-t-mobile-uk-o2-uk-and-t-mobile-usa

UNESCO. (2012). *Liberté de connexion Liberté d'expression – Ecologie dynamique des lois et règlements qui façonnent l'Internet*. http://unesdoc.unesco.org/images/0021/002160/216029f.pdf

United Nations (UN) Special Rapporteur on Freedom of Opinion and Expression, the Organization for Security and Co-operation in Europe (OSCE) Representative on Freedom of the Media, the Organization of American States (OAS) Special Rapporteur on Freedom of Expression and the

African Commission on Human and Peoples' Rights (ACHPR) Special Rapporteur on Freedom of Expression and Access to Information. (2011). *Joint Declaration on Freedom of Expression and the Internet.*

Van Schewick, B. (2010). *Internet architecture and innovation.* MIT Press.

Williamson, B., Black, D., & Punton, T. (2011, October). *The open internet – A platform for growth.* A report for the BBC, Blinkbox, Channel 4, Skype and Yahoo!

Wu, T. (2003). Network neutrality, broadband discrimination. *Journal of Telecommunications and High Technology Law, 2.*

Chapter 3
The Importance of Internet Neutrality to Protecting Human Rights Online

Andrew McDiarmid and Matthew Shears

3.1 Introduction

The history of the Internet has shown that it has tremendous capacity to advance human rights, in particular freedom of expression and related rights. Over two billion people around the world connect every day to access and share information and participate in wide-ranging aspects of social, economic, and political life. For individuals, connecting to the Internet provides access to an ever-expanding array of information resources and online services. At the same time, it offers opportunities for people to reach new audiences at very low cost compared to other forms of mass media. To an unprecedented degree, the Internet transcends national borders and reduces barriers to the free flow of information, enabling free expression, democratic participation, and the enjoyment of other rights.

At least, it can. Merely having Internet access is not sufficient to guarantee the full flowering of free expression and the other rights it enables, including the rights to freedom of assembly and association, the right to education, and the right to participate in cultural life. The Internet's power to transform communications and promote free expression and a pluralistic information environment flows from certain characteristics that have defined the Internet since its inception. These characteristics are not immutable, however, and are increasingly subject to pressure. To maximize the Internet's potential to advance human rights, the Internet must remain free from centralized controls, open to the fullest range of content and services, and truly global. Establishing rules to preserve net neutrality—or more precisely,

A. McDiarmid (✉)
Google, San Francisco Bay Area, California, USA

M. Shears
Center for Democracy and Technology, Washington, DC, USA

© Springer International Publishing Switzerland 2016
L. Belli, P. De Filippi (eds.), *Net Neutrality Compendium*,
DOI 10.1007/978-3-319-26425-7_3

Internet neutrality—is one way to prevent the imposition, by those in a position to control access, of structural inequalities that would distort this environment.[1]

Much writing and advocacy related to the Internet and free expression is concerned with state censorship and other curtailment of rights by governments. This is a critically important aspect of online free-expression advocacy, made ever more so by the ongoing revelation, as of this writing, of widespread surveillance of Internet traffic. But governments' duty to protect human rights extends beyond non-interference, particularly in the realm of communications and free expression.[2] And as the telecom sector is increasingly liberalized, private Internet access providers are in a position to control their customers' access to Internet content, often for purely commercial reasons. Discriminatory treatment of Internet traffic by access providers threatens Internet users' ability to seek, receive, and impart information of their own choosing, and the ability of entrepreneurs around the world to launch new communications tools and services that in turn can advance human rights. Fully protecting user choice and free expression and other rights online therefore requires that governments take steps to prevent access providers from taking actions that may interfere with users' enjoyment of those rights.

CDT's previous work has examined the need for rules to protect neutrality as the Internet evolves.[3] This paper seeks to frame the issue more directly in terms of Internet neutrality's role in fostering a range of human rights, including free expression, access to knowledge, and democratic participation. We also offer a set of principles to guide the enactment of rules to protect Internet neutrality.

3.2 Designed for Free Expression

In terms of its technical transmission architecture, the Internet has historically been indifferent to the content transmitted across it. Two fundamental design principles underlie this architecture: layering and the end-to-end principle. Layering creates a logical separation between network functions (such as the addressing and routing of information) and endpoint functions (such as the processing and presentation of content by servers, PCs, and smartphones). The end-to-end principle requires that networks take on only network responsibilities, leaving all other functionality to the endpoints.[4]

---

[1] CDT uses the term "Internet neutrality" to make it clear that neutrality principles should apply only to Internet access, not to non-Internet services offered over broadband infrastructure. We do not argue that neutrality obligations should apply to over-the-top services offered via the Internet.

[2] See infra note 25 and accompanying text.

[3] See, *e.g.* CDT, Preserving the Essential Internet, 2006, https://www.cdt.org/paper/preserving-essential-internet.

[4] See Saltzer et al. (1984), pp. 277–288; *see also* Brief of Internet Engineers, *FCC v. Verizon* (US Court of Appeals for the DC Circuit, 11-1355), http://www.fcc.gov/document/internet-engineers-amicus-brief-no-11-1355-dc-cir (a legal brief explaining the technical functionality of the Internet presented to the court considering a legal challenge to the US Federal Communications Commission's rules to establish Internet neutrality).

By analogy to the postal system, endpoints are like people writing and reading letters, while the primary function of ISPs' routers and switches is to read addresses and move information to its destination like the postal service. The result is a general-purpose network that accepts an ever-expanding array of content and applications—ranging from Skype to 'cloud' storage to personal websites. Within the Internet, networks receive and forward communications, without having to make an assessment of what the traffic is (*e.g.* whether it is an e-mail, a website, or a voice-over-IP call).

This approach permits the greatest level of flexibility for new uses of the Internet, making the Internet an unprecedented platform for free expression and innovation in communications. End users post any content and can invent wholly new applications and services without any changes to the underlying network. It enables any two Internet users—individuals, companies, websites, etc.—to communicate with each other without any need to get permission or make prior arrangements (other than purchasing basic access to the Internet) with their network providers or any other entity in between the two end points.[5] "The Internet is a general purpose technology that creates value not through its own existence, but by enabling users to do what they want. The Internet thus creates maximum value when users remain free to choose the applications they most highly value."[6]

This design has resulted in specific characteristics that support the Internet's power to promote free expression, access to knowledge, and democratic participation through ever-expanding means and opportunities for communication.[7] These defining attributes of the Internet include:

- **Global**: Absent interference, the Internet provides immediate access to information from around the world. For a user, it is as easy to send information to, or receive information from, a user on another continent as it is to communicate with a user in the building next door.
- **User-Controlled**: The Internet allows users to exercise far more choice than even cable/satellite television or shortwave radio. As the Internet exists now, a user can skip from site to site in ways that are not dictated by either the content providers or the access provider. User-controlled filtering tools can help users prevent unwanted content from reaching their computers.[8]
- **Decentralized**: The Internet is based on open technical standards and was designed to be decentralized. At the edges of the network, innovators can create a very wide range of applications and offer them without seeking approval or coordination of the entities operating the core of the network. This has meant that, compared to other forms of mass media, the Internet lacks the kind of

---

[5] See van Schewick (2010), pp. 72–75, 286–289 (discussing "end-to-end," "application-blind" network architecture).

[6] Engineers' brief, *supra* note 4.

[7] *See* CDT, *Regardless of Frontiers: The International Right to Freedom of Expression in the Digital Age*, April 2011, http://www.cdt.org/files/pdfs/CDT-Regardless_of_Frontiers_v0.5.pdf.

[8] See Morris and Wong (2009).

gatekeepers that exist in legacy print or broadcasting media and offers low barriers to access.

- **Open & Competitive**: The Internet is relatively unconstrained by scarce resources (as compared to, for example, radio and television broadcast channels) and can accommodate an essentially unlimited number of endpoints and speakers. Relative to mass media, there is much greater parity between large and small speakers online. Differences in resources notwithstanding, any individual can post content and make it accessible to the same global audience as that of large media companies.

While these characteristics have historically represented the status quo, access providers are increasingly technologically capable and economically motivated to act in ways that would alter these characteristics to the detriment of individuals' enjoyment of human rights. Internet neutrality is primarily concerned with preserving these characteristics, especially openness.

CDT defines Internet neutrality as the principle that providers of Internet access should not discriminate in their carriage of Internet traffic on the basis of its source, destination, content, or associated application.[9] Internet neutrality requirements are a key tool for addressing the risk that access providers will distort competition and reduce opportunities for free expression online (for example by slowing the traffic from services that compete with their own offerings). They are critical for ensuring that the Internet continues to promote openness, innovation, and human rights as the role the Internet plays in world economies, governance, and public discourse grows ever larger.

3.3   The Internet and Human Rights

The Internet reflects and has substantially advanced two central, forward-looking concepts of international free expression standards: borderlessness and choice. The Universal Declaration of Human Rights states, "Everyone has the right to freedom of opinion and expression; this right includes freedom to hold opinions without interference and to seek, receive and impart information and ideas *through any media and regardless of frontiers.*"[10] Similarly, Article 19.2 of the International Covenant on Civil and Political Rights states, "Everyone shall have the right to freedom of expression; this right shall include freedom to seek, receive and impart information and ideas of all kinds, *regardless of frontiers*, either orally, in writing or in print, in the form of art, or *through any other media of his choice.*"

As a decentralized global network, the Internet offers individuals the unprecedented power to seek and impart information across borders. It offers not

---

[9] Appropriate exceptions should be made for reasonable network management. CDT has written extensively on the practicalities of implementing Internet neutrality rules. *See generally* https://wwwcdt.org/issue/internet-neutrality.

[10] Article 19 (emphasis added).

only unprecedented global reach for individual speakers, but also unprecedented capacity for diverse information sources ranging from professional media sites to social networking sites, educational resources such as MIT Open Courseware,[11] and video platforms for audiences to choose from.

Accordingly, there is growing international consensus that the right to freedom of expression must be fully protected on the Internet. In 2011, UN Special Rapporteur for Freedom of Opinion and Expression Frank LaRue issued a landmark report on online free expression, calling the Internet "one of the most important vehicles by which individuals exercise their right to freedom of opinion and expression."[12] LaRue and the special rapporteurs on freedom of expression to regional human-rights bodies for Africa, the Americas, and Europe also jointly issued a set of principles for online free expression, including that "Freedom of expression applies to the Internet, as it does to all means of communication. Restrictions on freedom of expression on the Internet are only acceptable if they comply with established international standards."[13] The Human Rights Committee's ICCPR General Comment 34 specifies that protected means of expression "include all forms of audio-visual as well as electronic and internet-based modes of expression."[14] And in 2012 the Human Rights Council issued a resolution that the "same rights that people have offline must also be protected online, in particular freedom of expression."[15]

Moreover, free expression is an enabling right, the exercise of which feeds directly into the exercise of other social, cultural, economic and political rights, "such as the right to education[,] the right to take part in cultural life and to enjoy the benefits of scientific progress and its applications, [and] the rights to freedom of association and assembly."[16] And experience has shown how the Internet can empower not just individual free expression and access to information, but also political discourse, participation in culture, and economic development.[17] This magnifies the Internet's unique power to advance a range of human rights and underscores the importance of preserving that power through meaningful Internet neutrality rules.

---

[11] http://ocw.mit.edu.

[12] UN Human Rights Council, Report of the Special Rapporteur on the promotion and protection of the right to freedom of opinion and expression, Frank La Rue, May 2011, http://daccess-ods.un.org/access.nsf/Get?Open&DS=A/HRC/17/27&Lang=E.

[13] Frank LaRue, Dunja Mijatović (Organization for Security and Co-operation in Europe), Catalina Botero Marino (Organization of American States), and Faith Pansy Tlakula (African Commission on Human and Peoples' Rights), Special Rapporteurs' Joint Declaration on Freedom of Expression and the Internet, June 2011, http://www.oas.org/en/iachr/expression/showarticle.asp?artID=848&lID=1.

[14] UN Human Rights Committee, General Comment 34, ¶ 12.

[15] Human Rights Council, *The promotion, protection and enjoyment of human rights on the Internet*, A/HRC/RES/20/8, 17 June 2012, http://ap.ohchr.org/documents/dpage_e.aspx?si=A/HRC/RES/20/8.

[16] UN Special Rapporteur's Report, *supra* note 12.

[17] *See* CDT, *Regardless of Frontiers*, *supra* note 7; *see also* McKinsey (2012).

3.4 Internet Neutrality's Role in Fostering Human Rights

In human-rights terms, preserving Internet neutrality means preserving the power of individuals to make choices about how they use the Internet—what information to seek, receive, and impart, from which sources, and through which services. This in turn advances the other cultural and civil and political rights listed in the previous section.[18]

Violations of the neutrality principle that amount to blocking certain information resources or restricting what information Internet users can impart over their connection would have serious implications for the right to free expression. For example, blocking access to a particular lawful blog because its content is disfavored by the access provider would raise obvious concerns. Indeed, the blocking of Internet content by states has long been a leading concern of Internet-free expression advocates and was a major focus of the UN Special Rapporteur's report.[19]

In the Internet neutrality context, however, outright blocking often poses a much less realistic threat than the risk that access providers will seek to discriminate among different types or providers of Internet content. Discrimination among content can refer to either prioritizing or slowing down certain content for delivery over an access provider's network. When the net neutrality debate first flared in the US in the mid 2000s, broadband company executives made statements not about blocking per se, but about their desire either to obtain payment from the services their subscribers used or to enter into special arrangements with certain content providers to guarantee faster delivery speeds. This desire—to be paid by content providers for carrying their traffic—has continued to manifest in disputes over the terms by which large content networks (such as Google/YouTube) and large access providers (such as France Telecom—Orange) interconnect and exchange traffic.[20] And there appears to be a growing trend toward "sponsored data" arrangements,

---

[18] *See, e.g.*, Human Right Council, Report of the Special Rapporteur on the rights of peaceful assemble and association, Maina Kiai, May 2012, ¶ 32, http://www.ohchr.org/Documents/HRBodies/HRCouncil/RegularSession/Session20/A-HRC-20-27_en.pdf. ("The Special Rapporteur notes the increased use of the Internet, in particular social media, and other information and communication technology, as basic tools which enable individuals to organize peaceful assemblies.")

[19] *See supra* note 12, ¶ 31 ("States' use of blocking or filtering technologies is frequently in violation of their obligation to guarantee the right to freedom of expression." In addition, the report concludes that "while States are the duty-bearers for human rights, private actors and business enterprises also have a responsibility to respect human rights").

[20] *See* Spence (2013). Providers of Internet access have been roundly criticized for regulatory proposals to favor payment from content and application providers for the delivery of their traffic to Internet users. *See* Body of European Regulators for Electronic Communications, BEREC's comments on the ETNO proposal for ITU/WCIT or similar initiatives along these lines, November 2012, http://berec.europa.eu/eng/document_register/subject_matter/berec/others/1076-berecs-comments-on-the-etno-proposal-for-ituwcit-or-similar-initiatives-along-these-lines; CDT, *ETNO Proposal Threatens Access to Open, Global Internet*, June 2012, https://www.cdt.org/report/etno-proposal-threatens-access-open-global-internet.

particularly in the mobile market, under which content providers make deals with access providers to exempt their content and services from data usage caps.[21]

Discriminatory treatment of traffic has a more subtle but nonetheless meaningful impact on users' rights. First, the means of identifying traffic to carry out discriminatory treatment may impact the privacy of users' communications. In addition, choosing freely from among the myriad content, applications, and services available on the open Internet is an important part of the exercise of the right to free expression online. If access providers speed up or slow down access to certain sites, that choice risks becoming the illusion of choice, with users unwittingly steered toward particular content or services they might not have otherwise chosen.

Moreover, the Internet is not simply another mass medium for the one-way dissemination of content and information; it is also a platform for the development of new communications tools. Much like the way the free expression right is an enabler of other rights, the Internet is an enabler of varied, diverse media and services that in turn advance the enjoyment of free expression and other rights. Internet neutrality helps preserve a competitive market for such online content and services, fostering a diverse array of information sources and communication tools that enables the enjoyment of human rights by users of those tools. New competitors benefit tremendously from the open Internet's low barriers to entry. Once a company pays for its own Internet connection, it instantly gets access to the whole global network—a virtually infinite addressable market. Small providers of content, applications and services can compete directly for end users on a technologically neutral playing field, regardless of identity of the users' ISPs.

By contrast, if the Internet were to move in a direction where each ISP may determine whether and how fast its subscribers can access particular content and services, providers of online content and services would face a very different environment. Every new service would have to worry about how its traffic would be treated by various ISPs across the globe in order to be assured reaching the largest potential audience. And inevitably, some application providers would seek to gain competitive advantage by striking deals with ISPs for favorable treatment. As deals with ISPs became commonplace, anyone who did not strike such deals might face significant competitive disadvantages. Or in cases where paid priority was viewed as a necessity, content providers may choose to withhold their content from the customers of some access providers rather than pay. Whether through the onset of higher economic barriers to entry (such as a small startup in South America not having the leverage to pay to compete in foreign markets) or through refusals to serve certain markets deemed not worth the cost, the end result would be far fewer information sources and communications tools for Internet users.

Thus, the economic benefits of Internet neutrality—a neutral Internet that fosters competition among Internet-based services and economic development—also enhance the human rights benefits. By expanding the universe of information

---

[21] Data usage caps are numerical limits on the amount of data a subscriber to an Internet access provider may use per month. See *e.g.* Houghton (2012).

sources and services, this open, competitive environment supports user choice, free expression, access to knowledge and information, and public discourse and activism. The loss of a neutral platform for online services would undermine the ability of Internet users to exercise fully their fundamental rights online.

3.5   States' Role and Guiding Principles for Neutrality Rules

The Special Rapporteurs' Joint Statement on Freedom of Expression and the Internet, recognizing the Internet's power and the risk that interference with its use poses to free expression, included the following clear and specific call for the protection of Internet neutrality: "There should be no discrimination in the treatment of Internet data and traffic, based on the device, content, author, origin and/or destination of the content, service or application."[22] Enacting laws or regulations to protect Internet neutrality is one step states can take to heed this call and meet their obligation to protect the right to freedom of expression and opinion as well as other rights empowered by the Internet.

For state-owned access providers or providers with relatively direct ties to government, disproportionate or egregious interference with citizens' use of the Internet may well rise to direct violations of users' rights under the ICCPR if they do not meet the standard for permissible limitations.[23] But where Internet access services are privately run, even if competitively offered, discriminatory actions by these providers can also restrict rights. Indeed, the UN Special Rapporteur's report noted that "the private sector has gained unprecedented influence over individuals' right to freedom of expression."[24] And in such contexts where actions by private entities can restrict rights, the Human Rights Committee has advised that "the positive obligations on States Parties to ensure Covenant rights will only be fully discharged if individuals are protected by the State, not just against violations of Covenant rights by its agents, but also against acts committed by private persons or entities that would impair the enjoyment of Covenant rights in so far as they are amenable to application between private persons or entities."[25]

---

[22] *See supra* note 13, ¶ 5.

[23] General Comment 34, *supra* note 14, ¶ 7 ("The obligation to respect freedoms of opinion and expression is binding on every State party as a whole. ... Such responsibility may also be incurred by a State party under some circumstances in respect of acts of semi-State entities.") The UN Special Rapporteur's report, *supra note* 12, summarizes how, to be permissible under international human rights law, any such restrictions on free expression imposed by states must be (i) transparently described in law, and (ii) the least restrictive means of achieving a (iii) legitimate purpose as listed in Article 19.3 of the ICCPR.

[24] UN Special Rapporteur's Report, *supra note* 12, ¶ 44.

[25] UN Human Rights Committee, General Comment 31, *The Nature of the General Legal Obligation Imposed on States Parties to the Covenant*, Adopted 29 March 2004 (2187th meeting), ¶ 8, http://daccess-ods.un.org/access.nsf/Get?Open&DS=CCPR/C/21/Rev.1/Add.13&Lang=E; See also Human Rights Council, Report of the Special Representative of the Secretary-General on

Below, we offer five principles to guide the substantive development of Internet neutrality protections that can help states meet their duty to protect free expression and other human rights online.

There should be a clear expectation that Internet access services must be provided in a neutral manner, without discrimination based on the content, applications, or services subscribers choose to access. The core principle of Internet neutrality is that ISPs must not discriminate among lawful traffic based on its content, source, destination, ownership, application, or service. There is an emerging consensus among states and regions that have taken up Internet neutrality to prefer application-agnostic, i.e. nondiscriminatory, network management.[26] Reasonable, narrow exceptions should be permitted, but non-discrimination—including banning both prioritization and de-prioritization of traffic—must be established as the baseline expectation.

The scope of the neutrality obligation should be clearly defined and should account for the crucial distinction between Internet access services and specialized services. CDT prefers the term "Internet neutrality" because the goal is to preserve the openness of the Internet—as opposed to other, non-Internet services that also may be offered using broadband networks, such as stand-alone voice- or television-over-IP services. The neutrality and openness of the Internet platform can be adequately protected without foreclosing the use those networks for a wide range of non-Internet services on terms and conditions of network operators' own choosing. But the line between Internet access and other services not subject to a neutrality obligation must be clear; specialized services must be truly specialized in the sense of serving a specific and limited purpose. A service that provides a general-purpose ability to send and receive data communications across the entire Internet should not be eligible for treatment as a specialized service.

---

the issue of human rights and transnational corporations and other business enterprises, Ruggie (2011), (The Framework rests in part on states' obligation as to third parties, as well as the "corporate responsibility to respect human rights, which means that business enterprises should act with due diligence to avoid infringing on the rights of others.")

[26] *See, e.g.* US Federal Communications Commission, *Report and Order in the matter of Preserving the Open Internet* (GN Docket No, 09-191), Adopted 21 December 2010, http://hraunfoss.fcc.gov/edocs_public/attachmatch/FCC-10-201A1.pdf; Canadian Radio-television and Telecommunications Commission, *Review of the Internet traffic management practices of Internet service providers* (CRTC 2009-657), 21 October 2009, http://www.crtc.gc.ca/eng/archive/2009/2009-657.htm; Chile, Ley núm. 20.453 Consagra el Principo de Neutralidad en la Red para los Consumidores y Usarios de Internet, http://www.leychile.cl/Navegar?idNorma=1016570 (in Spanish); Netherlands, Telecommunications Act, adopted May 2012, discussion available at Door Ot van Daalen, "Netherlands First Country in Europe with Net Neutrality," *Bits of Freedom blog*, 8 May 2012, https://www.bof.nl/2012/05/08/netherlands-first-country-in-europe-with-net-neutrality/ (partial unofficial English translation available at https://www.bof.nl/2011/06/27/translations-of-key-dutch-internet-freedom-provisions/; Solvenia, Zakona o elektronskih komunikacijah (ZEKom-1) (Electronic Communications Act), adopted 20 December 2012, http://www.uradni-list.si/_pdf/2012/Ur/u2012109.pdf#!/u2012109-pdf (English summary available at http://radiobruxelleslibera.wordpress.com/2013/01/03/slovenia-reinforces-net-neutrality-principles/.

The neutrality obligation should apply equally to fixed and mobile Internet access services. In a converging world where wireless mobile connectivity is expected to make Internet access increasingly ubiquitous, failing to address mobile would leave a gaping hole in any policy meant to promote openness and nondiscrimination on the Internet. Mobile carriers may face some special technical challenges, relating to such factors as spectrum limitations and radio interference. Given these technical realities, what constitutes reasonable traffic management on a mobile data network may differ from the norm on fixed connections. But there is no reason to think that mobile ISPs need to discriminate among traffic based on content-related factors such as its source, ownership, application, or service. Core neutrality principles can and should apply to mobile Internet access services.

There should be clear guidelines for evaluating exceptions for reasonable network management practices. Rather than attempting to specify which particular technical practices are acceptable, Internet neutrality rules should establish clear but flexible criteria for assessing the reasonableness of network management techniques that deviate from the non-discrimination norm. As exceptions to the neutrality rule, reasonable network management activities should be consistent with international human rights standards regarding transparency, narrow tailoring, and proportionality. Wherever possible, traffic management practices should be content- and application-neutral. This is the most reliable way to ensure that traffic management is applied fairly and evenly, and that the ISP is not selecting which specific content or applications to favor or disfavor. The US Federal Communications Commission, the Body of European Regulators for Electronic Communications, and the French Autorité de Régulation des Communications éléctroniques et des Postes have all proposed criteria for assessing the reasonableness of network management practices.[27]

The neutrality obligation should not apply to over-the-top services available on the Internet. Internet neutrality must focus on the goal of preserving the Internet as a neutral, non-discriminatory transmission medium. Thus, the obligation should apply to access providers only, and not to the limitless array of content, services, and application available over the Internet. Concerns over market power, competition, or the human rights impact and obligations of these services are best addressed separately.

As the role of the Internet in the social, economic, and political areas of everyone's life grows ever greater, states must act to ensure that the enjoyment of human rights is protected. We strongly believe that rules based on these principles will help preserve the Internet's unique power to promote free expression and other rights.

---

[27] FCC *Open Internet Order*, *ibid.*; ARCEP (2012), pp. 24–26; BEREC (2012), p. 6.

References

ARCEP. (2012, September). *Internet and network neutrality: Proposals and recommendations* (pp. 24–26). http://www.arcep.fr/uploads/tx_gspublication/net-neutralite-orientations-sept2010-eng.pdf

BEREC. (2012, December). *Summary of BEREC positions on net neutrality* (p. 6). http://berec.europa.eu/files/document_register_store/2012/12/BoR_(12)_146_Summary_of_BEREC_positions_on_net_neutrality2.pdf

Houghton, B. (2012, October 1). Spotify Adds Germany's Deutsche Telekom to growing list of mobile deals. *Hypebot.* http://www.hypebot.com/hypebot/2012/10/spotify-adds-germanys-deutsche-telekom-to-growing-list-of-mobile-deals.html

McKinsey. (2012, January). *Online and upcoming: The Internet's impact on aspiring countries.* http://www.mckinsey.com/client_service/high_tech/latest_thinking/impact_of_the_internet_on_aspiring_countries

Morris, J. B., Jr., & Wong, C. M. (2009, Fall). Revisiting user control: The emergence and success of a first amendment theory for the Internet age. *University of North Carolina First Amendment Law Review, 8.* http://www.cdt.org/files/pdfs/morris_wong_user_control.pdf

Ruggie, J. (2011, March 21). *Guiding principles on business and human rights: Implementing the United Nations "Protect, Respect and Remedy" Framework.*

Saltzer, J. H., Reed, D. P., & Clark, D. D. (1984, November 4). End-to-end arguments in system design. *ACM Transactions in Computer Systems, 2,* 277–288. http://web.mit.edu/Saltzer/www/publications/endtoend/endtoend.pdf

Spence, E. (2013, January 20). Why Orange's dominance in Africa forced Google to pay for traffic over the mobile network. *Forbes.* http://www.forbes.com/sites/ewanspence/2013/01/20/why-oranges-dominance-in-africa-forced-google-to-pay-for-traffic-over-their-mobile-network/

van Schewick, B. (2010). *Internet architecture and innovation* (pp. 72–75, 286–289). MIT Press.

Chapter 4
Net Neutrality from a Public Sphere Perspective

Francesca Musiani and Maria Löblich

4.1   Introduction

The Internet impacts social communication and the public sphere, and this impact has consequences for the political shape of the communication order—therefore, for society as a whole. One important question in this regard is which regulatory framework is being developed for the Internet, and how this framework enables and at the same time restricts communication in the public sphere. Net neutrality is at the very core of this question: distribution channels can be used as a means to discriminate, control, and prevent communication. In other words, content and user behavior can be controlled through the architecture of the physical layer and the "code" layer of the Internet. The discussion on net neutrality touches fundamental values (public interest, freedom of expression, freedom of the media, and free flow of information), that communications policy authorities in liberal democracies frequently appeal to in order to legitimize their interventions in media systems. The implementation of these values, from a normative point of view, is seen as the precondition for media to create the public sphere—be it online or offline—and thus fulfill its function in society (Napoli 2001).

Differing concepts of the public sphere are present in the work of several authors. However, the concept developed by Jürgen Habermas (1989; Calhoun 1992; Lunt and Livingstone 2013; Splichal 2012; Wendelin 2011) is widely recognized as being the most influential. According to Habermas, the public sphere links citizens and power holders; it is "a realm of our social life in which something approaching public opinion can be formed." Habermas' concept of the public sphere centers on deliberation. Functioning deliberation requires that "access is guaranteed to all

F. Musiani (✉)
Institute for Communication Sciences (CNRS/Paris-Sorbonne/UPMC), Paris, France

M. Löblich
Ludwig-Maximilians-Universität of Munich, Munich, Germany

© Springer International Publishing Switzerland 2016   43
L. Belli, P. De Filippi (eds.), *Net Neutrality Compendium*,
DOI 10.1007/978-3-319-26425-7_4

citizens" (Habermas 1984, p. 49). This emphasis on access makes this concept of the public sphere particularly useful for an investigation of the net neutrality debate. Dahlgren (1995, 2005, 2010) developed Habermas' notion of the public sphere into an analytic tool in order to study the role of the media and the Internet vis-a-vis the public sphere. According to Dahlgren, the public sphere is "a constellation of communicative spaces in society that permit the circulation of information, ideas, debates – ideally in an unfettered manner – and also the formation of political will" (Dahlgren 2005, p. 148). Traditional media and online media play an important role in these spaces or "public spheres" (as there are distinct, sometimes overlapping social spaces that constitute different public spheres; Dahlgren 2010, p. 21).

Dahlgren (1995) distinguishes three analytical dimensions of the public sphere: the structural, the representational, and the interactional. The structural dimension refers to the organization of communicative spaces "in terms of legal, social, economic, cultural, technical, and even Web-architectural features" (Dahlgren 2005, p. 149). These patterns impact Internet access. The representational dimension directs attention to media output and raises questions concerning fairness, pluralism of views, agenda setting, ideological biases, and other evaluation criteria for media content. According to Dahlgren, representation remains highly relevant for online contexts of the public sphere. The interactional dimension focuses on the ways users interact with the media and with each other in particular online sites and spaces. In these "micro-contexts of every-day life" users deliberate on meaning, identity, opinions, or entertain themselves (Dahlgren 2005, p. 149).

We use these analytical dimensions as a heuristic framework to identify net neutrality areas that are relevant for communication studies; thus, each dimension serves as an entry point into a particular set of net neutrality issues. The structural dimension is an analytical starting point for examining the bundle of net neutrality issues that are related to access to the Internet infrastructure for individuals and collective entities. The representational dimension leads to the question of how net neutrality relates to online content. We refer to content "accessible in the public Internet," as opposed to secure or closed private networks (Marsden 2010, p. 29). The related issues are content diversity, control, and censorship of social communication—although, of course, net neutrality is just one aspect of these debates. The interactional dimension directs attention to the modes, cultures, and spaces of social communication online and whether they are affected by net neutrality. Closed systems or "walled gardens" will illustrate the extent to which the potential benefits of online interaction and deliberation can be impeded or lost.

Dahlgren had outlined these dimensions before the Internet became so widely diffused; thus, there is some overlapping when they are applied to online spaces. Content control carried out by Deep Packet Inspection (DPI)—packet filtering techniques examining the data and the header of a packet as it passes an inspection point in the network—may affect interacting users as much as media organizations. While Dahlgren pointed to the blurring of the representation and interaction dimensions in relation to the Internet, traditional mass communication categories such as "one-to-many" versus "one-to-one" can no longer be separated as clearly (Dahlgren 2005, pp. 149–150). However, by distinguishing access to Internet infrastructure, diversity of content transmitted via Internet infrastructure, and user interaction enabled through Internet infrastructure, these dimensions provide important analytical tools.

4.2 Structural Dimension: Access to the Network for Content Producers

Architectural, economic, and other structures shape the organization of communicative spaces and constitute the framework for different actors' access to Internet infrastructure. Net neutrality bears technical implications and economic consequences for audiovisual content producers, news media outlets, and other corporate content providers. These implications influence the definition and the implementation of the quality of service principle. This principle is essential for audiovisual service providers because video on demand needs to be delivered by strict technical deadlines ("real-time" traffic). Delays severely and negatively affect the viewing experience (van Eijk 2011, p. 9). By contrast, an email "just needs to get there as soon as (and as fast as) possible (so-called 'best-effort' traffic)" (Clark 2007, p. 705). Therefore, some authors make the point that network management can benefit content providers and consumers by making the flow of traffic more balanced, or smoother (Yoo 2012, p. 542).

In order to prevent network overload at times of peak usage, corporate content providers make quality of service one of their priorities. Google has built its own infrastructure of server farms and fiber-optic networks in order to store content and get it more quickly to end-users (Levy 2012). Economists have argued that producers of the next generation of online video, who depend "critically" on the prioritization of data, need a legal or quasi-legal assurance of their delivery (Hahn and Litan 2007, p. 605). Proponents of net neutrality, however, emphasize that the priority should be to keep the costs of market entry as low as possible for the "lowest end market entrants – application companies" (Wu and Yoo 2007, p. 591).

As the Internet becomes an increasingly important distribution channel for traditional media, the boundaries of old business models (television, telecommunication) blur. Problems arise with the interaction of content and networks (Vogelsang 2010, pp. 8–9). In the view of many scholars, deviations from network neutrality do not necessarily harm users and media organizations. However, these scholars generally acknowledge that situations where Internet service providers become content providers may favor the implementation of network management techniques in order to discriminate against competitors. Providers can exclude competitor content, distribute it poorly, or make competitors pay for using high-speed networks (Marsden 2010, p. 30; van Eijk 2011, p. 10). Critics fear a similar model, derived from cable TV industry, where cable providers "charge a termination fee to those who wish to get access to the user" (Marsden 2010, p. 18). In particular, this would mean a burden for new media businesses and non-commercial services, such as citizens' media and blogs. While large content providers can negotiate free or even profitable access, smaller content providers with less contracting power are forced to pay cable TV operators for access. As a result, net neutrality might be easily circumvented both by large content providers and ISPs (Marsden 2010, pp. 18, 101). While some scholars argue that antitrust and competition laws are sufficient to protect upstart content providers from negative consequences of vertical integration and concentration (Hahn and Litan 2007, p. 606), others argue that there are limits to competition in the access network market due to high fixed costs that restrict market entry (Vogelsang 2010, p. 7).

In Europe, a special concern is public service broadcasting. Many scholars demand an open and non-discriminatory access to distribution for this service. Several German authors, for instance, regard must-carry rules as a suitable instrument to secure the circulation of online services: They suggest introducing a classification of online services that fulfill indispensable functions for public sphere, contribute to the diversity of opinions, and, therefore, should enjoy the privilege of must-carry rules. They classify public service broadcasting as such an indispensable service (Holznagel 2010, p. 95; Libertus and Wiesner 2011, p. 88). The question remains, however, who decides which services should get this privilege and, in general, whether net neutrality will only apply to public service broadcasting (directing other content into the slow lane) or to all content providers (Marsden 2010, pp. 83, 98).

4.3   Representational Dimension: Diversity and Control of Content

A functioning public sphere is based on the representation of the diversity of information, ideas, and opinions (Dahlgren 2005, p. 149). Different technical practices of inspection or prioritization of data packets, for political or law enforcement purposes, shape net neutrality in various ways. They condition access and circulation of content and restrict the variety and diversity of such content.

A number of technical practices are currently available to governments and the information technology industry to control or restrict content. Examples are bandwidth throttling (the intentional slowing down of Internet service by an ISP), blocking of websites, prioritization of certain services to the detriment of others, and Deep Packet Inspection (DPI). The latter has several implications, beyond net neutrality, for privacy, copyright, and other issues. DPI may be implemented for a variety of reasons, including the search for protocol non-compliance, virus, spam, intrusions; the setting of criteria to decide whether a packet may go through or if it needs to be routed to a different destination; and the collection of statistical information (Bendrath and Mueller 2011; Mueller and Asghari 2012).

As a technology capable of enabling advanced network management and user service and security functions potentially intrusive or harmful to user privacy—such as data mining, eavesdropping, and censorship—DPI has been framed in a predominantly negative way. This is due to the fact that, even though this technology has been used for Internet management for many years already, some net neutrality proponents fear that the technology may be used to prevent economic competition and to reduce the openness of the Internet. Indeed, this has already happened. For example, in April 2008, Bell Canada was accused of using DPI technology to block peer-to-peer traffic generated not only by clients of its service Sympatico but also by other consumers relying on independent ISPs (Bendrath and Mueller 2011, p. 1153). Thus, net neutrality proponents argue that the purpose of DPI deployment is crucial and should be made as transparent as possible (Ufer 2010). Furthermore, the emphasis is put on the need to reflect further on the extent to which the employment of filtering techniques is bound to specific cultures. Blocking of content sometimes takes place in specific contexts where it is regarded to be harmful to the public or to some segment of the public, as is the case for hate speech. Some researchers warn that the role played by local values and cultures in the deployment of such measures should not be underestimated (Goldsmith and Wu 2006; Palfrey and Rogoyski 2006, p. 33). However, others emphasize instead that the implementation of these techniques, especially if bent to the requirements of political actors, may lead to biases in, blockings of, or censorship of the content of online communications. These scholars emphasize the power that ISPs have to "control access to vast expanse of information, entertainment and expression on the Internet" (Blevins and Barrows 2009, p. 41; Elkin-Koren 2006).

The intermediaries of the Internet economy have the technical means to implement traffic shaping practices, as well as a number of measures that are susceptible to affecting diversity of content on the Internet such as DPI or filtering. So far, the directive or mandate to shape traffic has often come from governments. The literature identifies two central motivations for political actors adopting these practices. First, they may be used by authorities as an investigation tool. ISPs are sometimes used as "sheriffs" of the Internet when they are placed in the position of enforcing the rules of the regime in which they are doing business (Palfrey and Rogoyski 2006). The use of these measures is also attributed to security purposes such as the fight against terrorism, child pornography, online piracy—with all the controversies this raises in terms of setting critical precedents (Marsden 2010, pp. 19, 67, 81)—or to allegedly protect largely shared values such as the protection of minors or the fight against hate speech (Marsden 2010, p. 102). These techniques are also used for law enforcement in the area of intellectual property protection. For example, in the infamous Comcast controversy of 2007, one of the first controversies labeled as net neutrality-related, the U.S. broadband Internet provider started blocking P2P applications, such as BitTorrent. The stated rationale was that P2P is used to share illegal content and the provider's infrastructure was not designed to deal with the high-bandwidth traffic caused by these exchanges. Accordingly, the cinema and music recording industry have repeatedly taken positions against net neutrality in their fight against "digital piracy" (Bendrath and Mueller 2011, p. 1152; Palfrey and Rogoyski 2006, p. 45). Civil society organizations and some political actors have vocally opposed both these sets of motivations, deemed as inadequate to justify an increased control of data and the invasion of freedom of speech rights (Libertus and Wiesner 2011, p. 87).

4.4   Interactional Dimension: "Walled Gardens"

Net neutrality breaches also have effects on the interactional dimension of the public sphere. The formation, in the landscape of information and communication technologies, of so-called "walled gardens"—the carrier offers service without access to the wider Internet, controls applications, and restricts non-approved content—has important implications for online interaction and illustrates the extent to which the potential advantages leveraged through online interaction and deliberation can be short-circuited by restrictions on software and content (Marsden 2010, p. 88).

The debate over the neutrality of the Internet is—perhaps surprisingly—often separated from a reflection on the attacks on the universality of the Web. However, the two largely overlap in the economic strategies of content providers and application designers on the Web and their effects on the network (Dulong de Rosnay 2011). The tendency to create "walled gardens" is perhaps the best illustration of this phenomenon. For example, social networking services harness users' personal data to provide them with value-added services but exclusively and specifically on their own sites. In doing so, they contribute to the creation of sealed "silos" of information, and they do not allow users to export or recover data easily. The "giants" of digital services manifest, more and more frequently, their intention to become broad social platforms underpinning the entire spectrum of web services using these strategies. In fact, their goal is oftentimes to direct users to specific commercial services, to closed economic systems and stores that control not only the software that can be installed on users' devices but the content (Zittrain 2008).

This is an issue of both application discrimination and content discrimination (Marsden 2010, p. 88). The ways in which content providers rely on applications that depend on major social networking players reinforces this logic of partition and gate-keeping. The walled gardens phenomenon has also been described as "balkanization" or "gilded cages." Hardware manufacturers also seek to ensure a "captive audience": The model proposed by Apple, notably, forbids providers of content and media to directly propose applications to users and prevents them from buying paid goods, such as music or digital books, outside of the Apple ecosystem (which includes, *e.g.* a partnership with Amazon).

Breaches of neutrality also affect the application layer itself. Carriers "offer exclusive, preferential treatment to one application provider," thereby creating walled gardens of preferred suppliers (Marsden 2010, p. 88). Search engines choose their answers to queries based on advertising revenue, while endorsement systems such as "Like" on Facebook and "+1" on Google, and social networking/recommendation systems such as the now-defunct Ping for iTunes, form a set of competing systems that affect the entire value chain of the Internet. The issue of "exclusivities"—especially in the mobile Internet—and of the mergers between communication operators and other stakeholders, such as Deezer and Orange, are further symptoms of the emergence of vertical conglomerates.

The walled gardens phenomenon, as an illustration of the interactional dimension of the public sphere, bridges the structural and representational dimensions by revealing the close connection between the diversity of content and the "diversity of stakeholders who have editorial control over that content" (Herman 2006, p. 116). The policy implemented by Apple in relation to applications developed by external actors is seen as a possible way to downplay unwelcome political and cultural ideas. Preventing an application from running on Apple devices may have immediate implications for diversity of political views. Similarly, an ISP may or may not allow users to select some of the Web sites contained or barred from the garden, thus hindering expressions of political and social significance with network management choices (Nunziato 2009, pp. 5–8). The isolation of content on specific networks or services from other content on the wider Internet, preventing broader interaction between them, is reinforced by the "cumulative effect" of walled gardens. If a sufficient number of people join a service and the service is able to reach a critical mass of users, the system becomes self-reinforcing. The companies managing them are able to move toward a quasi-monopoly (Marsden 2010, pp. 67, 186–194).

Legal scholar Christopher Yoo argued that ISPs and companies such as Apple may be considered as editors, endowed with "editorial discretion" and equipped with "editorial filters," because of their *de facto* right to remove inappropriate content (2005, pp. 47–48). He controversially points out that "the fact that telecommunications networks now serve as the conduit for mass communications and not just person-to-person communications greatly expands the justification for allowing them to exercise editorial control over the information they convey. In the process, it further weakens the case in favor of network neutrality" (Yoo 2005, pp. 47–48). In this view, net neutrality measures would be counter-beneficial as they would prevent ISPs from providing some guarantee of quality of content, when faced with information overload. For example, Blevins and Barrows (2009) stated that "certain ISPs may not want to carry speech that in their determination is indecent, pornographic, or related to hate groups or particular religious or political persuasions" (p. 38). However, the comparison made by Yoo with editorial rights of newsrooms (2005, pp. 46–47) appears inadequate, as journalism is a profession with its own logic, self-understanding, norms, rules, and programs, which do not apply to ISPs. Herman (2006) pointed out that broadband providers are not considered to be editors. In addition, giving editorial control to users of the Internet, rather than providers, best exemplifies democratic goals (Blevins and Barrows 2009, p. 41).

The issue of walled gardens and net neutrality is further compounded (and complicated) by the advent of the mobile Internet, for which the allotted bandwidth remains scarce. At the same time, mobile networks increasingly constitute the first "entry point" into the Internet for several regions in the world—first and foremost, Africa. Access restrictions on mobiles to certain protocols, such as Voice over IP (VoIP), and other limits, are officially justified by a poor allocation of band frequency. But they are often attributable, behind the scenes, to industrial battles. The model fostered by Apple's iPhone (and its "cousins", such as Amazon's Kindle tablet) contributes to the change in the market's power relations, by contributing to the shift of power from the operator to the hardware manufacturer (Curien and Maxwell 2011, p. 64).

Many of the most recent attempts to circumvent net neutrality directly involve mobile telephony. In the summer of 2010, Google and Verizon were discussing the prices that the "giant" of search would have to pay to the operator for a "preferential treatment" given to the videos of Google's subsidiary YouTube. The reasons why Google—previously very much in favor of Internet providers' independence—changed its position are numerous, but the first and foremost is the ongoing battle between Google's Android and Apple's iPhone. By blocking some of Google's applications—notably a system allowing to telephone via the Internet rather than the mobile network, and the applications for geolocalized advertisement—Apple has shown the force of a system installed behind a steely wall of exclusivity. Also, in order to be diffused on the iPhone, YouTube's videos need to be encoded in the H264 format, for which Apple has patents. Google has now replied with the WebM format, bought from On2 Technologies and transformed into an open web media project. The speed at which YouTube became the primary video streaming service on the Internet may reinforce this tendency to WebM, which has become the standard on all Chrome and Firefox navigators since April 2011. This battle between Google and Apple shows how, even if there is a diversity of applications serving the same end, the lack of openness of such applications limits interaction, at best, to within each of them, thereby greatly reducing interoperability and access.

The danger of these power plays has not gone unnoticed by scholars. Interviewed by the *New York Times* on November 14, 2010, Tim Wu—whose then-recently published book *The Master Switch* described the rise-and-fall cycles of great "communication empires" (Wu 2010)—gave a disenchanted view of the Cupertino firm and its now-deceased CEO Steve Jobs, noting that "firms today, like Apple, make it unclear if the Internet is something lasting or just another cycle … The man who helped create the personal computer 40 years ago is probably the leading candidate to help exterminate it. His vision has an undeniable appeal, but he wants too much control" (Wu and Bilton 2010).

4.5 Conclusions

Net neutrality is concerned with the organization of the online public sphere infrastructure, in particular its technical, and especially its economic and power structures. At the same time, net neutrality takes into account the interests of old and new content providers and of Internet users and Internet service providers. Large content providers such as Google and Facebook are not the only "gatekeepers" on the Internet. Internet service providers, perhaps more than any other entity, enable and constrain online communication. Net neutrality research takes their position into consideration, exploring how diverse interests can be balanced in the light of increased bandwidth usage, quality of service demands, and limited mobile Internet capacities.

A functioning public sphere is based on the representation of the diversity of information, ideas, and opinions. Traffic shaping and filtering measures are applied for economic reasons, but also for political and law enforcement ones. These measures can be fostered by other actors than Internet service providers.

The existence of "walled gardens" points to the fact that interaction in the online public sphere can be impeded by restrictions on software and content. In closed platforms, providers decide which applications, content, and information are allowed and which are not allowed within the service. Proprietary, closed systems set limits for connecting to the Web and pose limits to the user's individual capacity to refine or develop new applications based on existing ones. Users, when confronted to the net neutrality debates, are equipped with diverse and uneven tools. Not all users have the technical knowledge enabling them to make informed choices; these are therefore, out of necessity, often left outside the realm of political intervention and to the exclusive authority of the market. Thus, actors with large and multifaceted stakes in the Internet value chain are constantly on the verge of monopolizing a debate with underlying impacts on social architecture, fundamental freedoms, and the conditions for democratic expression.

There is some overlapping and interrelation between the dimensions, due to the blurring of categories in an online public sphere. However, the three analytical dimensions—access to Internet infrastructure, diversity of content transmitted via Internet infrastructure, and user interaction enabled through Internet infrastructure—highlight how a perspective grounded in communication studies can complement the frameworks offered in the economic and legal traditions, thereby offering a more robust basis for an informed debate on the issues raised by the contested net neutrality terrain. The public sphere perspective connects, for example, scholars interested in freedom of expression and speech with those concerned with issues of economic advantage, monopoly, and concentration. Several fundamental issues central to communication studies, which have been re-labeled as net neutrality—for example network (de-)centralization, bottleneck regulation, monopoly and competition, public service values—reappear in new forms in the Internet environment.

References

Bendrath, R., & Mueller, M. (2011). The end of the net as we know it? Deep packet inspection and Internet governance. *New Media & Society, 13*, 1142–1160. http://dx.doi.org/10.1177/1461444811398031

Blevins, J., & Barrow, S. L. (2009). The political economy of free speech and network neutrality: A critical analysis. *Journal of Media Law & Ethics, 1*(1/2), 27–48.

Calhoun, C. (Ed.). (1992). *Habermas and the public sphere*. Cambridge, MA: MIT Press.

Clark, D. (2007). Network neutrality: Words of power and 800-pound gorillas. *International Journal of Communication, 1*, 701–708.

Curien, N., & Maxwell, W. (2011). *La neutralité d'Internet*. Paris: La Découverte.

Dahlgren, P. (2005). The Internet, public spheres, and political communication: Dispersion and deliberation. *Political Communication, 22*, 147–162. http://dx.doi.org/10.1080/10584600590933160

Dahlgren, P. (1995). *Television and the public sphere*. London: Sage.

Dahlgren, P. (2010). Public spheres, societal shifts and media modulations. In J. Gripsrud & L. Weibull (Eds.), *Media, markets & public spheres. European media at the crossroads* (pp. 17–36). Bristol: Intellect.

Dulong de Rosnay, M. (2011). Réappropriation des données et droit à la rediffusion. *Hermès, 59*, 65–66.

Elkin-Koren, N. (2006). Making technology visible: Liability of internet service providers for peer-to-peer traffic. *New York University Journal of Legislation & Public Policy, 9*(15), 15–76.

Goldsmith, J., & Wu, T. (2006). *Who controls the Internet? Illusions of a borderless world*. Oxford: Oxford University Press.

Habermas, J. (1984). *The theory of communicative action* (Vol. I & II). Cambridge: Polity Press.

Habermas, J. (1989). *The structural transformation of the public sphere*. Boston: MIT Press.

Hahn, R., & Litan, R. E. (2007). The myth of network neutrality and what we should do about it. *International Journal of Communication, 1*, 595–606.

Herman, B. D. (2006). Opening bottlenecks: On behalf of mandated network neutrality. *Federal Communications Law Journal, 59*, 107–159.

Holznagel, B. (2010). Netzneutralität als Auf gabeder Vielfaltssicherung. *Kommunikation und Recht, 13*, 95–100.

Levy, S. (2012). Power House. Deep inside a Google data center. Wired, 17 October.

Libertus, M., & Wiesner, J. (2011). Netzneutralität, offenes Internet und kommunikative Grundversorgung. *Media Perspektiven, 2*, 80–90.

Lunt, P., & Livingstone, S. (2013). Media studies' fascination with the concept of the public sphere: Critical reflections and emerging debates. *Media Culture & Society, 35*, 87–96. http://dx.doi.org/10.1177/0163443712464562

Marsden, C. (2010). *Net neutrality. Towards a co-regulatory solution*. London: Bloomsbury Academic. http://dx.doi.org/10.5040/9781849662192

Mueller, M., & Asghari, H. (2012). Deep packet inspection and bandwidth management: Battles over BitTorrent in Canada and the United States. *Telecommunications Policy, 36*, 462–475. http://dx.doi.org/10.1016/j.telpol.2012.04.003

Napoli, P. (2001). *Foundations of communications policy: Principles and process in the regulation of electronic media*. Cresskill, NJ: Hampton Press.

Nunziato, D. C. (2009). *Virtual freedom: Net neutrality and free speech in the Internet age*. Stanford: Stanford University Press.

Palfrey, J., & Rogoyski, R. (2006). The move to the middle: The enduring threat of "harmful" speech to network neutrality. *Washington University Journal of Law and Policy, 21*, 31–65.

Splichal, S. (2012). *Transnationalization of the public sphere and the fate of the public*. New York: Hampton Press.

Ufer, F. (2010). Der Kampf um die Netzneutralität oder die Frage, warum ein Netz neutral sein muss. *Kommunikation und Recht, 13*, 383–389.

Van Eijk, N. (2011). Net neutrality and audiovisual services. *IRIS Plus, 5*, 7–19.

Vogelsang, I. (2010). Die Debatte um Netzneutralität und Quality of Service. In D. Klumpp, H. Kubicek, A. Roßnagel, & W. Schulz (Eds.), *Netzwelt – Wege –Werte – Wandel* (pp. 5–14). Berlin: Springer.

Wendelin, M. (2011). *Medialisierung der Öffentlichkeit. Kontinuität und Wandel einer normativen Kategorie der Moderne*. Köln: Halem.

Wu, T. (2010). *The master switch: The rise and fall of information empires*. New York: Knopf.

Wu, T., & Yoo, C. (2007). Keeping the Internet Neutral?: Tim Wu and Christopher Yoo Debate. *Federal Communications Law Journal, 59*, 575–592.

Wu, T., & Bilton, N. (2010). One on one: Tim Wu, author of 'The Master Switch' New York Times, 14 November. http://bits.blogs.nytimes.com/2010/11/14/one-on-one-tim-wu-author-of-the-master-switch/. Accessed 9 Aug 2015.

Yoo, C. (2005). Beyond network neutrality. *Harvard Journal of Law & Technology, 19*, 1–77.

Yoo, C. (2012). Network neutrality and the need for a technological turn in Internet scholarship. In M. E. Price, S. G. Verhulst, & L. Morgan (Eds.), *Routledge handbook of media law* (pp. 539–555). New York, Abingdon: Routledge.

Zittrain, J. (2008). *The future of the Internet and how to stop it*. New Haven & London: Yale University Press.

Chapter 5
Network Neutrality Under the Lens of Risk Management

Alejandro Pisanty

An original approach to Network Neutrality is presented. Violations of Network Neutrality are considered as risk and a risk management framework to deal with such violations is presented. This framework can be used by different parties in varied environments for dealing with preventive as well as reactive action in the face of violations by Internet Service Providers and other infringing parties. The framework includes an identification of the forms of Network Neutrality violations, their weighting by likelihood and impact, and actions for risk avoidance, detection, mitigation, business continuity, contingency planning, and prevention. The actions are shown in a graduated-response order so that scaling up towards the resolution of conflict or controversy around Network Neutrality violations can be properly planned and executed.

I propose to analyze the problem of Network Neutrality through the lens of risk management, *i.e.* to apply basic disciplines of risk management to the formulation and possible violations of the principle of Network Neutrality (NN). This perspective is productive in giving the violations a treatment that can be commensurate with their likelihood and impact as well as with the cost of their avoidance, mitigation, and remediation.

The components of risk management considered in this paper have been compounded from widely-used frameworks (Landoll 2011; Miller 1992; Oren 2001). Impact and likelihood are approximate and together with naming and defining the risk are part of risk identification. Avoidance and prevention are listed separately; avoidance assumes that violations to Network Neutrality exist, whereas prevention is action intended to cause the impede or forestall Network Neutrality violations.

A. Pisanty (✉)
National University of Mexico, Mexico City, Mexico

© Springer International Publishing Switzerland 2016
L. Belli, P. De Filippi (eds.), *Net Neutrality Compendium*,
DOI 10.1007/978-3-319-26425-7_5

5.1   Conceptual Framework for the Analysis

Network Neutrality is the principle—or extension of a more fundamental set of principles, among which the end-to-end principle (Van Schewick 2010) stands out—by which an Internet access provider (ISP) delivers Internet Protocol (IP) traffic to its users without discrimination of port numbers, protocols, origin, destination of contents of the communication carried by the IP packets. Common expressions of this principle include the expression "the five alls" meaning all ports, all protocols, all origins, all destinations, all contents are carried in a non-discriminatory fashion, which we use in communications by the Internet Society of Mexico and some of our teaching. The canonical reference for definitions of Network Neutrality is Wu (2003); further updates and discussion are available on Wu (n/d) and OFCOM (2011).

Several constraints apply to the above statement defining Network Neutrality for the purposes of this paper:

First, in actual practice it is impossible to comply with the "five alls" due to operational considerations. ISPs may need to block some ports and origins, in particular, due to Best Practice (or, in organizations like the IETF, Best Current Practice, BCP) recommendations (such as blocking port 25 to avoid the use of open relays for e-mail spam), traffic engineering and traffic shaping in order to provide acceptable service in the face of varying network conditions, response to attacks among which Distributed Denial of Service attacks (DDoS) are prominent, congestion, and other needs of network and service management. ISPs may also be forced to block some traffic for legal reasons, such as a prohibition, within a given country or territory, of providing certain contents (hate, racial or gender discrimination, child-abuse imagery, etc.).

Filtering and blocking may be operated by a wide variety of technical means. Among the simplest and most common are ACLs (Access Control Lists) in routers and switches, which filter out IP addresses or address blocks. Other simple filtering and blocking techniques are based on domain names, which in some cases has been attempted by tampering with the Domain Name System (DNS) close to the network core, with deleterious effects already described by Crocker et al. (2011).

Filtering, blocking and throttling are also known to be performed on the basis of Deep Packet Inspection (DPI), which allows the ISP or other operators to obtain information about the contents and other characteristics of the communication beyond the information contained in the IP packet headers. DPI is considered in itself a violation of the end-to-end principle to some extent. We will not enter the extensive discussion about this subject and consider it as a violation, or tool for Network Neutrality violations, when its use fits the definitions in this paper.

Taking these factors into account allows for a sharper definition of Network Neutrality, in particular by focusing on "discrimination." The most widely accepted definitions of Network Neutrality leave room for some actions to be considered non-violations even though they do not deliver the "five alls".

The allowance is thus made for legally-mandated blocking and filtering, as well as for filtering, blocking or throttling traffic for traffic engineering purposes. Traffic engineering is intended to optimize the operation of a network and to respond to contingencies; what it does not allow for is performing any of these actions selectively in order to favor some traffic over another for commercial reasons such as can appear when an ISP is vertically integrated or otherwise allied with a content provider, and the ISP in this case selectively eases the traffic from this provider against some or all others.

It is also generally accepted that if an ISP or similar provider is to incur in any of the above practices without violating Network Neutrality, the action should be in so far as possible legally motivated, temporary, and communicated to the user in a clear way (the transparency requirement).

There are also additional, important variations in these concepts depending on country and approach, particularly depending on whether the approach is market and competition oriented, regulatory, or legislative. At the time of this writing most countries have decided not to enact legislation mandating Network Neutrality and have not included it in the telecommunications regulations, so are mostly watching the situation evolve and allowing competition in open markets as a way to ensure that ISPs will provide access to the "five alls" except within the allowances already described. A few countries, such as the Netherlands and Chile, have laws mandating Network Neutrality, and they merit watching more closely for lessons learned.

Further precisions to the definition and our analysis in this paper refer to the provider involved; ISPs are but one widely accepted category and well-defined in national legislations, but variations may exist for differences in legislation or language or due to market structures.

We have designed our framework for managing violations to Network Neutrality at risk in a way that allows for broad variations in the uncertainty of the definition of Network Neutrality and the party potentially incurring in such violations. The risk management framework is designed to be robust against differences in definition over geography and time.

The subject of the violations is constructed as a broadly defined persona. Again, broad definitions are chosen in order to provide a robust framework.

The persona around which the framework is designed is mainly an individual Internet user who uses the Internet for access to information; interpersonal communication through e-mail, instant messaging and other text, sound and video, whether synchronous or asynchronous, one-to-one, one-to-many or many-to-many; interactions with and through online social networks, fora and communities; peer-to-peer, client–server, or otherwise; publish content online through social media, blogs, newspapers, online fora, scientific and academic publications, video and audio websites and portals, augmented- and virtual-reality spaces and others; purchase and sell physical and electronic goods and services; and many other activities as listed in surveys such as those performed by the Pew Trust in the US and INEGI and AMIPCI in Mexico.

In so far as possible, the persona definition is neutral and robust for differences in gender, nationality, place of residence, socio-economic status, age, and other demographic variables unless otherwise noted. Particular attention is paid to the non-commercial use of the Internet by the persona. However it is also assumed that the user represented in the persona may be making commercial use, as a buyer of goods and services, and a seller at least of personal services such as an employee, independent professional, or occasional seller. A different analysis applies to the enterprise, and it requires a different persona that may be studied later.

For the purposes of the framework, both wired and wireless communications are considered. Participants in the Network Neutrality debate in some jurisdictions make or try to make a strong distinction between both. This is due especially to the much stronger constraints that wireless communications face in provisioning bandwidth, throughput, tolerable latency and jitter, and their basic inputs such as spectrum allocations and antenna/cell locations.

The way to reconcile these two sets of constraints for the framework is to judge the reasonableness of operators' actions in each at given times. Special conditions may mitigate a harsh judgment of Network Neutrality violations for wireless operators if they face temporary congestion of their networks. These conditions may include network congestion, damages to the networks' links or active equipment, and other deliberate or accidental attacks, and may appear in natural disasters, violent social events, and non-violent but highly-attended or widely communicated social events.

For this framework, we are not making separate analysis for intentional and non-intentional violations. The usual distinctions of political, financial, etc. types of risk are agglomerated for simplicity. The actions suggested have been designed or selected, and ranked so that risk management is kept aligned and proportional.

Our main scenario, therefore, is one in which we seek to establish possible responses to deliberate violations of Network Neutrality due to commercial interest, and allow as well to some degree of politically generated filtering and blocking.

A key caveat[1] is that effective use of this method depends on ascertaining the existence, form and degree of the Network Neutrality violations. Tools such as those listed by BEREC and others in Europe (Potts 2015)[2] and those made available by m-lab[3] (or Measurement Lab) will be needed. In some cases, sampling and good statistics will be needed, as the burden of proof in complaints or litigation will be laid upon the users. Crowdsourcing is highly recommended for those cases.

5.2 Violations of Network Neutrality

Table 5.1 summarizes the approach. It is based on the consumer's point of view. A new table must be written for each stakeholder or a color, or graphic tool must be introduced to signal the different risk valuations and strategies that apply.

---

[1] Added for Compendium, September 2015.

[2] Potts (2015).

[3] http://www.measurementlab.net/.

Table 5.1 Risk management analysis of network neutrality violations

Risk name	Impact and probability	Avoidance	Detection	Mitigation	Response	Contingency plan	Continuity	Prevention
Blocking of: Port Protocol Source Destination Traffic pattern Content by DPI	P high I high	VPN unless blocked by ISP as well	Netalyzr Crowdsourcing Verification with sender or other third parties	VPN IP address spoofing Identity masking	Complaint Public complaint Public outrage campaign Lawsuit if laws broken	VPN Site provisioned by alternate ISP	Public advice Change supplier Redundant provisioning Lobby/pressure ISP or other infringing party Lobby/pressure parties which can force change of ISP conduct, such as consumer authorities and telecommunications, market and/or competition regulators	Consumer regulation Market and competition regulation Telecoms law NN law Strong consumer and citizen voice
Throttling for Own Client/Ally Political Other vertical Mislabeling	P high I variable	Hard (VPN may not cause significant relief)	Speed of downloads; connection-dependent process stability (*e.g.* SSH); Large samples needed	CDN run by OSP; cache or proxy; alternate unthrottled source (possibly P2P upload)	Complaint Public complaint Call for regulatory intervention Public outrage (harder than for blocking) Litigation	CDN Site provisioned by alternate ISP Patience	Patience	Consumer regulation Market and competition regulation Telecoms law NN law Strong consumer and citizen voice
Traffic management	P extremely high I variable	If within accepted rules, no action needed	ISP notices Netalyzr Crowdsourcing	If within accepted rules, no action needed, otherwise go to next line in table	If within accepted rules, no action needed, otherwise go to next line in table	If within accepted rules, no action needed, otherwise go to next line in table	If within accepted rules, no action needed, otherwise go to next line in table	If within accepted rules, no action needed, otherwise go to next line in table

(continued)

Table 5.1 (continued)

Risk name	Impact and probability						
	Avoidance	Detection	Mitigation	Response	Contingency plan	Continuity	Prevention
Failure to communicate to users Absence of advice Misleading advice Temporary measures made permanent	Double ISPs (assuming no collusion)	Verify with third parties News Social media Crowdsourcing	Create own warning and circulate; make viral through social media	Create own warning and circulate; make viral through social media Lobby/pressure ISP and parties with power over its conduct	Create own warning and circulate; make viral through social media Lobby/pressure ISP and parties with power over its conduct	Create own warning and circulate; make viral through social media Lobby/pressure ISP and parties with power over its conduct	Change supplier if market and rules allow Call on regulators for telecommunications, competition, consumer rights

P probability or likelihood, *I* impact

Notes to the table:

1. VPN means "virtual private network." It is potentially useful to circumvent Network Neutrality violations by not obscuring to the ISP the IP address, domain name, or other revealing characteristics of the website, email destination, etc. with which the user communicates

2. "Netalyzr" is software from the University of California at Berkeley which allows users to identify a large set of features of Internet connections, including proxies they have not set, inaccessible ports, IP addresses, and other potential Network Neutrality violations. It is used in this paper to represent both the specific Netalyzr software and any other user-operated software tools that allow users to detect whether some ports, protocols, communication origins, destinations or contents are not accessible to them. The use of these tools is more effective and credible after proper training and may need considerable sampling for definitive results. For example, Netalyzr lights an alarm when IP address and domain name do not match "whois" records; this may be due to supplantation, man-in-the-middle (MITM) attacks, Network Neutrality violations, or decisions by the portal owner to use a CDN. This last situation is not uncommon for large media, online services, and OSPs. The user must interpret the results with great care

3. The detection of throttling may be much more difficult than the detection of outright blocking. Numerous measurements with quality tools, with a good sampling design, may be needed in order to prove it definitively. In throttling, the ISP may use a large variety of techniques to diminish the speed at which certain selected communications operate. The user may perceive throttling through slow downloads, broken connections due to timeouts, pixelization and freezing in images and video, and related phenomena. These events are also usual in some underprovisioned or congested networks, may be occasional even when not deliberate, and, therefore, may be attributed to uncertain causes. Therefore, the infringing ISP may deflect complaints and criticism by placing the cause of the events on the user's side or on the vagaries of the best-effort approach of Internet communications embedded in the protocols and design

4. Unless the user has a strong service-level agreement (SLA) with the ISP, a number of complaints may be dismissed as mentioned for throttling. Strong SLAs usually contain definitions, expected levels of availability, upper bounds on "ping" times, delay, and jitter in communications, as well as penalties for violations. They are not common for individual Internet users (home or small-business contracts). When they are available, they are costly and mostly oriented to business contracts. This paragraph covers "response"

5. Impact and probability must be determined for each risk and in each different set of conditions (time, place, stakeholders, intended or actual action). The impact of ISP actions on Network Neutrality is deemed high if the actions are liable or proven to hamper seriously the user's ability to communicate, and low if the opposite is the case or if avoidance and mitigation are readily available. The probability of each risk is assessed on grounds of history. Thus, for example, port blocking to impede access to VoIP is assessed a high probability because it has reported in numerous occasions in several different countries

Entries in the table indicate the actions the user should consider performing according to the risk described in the line in which the cell is found, and for the risk-management action indicated in the column. When more than one action is listed, the order in the list is the order of escalation suggested. For example, a user who finds that a certain port is closed by her ISP should first complain to the ISP and request for the port to be opened; if this does not produce the desired effect, or an explanation why the ISP will not open the port, the user should bring a formal complaint to the appropriate authority (telecommunications regulator, competition authority, consumer defense authority or organization, etc.). Should this in turn fail, one option for the user is to create pressure on the ISP through a public outcry, maybe using social media for the purpose. The order of escalation should be clear in this example.

Another table of interest would perform and summarize the analysis for a provider of services over the Internet (OSP) which could be affected by violations to NN by an ISP or carrier on which the OSP relies, either by contract or as an unavoidable intermediary in the Internet interconnection ecosystem.

The individual user's concerns with Network Neutrality revolve around the fulfillment of the principle's "five alls"—unfettered access to all protocols, all ports, all contents, all origins, all destinations of Internet communications, barring well-defined and limited exceptions for traffic management and security.

Thus, the individual user's concerns are affected when an ISP limits or diminishes access in ways that to which the user is sensitive. Not being able to access some ports, protocols, etc. hampers the Internet user experience and may infringe consumer or citizen rights, thus spanning a spectrum that goes from the technical through the commercial and potentially all the way to the political.

The general Internet user may face Network Neutrality violations with but limited tools to detect them, to pinpoint which they are, to react to them, and in other ways to prevent and avoid them. It is in the interest of global stewardship of the Internet, therefore, that Network Neutrality violations be easily detected, and that users have ways to deal with them. Further, in contrast to other stakeholders, design for users must be based on the assumption that the user has frugal—at best—economic resources, very limited technical knowledge, extremely limited technical tools, and near-nil political clout at the individual level (and in most countries and conditions, nil collective power as well).

The OSP's concerns are ability to reach all users, ability to reach all clients, the quality of user experience and the factors this in turn is measured by, and unfettered access to and through infrastructures such as CDNs which may form complex layers between the OSP, its users and its clients.

The OSP's actions will differ from an individual user's in some significant aspects. The OSP may be able to negotiate directly with an ISP or carrier, or lobby a regulatory agency or even a legislature where the individual user can't, for example, given the power that is granted on the OSP due to its corporate nature and economic value *vis á vis* the limited power of an individual consumer—further, in a foreign jurisdiction.

The individual user's and the OSP's interests—and therefore to some extent risks—may become aligned in cases such as that in which the user's interest is to access and use the OSP's services and these are blocked, throttled, or in some other way affected negatively by Network Neutrality violations by intermediaries.

Risk sharing or risk transfer has not been considered in the table. The possibilities of transferring violations of Network Neutrality to third parties in a meaningful way or of spreading the risk through sharing have been considered to make little or no sense at this stage and therefore excluded from the study for now.

To further facilitate use of the table an example is provided:

Assume that a port or set of ports are being blocked by an ISP, corporate part or ally of a telephony company, in order to impede the use of an application such as VoIP (voice over IP) or IP telephony. This could be done by the company in order to preserve its source of income in conventional telephony against the competition of the much cheaper or free VoIP service. The user's conduct following the table would start in row 1 of the table.

a. The user's first need is to establish with reasonable certainty that the port blocking condition is indeed in operation. To detect this she can:

    i. Use the same equipment in a different network and find that in this new one the service is not blocked.

    ii. Connect to a VPN and find that using the VPN the service is not blocked. This assumes that the VPN is not blocked by the ISP and that the service is not blocked by the VPN.

    iii. Run software such as Netalyzr, which will tell the user whether some port numbers or ranges are found blocked, and provide some other diagnostics which could also be useful to dissect the situation.

b. Once the user has certainty that the ISP is violating Network Neutrality by blocking port numbers she can:

    i. Call the ISP and find out whether this is a deliberate condition or an accidental one.

    ii. In case it is accidental the user can have the condition lifted by the ISP.

    iii. In the case that the port blocking is intentional the user can request its lifting, starting through customer service and its escalation.

c. Should the above steps fail the user may have one course of action left which is to go public with her complaint, starting with social media, consumer associations, consumer authorities, telecommunications regulators, competition authorities, and media and social media campaigns. The specifics of each case will be determined, among other factors, by the applicable legislation, whether the legislation is enforced, etc.

d. Mitigation. The user may find a workaround to get to the contents or services being blocked, by using a VPN or an alternate ISP. This in turn may require changing physical location, to an Internet café, academic facility, or other that doesn't suffer from the port blocking.

e. Contingency plan. The user need be prepared to detect the port blocking and enact the mitigation actions immediately, for which access to a VPN must have been obtained in advance (*e.g.* generating an account, paying for it, and testing regularly that it is available and fulfills the purpose).

f. Continuity plan. The user continuity plan will be a combination of the counter-measures already listed, and will be deprecated once regular access conditions have been reestablished.

g. Prevention. Preventive measures against port blocking directed to impede access to defined services require inducing change in the ISP's behavior. In order, the measures are complaints and protests directly to the ISP, public campaigns that force the ISP to change, or the enactment of regulatory or legislative measures. This succession matches well the history of Network Neutrality legislation In the Netherlands.

References

Crocker, S., Dagon, D., Kaminsky, D., McPherson, D., & Vixie, P. (2011, May). *Security and other technical concerns raised by the DNS filtering requirements in the PROTECT IP Bill*. http://www.shinkuro.com/PROTECT%20IP%20Technical%20Whitepaper%20Final.pdf

Landoll, D. J. (2011). *The security risk assessment handbook* (2nd ed.). Boca Raton, FL: CRC Press.

Miller, K. D. (1992). A framework for integrated risk management in international business. *Journal of International Business Studies, 23*, 311–331. http://www.jstor.org/stable/154903

OFCOM. (2011). *OFCOM's approach to net neutrality*. Retrieved from http://stakeholders.ofcom.org.uk/binaries/consultations/net-neutrality/statement/statement.pdf version of Nov. 24 2011.

Oren, S. (2001). *Market-based risk mitigation: Risk management vs. risk avoidance*. http://www.pserc.wisc.edu/ecow/get/publicatio/2001public/marketbasdriskmitigation-v2-oren.pdf

Potts, M. (Ed.) (2015). SMART 20012/0046, Deliverable D8: Third Experts Workshop Report, *Study on European Internet Traffic: Monitoring Tools and Analysis*. Retrieved from http://internet-monitoring-study.eu/images/workshop3/Workshop3_report.pdf

Van Schewick, B. (2010). *Internet architecture and innovation*. Cambridge, MA: MIT Press.

Wu, T. (2003). Network neutrality, broadband discrimination. *Journal of Telecommunications and High Technology Law, 2*, 141. http://papers.ssrn.com/sol3/papers.cfm?abstract_id=388863

Wu, T. (n/d). http://timwu.org/network_neutrality.html

Chapter 6
There's No Economic Imperative to Reconsider on Open Internet

Benoît Felten

6.1 Introduction

The debate on the neutrality of Internet access isn't new, and if its intensity varies over time, it has for a long while tainted the relationship between Internet Service Providers (ISPs) and Online Service Providers (OSPs). This paper was first published in April 2013 as a reaction to two particular traffic management approaches which framed the network neutrality narrative between the end of 2012 and the beginning of 2013. Such approaches are still very actual within the network neutrality debate and need to be mentioned, by way of introduction.

First, an approach sponsored by ETNO (European Telecom Network Operator's Association), has led to intense pressure within the International Telecommunications Union (ITU) aiming at enforcing a substantial change in Internet network economic principles.[1] The aim was to introduce international IP traffic compensation mechanisms similar to those that prevailed in PSTN networks. At the end of the annual conference of the ITU in Dubai in early December 2012, the proposed motions to that effect were rejected.

The second approach, which is not specific to France but has been particularly visible there in early 2013, is the reluctance of certain ISPs to properly dimension the interconnection links between them and certain large OSPs. This reluctance has led to degradation of the quality of service perceived by the users of these ISPs and sometimes even attracted the scrutiny of policy makers and the regulator. In January

This research was sponsored by Google, although the opinions and views expressed are independent and not a representation of the company's policies.

[1] *"Net neutrality debate goes to the ITU WCIT"* (http://www.diplomacy.edu/blog/net-neutrality-debate-goes-itu-wcit).

B. Felten (✉)
Diffraction Analysis, Paris, France

© Springer International Publishing Switzerland 2016
L. Belli, P. De Filippi (eds.), *Net Neutrality Compendium,*
DOI 10.1007/978-3-319-26425-7_6

2013, the French ISP "Free" decided to block its clients' access to the sponsored links and advertisements of Google-owned Doubleclick, Google Syndication and Google Analytics.[2] It was a clear violation of the Internet neutrality principles to which French officials have always declared their support. The aim of this report is to present, in a dispassionate way, the economic mechanisms that allow the Internet to function; and to explain how various solutions exist to solve issues raised by Internet traffic management on ISP networks. These solutions do not require for traffic to be degraded, and neither do they justify reconsidering an open Internet.

6.2 The Consequences of Traffic Discrimination

The Internet's success can be attributed to a few simple network management principles including the adoption of open standards like IP,[3] which give users choice and control over their online activities. These principles lead to the following:

- No single player—public or private—has control over access to the Internet
- No blocking or degrading of lawful Internet traffic. There are no good reasons—outside of managing networks to prevent DOS attacks, spam, and other malware—for a broadband provider to block or degrade Internet traffic.

The openness of the telecoms infrastructure consumers use to access the Internet is a vital component of the broader concept of the open Internet. An open Internet means:

- innovation and business opportunities
- consumers enjoy greater choice
- citizens around the world participate in a free and open debate
- jobs and economic growth

Nonetheless, a number of ISPs believe that these principles are secondary to what they perceive as profitability imperatives, and their arguments to reconsider Internet neutrality are essentially as follows:

- ISP subscribers use the Internet more and more, therefore the traffic generated keeps increasing. In order to face these traffic increases, ISPs need to redimension their networks. Since this traffic comes from OSPs, the ISPs want them to contribute to these investments.
- Since the early days of the commercial Internet, large players (ISPs and OSPs) avoid mutual payment for traffic by establishing handshake agreements called peering agreements. These deals are dimensioned on the basis of the peak capacity they can handle, and some ISPs denounce their asymmetry: most of these deals were established in the days of dial-up access when phone lines offered very low but symmetrical capacity.

---

[2] "Si Free bloque la pub, c'est pour faire payer Google" (http://www.telerama.fr/medias/si-free-bloque-la-pub-c-est-pour-faire-payer-google,91554.php).

[3] Internet Protocol.

Some ISPs it seems are willing to not only express their distaste for Net Neutrality but actually act upon it: 'Voice on the Net Coalition Europe' tracks[4] a number of Internet neutrality violations, particularly (but not only) related to Voice over IP usage over mobile networks. In addition to these are the recent events initiated by ISP Free in France. Most violations aim at limiting or forbidding a use of the open Internet that would compete with the ISP's existing services. In the case of Free, the French press[5] suggests another explanation: these arbitrary discriminations would aim specifically at targeting Google, a major player in online advertising and an OSP with whom Free allegedly has under-provisioned peering capacity. Free's aim therefore would be to show Google that certain advertising revenues can be selectively targeted, thus hurting Google's bottom line directly.

In this interpretation, it becomes difficult to dissociate open access to Internet and economic considerations. While they are separate issues, in this instance content discrimination it seems was used as leverage for a commercial negotiation. And even if Free's initiative ended up being very short (for the time being) it has had important consequences during the few days it was in place, causing an immediate[6] fragmentation of the French Internet ecosystem.

6.3 Solutions for Internet Traffic Management

The prime economic principle of Internet traffic is that dimensioning of the links that carry the traffic (Internet traffic or any other traffic) is done exclusively on peak requirements. That means that the links are established to be able to sustain a given traffic peak, but once that dimensioning is established, there's no variable cost to handling traffic (except for transit contracts specifically priced that way). As a consequence, when the network is mostly idle (in the middle of the night for example) if a subscriber accesses a certain amount of data or doubles that amount, it has no economic impact for any of the players in that 'transaction'.

The traffic management costs for an ISP are mainly investment and maintenance costs at three levels in the network:

---

[4] "Comments on the European Commission's Public Consultation on specific aspects of transparency, traffic management and switching in an Open Internet" (October 2012, Voice on the Net Coalition Europe) & "Non Exhaustive Identification of Restrictions on Internet Access by Mobile Operators" (http://www.scribd.com/doc/98641591/VON-Europe-Non-exhaustive-Indentification-of-Restrictions-on-Internet-Access-by-Mobile-Operators).

[5] "Le Bras de Fer Free-Google n'est pas fini", Les Echos 08/01/2013.

[6] French content editors whose revenues would have been directly impacted by the block instituted by Free quickly put in place scripts to identify Free's customers surfing on their websites, and informed them of the block, its consequences and their intention to block Free users in turn if the ad blocking continued. See for example a screen capture of MediaEtudiant.fr on January 4th, 2013: https://twitter.com/ThierryDebarnot/status/287198222110318592/photo/1.

- provisioning of access equipment and investment in related access infrastructure;
- provisioning of aggregation and transport network equipment and possible investment in related infrastructure
- provisioning of interconnect links to manage traffic from or to external networks

This last item is at the heart of the demands of the ISPs for changes in the relationship between them and the OSPs. It's worth examining in more depth the nature of these relationships and the way they can be financially optimised.

Solutions for an ISP to handle external traffic. *Source*: **Diffraction Analysis, 2013**

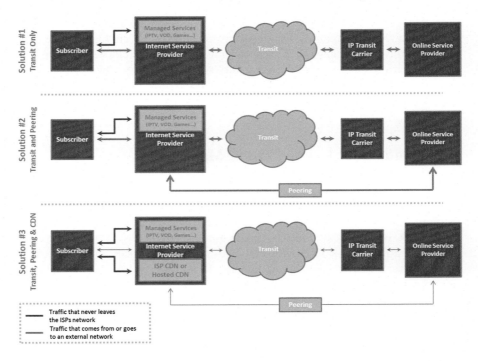

One aspect that is often overlooked in discussions about traffic management is that the data that flows inside the ISP's network has no impact on interconnection costs. The term "Internet Service Provider" is—in that sense—a misnomer since these players today offer many services other than Internet access to their customers (IP television, telephony, online gaming, content hosting, etc.). These services don't generate traffic that requires any interconnection but still represent important data flows: when a user watches TV at home using the ISP's set-top box, the user's access line (and a part of the transport network) is heavily used but there is no interconnect traffic between the ISP and an OSP.

When the traffic crosses to an OSP's network, there are essentially three non-exclusive ways to deal with that traffic as highlighted in the exhibit above:

- The first is for that traffic to be carried through a transit link. Transit links are connections between an ISP and a transit carrier which is connected to many networks worldwide and offers a global interconnect service. Transit is paid for, and the prices aren't always fixed (some deals establish a capacity cap for a given price, others are billed at the end of contract periods on the basis of what the peak actually was). Transit is a very competitive market in Western Europe, and the prices continue to decline. It's the default interconnection mechanism in the Internet value chain and all ISPs, as well as all OSPs (at the other end of the chain) rely on it one way or another.
- When an ISP and an OSP see an important flow of traffic between their networks, they must dimension for more transit, which has an impact on their cost base. It may become interesting for them to establish a direct link (called a peering link) between their networks to manage specifically that part of the traffic.[7] The vast majority of these peering agreements are not compensated financially: they allow both parties to save money on transit for the traffic between them. A recent OECD study analyzing over 142,000 peering agreements[8] found that 99.5 % of these aren't concluded with a written contract. Peering is simply part of the normal function of the Internet economy, a fact that is accepted by (almost) all players in the ecosystem.
- Finally, there's a third solution for an ISP to optimize external traffic and save on interconnection costs, which is to host the content most accessed by its users inside its network. There are two ways this can be done. The first is a commercial agreement with a company offering Content Delivery Network services (or CDN) which then hosts servers inside the ISP's network on which the most popular Internet content for that ISP is transmitted and stored during off-peak hours. OSPs who wish for their content to be thus distributed also sign a commercial agreement with the CDN provider. The second approach is the OSP's direct hosting of its content inside the ISP's network as part of a deal between OSP and ISP that can be financially compensated or not. In both cases, the amount of transit or peering capacity required to handle the external traffic is lowered as the most intense traffic to the ISP's subscribers is now hosted on its home network. Also, note that some ISPs compete with commercial CDN companies by offering their own replication services directly to the OSPs.

---

[7] Note that peering can also be established via third-party networks or transit carriers, which the exhibit in page 3 does not display for readability's sake. A more detailed representation of all traffic management options can be found in 'How the' Net Works: an introduction to peering and transit', Rudolf van der Berg, Ars Technica 2008.

[8] Internet Traffic Exchange—Market Developments and Policy Challenges, Dennis Weller, Bill Woodcock—2012.

6.4   Cost Mitigation in Internet Traffic Management

The costs of the different solutions mentioned above vary, of course, depending on the nature of the players involved and the traffic flows between them. It is possible however to examine the types of investment and recurring costs that each of these solutions requires in a simple manner:

Investment and recurring costs of various traffic management solutions

Chosen solution		For the ISP		For the OSP	
		Investment	Recurring costs	Investment	Recurring costs
Transit		– Routers for the links – Physical interconnect	– Payment to the transit carrier based on the peak capacity or actual traffic peaks	– Routers for the links – Physical interconnect	– Payment to the transit carrier based on the peak capacity or actual traffic peaks
Peering		– Routers for the links – Physical interconnect		– Routers for the links – Physical interconnect	
CDN	Commercial		– Subscription to the commercial CDN service		– Subscription to the commercial CDN service
	Bilateral agreement		– Server hosting if the ISP bears all or part of these costs	– Content servers	– Server hosting if the OSP bears all or part of these costs
	ISP	– Set-up of the ISP's CDN service (will generate revenues)			– Subscription to the ISPs CDN service

Source: Diffraction Analysis, 2013

One sometimes hears the argument that OSPs are 'free riders' on the access networks and that this justifies examining their financial contribution to the traffic handling costs inside the ISP networks. The table above clearly shows that OSPs invest or pay recurring costs in the same way as ISPs for all traffic management solutions. The 'free rider' argument focuses on what happens on the ISP's network and ignores both the recurring and transit costs of the OSPs, not to mention the significant investment that they consent to bring the traffic as close as possible to the end-users. OSPs are important investors or co-financiers of international, European and national fiber transport links. For example, both Google[9] and Facebook[10] co-invest in Asian transport backbone networks. In October 2012, Facebook announced the construction of an 8000 km European backbone to bring traffic from its hosting sites in Sweden as close as possible to its users.[11] OSPs invest in transport networks, hosting facilities and shared structures where traffic can be exchanged.

The argument that the OSPs are 'free riders' is unfounded also because it can easily be turned around: when an Internet user accesses content on the other side of the globe via a peering agreement, the distances covered by the ISP's access and transport network are minuscule compared to those of the transport network of the OSP. Since the main investment cost of a fiber network is distance, the OSPs could easily argue that the ISPs benefit from that portion of their network free of charge.

Finally, and it's probably the main point of the discussion, the ISPs are already paid by their subscribers to handle the traffic that these subscribers want to access. The economic analysis shouldn't be focused on what happens upstream, it should be focused on what happens downstream. Supposing for 1 min that traffic management costs became unbearable because of increased end-user demand (which is far from being the case today as shown below), it is first and foremost in that direction that ISPs should look for additional revenues.

The French regulator (ARCEP) has done a detailed analysis of traffic management costs for French ISPs in a study published in 2012.[12] The following exhibit summarizes the results of the cost modeling done by ARCEP:

Estimated cost spread of a consumer ADSL customer in France. *Source*: **ARCEP Modeling, 2012**

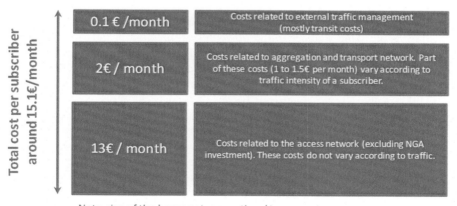

Note: size of the boxes not proportional to amounts

---

[9] Global Consortium to Construct New Cable System Linking US and Japan to Meet Increasing Bandwidth Demands, Google (http://googlepress.blogspot.nl/2008/02/global-consortium-to-construct-new_26.html).

[10] Facebook invests in APAC Undersea Cable, ZDNet, Juillet 2012 (http://www.zdnet.com/facebook-invests-in-apac-undersea-cable-7000000367/).

[11] Entretien avec Jay Parikh—VP, Infrastructure Engineering, Facebook à Structure Europe (http://new.livestream.com/gigaom/structureeuroday2/statuses/4942815).

[12] Rapport au Parlement et au Gouvernement sur la neutralité de l'Internet, ARCEP 2012.

The amounts that are the subject of the whole peering debate in France are included in the 0.1 Euros per month per subscriber shown above. According to market data provided by ARCEP[13] that would represent a total amount for the whole of the wireline market in France of around 26.57 m€ per year. Another way of looking at it is to calculate that the amount in question represents 0.28 % of Free's average revenue per user, or 0.27 % of Orange's.[14]

More generally, an ISP reluctant to increase its peering capacity with an OSP despite an influx of traffic must still handle that traffic, which consequently travels through a transit link. Either the latter's cost increases to manage that additional traffic or the transit link is deliberately under-provisioned, and the quality delivered to end-users is degraded. Alternatively, setting up a CDN through a bilateral agreement would allow for a minimal investment to significantly reduce the transit bill.

Considering how low the amounts in question are and how simple the economic arbitration seems to be between modest investment in capacity and growing transit costs, it's hard to understand why the debate is getting so much attention.

6.5   Achieving Economic Efficiency in Traffic Management

The interconnection debate is clearly a piece in a larger whole, only part of which is explicit.

ISPs first argue that traffic asymmetry is the reason why they only recently started taking a stance on this issue. It's a startling statement, firstly because an interconnection link between two players has no direction and the cost to establish this link is the same whether traffic flows in one direction or the other; secondly because the traffic asymmetry is a direct result of the asymmetry in the access network. It's hard to imagine ISPs, a few years down the line, being willing to pay OSPs when the traffic flows invert as has already been witnessed on some FTTH networks in the Nordic countries[15] because symmetrical access generates more uplink traffic from customers than downlink.

Another argument put forward by ISPs is that the significant investment, current and future, in access network upgrades is made necessary by the increase in traffic. While factually true, that statement deserves deeper examination. Since networks are dimensioned for traffic peaks, the most traffic-intensive services, i.e., video applications, are the ones that drive the technology choices for network upgrades. The main video application for residential ISP customers in France (and elsewhere) is IP television. The traffic flows from IP television are increasingly HD, delivered

---

[13] Observatoire trimestriel des marchés de DETAIL des communications électroniques (services fixes haut et très haut débit) en France—3ème trimestre 2012—résultats provisoires, ARCEP.

[14] ARPU sources: Résultats financiers de Free à mi-2012 and Résultats financiers d'Orange à fin 2011.

[15] Analysis of FTTH Service Portfolios, Yankee Group/FTTH Council Europe, 2009.

on large screens and they dwarf in size any other traffic flow on the network (including OSP video flows). It would be disingenuous to suggest therefore that the technology choices and the related investment in the network upgrade are a result of the Internet traffic increase only: clearly the most significant traffic flows are managed IPTV service flows, unrelated to OSP content.

Also, as stressed above, Internet traffic increase leads OSPs to invest in infrastructure (hosting facilities, regional, national and international networks) and increase their recurring transit costs.

Finally, it's important to keep in mind that the online advertising market, which is the lifeblood of the OSPs in France, is tiny in size compared to the access market. According to ARCEP[16] the total revenue of ISPs on the end-user market will represent around 41.8 billion Euros[17] in France in 2012 versus an online advertising market estimated at 2.7 billion Euros.[18] That's a little above 1:15 in terms of economic weight differential between OSPs and ISPs.

The paradox of the current debate is that online content and applications drive demand for Internet access and therefore represent a significant portion of the ISPs' revenues. A 2011 study interviewing a representative panel of 1000 French Internet users concluded that 38 % of them would be likely or very likely to pay more for a faster Internet access offer if it was available to their home.[19]

6.6 Conclusion

In the end, it's hard to figure out exactly what outcome the ISPs expect from this debate. Solutions to reduce the external interconnection costs while increasing quality of service for the end users exist, and incidentally are part of the announcements made by ISP Orange on the evolution of its broadband offers.[20] The debate, additionally, concerns very small amounts compared to the global economy of Internet access.

ISPs seem to wish for an intervention of policy makers that ideally lets them ignore net neutrality or, at the very least, lets them bill for peering to these OSPs with whom they exchange traffic. They hope perhaps that such a commercial

---

[16] Observatoire des marchés des communications électroniques en France 3 ème trimestre 2012— résultats définitifs.

[17] For this calculation, we used ARCEP's numbers for 2012 Q3 (Observatoire des marchés des communications électroniques en France 3 ème trimestre 2012—résultats définitifs) and projected evolution linearly to the end of 2012 to reach our estimated number of 41.8 bn€.

[18] 8ème Observatoire de l'Epub—Capgemini Consulting à l'initiative du SRI.

[19] To the question "If there was a faster Internet connection available for your household to what extent would you be likely or unlikely to pay more for this service?", 38 % answered "very likely" or "likely." Source: ICM Consumption Broadband 2011.

[20] Orange et Akamai forment une alliance stratégique pour la diffusion de contenus (http://www.orange.com/fr/presse/communiques/communiques-2012/Orange-et-Akamai-forment-une-alliance-strategique-pour-la-diffusion-de-contenus).

mechanism will let them regulate financially the amount of traffic that comes onto their networks and thus minimize the impact of OSP services that may compete with the ones they offer to their customers.

Unfortunately, the establishment of mandatory paid peering would most likely not have the expected results. 'Paid peering' as it currently exists is not the prevailing practice in the market. It's essentially uneconomical between large players and while it can be the result of peering negotiations, it's generally the mutually agreed result of an imbalance in respective sizes. The choice of settlement-free peering, on the other hand, is meaningful for both parties since it allows them to deliver a better quality of service while both save money on transit. A mandatory paid peering relationship would lock the OSP in a commercial deal with a fixed cost whereas transit is a competitive and fluid market. It would become very hard to figure out of the benefits of paid peering for large OSPs, and they would most likely prefer transit, a more transparent and flexible solution. Both players would be penalized financially, the whole Internet economy would suffer, and ISPs even more so than other players.

Furthermore, even supposing such deals were economically viable, the evolution of these deals over time would likely not be favourable to ISPs as traffic flows start balancing out with symmetry—or at least decent upload capacity—being deployed in next-generation access networks. One can guess that ISPs would switch from being fervent supporters of 'mandatory paid peering' mechanisms to being ardent opponents of them in a few years.

Finally, by penalising peering, a regulatory intervention to mandate paid peering would favor transit to the detriment of quality of service offered to end-users since more intermediaries would be involved in content and application delivery. Additionally, it would also penalize and maybe eliminate small ISPs, who would not represent large enough footprints to justify a paid peering agreement with anyone else in the ecosystem.

In conclusion, it seems important to stress that solutions to optimize traffic exist and are very affordable; despite what they may sometimes suggest, ISPs are trapped in neither unsolvable technical issues nor unbearable economic situations. The financial importance of traffic management is modest, the model has been working since day one of the Internet and allows all players in the ecosystem to operate at low costs. It would be counter-productive to challenge those mechanisms and therefore break the fragile balance that allows Internet users to access the content they seek in the best conditions without any player in the ecosystem being in a position to decide what they may or may not access.

Chapter 7
Net Neutrality and Quality of Service

Louis Pouzin

7.1 Introduction

The terminology "Net Neutrality" associates two words for which there is no precise definition. Thus, we must define here the meanings we use in the body of the present document.

"Net" is an abbreviation for Internet. But what is Internet? Initially, in 1973, the term became used as a short for internetwork, that is a set of interconnected packet switching networks. The term "catenet" was proposed (Pouzin 1973, 1974) for this level of communication infrastructure. Actually over the years people kept using the word internet to mean anything and everything (hardware, software, applications, services) including catenet itself. Thus, the meaning of the word "internet" became a hodgepodge of fuzzy interpretations and misconceptions making unlikely any public rational consensus on desirable policies and improvements.

In this document, "net" means "**catenet**".

Neutrality is often understood as non partisan, when bringing up several viewpoints or proposing various alternatives to a disputed resolution. This is a human or institutional posture. When associated with (computer) network it is literally meaningless. Nevertheless, people somehow invent their own interpretation of network neutrality fitting their concerns. Usually, their perception derives from a feeling of being unfairly discriminated in ways they get network service. At the same time, they cannot advance technical specifications intended to make the network neutral.

Caveat In the USA the term "network neutrality" stems from a rather different perspective than in other countries. More details shall be found at the end of this article.

Implementation of the net neutrality principle

L. Pouzin (✉)
EUROLINC, Paris, France

© Springer International Publishing Switzerland 2016
L. Belli, P. De Filippi (eds.), *Net Neutrality Compendium*,
DOI 10.1007/978-3-319-26425-7_7

The immediate question is: what is the principle?

Many people think that all packets should be handled equally. E.g. packets sent to a high bandwidth destination would be delayed so that they would not exceed the number of packets sent to a low bandwidth destination. Or packets carrying voice conversation would have to wait for an available slot in a common output queue, etc.

A quick scan for "network neutrality" in a search engine turns up scores of references, *e.g.* (http://www.ocf.berkeley.edu/~raylin/whatisnetneutrality.htm), based on various usage assumptions and network characteristics.

It is clear that interpretations vary with net operators, content providers, and end users.

An example is a set of principles worked out in Norway (Norway Gets Net Neutrality—Voluntary) in 2009. For a time this was hailed as a model of a broadly agreed consensus. However, in 2012 this agreement fell apart (Norway ISP Ends Net Neutrality Support), due to a major increase in bandwidth requirements for video traffic.

7.2 Net Operators

Net operators endeavor to handle data within the technical constraints of the service expected by end users, *e.g.* interactive session, transaction, file transfer, voice conversation, web page, voice or video streaming, real-time. Each type of service usually expects a minimum transit delay, or a minimum bandwidth, or a stable delivery rate. Fulfilling all these constraints at any time cannot be achieved without monitoring data flows and moving packets within specific time frames. In case of bandwidth shortage, some arbitration is needed among flows so that the service degradation perceived by users remains tolerable. Obviously there is no magic recipe to guarantee that all users perceive an equal degree of degradation.

When bandwidth shortage is severe it may be necessary to delay some high bandwidth flows, which reduce low bandwidth ones to a trickle. That is, some types of less demanding users get priority. This is service management.

Typically from their source to end users data flows are carried through more than one operator. Nets are usually independent systems applying their own service management policy. Therefore, one should not expect a natural built-in consistency among all operators. Mutual adjustments result from experience, proper selection of net partners, and administrators preferences.

7.3 Content Providers

A content provider could be, for example, a heat sensor, a camera, a PC or a data center that is, any computing system collecting or serving data, but not a packet carrier. They are connected to one or more nets and are used remotely in interactive, transaction or streaming mode or file transfer. As long as their traffic flow is substantially lower than the net capacity there is no specific issue to be raised. On the other hand, providers may not receive data in time, or they may exhaust the net capacity.

Net overload or insufficient data collection frequency may cause provider's data loss, which might be mitigated with buffering (storage) and compression, if applicable by providers. Statistics collection is presumably more tolerant to some minimal data loss. Alarms are not.

Massive provider data transfer is more likely to trigger congestion in a part of the net. This is unwelcome by net operators, and a major bone of contention with content providers. This is not a matter of technical arguments. The crux of the matter is money: who should pay for increasing net capacity. Is more capacity really justified, when more than half a web page is preempted by unwanted publicity and visual gadgets? Why is the provider not applying better data compression?

7.4 End Users

A dominant majority of end users are not (interested in becoming) net experts. They pay their ISP, and other providers, for various services, net access, search engines, email, social nets, banking, travel services, phone, music, TV, etc. They feel ripped off when the service is slow, broken, or error 404 (typical diagnostic for a missing page). There could be a number of reasons for the degradation, ISP or net adapter, some operator trouble, a slow application server, a bugged DNS, a clumsy routing through the net, a virus, or other. For the user, it's the "internet". After several calls to support, and much wasted time, he blames the net operator, which has a reputation of favoring some profitable clients, to the detriment of his kind of user. Adding to the picture a one-sided contract whereby the user is under threat of being cut off the net while the operator or ISP is immune from complaints. In conclusion, the net is not neutral, not to say crooked.

7.5 Conflict Generators

Users reactions may be partially subjective, but quite predictable. As ISP/operator contracts are one-sided and exclude any quality of service evaluation, users may think they pay for other users enjoying better service, and it's certainly true in some areas of the net. Without factual observation of the service characteristics, there cannot be any credible assertion of neutrality. The result is an endemic user suspicion and frustration. Nevertheless the net neutrality they call for may be just a mirage.

As long as running applications are allocated needed resources, users are generally satisfied. When bandwidth shortage occurs the internet infrastructure is presently not able to smooth out every demand peak, and some or all users start observing partial service degradation. It is easy to blame network operators for inefficient network management, and in particular for giving priority to some contents or some customers that are financially more rewarding. In simple cases it may be possible to bring evidence of such a policy, and sue an operator for unfair practice, *e.g.* if the network operator is a monopoly with financial interests in specific content providers or consumers.

However, very few users have enough resources and expertise to dig into frequent complex network configurations where multiple providers and consumers are sharing pools of dynamically allocated bandwidth. Further research and measurement tools are necessary to identify, visualize, experiment, and control critical network resources. A research trail, dubbed "network tomography" (OFCOM 2015; Predictable Network Solutions Limited 2015) seems to open new avenues. Practical operable tools should not be expected in a very short term.

A conclusion may be drawn from such studies: there are no simple tricks to make the internet "neutral". At this time casting network neutrality in well-wishing declarations, or worse in laws, shall presumably entail more delays in reaching stable solutions. A more practical approach is QoS.

7.6 Quality of Service (QoS)

Initial QoS definition for telecommunications was produced by ITU in 1994. Its definition for computer networks was more arduous due to environment complexity, which keeps growing. An overview is in Wikipedia (http://en.wikipedia.org/wiki/Quality_of_service). Selected research articles have elaborated solutions applicable to the net (Boutaba et al. 2010; Aib and Boutaba 2007; Xiao and Boutaba 2005). Hence best effort, meaning no QoS, is no longer the essence of the net. End-to-end flow characteristics are now predictable.

A significant result is a new business model for the net. An operator or ISP is in a position to offer users differentiated classes of guaranteed service. In return a user is in a position of checking that he gets what he pays for, or claiming compensation. What other users are getting becomes immaterial. Each user pays for his own QoS. Net neutrality no longer makes sense in the net context. Users may resent the same QoS being charged at lower fees to some clients, and complain about unfair competition, but this would be a strictly commercial dispute unrelated to the net operation.

As it occurs, QoS may not be implemented properly. Some net or ISP may enforce filtering based on content technical characteristics. E.g. it is reasonable to defer the delivery of huge attachments to a low bandwidth device. Thus, users need well-documented information on conditions, which could interfere with QoS. Options should be available to let users arbitrate between options, *e.g.* cutting video or images to speed up delivery.

Who is charged for QoS? Even though the subject appears more commercial than technical, it may have a strong influence on traffic. Some content providers can flood the net, in clogging all service classes. Unless a minimum QoS is maintained in each class some users could be denied service. That is, traffic thresholds may be needed to limit production or consumption during peak times (similar to electricity distribution). Content providers and users contribute to net load, and should be charged to facilitate traffic smoothing.

7.7 More Insidious Service Distortions

There are more factors potentially distorting service. E.g. a file transfer class may be limited to very short files, a video channel may reduce image resolution, etc. Such constraints may not be attractive to users, but on a competitive market they could hopefully find better providers.

Presently accessing internet services requires either an IP address or a domain name. Web applications are often designed only for domain names. These names are registered in the DNS, a directory fed by a private company (Verisign) under contract with ICANN, a private monopoly imposed by the US government without any international legitimacy. Domain name rental fees paid by users crawl up the food chain to ICANN through retailers (registrars) and Verisign.

Apart from this cash cow scheme there is a neutrality issue. Like any monopoly, ICANN protects its turf against competition: its DNS contains only names paying a rental fee. There are non-ICANN DNS (http://en.wikipedia.org/wiki/Alternative_DNS_root) containing more domain names that are not in the ICANN DNS. However, ISPs, browsers and mailers on the market know only the ICANN DNS, a blatant case of abuse of dominant position. This may be fixed, but needs a user's initiative, a common deterrent.

Another case observed in some hotels and institutions is a denial of net access when the user's device has been set with non-ICANN DNS addresses. This is rather surprising since other institutions have no need to protect the ICANN monopoly nor the NSA tracking.

Being under US government proclaimed jurisdiction, the ICANN DNS content is monitored, if not altered, out of users knowledge. Personal and confidential information can be collected from DNS servers. A going study (DNS Privacy Considerations 2015) uncovers a gamut of surreptitious spying traffic showing that "the lack of privacy protections in the DNS is actively exploited". Hence, users may have solid reasons for not using the ICANN DNS.

As pointed out above data flow characteristics are not the only factors bearing on users satisfaction. Monopolies limiting service availability and controlling tariffs create more market distortions than open competition. Security and privacy violations, de facto hidden to users, are even more discriminating than some suspicious traffic management.

7.8 Conclusions

The best effort internet service shows its age (1983). QoS is sorely needed for critical applications. However upgrading the present infrastructure appears doomed to a fate similar to IPv4–IPv6 upgrading. Actually class 0 of QoS is what we have, and what many people are satisfied with. It is ample time to start building a new infrastructure.

7.9   Appendix: Net Neutrality in the USA

When there is no data communication regulation by the government, the situation is termed "net neutrality", or "internet freedom" in propaganda literature. It is usually pushed by major content providers and network operators, but not by users.

In February 2015, the Federal Communications Commission (Federal Communications Commission and Open 2015; 13 things you need to know about the FCC's Net Neutrality Regulation 2015) (FCC) decided to regulate "broadband", that is Digital Subscriber Line (DSL), 256 Kbits/s and higher. Called "Open Internet" by the FCC, the rules are considered antagonistic to net neutrality by powerful lobbies, which may sue the FCC and get the rules overturned by a court.

In a nutshell the rules boil down to: (1) No blocking, (2) No throttling, (3) No fast lanes.

Due to the peculiar political environment, further development on net neutrality in the USA is out of the scope of this article.

References

13 things you need to know about the FCC's Net Neutrality Regulation (2015, March) http://www. cnet.com/news/13-things-you-need-to-know-about-the-fccs-net-neutrality-regulation/

A Study of Traffic Management Detection – Methods & Tools, Predictable Network Solutions Limited, www.pnsol.com (2015, August) http://stakeholders.ofcom.org.uk/binaries/research/ technology-research/2015/traffic-management-detection.pdf

Aib, I., & Boutaba, R. (2007). Business-driven optimization of policy-based management solutions. 10th IFIP/IEEE international symposium on integrated network management (IM 2007), Munich, Germany.

Boutaba, R., Limam, N., & Xiao, J. (2010). Autonomic principles for service management: performance, fairness and stability. *Proceedings of the 2nd International Symposium on IT Convergence Engineering (ISITCE)*, Pohang, Korea, 19–20 August 2010.

Federal Communications Commission, Open Internet (2015, February) https://www.fcc.gov/ openinternet

Norway Gets Net Neutrality—Voluntary, but broadly supported http://arstechnica.com/tech-policy/2009/02/norway-gets-voluntary-net-neutrality/

Norway ISP Ends Net Neutrality Support http://news.heartland.org/newspaper-article/ norway-isp-ends-net-neutrality-support

Pouzin, L. (1973, October). Interconnection of packet switching networks, INWG note 42. http:// www.xn--brwolff-5wa.de/public/pouzin-1973-catenet.html

Pouzin, L. (1974, May). A proposal for interconnecting packet switching networks, *EUROCOMP* (pp. 1023–1036). Brunel University (I. Auerbach (Ed.). The Auerbach Annual – 1975 Best computer papers, 105–117).

DNS Privacy Considerations, RFC 7626 (2015, August) https://www.rfc-editor.org/info/rfc7626

Traffic Management Detection Methods & Tools, OFCOM (2015, August) http://stakeholders. ofcom.org.uk/market-data-research/other/technology-research/2015-reports/ traffic-management

Xiao, J., & Boutaba, R. (2005, December). QoS-aware service composition and adaptation in autonomic communication. *Journal on Selected Areas in Communications, IEEE, 23*(12), 2344–2360.

Chapter 8
A Discourse-Principle Approach to Net Neutrality Policymaking: A Model Framework and Its Application

Luca Belli, Matthijs van Bergen, and Michał Andrzej Woźniak

8.1 Introduction

The question of whether and how to protect the principle of network neutrality ("NN") is currently one of the most hotly debated topics of Internet policy around the world. As the name may already suggest, NN is essentially a non-discrimination principle that applies to the transmission of Internet traffic. It prescribes that, in principle, all Internet traffic should be transmitted on an equal basis, or at least in a manner that does not favour or disfavour particular users, applications, content, services or devices. The need to protect NN through law and policy is widely perceived as a result of the discriminatory treatment of Internet traffic which some Internet providers have begun to engage in (BEREC 2012) while others have publicly announced their wish to do so.[1] Such discriminatory treatment has the potential to restrict the freedom of Internet users to receive and impart information and use or run services and devices of their choice.

Indeed, while competition and the desire for profit-maximisation provide an important incentive for network operators to not unfairly discriminate in the transmission of Internet traffic, market failures[2] and vertical integration of operators and

---

[1] See *e.g.* KPN (2011) and ETNO (2012).

[2] For example, in many markets operators arguably enjoy a termination monopoly to reach the users who subscribe to their Internet access services. This enables the so-called 'Tony Soprano vision of networking' (a term credited to Tim Wu, besides 'net neutrality'), where Internet providers can extract 'protection money' from providers of online content and/or applications, by threat-

L. Belli (✉)
Fundação Getúlio Vargas Law School, Rio de Janeiro, Brazil
e-mail: luca.belli@fgv.br

M. van Bergen
ICTRecht & Leiden University, Brussels, Belgium

M.A. Woźniak
Free and Open Source Software Foundation & Warsaw Hackerspace, Warsaw, Poland

© Springer International Publishing Switzerland 2016
L. Belli, P. De Filippi (eds.), *Net Neutrality Compendium*,
DOI 10.1007/978-3-319-26425-7_8

online service providers appear to result in perverse incentives to violate net neutrality and to restrict or interfere with Internet users' fundamental rights and, ultimately with their freedom of choice.[3]

Discriminatory treatment of Internet traffic not only has the potential to jeopardise Internet users' right to impart and receive information, ideas and services without interference, but also to hinder competition, and to reduce the economic and social value resulting from the openness and peer to peer nature of the Internet.[4]

Over the past years, national regulators, as well as international organisations, have been producing an increasing amount of research looking for a NN formula able to sustainably preserve an open and decentralised Internet ecosystem. This article describes the process and result of a multistakeholder effort organised within the Dynamic Coalition on Network Neutrality ("DCNN"), a component of the United Nations Internet Governance Forum (IGF), established to promote debate on NN and elaborate a Model Framework for the protection of NN through policy and legislation.

The interest of a Model Framework on Network Neutrality has been stressed, since 2009, by the Council of Europe (CoE) Committee of Ministers[5] and reiterated during the CoE Multi-Stakeholder Dialogue on Network Neutrality and Human Rights (CDMSI 2013), the event that triggered the creation of the DCNN. The elaboration of the Model Framework on Network Neutrality has been coordinated by two of the authors of this paper that, at the time of the elaboration, were serving as NN experts for the CoE. One of the main goals of such effort was to deliver policy elements to the CoE Steering Committee on Media and Information Society (CDMSI), to be used for the elaboration of a NN recommendation of the CoE Committee of Ministers.[6] Important requirements for the Model Framework on NN were therefore the compliance with and promotion of international human-rights

---

ening to put the traffic towards their users on a slow lane, or not deliver it at all. Another problem is that the market for Internet access services is oligopolistic. In this respect, the Netherlands Bureau for Economic Policy Analysis has asserted that "one cannot be optimistic about the intensity of competition [in the telecoms sector]. Moreover, if providers make their networks "less neutral" by implementing network bias practices, the intensity of competition decreases further. " (CPB 2010) At the EU level, the Universal Service Directive (*i.e.* directive 2002/22/EC) has strengthened consumer protection, fostering better consumer information pertaining to supply conditions and tariffs in order to allow them to more easily switch providers, thus promoting competition in the electronic communications markets. However, as pointed out by BEREC several types of discriminatory practices are particularly widespread at the European level (BEREC 2012).

[3] See *e.g.* CPB (2010) and BEREC (2012).

[4] See *e.g.* van Schewick (2010), BEREC (2012), and Belli and van Bergen (2013).

[5] Particularly, para 9 of the Declaration of the Committee of Ministers on network neutrality affirms that net neutrality "should be explored further within a Council of Europe framework with a view to providing guidance to member states and/or to facilitating the elaboration of guidelines with and for private sector actors in order to define more precisely acceptable management measures and minimum quality-of-service requirements"

[6] The report containing the Model Framework was delivered to the CoE on 6 December 2013. See Belli and van Bergen (2013).

standards and also the 'scalability', which in this context means being easily implementable and applicable across different national legal systems.

This article will briefly describe the conceptual framework that led to the elaboration of a net neutrality policy-blueprint (Sect. 8.2) and the participatory process put in place by the DCNN in order to craft the Model Framework (Sect. 8.3). Lastly, we will provide the result of such process and elaborate on its concrete application (Sect. 8.4). The goal of this paper is, on the one hand, to highlight that open and participatory processes can be regarded as a viable way to develop sustainable Internet policy and, on the other hand, to provide a concrete example of such processes and their potential outcomes. The establishment of the DCNN aimed at channelling expertise coming from a variety of stakeholders towards the creation of a sustainable policy blueprint. The main goal of the Model Framework is to help clarify the NN debate and to propose a policy suggestion aimed at preserving the ability of every Internet user to freely receive and impart information as well as innovation via the Internet. To this end, the first article of the Model Framework aims at bridging a dialectic lacuna, by precisely defining the network neutrality principle. Consequently, the Model delineates the limits of the NN principle as well as the criteria according to which it should be applied. Furthermore, the Model suggests an enforcement mechanism that seems essential to implement such a crucial principle in an appropriate fashion.

8.2   A Discourse-Principle Approach

According to Jürgen Habermas' discourse principle, the only norms that one can claim to be valid are those meeting—or having the possibility to meet—the approval of all the participants in a practical discourse. Hence, Habermas argues that norms' legitimacy should not be based on their "formal-semantic properties" but should rather be guaranteed by the formal conditions that allow "rational will formation" through participation in this discourse.[7]

However, the philosopher acknowledges that, in spite of how sophisticated can be the efforts to achieve a consensual rule on a purely rational basis, human beings' lack of "perfect knowledge" inexorably leaves them in a state of uncertainty regarding whether the rules elaborated by them have truly been crafted according to the discourse principle. For this reason the most suitable solution—or the one with the least hindrance, depending on the point of view—is to undertake a participatory process through which the elaboration of the rule is legitimised by participants' free contribution on an equal footing,[8] in order to put in place "a cooperative search for truth, where nothing coerces anyone except the force of the [most persuasive] argument".[9]

---

[7] See Shelly (1993), pp. 65–67.

[8] Here, the expression "equal footing" should be interpreted as lack of negative discrimination with regard to the possibility to participate in a debate.

[9] See Habermas (2001), p. 198.

To foster the aforementioned Habermasian approach to policy development, all interested individuals should have the possibility to express their opinions and provide their inputs through transparent and participatory processes. Openness and transparency seem essential preconditions for the consideration of the wider number of standpoints as well as possible externalities linked to a specific policy subject (Belli 2015a, b). To this latter extent, Froomkin has stressed that the achievement of the Habermasian practical discourse depends on how closely the participants to this collaborative effort manage to approach "an ideal in which (1) all voices in any way relevant get a hearing, (2) the best arguments available to us given our present state of knowledge are brought to bear, and (3) only the unforced force of the better argument determines the 'yes' and 'no' responses of the participants".[10] However, it is important to note that only in an ideal—and particularly difficult to realise—situation it is possible to fulfil completely the conditions above. Therefore, considering the practical difficulties to realise an ideal practical discourse, "something less than the "best" might also be a practical discourse".[11]

The Internet standards elaboration process developed by the Internet Engineering Task Force (IETF), can be argued to form such a near fulfilment of the practical discourse conditions. This process is open to every interested Internet user and based on the collaborative development of Requests for Comments (RFCs) through online and onsite interactions taking place via publicly archived mailing-lists or during open workshops. The purpose of the mailing-list interaction is to facilitate the participatory process that leads to the crystallisation of "rough consensus" through the confrontation of rational arguments. In this way, the proposed standards are commented and refined in order to become draft-standards, ready to be adopted uniquely by reason of their rational efficiency.[12] Indeed, the IETF standardisation process is traditionally based on "rough consensus and running code." (Hoffman 2012) The content of the draft standards—defined "Internet Drafts"—is defined by the IETF working groups through a "rough consensus" process, whose aim is to let the dominant view of the working group emerge in the form of a general sense of agreement (Bradner 1998).

Once consensus emerge within the IETF working group, the Draft may acquire the status of Internet Standard only when all IETF members are given the possibility to comment on it through a "Last Call" for comments (Bradner 1996) and it is demonstrated that it can empirically "run" *i.e.* the technical specifications have reached technical maturity and can be implemented in multiple interoperable software applications. Such requirements are certified by the IETF Internet Engineering

---

[10] See Froomkin (2003), p. 771.

[11] *Ibid.*, p. 776.

[12] Although Internet standards are mainly adopted by reason of their efficiency, it has been eloquently demonstrated that they have highly political connotations. To this extent, Laura DeNardis highlights that "[…] protocols are political. They control the global flow of information and make decisions that influence access to knowledge, civil liberties online, innovation policy, national economic competitiveness, national security, and which technology companies will succeed." See: DeNardis (2009), p. 6.

Steering Group (IESG) that encompasses the IETF Area Directors and whose approval allows the draft to be published as an official IETF standard, *i.e.* a RFC, by the RFC Editor. Lastly, the standards are voluntarily adopted by market players, such as network operators, software developers or online service providers.

It is important to note that the abovementioned process, which has proved reliable for the elaboration of technical standards, may be reproduced for the elaboration of policy standards or regulatory models. To this end, open working groups can be created to analyse specific policy subjects rather than technical ones and may interact via mailing-list and in physical meeting to develop policy and regulatory proposals through rough consensus processes. Such proposals may subsequently be approved, if deemed as "runnable"—i.e. concretely applicable within national legal systems—and voluntarily adopted by national regulators or inspire legislators and international organisations' policy-making efforts. In the light of this possibility, the IETF open standardisation process has been reproduced within the DCNN to conceive a model framework that could act as an open NN standard. The goal of this experiment was to elaborate a policy blueprint that could serve as an 'open regulatory standard' to be voluntarily adopted by national or international policymakers. Although very few IGF Dynamic Coalitions have produced concrete outputs so far, the reproduction of the IEFT modus operandi within an IGF Dynamic Coalition is not prohibited and the elaboration of policy or regulatory standards is, therefore, possible and delegated to each coalition's self-organisation.

8.3 A Net Neutrality Policy-Blueprint

As it has been pointed out in Part I, the participatory process put in place through open, inclusive and transparent email interaction has the potential to make the Habermasian practical discourse a (close) reality. Indeed, although mailing-list debates have obvious benefits and disadvantages,[13] it cannot be denied that they can be utilised as true debate-arenas, aimed at facilitating a "rational-will formation" process via open debates, which may be a close approximation of the Habermasian practical discourse.

Such a process is particularly beneficial to analyse the potential externalities that may be determined by specific Internet policies while considering the good (and bad) practices already adopted at both national and international level. The consideration of the various facets of a policy issue through an open and multistakeholder dialogue has indeed the potential to allow the elaboration of "scalable and innovation-enabling"[14] policies. The DCNN has therefore been established in order to transpose the practical discourse approach that characterises Internet standardisa-

---

[13] Particularly, Michael Froomkin highlights that, on the one hand, "much more parallel discourse is possible, which increases the chances of everyone having his or her say" whilst, on the other hand, merely virtual interactions make it "much easier to ignore people". See: Froomkin (2003), p. 799.

[14] See OECD (2011), p. 4.

tion into an IGF-based working group dedicated to net neutrality policy-analysis. IGF Dynamic Coalitions' self-organised, bottom-up and collaborative nature lends itself very well to the reproduction of the modus operandi that characterises the IETF working groups. Particularly, the creation of an open, inclusive and transparent discussion-platform is an essential requirement for the establishment of a dynamic coalition and, at the same time, a fundamental precondition to foster the confrontation of arguments leading to the formation of the rational will. Such open and multistakeholder approach is generally considered as beneficial for the development of consensus-based internet policies (OECD 2011) and seems particularly valuable for the elaboration of an efficient NN framework. Indeed, the NN debate is at the crossroad of highly contentious technical, economic and social issues (Marsden 2010; Belli and De Filippi 2013) and the large spectrum of stakeholders involved in the debate emphasises the interest of analysing this issue through a participatory and multistakeholder process.

The Multi-Stakeholder Dialogue on Network Neutrality and Human Rights, a conference organised under the auspices of the Council of Europe in May 2013 (CDMSI 2013), demonstrated the interest of a multi-faceted analysis of the NN debate and offered the participants the possibility to organise the inception of the DCNN. The CoE conference shed light on the Internet-traffic-management (ITM) techniques' potential to jeopardise the full enjoyment of fundamental rights while conferring network operators a true position of gatekeepers. The goal of the DCNN was indeed the creation of an open and multistakeholder working group able to produce a model regulatory framework protecting NN. In the view of the CoE conference participants, the elaboration of a model framework would be instrumental to provide concrete guidance on the protection of internet users fundamental rights whilst preserving the "public service value of the Internet" (CDMSI 2013).[15]

The DCNN was established with the goal of providing a discussion platform—open to all interested stakeholders—for the elaboration of a Model Framework on Network Neutrality. To this end the DCNN mailing-list has been publicly advertised (Belli 2013) and opened to any interested stakeholder. Mailing-list subscribers[16] participate on an equal footing in spite of their DCNN membership,[17] and can be categorised in five stakeholders groups: governmental entities; private-sector entities; non-governmental organisations; technical community; and academia. Mailing-list's discussions have been moderated by a coordinator, acting as an IETF working group chair, and only one "on-line vote" has been called for, in order to solve a terminology controversy.[18] Lastly, in the interest of transparency, the DCNN mailing-list archives have been kept public.

---

[15] See Council of Europe (2007).

[16] The total list-members number has evolved from 12, on 1st August 2013, to 82 on 1st October 2013.

[17] A complete list of DCNN members is available on http://www.networkneutrality.info/members.html.

[18] The vote was aimed at democratically choosing between Internet Access Provider (IAP), Internet Service Provider (ISP) or Internet Connectivity Provider (ICP). 74, 4 % of voters expressed a preference for the term ISP.

The first draft model framework has been elaborated utilising elements from two model laws, submitted by Luca Belli and Matthijs van Bergen to the Multi-Stakeholder Dialogue on Network Neutrality and Human Rights. Subsequently, two comment periods—the first one lasting 30 days and the second one 10—have been organised in order to reply to allow all interested stakeholder to participate in a public consultation, initiated with a "Request for Comments" on the draft model. Lastly, a third comment period has been established to allow final remarks and objections on the consolidated version of the model. The Model Framework on Network Neutrality is, therefore, the product of an open and cooperative effort and should be considered as a "policy blueprint" providing guidance on how to safeguard network neutrality. The Model Framework has been presented at the IGF meeting of the DCNN and subsequently submitted to the CoE CDMSI, which used it as working material for the elaboration of a CoE recommendation on Network Neutrality. The use or adoption of this model framework—or parts of it—should be undertaken on a merely voluntary basis and exclusively driven by the efficiency of its provisions.[19] The text of the model framework is reproduced below together with some guidelines aimed at facilitating the comprehension of its rational as well as its application.

8.4 The Model Framework and Its Application

The main goal of the Model Framework is to help clarify the NN debate and to present a way forward for NN regulation. To this end, the first article of the Model aims at bridging a dialectic lacuna, by defining the NN principle. Consequently, the Model delineates the limits of the NN principle as well as the criteria according to which it should be applied. Furthermore, the Model suggests an enforcement mechanism, essential to appropriately implement NN.

8.4.1 The Model Framework on Network Neutrality

1) *Network neutrality is the principle according to which Internet traffic shall be treated equally, without discrimination, restriction or interference regardless of its sender, recipient, type or content, so that Internet users' freedom of choice is*

---

[19] To this end, the European Parliament has taken inspiration from the model framework while amending the net neutrality provisions contained in the European Commission's proposal for a 'Connected Continent' regulation. Compare the Model Framework on Network Neutrality and the net neutrality provisions (particularly the net neutrality principle's definition) of the *European Parliament legislative resolution of 3 April 2014 on the proposal for a regulation of the European Parliament and of the Council laying down measures concerning the European single market for electronic communications and to achieve a Connected Continent.*

not restricted by favouring or disfavouring the transmission of Internet traffic associated with particular content, services, applications, or devices.

2) *In accordance with the network neutrality principle, Internet service providers shall refrain from discriminating, restricting, or otherwise interfering with the transmission of Internet traffic, unless such interference is strictly necessary and proportionate to:*

give effect to a legislative provision or court order;

preserve the integrity and security of the network, services and the Internet users' terminal equipment;

prevent the transmission of unsolicited communications for direct marketing purposes to Internet users who have given their prior consent to such restrictive measures;

comply with an explicit request from the subscriber, provided that this request is given freely and is not incentivised by the Internet service provider or its commercial partner;

mitigate the effects of temporary and exceptional network congestion, primarily by means of application-agnostic measures or, when these measures do not prove efficient, by means of application-specific measures.

3) *The network neutrality principle shall apply to all Internet access services and Internet transit services offered by ISPs, regardless of the underlying technology used to transmit signals.*

4) *The network neutrality principle need not apply to specialised services. Internet service providers should be allowed to offer specialised services in addition to Internet access service, provided that such offerings are not to the detriment of Internet access services, or their performance, affordability, or quality. Offerings to deliver specialised services should be provided on a non-discriminatory basis and their adoption by Internet users should be voluntary.*

5) *Subscribers of Internet access service have the right to receive and use a public and globally unique Internet address.*

6) *Any techniques to inspect or analyse Internet traffic shall be in accordance with privacy and data protection legislation. By default, such techniques should only examine header information. The use of any technique which inspects or analyses the content of communications should be reviewed by the relevant national data protection authority to assess compliance with the applicable privacy and data protection obligations.*

7) *Internet service providers shall provide intelligible and transparent information with regard to their traffic management practices and usage policies, notably with regard to the coexistence of Internet access service and specialised services. When network capacity is shared between Internet access services and specialised services, the criteria whereby network capacity is shared, shall be clearly stated.*

8) *The competent national regulatory authority shall:*

be mandated to regularly monitor and report on Internet traffic management practices and usage policies, in order to ensure network neutrality, evaluate the potential impact of the aforementioned practices and policies on funda-mental rights, and ensure the provision of a sufficient quality of service and the allocation of a satisfactory level of network capacity to the Internet. Reporting should be done in an open and transparent fashion and reports shall be made freely available to the public;

put in place appropriate, clear, open and efficient procedures aimed at addressing network neutrality complaints. To this end, all Internet users shall be entitled to make use of such complaint procedures in front of the relevant authority;

respond to the complaints within a reasonable time and be able to use necessary measures in order to sanction the breach of the network neutrality principle. This authority must have the necessary resources to undertake the aforemen-tioned duties in a timely and effective manner.

9) *Definitions*

The "Internet" is the publicly accessible electronic communications network of networks that use the Internet Protocol for communication with endpoints reachable, directly or through network address translation, via a globally unique Internet address.

The expression "Internet service provider" refers to any legal person that offers Internet access service to the public or Internet transit service to another ISP.

The expression "Internet access service" refers to a publicly available elec-tronic communications service that provides connectivity to the Internet, and thereby provides the ability to the subscriber or Internet user to receive and impart data from and to the Internet, irrespective of the underlying technol-ogy used to transmit signals.

The expression "Internet transit service" refers to the electronic communica-tions service that provides Internet connectivity between Internet service providers.

The expression "Internet traffic" refers to any flow of data packets transmitted through the Internet, regardless of the application or device that generated it.

The expression "specialised services" refers to electronic communications ser-vices that are provided and operated within closed electronic communica-tions networks using the Internet Protocol, but not being part of the Internet. The expression "closed electronic communications networks" refers to net-works that rely on strict admission control.

The expression "application-agnostic" refers to Internet traffic management practices, measures and techniques that do not depend on the characteristics of specific applications, content, services, devices and uses.

The expression "subscriber" refers to the natural or legal person who has entered into an agreement with an Internet service provider to receive Internet access service.

The expression "Internet user" refers to the natural or legal person who is using Internet access service, and in that capacity has the freedom to impart and receive information, and to use or offer applications and services through devices of their choice. The Internet user may be the subscriber, or any per-

son to whom the subscriber has granted the right to use the Internet access
service s/he receives. Any legal person offering content and/or applications
on the Internet is also an Internet user.

8.4.2   The Application of the Model Framework

Article 1 of the Model first defines NN and subsequently explains the aim of this
principle. NN is essentially a non-discrimination principle which applies to the
transmission of Internet traffic.

According to this principle, all Internet traffic is to be transmitted equally and
without discrimination, restriction or interference, regardless of:

- the type or content of the traffic;
- the identity of its sender or recipient;
- the nature of the discrimination, restriction or interference (technical, financial,
  or otherwise).

Therefore, it may be argued that NN plays a pivotal role in enhancing freedom of
choice, freedom of expression, privacy and self-determination of all Internet users,
while fostering media pluralism and economic innovation (Kocsis and Weda 2013).

From these values, freedom of choice requires an additional comment. Choice
can be available to subscribers on many levels—from the level of an ISP offering an
Internet access service, through a level of particular service providers on the Internet,
providing certain kind of services and competing with one another, down to a choice
of a particular offering within a given service of a given service provider (for
instance, a given article on a website). It is crucial that this choice, on all its levels,
is preserved, so that subscribers can make independent choices at any time.

Specifically, choice in the form of deciding on a package of Internet access bun-
dled with certain services (for instance, a zero-rated social network and a prioritized
VoIP offering of ISP's business partners), once per a long-term contract commitment, is not conducive to the permission-less innovation principle that allowed the
Internet to flourish. It is hard to anticipate when a new social network or VoIP offering eclipses the currently-popular ones, but this process—along with subscribers'
choice and ability to innovate—should not be hampered by such long-term
commitments that inevitably favour the established front-runners, rather than fostering the emergence of innovative services and applications.

In accordance with the network neutrality principle, ISPs must manage Internet
traffic in a non-discriminatory fashion. A prime example of a non-discriminatory
transmission mode is First-in, first-out, or "FIFO" transmission of Internet packets.
Besides FIFO there is a multitude of other queuing and transmission policies that do
not depend on the characteristics of specific applications, content, services, devices
and uses. Net neutrality prescribes that ISPs must in principle apply only such "appli-

cation-agnostic"[20] forms of Internet traffic management ("ITM"), while any application-specific discrimination, restriction or interference is only allowed if strictly necessary for and proportionate to any of the legitimate aims listed in article 2. The application of article 2 should be put in place through the following 'five-step test':

1) It should first be established whether or not an interference, restriction or discrimination has occurred. Any ITM that is not application-agnostic should be deemed as discrimination, restriction or interference (in short: interference);
2) the second step is to determine whether the interference in question is prescribed by the agreement between the ISP and its subscriber. If the agreement does not provide a sufficiently foreseeable ground for the interference, it is illegal. If the interference is prescribed by the agreement, we proceed to step three;
3) the third step consists in establishing whether the interference was applied for a legitimate aim. The purpose of the ITM measure must correspond with at least one of the legitimate aims, which are listed exhaustively in article 2, indents *a* to *e*;
4) the fourth step consists in determining if the measure is necessary in an open, end-to-end network. Can't the problem be properly solved at the edges? If there is no valid reason to implement a centralised measure to solve a specific problem, then the measure is not consistent with the network neutrality principle;
5) the fifth step consists in assessing the proportionality of the ITM measure. Notably, it should be evaluated whether the benefit brought by the specific measure exceeds its possible disadvantages and whether it is possible to utilise a different, less discriminatory and possibly more efficient measure in order to achieve the same purpose.

Similar to the way the European Court of Human Rights ("ECtHR") leaves a wider or smaller margin of appreciation to member states in certain situations, national courts and regulatory authorities can leave a wider or smaller margin for ISPs to decide which ITM measures are necessary and proportionate. When competition is strong, switching is easy and transparency is optimal, courts and regulators can leave a wider margin of appreciation to ISPs. When the technical community is divided concerning the discriminatory nature of a particular ITM measure, or about its efficiency or proportionality, the margin of appreciation can be left wider as well.[21]

---

[20] For further information about the concept of application-agnostic traffic management, see van Schewick (2012) while for a concrete application of such management see Bastian et al. (2010).

[21] As the state of the art evolves, it may at some point become clear that a certain application-specific measure which previously was broadly considered necessary and proportionate, gradually becomes inefficient and disproportionate by comparison to new measures, particularly if those measures are (more) application-agnostic. Therefore, it may be argued that the margin of appreciation becomes smaller when discriminatory ITM measures become more outdated in the light of newer, more efficient and/or more application-agnostic measures. We can imagine a 'cycle' where the same application-specific measure is first clearly necessary and proportionate, then gradually devolves and becomes less efficient at achieving its purpose compared to the state of the art, to a point where the measure is merely acceptable under the margin of appreciation for ISPs, while

It is important to note that such interference could take forms other than purely technical—for instance, subscribers could be charged more for a certain kind of traffic, or for traffic related to a certain application. One specific example is zero-rating, a practice allowing consumers to access specific services, applications or content for free by moving the cost from consumers either to the application provider or to the platform owner. As such, specific traffic (*e.g.* to/from ISP's own services, or its business partners) is favoured by the ISP by not being counted towards subscribers' monthly transfer limit, or not being charged for at all. This effectively means that the rest of subscribers' traffic is discriminated against financially. Such practices should be considered as within the scope of the Model Framework and, accordingly, should be subjected to the five-step test.

Article 2 delineates a limited number of legitimate aims for interferences. In accordance with indent a, an ISP is permitted to comply with a specific legislative provision or a court order prescribing an interference.

Indent b provides that interference may be justified if necessary to safeguard the integrity and security of the network, services and Internet users' terminal equipment. As an example, the blocking of (D)DOS traffic and malware can be mentioned.

Furthermore, it is important to note that in many European jurisdictions—at least in those within the EU—it is forbidden to send unsolicited electronic communications for direct marketing purposes, commonly referred to as "spam".[22] Although the problem of spam can also be dealt with at the 'edge', *e.g.* by filtering at the mail server, it may be considered wasteful if all spam traffic, which is said to constitute about 70–80 % of all e-mail traffic (Internet Society 2012), is first delivered to the end-point, taking up network capacity in the process, only to be discarded immediately after delivery. Therefore, filtering illegal spam at the network level forms a legitimate purpose. However, since filtering techniques always carry a risk of over-blocking, the model requires the consent of the receiving subscriber in order to put in place spam filtering at the network level (which may be less granular and less precise, compared with application-level filtering). In addition, although consent of the sending subscriber to filter outgoing spam is not necessary (indeed, it seems unlikely that a spammer would ever express it), article 2 indent c requires that the least restrictive and least discriminatory method that is still sufficiently effective, is used.

If a subscriber wishes that certain application-specific ITM measures be taken by the ISP, the ISP may comply with such request, in accordance with indent d. For example, this may involve Internet access services where the ISP is explicitly requested to filter out material that the subscriber objects to for religious reasons, or that is not deemed as suitable for children. Such filtering measures can also be performed at the edges, but if the Internet user prefers that the ISP takes care of this task, and the ISP offers this functionality, this should be allowed. It is also conceivable that certain Internet users may wish to prioritise traffic relating to certain favourite applications.

---

finally becoming unacceptable and disproportionate in the light of the development of newer and less discriminatory alternatives.

[22] See Directive 2002/58/EC (known as the e-Privacy Directive), article 13.

The implementation of such an option (prioritisation or blocking/filtering of certain traffic per user request) in a way that leaves the Internet user in sufficiently direct control over what applications get priority and when—*i.e.* not by picking a plan that is set for the entire contract term, rather selecting applications that are to be prioritised with possibility to change it at any time, or at the very least once per billing period—would be in accordance with the model. ISPs and their commercial partners may not, however, provide any monetary or other incentives (such as discounts or free items) for Internet users to accept or request discriminatory ITM measures. Such measures should also be explicitly opt-in.

Lastly, it should be noted that, in the event of temporary and exceptional network congestion, it may be necessary to implement certain protocol-specific measures, such as prioritising traffic pertaining to real-time applications that are particularly sensitive to delay and jitter, such as (video) calling or gaming, over less time-sensitive applications, such as file sharing and e-mail. Indent *e* of article 2 leaves room for such interferences, but as it explicitly underlines: protocol-agnostic measures should be used if they are sufficiently effective in achieving the legitimate aim, whereas protocol-specific measures can only be justified if they prove more effective and/or efficient than any available application-agnostic alternatives. As such, ISPs may handle congestion giving preferential treatment protocols supporting latency-sensitive applications such as VoIP but may not prioritise only selected VoIP services.

The network neutrality principle should apply to both wired and wireless forms of Internet access services, regardless of the technology used to transmit signals (*e.g.* Ethernet, WiFi, or HDPA).

Importantly, article 2 gives no room for 'pay-for-priority' business models on the Internet. The mere fact that some entities may be willing to pay ISPs for implementing certain discriminations, restrictions or interferences, such as prioritising, throttling or blocking specific Internet traffic, does not constitute a legitimate aim for such interferences. However, such business models are not banned *in toto*, for they may be implemented through specialised services.

Indeed, in accordance with article 4, the network neutrality principle need not apply to specialised services, which may utilise the Internet Protocol, but which are offered on closed networks which are not part of the Internet and utilise strict access control. Examples of such services include certain IP-TV and VoIP services, often offered as a part of a 'triple play' package, where the subscriber of Internet access service also receives a 'set-top' box and digital home phones. We can also imagine certain e-health applications and other types of applications that have particularly high security requirements (a good rule of thumb is that anything connected to the Internet can be broken into or compromised), a high sensitivity to latency and jitter and a sufficiently high value to justify investments in closed networks providing specialised services besides the open Internet. In the future we may expect to see less IP-TV and VoIP services offered as specialised services, because many Internet access services now offer sufficient bandwidth to enable on demand real-time streaming of 1080p resolution HD content (content distribution networks are helpful here as well), and Skype, Vonage, Tox and other Internet-based VoIP-applications normally have better sound quality than PSTN phone lines, while their quality can be considered comparable to specialised VoIP-services, unless they are being blocked or throttled, or if there is an exceptionally high level of congestion.

However, specialised services must not be offered in such a way that would degrade the quality of Internet access services below satisfactory levels and, if capacity is shared between Internet access services and specialised services, the ISP must clearly state this and the criteria whereby this sharing takes place. To this extent, regulatory authorities have the ability to set minimum requirements for the quality of Internet access services.

It is important to stress that specialised service do not constitute a substitute for Internet access services (for instance, in a form of ISP-provided intranet, based on Network Address Translation allowing for access to the broader Internet without possibility of receiving an external IP address), nor for any service already available on the public Internet, and therefore cannot be marketed as a substitute for them. It is provided by the ISP for a fee on a specially-requested basis and offers enhanced functionalities (assured quality of service, speed or security, etc.), whose level or type is not readily available on the public Internet. It relies on strict access control, although it is offered to the public and is conveyed via physically or logically separate infrastructure from the one used to convey Internet traffic.

Physical separation implies that specialised services and Internet traffic are transported over separate equipment. Logical separation implies that specialised services and Internet traffic use the same physical equipment but the network operator dedicates specific and clearly defined resources for each type in a manner functionally equivalent to physical separation—that is resources are allocated upfront and cannot be reallocated without explicit modification of the service agreement. Such resources should also not be possible to dynamically (re)allocate.

In accordance with article 5 of the Model, all Internet users have the right to a public IP address. A public IP address enables Internet users to be more than passive consumers of online content and applications, but to be equal participants in the exchange of ideas, thoughts, information, services and applications online. This requirement can be expected to speed up adoption of IPv6 and reduce adoption of carrier-grade NAT, which may determine a variety of problems such as transforming 'big routers in big firewalls'.[23]

Article 6 requires that any technique to inspect or analyse Internet traffic shall be limited to header information by default, and be reviewed by the relevant data protection authority if the contents of traffic are inspected or analysed.

Article 7 poses an obligation on ISPs to provide clear information about their traffic management policies. In order to provide the required transparency and information for users to base their choices for particular Internet access services on, ISPs must advertise the minimum bandwidth allocated to the Internet access service of the subscriber during the peak congestion levels on the ISPs network. This may be in addition to the theoretical maximum bandwidth levels that most ISPs currently advertise with.

---

[23] See *e.g.* Donley et al. (2013) and McAuley (2012).

Article 8 provides that regulatory authorities should have sufficient means and legal powers to enforce effectively net neutrality. The competent authority must regularly monitor and report on the compliance with net neutrality. The report by BEREC on traffic management practices (BEREC 2012) could serve as a basis for such reporting, while the Model additionally prescribes that regulatory authorities must be properly equipped to assess net neutrality from a human rights perspective.

Lastly, article 8(b) of the Model grants Internet users the right to file net neutrality infringement complaints with the regulatory authority as well as the competent court.

8.5   Conclusion

The Model Framework can be seen as the first regulatory standard produced by an IGF Dynamic Coalition. The value of the model framework is therefore not limited only to its content but also to its development process. Indeed, the development of the model framework has indubitably shown that the IGF can produce concrete outcomes that may be used, on a voluntary basis, to nurture national or international policy-making efforts.

However, due to the non-existence of an IGF procedure comparable to the IETF Last Call as well as to the lack of an IGF organ analogue to the IESG, the DCNN model framework cannot be considered as having the same status as an IETF standard and could be rather compared to an Internet Draft. To this end the 2014 IGF Chair's Summary called for the development of "a process that allow[s] the entire IGF community to weigh in and validate the findings of the [DCNN]."[24] Such process would be analogous to the IETF-wide Last Call, which aims at "getting the attention of people who weren't following the progress of the draft [and] get community-wide discussion on documents before the IESG considers them". In order to put in place an IGF equivalent to the Last Call process a Request for Comments aimed at developing a Policy Statement on Network Neutrality, based on the model framework, has been organised. The result of such process is described in the last article of this book.

References

Bastian, C., Klieber, T., Livingood, J., Mills, J. & Woundy, R. (2010, December). An ISP congestion management system. RFC 6057. https://tools.ietf.org/html/rfc6057#page-9

Belli, L. (2013, July 24). A new arrival in the IGF family: The dynamic coalition on network neutrality. Retrieved from http://www.medialaws.eu/a-new-arrival-in-the-igf-family-the-dynamic-coalition-on-network-neutrality/

---

[24] See IGF Chair (2014), p. 10.

Belli, L. (2015a, May). A heterostakeholder cooperation for sustainable internet policymaking. *Internet Policy Review, 4*(2), 1–21.

Belli, L. (2015b). *De la gouvernance à la régulation de l'Internet*. Paris: Berger-Levrault.

Belli, L., & De Filippi, P. (Eds.). (2013, October). *The value of network neutrality for the internet of tomorrow*. 1st Report of the Dynamic Coalition on Network Neutrality.

Belli, L., & van Bergen, M. (2013). Protecting human rights through network neutrality: Furthering internet users' interest, modernising human rights and safeguarding the open internet. Council of Europe. CDMSI (2013) Misc 19.

BEREC. (2012, May 29). A view of traffic management and other practices resulting in restrictions to the open Internet in Europe. Findings from BEREC's and the European Commission's joint investigation. BoR (12) 30.

Bradner, S. (1996). The internet standards process – revision 3, request for comments: 2026.

Bradner, S. (1998). IETF Working Group Guidelines and Procedures, request for comments: 2418.

CDMSI. (2013). Council of Europe multi-stakeholder dialogue on network neutrality and human rights Strasbourg, Outcome Paper prepared by Luca Belli. CDMSI (2013) misc18E.

Council of Europe. (2007). Recommendation CM/Rec(2007)16 of the Committee of Ministers to member states on measures to promote the public service value of the Internet.

CPB. (2010, September 23). *Memo: Response to public consultation on internet and net neutrality*. The Hague: Netherlands Bureau for Economic Policy Analysis.

DeNardis, L. (2009). *Protocol politics: The globalization of internet governance*. Cambridge, MA: MIT Press.

Directive 2002/58/EC of the European Parliament and of the Council of 12 July 2002 concerning the processing of personal data and the protection of privacy in the electronic communications sector (Directive on privacy and electronic communications).

Donley, C., Howard, L. Kuarsings, V., Berg, J., Doshi, J. (2013, September). Request for comments: 7021, Assessing the Impact of Carrier-Grade NAT on Network Applications. http://www.rfc-editor.org/rfc/rfc7021.txt

ETNO. (2012, September). Paper on Contribution to WCIT. ITRs Proposal to Address New Internet Ecosystem. http://www.etno.eu/datas/itu-matters/etno-ip-interconnection.pdf

Froomkin, M. (2003, January). Habermas@discourse.net: Toward a critical theory of cyberspace. *Harvard Law Review, 116*(3), 749–873.

Habermas, J. (2001). Discourse ethics: Notes on a program of philosophical justification. In *Moral consciousness and communicative action* (Studies in Contemporary German Social Thought)

Hoffman, P. (Ed.). (2012). The Tao of IETF: A Novice's Guide to the Internet Engineering Task Force. IETF Trust. http://www.ietf.org/tao.html

IGF Chair. (2014). Connecting Continents for Enhanced Multistakeholder Internet Governance. IGF 2014 Chair' s Summary. Istanbul, Turkey.

Internet Society. (2012, October 11). Combating spam: Policy, technical and industry approaches. http://www.internetsociety.org/sites/default/files/Combating-Spam.pdf

Kocsis, V., & Weda, J. (2013, June 12). The innovation-enhancing effects of network neutrality, study commissioned by the Dutch Ministry of Economic Affairs, Amsterdam.

KPN. (2011, May 10). KPN Investor Day: Group Strategy. Strengthen – Simplify – Grow. http://pulse.companywebcast.nl/playerv1_0/default.aspx?id=12193&bb=true&swf=true

Marsden, C. (2010). *Net neutrality: Towards a co-regulatory solution*. London: Bloomsbury Academic.

McAuley, C. (2012, February 14). 3 things you need to know about carrier-grade NAT. http://blogs.ixiacom.com/ixia-blog/carrier-grade-nat-testing/

OECD. (2011). Communiqué on principles for internet policy-making. Retrieved from http://www.oecd.org/internet/innovation/48289796.pdf

Shelly, R. (1993). Habermas and the Normative Foundations of a Radical Politics. Thesis Eleven, no. 35.

Van Schewick, B. (2012, June 11). Network Neutrality and Quality of Service: What a Non-Discrimination Rule Should Look Like.

Van Schewick, B. (2010). *Internet architecture and innovation*. Cambridge, MA: MIT Press.

Part II
A Regulatory Perspective on Net Neutrality

This section offers a collection of independent analyses exploring existing and proposed regulatory approaches to net neutrality and scrutinise the justifications that support the network neutrality principle. Given the transnational nature of the Internet, net neutrality can be better addressed through international cooperation. Yet, harmonisation at the international level might be difficult to achieve, as different countries are currently addressing the issue in different manners, thus fostering potentially conflicting approaches to what would constitute an infringement of Net Neutrality principles. Indeed, the interpretation and implementation of Net Neutrality provisions currently lies at the core of on-going regulatory debates, both at both domestic and international level.

The regulatory debate on network neutrality started in 2005, in the U.S., with the adoption of a Policy Statement[1] by the Federal Communications Commission (FCC) presenting a set of principles to preserve and promote the open and interconnected nature of the publicly accessible Internet. The question of Network Neutrality subsequently became central to the European regulatory agenda in 2009, during the revision of the Telecom package. The process encouraged some EU member states to elaborate national approaches to network neutrality, some of which were eventually implemented into domestic law (notably in the Netherlands and Slovenia).

In 2013, the Model Framework on Network Neutrality[2] initiated by the Council of Europe and developed by the Dynamic Coalition on Network Neutrality provided a set of recommendations on how to enshrine Network Neutrality principles into domestic law. In September 2013, the European Commission proposed a new Regulation laying down measures concerning the European single market for electronic communications,[3] which included specific provisions on Network Neutrality.

---

[1] The FCC Policy Statement is available at: https://apps.fcc.gov/edocs_public/attachmatch/DOC-260435A1.pdf.

[2] See Belli L, van Bergen M. & Woźniak M. Chap. 8.

[3] Regulation of the European Parliament and of the Council laying down measures concerning the European single market for electronic communications and to achieve a Connected Continent — COM(2013) 627. See: http://ec.europa.eu/digital-agenda/en/news/regulation-european-parliament-and-council-laying-down-measures-concerning-european-single.

In April 2014, the European Parliament adopted the first reading of the "Connected Continent" Regulation including net neutrality provisions, which prohibit the deployment of discriminatory traffic management on public electronic networks. After the adoption of a political agreement, in March 2015, the EU Council of Ministers started the informal "trialogue" negotiations leading to another political agreement with the EU Parliament and the Commission. The EU Parliament may still amend the trialogue proposal, and some key elements of the regulation may still be modified.

As is commonly the case, the devil is in the details and the definition of apparently technical elements may have considerable juridical and economic consequences. As illustrated by Frode Sørensen in his paper on "The Net Neutrality Service Model and Specialised Services", the debate is still open with regard to what constitutes a "specialised service"—*i.e.* a service that relies on access restrictions and Internet traffic management (ITM) techniques guaranteeing specific quality level, therefore not qualifying as an Internet access service. Understanding what this means in practice is an important precondition for the proper implementation of network neutrality regulations in Europe and elsewhere. Indeed, similar questions are being addressed in a variety of countries although national regulatory agencies may have different interpretations of the network neutrality principle thus fostering heterogeneous approaches. In Latin America, for instance, network neutrality is heavily debated in countries such as Argentina, Colombia and Ecuador, and legislation has already been enacted in a few countries, including Chile, Peru, and, more recently, Brazil. Yet, controversies exist with regard to the implementation of certain provisions, and, in particular, as regards the interpretation of established exceptions to the Net Neutrality principle. In this respect, Patricia Vargas-Leon's paper provides a comprehensive overview of the various Net Neutrality laws enacted and/ or proposed in Latin America and identifies the most important differences that subsist amongst these laws.

In Chile, the first Net Neutrality law[4] was enacted in 2011, as a modification of the Chilean general telecommunications law promulgated in 1982. The law establishes a duty for every Internet Service Provider (ISP) to provide non-discriminatory treatment to anyone using content or services for legal purposes. Yet, ISPs are given the discretion to determine ultimately what qualifies as a legal or illegal purpose. Besides, despite the enactment of Net Neutrality provisions, law enforcement may face difficulties, and many ISP have been accused of slowing down the speed of specific online services, such as YouTube or peer-to-peer networks. In Peru, net neutrality principles were incorporated into domestic law in 2012, through a bill[5]

---

[4] The net neutrality law in Chile is officially known as "Law 20453", or "Ley que establece la neutralidad de la red para consumidores y usuarios de Internet" ("Law that establishes the net neutrality for consumers and internet users").

[5] On July 20th, 2012, the Peruvian government enacted the law titled "Ley de promoción de la banda ancha y construcción de la red dorsal nacional de fibra óptica", ("Law to Promote the Increasing of Broadband and Construction of National Fiber Optic Backbone"), officially law 29904.

designed to promote the development, use and massive access to high-speed Internet connectivity. The law made it illegal for ISPs to block, interfere, discriminate or restrict the right of any Internet user to use an application, regardless of its nature, origin, or destination. Yet, just like the Chilean law, the law leaves it to the ISPs to determine what constitutes "arbitrary" practices when it comes to the respect of the Net Neutrality principle. Finally, after 5 years of debate, the Brazilian Senate adopted the Marco Civil da Internet no Brasil,[6] which specifically endorses the Net Neutrality principles by prohibiting ISPs from discriminating amongst different packets. Yet, exceptions to the general principle are not clearly specified, since those have to be implemented, at a later stage, by the executive branch.

The regulatory debate in Mexico is analysed by Alejandro Pisanty in his paper on "Network Neutrality debates in Telecommunications Reform", which presents a summary of the net neutrality debates in the legislative process taking place between 2013 and 2014. The author highlights that a major telecommunications law and market reform is taking place in the country and network neutrality may be considered as a useful test case to measure how convergent the legislation can be and to identify policy elements that can be translated into other markets. This reform is particularly interesting because it occurs in the absence of any common-carriage tradition but at the same time as must-carry, must-offer provisions are being introduced concerning the television market, for the first time. As a result, Network Neutrality has become a rallying cry for public demonstrations and other protests against the reform project. The paper describes and interprets the major economic forces, ideological and political trends that can be observed in Mexico, with a view toward their application to other geographies and contexts.

With regard to Australia, Angela Daly explains that the situation is much less mature. In her paper, the author highlights that although the country has been lagging behind in the regulatory debate, it is now catching up with the recent developments happening both in Europe and in the U.S. While there is still no network neutrality regulation in place (or even proposed) in Australia, it is nonetheless regarded as one of the major issues on the public agenda for Internet regulation. The 2012 Convergence Review Final Report specifically addressed the issue, pointing to content-related competition as one area where new policy and regulation should be implemented. However, following the federal elections in 2013, most of these recommendations were effectively abandoned as the new government was not supportive of any reform in this area. Today, there are therefore no plans to introduce Net Neutrality provisions into Australia legislation. Infringement to Network Neutrality can thus only be dealt with through the perspective of competition law, as a generic body of law which does not, however, specifically refer to Network Neutrality as principles that ought to be enshrined in the law.

Lastly, the most recent regulatory development regarding net neutrality in the Northern Hemisphere are analysed by Roslyn Layton, Joe McNamee and Maryant Fernandez. In her paper on a "Test of the FCC's Virtuous Circle: Preliminary results

---

[6] On April 23rd 2014, the Brazilian Senate passed what is known as the "Marco Civil Da Internet" ("Civil framework for the Internet"), officially law 12965.

for edge provider innovation and investment by country with hard versus soft rules", Roslyn Layton elucidates the design of an empirical assessment of the theory of the "virtuous circle of innovation", according to which the growth of content and applications stimulates demand for Internet subscriptions, which generates revenue for operators that consequently invest in infrastructure. This theory, the author argues, is frequently used to back network neutrality policies' benefits with regard to encouraging broadband providers to expand their networks and invest in new broadband technologies.[7] As such, users buy subscriptions to access the Internet, bringing revenue to broadband Internet access providers (BIAS), which then invest in infrastructure for networks. Layton offers a random effects model developed to test the outcome of edge provider innovation by country based upon the type of net neutrality rules as well as the impact for BIAS investment from 2000 to 2014. The investigation finds a significant and positive correlation for countries with soft forms of net neutrality rules (guidelines, codes of conduct, and multistakeholderism) and the incidence of local country edge provider innovation for mobile applications. No benefits for edge provider innovation were observed in countries with hard rules (legislation or regulation). No correlation was observed between the presence of net neutrality rules and increased investment.

Joe McNamee and Maryant Fernandez conclude this section, offering a critical analysis of the political negotiations occurring at the European Union level. With an "Analysis of the European Union's Trialogue Compromise" the authors present the intense rounds of negotiations that occurred, from 2013 until 2015, between the European Commission, the European Parliament and the Council of the European Union—the so-called "trialogue negotiations". The authors illustrate the difficulties encountered by these three institutions in the process of reaching a political compromise. Then they proceed to delineate the various elements of the current compromise that need further clarification and improvement, which concern, most notably, the definition of appropriate traffic management practices, with particular regard to congestion management; the tendency towards the privatisation of law enforcement and its potential risks of censorship; and the thorny issues of price discrimination and specialised services.

---

[7] E.g. FCC Report and Order Preserving the Open Internet (2010), available at https://apps.fcc.gov/edocs_public/attachmatch/FCC-10-201A1_Rcd.pdf.

Chapter 9
Specialised Services and the Net Neutrality Service Model

Frode Sørensen

9.1 Introduction

This paper contains a dual presentation of the net neutrality service model as developed through several years of public discourse about regulatory approaches to net neutrality. Particularly in Europe, this model which is used to differentiate between Internet traffic considered *in scope of* net neutrality and specialised services *exempted from* net neutrality assessment, has gained prominence trough the political process aiming at a "Connected Continent".

The term "specialised service" has subsequently often been replaced to with rather general terms such as "services other than Internet access services" or "non-broadband Internet access services". This paper, however, uses the descriptive name "specialised service".

The first part of the paper presents the historical evolution of the specialised service concept, from the inception of the idea until the more formal definitions prepared by BEREC and EU's political institutions. The discussion about specialised services also has an international dimension, through FCC and IGF Dynamic Coalition on Net neutrality. However, there is still a need to converge the different frameworks into a coherent net neutrality service model.

The second part of the paper elaborates how the service model containing the two distinct service categories, Internet access services and specialised services, can be understood as a method for traffic separation leading to safeguards preventing degradation of the Internet access services. The definitions of the service categories and the criteria for exceptions from the net neutrality principle for the Internet access service, so-called reasonable traffic management, are also discussed.

F. Sørensen (✉)
Norwegian Communications Authority, Lillesand, Norway
e-mail: frode.sorensen@nkom.no

© Springer International Publishing Switzerland 2016
L. Belli, P. De Filippi (eds.), *Net Neutrality Compendium*,
DOI 10.1007/978-3-319-26425-7_9

9.2   On the Origin of Specialised Services

9.2.1   The Beginning

Tim Wu introduced the "net neutrality" concept more than 10 years ago, and in 2005 Federal Communications Commission (FCC) launched its open Internet principles. These two events can be seen as the very first steps in the development of a net neutrality policy, though the essence of net neutrality could already be found in the Internet's underlying functioning.

The Norwegian Communications Authority (Nkom) was the first in Europe to establish a regulatory platform for net neutrality. Nkom based its work on co-regulation, and Norwegian guidelines for net neutrality were introduced in February 2009. These guidelines implicitly discuss specialised services and state that "if the physical connection *is shared with other services*, it must be stated clearly how the capacity is shared between Internet traffic and the other services".[1]

In October 2009, FCC published a Notice of Proposed Rulemaking, and in December 2009 FCC introduced rules for preserving a free and open Internet. These two documents explicitly address specialised services but do not define the term. However, the latter document refers to "*specialized services, such as existing facilities-based VoIP*".[2]

Net neutrality was intensely debated during the political process that led to a revised European regulatory framework in December 2009. The framework aims to promote competition among service providers, and concerning net neutrality, transparency is emphasised as a tool to enable end users to switch providers when necessary.

9.2.2   BEREC's Definitions

In 2010, BEREC established its Net Neutrality Expert Working Group, under the chairmanship of Nkom, with the purpose of studying practical methods for the application of the net neutrality provisions of the 2009 European regulatory framework. Due to the emphasis placed on transparency in the regulatory framework, the first report from the group was "Guidelines on transparency in the scope of net neutrality", closely followed by "Framework for quality of service in the scope of net neutrality".[3]

The *Framework* for quality of service published in 2011 represents BEREC's first step in the analysis of Article 22(3) of the USD on the prevention of service degradation. This report introduces main categories of service offers that ought to

---

[1] Nkom (2009).
[2] FCC (2010).
[3] BEREC (2011).

be considered by regulators when assessing the net neutrality situation in the market: Internet access services and specialised services, two service categories that share capacity on the end-user's broadband connection, also referred to as "the two lanes".

The *Guidelines* for quality of service in the scope of net neutrality[4] came in 2012, and introduced definitions for the service categories. The Guidelines presented a complete service model for regulatory assessment of net neutrality. The Internet access service is defined as a service that provides connectivity to the Internet, while specialised services are provided over virtual or physical networks distinct from networks constituting the Internet, but that will typically operate over the same infrastructure.

Furthermore, as the European regulatory framework from 2009 did not mandate net neutrality, two versions of the Internet access service are defined: unrestricted and restricted Internet access services. *Unrestricted* services provide access to all applications and all end-points on the Internet except reasonable traffic management while *restricted* services may also include unreasonable traffic management (such as the blocking of individual applications).

Assessment of the net neutrality situation in the market can thus be carried out on the basis of two methods: First, an assessment can be made of whether Internet access services are generally degraded, typically in comparison to specialised services. Second, an assessment can be made of whether *individual applications* that use Internet access services are being degraded; in other words, check the penetration of restricted Internet access services.

9.2.3 The European Legislative Process

When the European Commission on 11 September 2013 published its proposal for a Regulation to achieve a "Connected Continent", the regulatory goal of promoting net neutrality was proposed converted to a "freedom" for Internet users. The proposal contained net neutrality provisions acknowledging a service model consisting of the Internet access service and specialised services.

In BEREC's statement on the proposal, we read that: "BEREC welcomes the Commission's acknowledgment of the existence of specialised services alongside and distinct from internet access services (IAS). However, BEREC believes the relevant definition does not adequately capture their provision within closed networks and so risks hindering NRAs' capacity to apply open Internet standards to IAS and to determine the acceptable relationship between IAS and specialised services."[5]

After extensive discussion in the committees of the European Parliament, the vote during the plenary meeting on 3 April 2014 resulted in the adoption of several

---

[4] BEREC (2012a).
[5] BEREC (2013).

net neutrality provisions that strengthened the definitions of the two service categories. The wording of a number of articles was amended, to some extent in line with BEREC's suggestions.

BEREC expresses support for the European Parliament's work on promoting the principle of net neutrality, and clarifies in regard to the service model that "BEREC considers that specialised services should be clearly separated (physically or virtually) from internet access services at the network layer, to ensure that sufficient safeguards prevent degradation of the Internet access services."[6]

Finally, on 30 June 2015 an agreement about *European net neutrality rules* was reached between the Commission, the Parliament and the Council of EU[7] and the common position of this "trilogue" was forwarded to formally approval by the Council and the Parliament.[8]

9.3   The Net Neutrality Service Model Explained

The net neutrality service model with the two service categories has been developed to provide a balanced approach to net neutrality. The aim of the model is to protect net neutrality for Internet-based applications while allowing alternative approaches to quality of service and business models for specialised services.

9.3.1   The Practical Side of the Discussion

Since 2009, the net neutrality debate in Europe has been constantly evolving, and the "specialised service" concept has become a major issue in the debate. How should we understand this concept? What does it mean in practice? Which specific services does it refer to? While looking for answers to these questions, we get to the very core of the discussion about the "net neutrality service model": how specialised services relate to the Internet.

To start with the practical side of the discussion: specialised services already exist today. They consist of traditional services that have migrated to IP technology, such as *facilities-based* VoIP and IPTV. However, they can also be used to provide new services, and e-health seems to be the most prominent example that is being highlighted by stakeholders.

How one actually defines specialised services is important, as it should not include *Internet-based applications* which are increasingly used as a substitute for legacy services. Such Internet-based applications are often termed "over-the-top"

---

[6] BEREC (2014).

[7] European Commission, 30 June 2015, Commission welcomes agreement to end roaming charges and to guarantee an open Internet.

[8] Council of the European Union, 8 July 2015, Press release: Council confirms agreement with EP.

and include such applications as peer-to-peer voice over IP (*e.g.* Skype) and video streaming.

The "over-the-top" phrase indicates that there are two layers: the application layer and the network layer. The application layer is placed on top of and clearly separated from the network layer, which facilitates the development and deployment of new applications. This separation makes the Internet a general purpose network where the end-users have the possibility to use applications of their choice, or even to develop new ones, independently from the network operator's permission.[9] This is the basis for the enormous innovation in content and applications on the Internet that we have witnessed in recent years.

9.3.2   How to Define Specialised Services

Net neutrality is the principle that all Internet communications shall be treated equally. Equal treatment of traffic means that the traffic is transmitted irrespective of content, application, service, device, and irrespective of the sender or receiver. The latter element means that transmissions shall be carried out equally for different end-users, including content and application providers.

Up to the present moment, it seems that the understanding of what net neutrality is and what it is not has matured significantly. A consensus was established relatively early that net neutrality applies to the Internet, and not to other forms of electronic communications networks. Essential concepts in this context are so-called "specialised services", i.e. services that are not Internet access services.

The Norwegian guidelines for net neutrality stipulate that "if the physical connection is shared with other services, it must be stated clearly how the capacity is shared between Internet traffic and the other services." When the guidelines were established in February 2009, specialised services were not a familiar concept, and, therefore, this term was not explicitly used. The FCC has not defined specialised services in detail, but wrote, for example, about "specialized services, such as existing facilities-based VoIP" in its Report and Order in December 2010.

In 2011, BEREC established this definition of specialised services: "Specialised services are electronic communications services that are provided and operated within closed electronic communications networks using the Internet Protocol. These networks rely on strict admission control and they are often optimised for specific applications based on extensive use of traffic management in order to ensure adequate service characteristics."[10]

---

[9] Daigle (2014).
[10] BEREC (2012b), p. 27.

Furthermore, the Model Framework on Network Neutrality[11] of the IGF Dynamic Coalition on Net Neutrality defines specialised services as "electronic communications services that are provided and operated within closed electronic communications networks using the Internet Protocol, but not being part of the Internet. The expression 'closed electronic communications networks' refers to networks that rely on strict admission control."[12]

Even though the terminological choice of the European net neutrality rules proposed on 30 June 2015, as well as the US net neutrality rules published by FCC on 26 February 2015, has been rather to refer to specialised services as "services other than Internet access services" or "non-broadband internet access services", these services are still essential to the understanding of regulation of net neutrality.

9.3.3   Borderline Cases

Since the whole idea underpinning net neutrality is to ensure equal treatment of traffic, and specialised services are exempted from net neutrality considerations, it is of utmost importance to properly frame these services in order to avoid they have a negative impact on Internet traffic. Particularly, it seems essential to keep specialised services separated from Internet traffic so that the provision of the latter does not impair the former. On the contrary, the lack of separation may effectively undermine the foundation of net neutrality. Because how will mutually neutral handling of traffic help if external conditions degrade the capacity of the Internet access service as a whole?

Specialised services can help to guarantee the quality of certain forms of communication. As the definition of BEREC stresses, such services could be optimised for specific purposes. A typical example is real-time services such as telephony and the like. Specialised services can be provided with support for quality of service by having the services set up in networks where capacity is dimensioned according to the amount of traffic, and the traffic load is made predictable based on access control (typically based on subscriptions).

Quality of service to specialised services is not ensured by giving these services an explicit higher priority level than the Internet access service, but rather by having adequate capacity reserved for the specialised services without this being done at the expense of Internet traffic. Internet traffic has its own capacity scaled according to the contractual access speed. (The latter should not be understood as if the Internet

---

[11] The *Model Framework on Net Neutrality* has been developed subsequent to the Council of Europe organising its Multi-Stakeholder Dialogue on Network Neutrality and Human Rights, in May 2013. See Council of Europe Multi-Stakeholder Dialogue on Network Neutrality and Human Rights Strasbourg, Outcome Paper prepared by Luca Belli. The framework has been established by the *IGF Dynamic Coalition on Net neutrality*, and the launch itself was made at the Internet Governance Forum in October 2013. See http://www.networkneutrality.info.

[12] See Model Framework on Network Neutrality, para. 9.f. available at http://www.networkneutrality.info/sources.html.

access service has an absolute guarantee of the speed, but this is based on statistical calculations.)

The importance of separate capacity for the two service categories is also very evident in the BEREC definition of specialised services. These services are offered in "closed networks" that make it possible to *separate* this traffic from Internet traffic. FCC calls this to *isolate* the capacity used by the two service categories.[13] Both service categories are typically transmitted over the same physical infrastructure, in which case sufficient resources are to be available for the specialised services and Internet access service in their own "virtual networks".

Such "closed networks" can help to ensure that specialised services do not have a negative impact on the Internet access service, nor degrade it. This is already clear from the 2009 European regulatory framework: "*In order to prevent the degradation of service and the hindering or slowing down of traffic over networks,* Member States shall ensure that national regulatory authorities are able to set minimum quality of service requirements on an undertaking or undertakings providing public communications networks" (USD 22.3).

9.3.4   The Devil Is in the Details

Having said this, it is also important to emphasise that there is nothing negative in traffic management in itself. Traffic management is called for if one is to handle efficiently the traffic in the networks. In connection with net neutrality, a distinction is made between reasonable and unreasonable traffic management. *Unreasonable* traffic management is basically traffic management that provides non-neutral transmission of different types of traffic, thus unreasonably limiting end-users freedom to impart and receive information. But exceptions to the general rule of equal treatment are needed and have to be considered reasonable in specific cases.

BEREC has defined four assessment criteria for *reasonable* traffic management: non-discrimination of content and application providers, end-user control, application agnosticism and proportionality.[14] BEREC also emphasises that these criteria should not only apply to technically implemented traffic management but also to other restrictions such as for example, described in contractual terms.

Typical exceptions which may be considered reasonable are: (1) orders given in statutory bodies of law and court decisions, (2) measures to ensure the integrity and security of the network, (3) the prevention of unsolicited communication, (4) measures based on an explicit request from the end user and (5) handling of special situations relating to congestion management.

Most of these exceptions are easy to understand. Net neutrality should not be used to legitimise illegal or harmful activities (items 1 and 2). The problem of spam and the like must be handled efficiently (item 3) and the end users must be able to

---

[13] FCC (2015).
[14] BEREC (2012c).

protect themselves within their own access when this does not affect others, such as parental control (item 4).

The exception to net neutrality that is the most complex is how to deal with congestion. The way the Internet is constructed means that congestion will necessarily occur from time to time. Internet service providers' main measure to deal with congestion is to build capacity in the network in accordance with the subscription contracts they have. Moreover, short-term congestion is automatically handled by built-in mechanisms in IP technology, also referred to as "congestion control".

If there is a need to manage the traffic load above and beyond this, the mechanisms that handle the various applications neutrally (application-agnosticism) and allow an end user to decide what his available capacity will be used for (end-user control) should be preferred. Only in special situations where this is not possible in practice, should it be necessary to make use of application-specific methods for congestion management.

9.3.5   Toward Pan-European Net Neutrality

It is generally a positive development that the situation is moving from a fragmented approach in various countries toward a common European approach to net neutrality. The service model consisting of the two categories of services, i.e. Internet access service and specialised services, is an important foundation for efforts to unite on a common understanding of net neutrality regulation.

However, there is still a need for clarification in order to foster a better understanding of the model:

- The model assumes that the two service categories are defined as clearly as possible, so that there is no manipulation regarding which label you put on the service provided.
- Furthermore, if the model is to work, it is essential that resources to the service categories are separate at the network layer to avoid degradation of the Internet access service.
- And finally, management of "traffic jam" (congestion) is by and large done irrespective of the applications, and only in special situations where this is not possible, may it be application-specific.

There still appears to be a need for further clarifications to the net neutrality rules. The "specialised services" concept is now well-known, and with the help of regulatory guidelines explaining the implementation of the rules, this has the potential to be made into a precise and enforceable regulatory tool.

With wishes for an open Internet in a modern Europe!

References

BEREC. (2011). *A framework for QoS in the scope of net neutrality*, see: http://berec.europa.eu/
doc/berec/bor/bor11_53_qualityservice.pdf

BEREC. (2012a). *Guidelines for QoS in the scope of net neutrality*, see: http://berec.europa.eu/
eng/document_register/subject_matter/berec/download/0/1101-berec-guidelines-for-quality--
of-service-_0.pdf

BEREC. (2012b). *Guidelines for QoS in the scope of net neutrality* (p. 27).

BEREC. (2012c). *BoR (12) Summary of BEREC positions on net neutrality.*

BEREC. (2013). *Statement on the publication of a European Commission proposal for a
Regulation*, see: http://berec.europa.eu/eng/document_register/subject_matter/berec/
download/0/2922-berec-views-on-the-proposal-for-a-regula_0.pdf

BEREC. (2014). *Views on the European Parliament first reading legislative resolution on the proposal for a Regulation*, see: http://berec.europa.eu/eng/news_consultations/whats_new/
2203-berec-publishes-its-views-on-the-european-parliament-first-reading-legislative-
resolution-on-the-european-commissions-proposal-for-a-connected-continent-regulation

Daigle, L. (2014). *Permissionless innovation – openness, not anarchy*, http://www.internetsociety.
org/blog/tech-matters/2014/04/permissionless-innovation-openness-not-anarchy

FCC. (2010). *Report and order, preserving the free and open Internet*, see: https://apps.fcc.gov/
edocs_public/attachmatch/DOC-303745A1.pdf

FCC. (2015). Report and Order on Remand, Declaratory Ruling, and Order on the Matter of
Protecting and Promoting the Open Internet. GN Docket No. 14-28.

Nkom. (2009). *Norwegian guidelines for neutrality on the Internet*, see: http://eng.nkom.no/tech-
nical/internet/net-neutrality/the-norwegian-model

Chapter 10
Net Neutrality: An Overview of Enacted Laws in South America

Patricia Adriana Vargas-Leon

10.1 Introduction

Although the Internet was created as a technology without a unique point of control, governments and private corporations increased their efforts to control the Internet infrastructure and traffic pursuing their own interests (Horvitz 2013). In this scenario and in the face of a fast growing Internet penetration rate, the role of those who control the Internet infrastructure is one of the main issues of public debate. Worldwide, government authorities see themselves forced to analyze the conditions offered by Internet service providers (ISPs) and the responsibilities these companies have to their customers. The main point of discussion is whether the market of Internet access should be regulated or not, is a discussion known as the network neutrality (or net neutrality) debate (Hahn and Wallsten 2006; Krämer et al. 2013).

With this context in mind, between 2010 and 2014, four South American governments from Chile, Colombia, Peru and Brazil enacted net neutrality laws, while Argentina and Ecuador are debating the subject also at a legislative level.

10.2 Net Neutrality Debate

There is a general agreement to consider net neutrality as a principle according to which the Internet traffic should be treated equally (Cullell-march 2012; Wu 2003). The net neutrality debate includes the Internet users' rights to get access to the content, services and applications over the Internet without any kind of interference from Internet service providers or government agencies. Acting in any other way indicates an act of discrimination (Hahn and Wallsten 2006). At the same time, it also includes

P.A. Vargas-Leon (✉)
School of Information Studies, Syacuse University, Syacuse, NY, USA

© Springer International Publishing Switzerland 2016
L. Belli, P. De Filippi (eds.), *Net Neutrality Compendium*,
DOI 10.1007/978-3-319-26425-7_10

the right of Internet service providers to remain free of responsibility for the transference of contents and applications considered illegal or undesired by third parties (EDPS 2011; Mueller 2007). From an academic point of view, net neutrality is considered a principle to guide Internet policies both, at a national or international level (Mueller 2007). If intended to be a universal rule, any exception to the net neutrality principle should be included in a specific national statute and must be established alongside the obligation of non-discrimination (Cortés 2013). If such precaution is not included, general phrases or categories, such as, "reasonable management" could invalidate the warranty of a neutral network (Cortés 2013; Mueller 2007).

10.3   Controversy

The net neutrality principle avoids discrimination in electronic telecommunications, however, it does not mean Internet for everyone or Internet for a fair price; net neutrality exists even if ISPs offer contracts with different levels of connection with different prices (Cerda Silva 2013). Net neutrality only guarantees that the quality of service won't be affected by actions of the ISPs either slowing communications, conditioning access to the use of certain equipment or hindering access to certain services or content (Cortés 2013).

As a normative principle and within the public debate, net neutrality has two very important connotations (Mueller 2007):

1. Bandwidth regulation
   The term bandwidth refers to high-speed access to Internet traffic (BFA 2014). Considering this point specifically, there is a concern for the fact that bandwidth providers could adopt practices differentiating the Internet packages speed
2. Universal access to Internet resources
   The Universal access derives from the "end-to-end" principle, according to which, the specific functions of any application lie at the beginning and at the end of the communication process (Saltzer et al. 1984). On this matter, there is a policy concern that ISPs could block the access to any source of information on the Internet or limit any kind of content, applications or services.

10.4   Net Neutrality Laws in South America

Usually, net neutrality is discussed as a subject of national legislation (Mueller 2007); in this way, as it will be demonstrated in this paper, the South American net neutrality laws have important distinctions. Just to mention the most basic difference, Chile has an exclusive law to regulate the net neutrality principle, while Colombia, Peru, and Brazil have laws that regulate the subject alongside with others in a broader framework. The specific provisions about net neutrality and the particular characteristics of the situation that surround their creation will be explained in the next paragraphs.

10.4.1 Chile

The net neutrality law in Chile was the result of previous facts, where the biggest telecom companies were questioned about their practices over Internet traffic, the poor quality of service and the lack of transparency about their operations (Cerda Silva 2013). By 2003, an Internet service provider (ISP), Voissnet, engaged in a judicial battle against the biggest broadband provider in Chile, Telefónica de Chile,[1] or only Telefónica.

Voissnet S.A. is a local Internet service provider, and in 2003 the company offered more convenient prices to Internet users than Telefónica de Chile regarding the Voice over Internet Protocol (VoIP). In this scenario, Telefónica took action to obstruct and slow down Voissnet services (Silva 2007). Voissnet sued Telefónica and accused the company of unfair practices hindering free competition (ITU 2007; Silva 2007). Telefónica's argument for the defense was based on the lack of a specific regulation for the provision of broadband services, and therefore, the company considered that the restriction over the Voissnet servers was legal. Telefónica also accused Voissnet of unfair competition for offering public telephony services without a proper license and without compensating them for the cost of their networks (ITU 2007).

In 2007, the court forbade Telefónica from imposing limitations and restrictions over the competition in the fixed telephony business. However, because Chile does not belong to the case law system, the court ruling was not mandatory for similar cases. Subsequently, the court also ruled over cases involving free competition among mobile broadband and p2p services. After continuous claims of the civil society, the quality and transparency of the telecommunications service was included in the legislative branch agenda and the result would be what today is known as the first net neutrality law in the world (Cerda Silva 2013).

The net neutrality law in Chile, officially known as "Act 20453", or "Ley que establece la neutralidad de la red para consumidores y usuarios de Internet" ("Act for establishment of network neutrality for Internet users"), was enacted in 2010. Act 20453 is a modification of the Chilean General Telecommunications Act enacted in 1982[2] (Bourreau et al. 2014; CNC 2010).

The net neutrality principle and its exceptions are incorporated in article 24H, paragraph a) of Act 20453:

---

[1] By 2003, and still today, Telefónica de Chile (subsidiary of the Spaniard company with the same name) controlled the 53.2 % of the land lines and its operator, Movistar, controlled the 78 % of the Internet connections (Subtel 2013).

[2] Telecom Law N° 18168.

Act 20453.- Act for establishment of net neutrality for Internet users
> Article 24 H. - The broadband operators and Internet service providers that provide connectivity services between users or users' networks and the Internet:
>
> Cannot arbitrarily block, interfere, discriminate, obstruct or restrict users' rights to use, send, receive or offer any type of content, application or legal service through Internet, just like any other type of activity or legitimate use performed through the Internet. In this way, they [the broadband operators] must offer to each user Internet access or connectivity service to the Internet service provider according the case, which does not distinguish arbitrarily content, applications, services, according their source or ownership, taking into account the different configurations of Internet access according the users' contracts.
>
> Despite of everything, the broadband operators and the Internet service providers may take required measures or actions in order to manage the traffic and administrate the network in the exclusive framework where the activity was authorized, as long as such measures are not directed to conduct actions that affect or may affect the free competition.
>
> Broadband operators and Internet service providers will procure to preserve the users' privacy, protection against malware and the security of the network. In this way, they also can block the access to specific contents, applications or services, followed by the express request of the user, and at its own expense.
>
> Under no circumstances, this blocking must affect arbitrarily the Internet service providers and their applications on the Internet (author's translation) (CDC 2010).

As it was approved, Act 20453 creates a new group of guarantees and rights for Internet users, at the same time that it regulates new rights and duties for the ISPs, such as (BNC 2010; Cerda Silva 2013):

1. ISPs are required to inform Internet users about the different service plans and keep them informed about the changes in their service
2. ISPs are required to refrain from interfering in communications among Internet users

However, the Chilean net neutrality law also has some unclear sections and was criticized for this reason (DG 2010; Henriquez 2015):

1. The net neutrality principle is a duty for every ISP; the definition of ISP[3] contained in the law is broad enough to include the Chilean government itself. This is very important for Chile, where the government provides Internet connections to part of the population because the government is subject to the same rules as private ISPs.
2. When Act 20453 established that ISPs must not "arbitrarily" interfere with Internet traffic, it leaves a possibility for the same ISPs to exercise "non-arbitrary" actions according their own criteria. In this regard, ISPs have some independence to measure their technical indicators about quality of service and decide the length of time to re-establish the service in case of failure. Internet users will have to audit the process themselves.

---

[3] A natural person or corporation that provides connectivity services among Internet users and Internet networks.

Moreover, because ISPs would have the capacity to exercise non-arbitrary actions, it is also possible the existence of contradictory criteria among multiple ISPs.

On this particular subject, Chilean jurisprudence defines something "arbitrary" as something that lacks justification, with no motive or cause, or when it is just the result of someone's will or whim.

3. The integration of multiple devices to the network is allowed as long as it does not affect the quality of service. If the quality of service gets saturated, ISPs are entitled to interfere to control the Internet traffic, which can affect the P2P networks or video reproduction.
4. There is no standard format to deliver the information to Internet users; each ISP produces its own format publication and sends it to the users. This makes difficult to Internet users to choose the best option for them.

The law also establishes that net neutrality is only guaranteed as a right to use contents or services for legal purposes; therefore, if the use of contents or services were illegal, ISPs would be authorized to act against the net neutrality principle. This provision seems to give authority to ISPs to qualify whether an activity is legal or illegal. One of the clearest examples could be blocking a specific site because of what ISPs consider a violation of intellectual property rights.

On March 11th, 2013, the Chilean regulator, the Secretariat of the Ministry of Transport and Telecommunications—SUBTEL, enacted the administrative regulation that sets the characteristics and conditions of net neutrality in the Internet service, officially known as "Decreto 368" (Decree 368) (MTT 2011). Decree 368 forbids the arbitrary blocking of applications, services and content on the Internet, and demands that ISPs establish clear conditions for their service. As established in the article 7, traffic shaping is regulated, but not forbidden (Sturm 2011). ISPs only can affect the quality of the contracted service and execute actions to address the traffic shaping and the net administration, exclusively within their field of authorized action and, as long as those actions do not affect the free competition. If ISPs execute traffic shaping actions, they must inform of this situation through a clear publication (MTT 2011).

Finally, it is important to mention that, despite the existence of a net neutrality law, by 2013 some telecommunication companies in Chile, such as VTR Banda Ancha (Chile) S.A. were accused by civil society organizations of slowing down the speed of specific online services, such as YouTube and P2P networks. VTR could not justify these practices, and is not the only one ISP involved in this type of activity (ONG Civico 2013). At the beginning of 2013, it also became public that telecom companies in Chile share among each other segments of fiber optic cable in an undetermined number of sites. This information is not available for the public. On February 27th, 2015 some of the telecom companies that were paying for redundant links, (in order to guarantee high availability) noticed that their fibers go through the same routes. However, each telecom company charged exclusively for using the same fiber. Despite this irregular situation, actions of the regulator do not address this problem. So far, when is about net neutrality, SUBTEL only has required to the telecom companies to eliminate of their plans the free access to social networks, because they break the law by providing a discriminatory access to content or applications (Henriquez 2015).

10.4.2 Colombia

Deliberations about net neutrality in Colombia were preceded by a polemic debate about intellectual property rights on the Internet. On April 14th, 2011, the Minister of Justice, Germán Vargas Lleras, presented a bill called "Derechos de Autor en Internet" ("Intellectual property rights on the Internet"). The goal of the bill was that authors could request ISPs to remove their creations from the Internet when their intellectual property rights were not respected (La Rotta 2011). According to the bill, the ISPs are responsible for the distribution of content legally protected through their networks (Bossio 2011). In November, 2011, when the bill was put to a vote, it was not approved by the Colombian Senate because Act 1450, passed 6 months before, granted legal protection to the net neutrality principle (Bossio 2011; La Rotta 2011).

On June 16, 2011, the Colombian government enacted the "Plan Nacional de Desarrollo 2010–2014" (PND) ("National Development Plan 2010–2014"), officially Act 1450, the leading document for public policy in Colombia during the Santos administration (Penarredonda 2015; TeamWork 2011). Each President must present his/her national plan for development to the Congress within 6 months after beginning his/her administration. The document contains the main objectives for Colombia for the next 4 years of the new Presidential administration and the obligations to be met by state agencies (Penarredonda 2015).

The article 56 of the Act 1450 includes the principle of net neutrality:

Act 1450.- Act to issue the National Development Plan 2010–2014
    Title III. Mechanisms for implementing the plan
    Chapter 2. Sustainable growth and competitiveness
    2.2 Information and communication technology
    [...]
    Article 56°. Internet neutrality. Internet service providers:

1. Notwithstanding the provisions of Act No. 1336[4] of 2009, Internet Service Providers won't be able to block, interfere with, discriminate against or restrict the right of any Internet user to use, send, receive or offer any licit content, application or service on the Internet. In this sense, they shall offer to each user, Internet access or connectivity, without making arbitrary distinctions between content, applications or services on the basis of the origin or ownership thereof. Internet Service Providers shall make offers according to the needs of the market segments or their users based on their use and consumption profiles, and this shall not be understood as discrimination.

---

[4] Act 1336 from 2009 was created to fight against child pornography in the Internet.

2. Internet Service Providers may not limit the users' right to add or use any kind of instruments, devices or equipment on the network, as long as they are legal and do not harm or adversely affect the network or the quality of the service.
3. Internet Service Providers shall offer to the users parental control services for illegal content, and shall provide users with clear information in advance, regarding the scope of such services.
4. Internet Service Providers shall publish on their website information about the Internet access offered, the speed and quality of the service, making a distinction between national and international connections, and shall include information about the nature and guarantees of the service.
5. Internet Service Providers shall implement mechanisms to preserve the users' privacy, protect them against viruses and ensure security on the network.
6. Internet Service Providers shall block access to certain content, applications or services, only upon express request of the users.

Paragraph. The Communications Regulatory Commission (Comisión de Regulación de Comunicaciones) shall regulate the terms and conditions for the implementation of the provisions of this section. The initial regulation shall be issued within six months following the entry into force of this law (author's translation) (CDC 2011).

Differently from the Chilean law, the Colombian law uses the term "licit" content or service, instead of "legal". However, in practical terms this does not imply major changes. Regarding the use of the word "arbitrary", the same critiques to the Chilean law apply to the Colombian. However, in the Colombian case, there is a lack of an authoritative legal source to define what arbitrary means. This is an absolute competence of the regulator.

On December 16th, 2011, the Colombian regulator, the "Comisión de Regulación de Comunicaciones"—CRC, enacted the administrative regulation 3502 (Ledesma 2011). The administrative resolution, just like section 1 of the article 56 of the law, leaves a possibility for the ISPs to offer services of Internet access for a price according to the needs of the market. By allowing the ISPs to make these offers, it may be possible for them to offer plans of Internet mobile services, which are oriented to offer services the ISPs want to offer, such as specific social networks, email or chat services. This practice has been explicitly prohibited by the net neutrality legislations from Chile and the Netherlands (Casasbuenas 2013).

In reference to traffic shaping, this is regulated only when it is oriented to (CRC 2011):

- Secure the reduction of network congestion
- Secure the integrity of the network
- Secure the quality of service
- Prioritize generic types or classes of traffic according to the requirements of quality of service (QoS) of such traffic
- Provide services or capabilities according to the user's choice to address the technical requirements, standards or best practices adopted by Internet governance initiatives or standard organizations.

Alongside with the regulation 3502, the CRC created a package of regulations related to the net neutrality legislation, in order to promote the digital ecosystem. This is important because, by December 2011, Colombia was the second nation-state in South America that was offering the fastest speed after Chile. The complementary regulations included: (1) Promotion of content and applications (Regulation CRC 3501—12/5/2011), (2) Promoting infrastructure (Regulation CRC 3499—12/5/2011), (3) Promoting services and Internet users' protection (Regulation CRC 3503—12/16/2011) (CDQ 2011).

Despite the new legislation and regulations, at the beginning of 2015, with the new Santos administration, the Executive branch submitted a new PND to the Colombian Congress to be approved. The article 206 of this document overturns the article 56 of the previous plan, which is the one that contains the net neutrality provisions. Facing critiques because of this situation, the former minister of Information and Communication Technology, Diego Molano, claimed that there is no possibility of overturning the net neutrality principle, since the law 1450 only sets a timeline for the regulator to establish conditions related to the net neutrality. According to Mr. Molano, this task is already completed with the resolution 3502 and complementary ones (Penarredonda 2015; Semana 2015).

Although the debate does not end yet, there is a fair question to ask: if the law that establishes the net neutrality principle is overturned, can the administrative regulation 3502 (and complementary regulations) to remain in force?

Colombia belongs to the civil law system, in which, administrative resolutions like 3502 require a previous law that establishes their creation. Once the "original law" is overturned, the administrative regulation may be unapplied any time as it no longer has legal grounds to exist. If the net neutrality principle loses "legal status" (as it only would exist as part of the administrative regulation), the principle can be challenged in Court by private companies for being illegal (Penarredonda 2015; Rubio Correo 2011). On this matter, it is not clear what will happen in Colombia.

10.4.3 Peru

In Peru, the net neutrality principle has had an administrative regulation since 2005. In that year, the Peruvian regulator, the "Organismo Supervisor de Inversión Privada en Telecomunicaciones" (Supervisory Agency for Private Investment in Telecommunications)—OSIPTEL approved the "Reglamento de Calidad de los Servicios Públicos de Telecomunicaciones – Resolución de Consejo Directivo N° 040-2005-CD/OSIPTEL" (Regulation of Quality of Public Telecommunications Services—Board Resolution No. 040-2005 CD/OSIPTEL) (Morachimbo 2012). This administrative regulation established in article 7 that Internet service providers and network operators could not block or limit any application to what the regulator called the path "user-ISP-ISP-user". Exceptions only would be allowed with previous approval from OSIPTEL (OSIPTEL 2005).

OSIPTEL's regulation lacked legislative authority (as it was part of the administrative regulation and not an act itself). In that way, as previously explained in the Colombian case, any ISP could challenge this regulation as an illegal provision. At that time in Peru, ISPs were offering to their clients "special deals," which contained limitations in the service in exchange for a reduction in the monthly fees. Clients were not properly informed about this matter, and these practices were considered "inappropriate" under article 7 (Bossio 2013).

At a legislative level, the net neutrality debate in Peru started in 2009 after the Peruvian government followed free market policies for nearly 20 years, which included the telecommunications sector. On July 20th, 2012, the Peruvian government enacted the act titled "Ley de promoción de la banda ancha y construcción de la red dorsal nacional de fibra óptica" ("Act for Broadband Promotion and National Optical Fiber Backbone Network Construction"), officially Act 29904. As included in the title, Act 29904 was created to promote the development, use and massive access to the Internet permanently at high speed. Act 29904 included net neutrality provisions, making illegal for an ISP to block, interfere with, discriminate or restrict the right of any Internet user to use an application, regardless of origin, destination or type of user (LAT 2012).

Article 6 of Act 29904 includes the net neutrality principle:

> Act 29904.- Act for Broadband Promotion and National Optical Fiber Backbone Network Construction
> [...]
> Article 6. – Freedom to use applications or broadband protocols
> Internet service providers will respect the net neutrality, according to which, they cannot arbitrarily to block, interfere, discriminate or restrict Internet users' rights to use an application or protocol, independently of its origin, destiny, nature or ownership.
> When is about the net neutrality principle, the telecommunications regulator – OSIPTEL decides what actions will not be considered arbitrary practice (author's translation) (CNP 2012).

According to Act 29904, ISPs cannot limit Internet users' rights to use any type of application or protocol and cannot restrict, block or arbitrarily disable functions or characteristics of the devices that prevent the free use of those protocols. As it is written, the Peruvian law can be criticized for the same reasons that the Chilean and the Colombian laws for the use of the word "arbitrary". In the Peruvian case, there is also a lack of an authoritative legal source to define what arbitrary means. However, differently from the Chilean and Colombian cases, the definition of what an arbitrary situation is became an absolute attribution of the regulator. On this matter, the regulator capabilities, the administrative regulation created for the implementation of Act 29904, Supreme Decree 014-2013-MTC (enacted on November 4th, 2013) entitles OSIPTEL to "grant permission" in advance to ISPs to go against the net neutrality principle in two situations: (a) when there is a judicial mandate and (b) in case of an emergency situation (MTC 2013). The last exception, referred as an "emergency situation," lacks any further explanation or guidelines to determine what an emergency situation is. Because of this last provision, the regulator takes a key role in the traffic and network management.

Regulation 014-2013 has provisions about traffic shaping, which is also subordinated to OSIPTEL's previous approval. According to article 10, when one or more ISPs pretend to implement traffic management actions, they must have OSIPTEL's previous approval. However, there are two exceptions to this rule: (1) when there is precedent by OSIPTEL and (2) a judicial mandate. In any case, OSIPTEL must make available its decisions related to the traffic shaping indicating the name of the ISP or ISPs that requested to make changes in the traffic of the Internet packets (MTC 2013).

Since 2012, and according the provisions of Act 29904, OSIPTEL has proposed to change the conditions to use telecommunications public services, which are part of the telecommunications services' contracts in Peru. As proposed, the new text should be:

> Article 67-Ao.- Content access, use of Internet protocols and applications
>
> The subscriber has the right to access any application service, using any protocol of the Internet and send or receive any content under the current legal system.
>
> The operator will be prevented to limit or block subscriber access to content, applications that are available for service, or an Internet protocol, except in those cases where such restriction or blockage occurs because of reasons supported and for which OSIPTEL has expressed its consent or mandated standards in this area.
>
> When operating companies provide Internet access services, tariff plans shall not limit, restrict or block access to certain applications or protocols for Internet content (Bossio 2013).

The Peruvian Congress did not pass these changes but decided to pass regulation complementary to Act 29904 and regulation 014-2013. On September 22nd, 2013, the Peruvian Congress passed the law titled "Ley que establece medidas para fortalecer la competencia en el Mercado de los servicios publicos moviles" ("Act to establish actions to strengthen competition in the market for mobile public services"), officially Act 30083. As mentioned, act 30083 is considered a complementary law to the net neutrality provisions.

The purpose of Act 30083 is strengthening the competition and expanding the market of mobile devices by inserting virtual mobile operators and rural mobile operators. On August 4th, 2015, the Ministry of Transport and Communications (MTC) enacted the administrative regulation of Act 30083, Supreme Decree 004-2015-MTC. In order to fulfill the mandate for which both, the law and the administrative regulation were created, they included the net neutrality as an obligation for network operators, virtual mobile operators and rural mobile operators (Pautasio 2014, 2015).

> Act 30082.- Act that establishes measures to strengthen competition in the market for public mobile services
>
> [...]
>
> Article 8.- Agreements between mobile network operators and virtual mobile operators
>
> [...]
>
> The conditions for concluding agreements between mobile network operators and virtual mobile operators are the following ones:
>
> 8.1.- Agreements subscribed between virtual mobile operators and network mobile operators should be based on the principles of neutrality, non-discrimination, equal access, and free and fair competition. Its implementation should take place in the terms and conditions negotiated in good faith between the parties.
>
> [...]
>
> Article 12.- Signing agreements
>
> The agreements signed between mobile network operators and rural mobile operators:

12.1 are based on the principles of neutrality, non-discrimination, equal access, and free and fair competition. Its implementation should take place in the terms and conditions negotiated in good faith between the parties (author's translation) (CNP 2013).

Since the administrative regulation was enacted recently, at the beginning of August 2015, more time will be needed to assess the results of this new policy.

10.4.4   Brazil

After 5 years of debate, on April 23rd, 2014, the Brazilian Senate passed what is known as the "Marco Civil Da Internet" ("Civil framework for the Internet"), officially Act 12965. The initial project was submitted for discussion on October 29, 2009 (FGV 2014), and like the Peruvian and Colombian law, the Brazilian legislation was not created to address the net neutrality principle exclusively. Marco Civil was created to address two specific problems: (a) to guarantee the net neutrality and (b) to preserve the Internet users privacy (FGV 2014; Gutierrez 2014). In this way, the original bill had three elements: (a) freedom of expression online, (b) protection of privacy and personal user data on the web and (c) network neutrality (Mari 2013). By 2010 the project known as Marco Civil was described by the Ministry of Justice, Luiz Paulo Barreto, as "The Constitution of the Internet" in Brazil (G1 2010).

Broadband providers were the biggest rivals of the project, which was about to be dismissed in the Brazilian Congress. However, the surveillance activities of the U.S. government revealed by Edward Snowden brought the debate back to the political agenda (Gutierrez 2014; Mari 2013). Specifically in Brazil, net neutrality advocates propose to treat the Internet as public utility, because the telecommunications business tends to reduce the number of providers so that many of them operate almost as monopolies (Lehman 2014).

Act 12965 incorporates all the net neutrality rights, limitation of responsibility for the intermediaries, freedom of expression and guarantees for Internet users' privacy. The law also establishes who the main stakeholders are and their responsibilities in the online environment (FGV 2014). The articles 9 of the law contain a specific reference to the net neutrality principle:

Act 12965.- Marco Civil Da Internet
   Chapter III.- Provision of Connection and Internet Applications
   Section I.- Of the Network Neutrality
   Art. 9.- The party responsible for the transmission, switching or routing has the duty to process, on an isonomic basis, any data packages, regardless of content, origin and destination, service, terminal or application.
   §1° The discrimination or degradation of traffic shall be regulated in accordance with the private attributions granted to the President by means of Item IV of art. 84 of the Federal Constitution, aimed at the full application of this Law, upon consultation with the Internet Steering Committee and the National Telecommunications Agency, and can only result from:
   I. – technical requirements essential to the adequate provision of services and applications; and
   II. – prioritization of emergency services.

§2° in the happening of discrimination or degradation of traffic provided in §1°, the responsible entity mentioned in Art. 9 must:

I.- abstain from causing damages to users, as set forth in art. 927 of Law no. 10.406, January 10th, 2002 – the Civil Code;

II.- act with proportionality, transparency and isonomy;

III.- provide, in an advanced notice, in a transparent, clear and sufficiently descriptive manner, to its users, the traffic management and mitigation practices adopted, including those related to network security; and

IV.- offer services in non-discriminatory commercial conditions and refrain from anti-competition practices.

§3° when providing internet connectivity, free or at a cost, as well as, in the transmission, switching or routing, it is prohibited to block, monitor, filter or analyze the content of data packets, in compliance with this article (cgi 2014).

From the text of the law, it is clear that there cannot be special prices for special content, which ensures the basic premises of the net neutrality principle. However, regarding the exceptions to the net neutrality principle itself, the Brazilian law is as unclear as those of the other nation-states analyzed in this paper. Exceptions are not clearly specified.

According to the section 1 of article 9, the "discrimination or degradation of the traffic" is an aspect that will be regulated by the Executive branch, after consultation with the Internet Steering Committee and the National Telecommunications Agency. Those exceptions are supposed to be contained in the administrative regulation, which was not published yet. In any case, the law does not mention transitory provisions for traffic shaping, and regarding the specific request of a user to block a site, the law does not mention anything either.

During the 5th Forum of the Internet, held in Salvador in July 2015, participants drafted the "Charter of Salvador," which requires all Internet regulation to be open to the public online and in a participatory platform for discussion, just as Marco Civil was discussed. The general concern of consumer associations in Brazil is that this delay in the process or enacting the administrative regulation may be used to disclaim the principles established in Marco Civil (Bruno 2015). The debate still continues (Fig. 10.1 and Table 10.1).

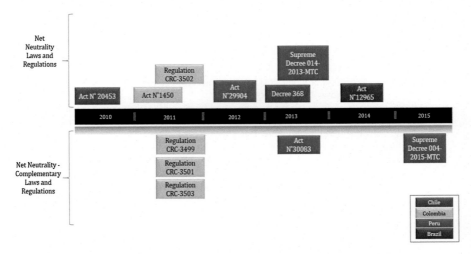

Fig. 10.1 Timeline net neutrality legislations overview in South America

Table 10.1 Net neutrality legislations in South America—comparison overview

	Category			
Nation-state	Exceptions to the net neutrality principle contained in the law and the administrative regulation	Regulator capabilities (provisions included in the law and administrative regulation)	Administrative regulation enacted	Traffic shaping according the administrative regulation
Chile	1. Security in the network 2. User specific request	SUBTEL, the regulator, is entitled: 1. To request from the ISPs information to verify the authenticity of the indicators related to the Internet service contracts, and therefore, to supervise the ISPs activity. SUBTEL also must approve the protocols to read the indicators. 2. To apply fines to those ISPs that do not follow the net neutrality principle 3. To create the administrative regulation to apply the law alongside with the Ministry of Communications	Yes	Allowed and regulated
Colombia	The law does not establish exceptions	CRC, the regulator, is entitled: 1. To create the specific administrative regulation of the law 2. To create additional regulations pursuing the improvement of services and protection of Internet users and the net neutrality itself	Yes	Allowed and regulated

(continued)

Table 10.1 (continued)

Nation-state	Exceptions to the net neutrality principle contained in the law and the administrative regulation	Regulator capabilities (provisions included in the law and administrative regulation)	Administrative regulation enacted	Traffic shaping according the administrative regulation
	Category			
Peru	When there is a previous authorization of the regulator in case of: 1. A judicial mandate 2. When there is an emergency situation	OSIPTEL, the regulator, is entitled: 1. To determine when a specific practice goes against the net neutrality principle (what practices are arbitrary and which ones are not) 2. To impose fees for arbitrary practices according its own discretion having in consideration the provisions of the administrative regulation 3. To "Grant permission" in advance to ISPs to go against the net neutrality when there is a judicial mandate and in case of an "emergency situation" 4. To "Approve in advance" changes in the traffic shaping upon request of one or more ISPs	Yes	Allowed and regulated
Brazil	The law does not establish exceptions and entitles the Executive Branch to determine what the exceptions will be. If exceptions are granted, they will be established by the administrative regulation, which was not published yet	There is no mention in the law about the regulator specific functions	No	Not known yet

10.5   Conclusion

The goal of this paper was to provide an overview of the net neutrality legislation enacted in South America, considering aspects such as exceptions to the net neutrality principle, ambiguity in the legal language, regulators' powers and traffic shaping.

Although the net neutrality debate's main point of discussion is that there is no special payment for special content, circumstances that prompt legislations over the subject may be extreme and so are the exceptions to the principle. So far, four South American governments enacted legislations in favor of net neutrality and others are discussing the subject.

In general terms, there are some important distinctions to consider among the Chilean, Colombian, Peruvian and Brazilian situations:

Originally, in Peru and Colombia there was not a significant or meaningful public debate on the net neutrality principle, except in Congress and a few civil society organizations. However, between 2013 and 2015 the debate on the subject has reborn; in the Peruvian case because of the enactment of complementary laws to the net neutrality principle itself, and in Colombia because of the possibility of overturn the original statutory provisions about net neutrality.

In Chile and Brazil there were long discussions about the subject within media, civil society, Congress, Judicial and Executive branch. The discussion remains because of arbitrary actions of ISPs in Chile and the creation of the administrative regulation in Brazil.

The Colombia statute does not include specific exceptions to the net neutrality principle, as the Chilean and the Peruvian do. The Brazilian law does not mention anything either and the administrative regulation was not published yet.

The Chilean and Peruvian law grant general and broad powers to the regulator to determine what practices are considered (or not considered) against net neutrality. The Colombian and Brazilian legislation do not grant any power to the regulator.

Provisions on traffic shaping are different in each case. However, the rule is that it is not forbidden, but regulated.

As a policy change, net neutrality legislation in Latin America is still new and each nation-state has different circumstances to deal with. As a matter of fact, even after net neutrality statutes were enacted, civil society organizations reported that even having this type of law, ISPs continue trying to find loop holes or vague legal provisions which allow them to manipulate the Internet traffic. Facing these circumstances, alongside with the particularities of a specific market, the problem of an unclear legislation is a challenge for regulators, policy makers and Internet users, a problem that must be addressed in the near future in order to guarantee the goal of these laws, which is to keep a neutral Internet.

References

BFA. (2014). *Broadband for America. ¿Qué es banda ancha?* Retrieved June 24, 2014, from http://www.broadbandforamerica.com/es/¿qué-es-banda-ancha

BNC. (2010). Historia de la Ley N° 20.453 Consagra el Principio de Neutralidad en la red para los consumidores y usuarios de Internet. Santiago de Chile.

Bossio, J. (2011). Columna: Compartir no es robar. Retrieved August 7, 2014, from https://lineadevista.lamula.pe/2011/04/17/compartir-no-es-robar/jorgebossio/

Bossio, J. (2013). La neutralidad de la red y los derechos de los usuarios de Internet en el Perú. Retrieved August 6, 2014, from https://redaccion.lamula.pe/2013/04/13/la-neutralidad-de-la-red-y-los-derechos-de-los-usuarios-de-internet-en-el-peru/jorgebossio/

Bourreau, M., Kourandi, F., & Valletti, T. M. (2014). Net neutrality with competing internet platforms. In *CEPR Discussion Paper No. DP9827.* Retrieved from http://papers.ssrn.com/abstract=2444828

Bruno, A. (2015). Entities ask agility in the regulation of "Marco Civil." Retrieved August 5, 2015, from http://nic.br/noticia/na-midia/entidades-pedem-agilidade-na-regulamentacao-do-marco-civil/

Casasbuenas, J. (2013). Neutralidad en Internet: Factor que potencia el cierre de la brecha social digital. Retrieved August 8, 2014, from http://www.colnodo.apc.org/documento.shtml?apc=f-xx-1-&x=3603

CDC. (2010). *Camara de Diputados de Chile. Proyectos de Ley. Consagra el principio de neutralidad en la red para los consumidores y usuarios de Internet.* Chile. Retrieved from http://www.camara.cl/pley/pley_detalle.aspx?prmID=5300&prmBL=4915-19

CDC. Ley 1450 de 2011, por la cual se expide el plan nacional de desarrollo, 2010–2014 (2011). *Colombia: Republica de Colombia. Diario Oficial.* Retrieved from http://www.mintic.gov.co/portal/604/articles-3821_documento.pdf

CDQ. (2011, December 20). CRC establece medidas de promoción del ecosistema digital. *La Cronica Del Quindio.* Bogota, Colombia. Retrieved from http://www.cronicadelquindio.com/noticia-completa-titulo-crc_establece_medidas_de_promocion_del_ecosistema_digital-seccion-economicas-nota-40294.htm

Cerda Silva, A. J. (2013). Neutralidad de la red y libertad de expresion. *Cuestion de Derechos,* (4). Retrieved from http://www.cuestiondederechos.org.ar/pdf/numero4/Articulo-5.pdf

cgi. (2014). *CGI.br – Marco Civil Law of the Internet in Brazil.* Retrieved July 10, 2014, from http://www.cgi.br/pagina/marco-civil-law-of-the-internet-in-brazil/180

CNC. (2010). *Ley de Neutralidad de la Red, Pub. L. No. 18168.* Chile: Biblioteca del Congreso Nacional de Chile. Retrieved from http://www.leychile.cl/Navegar?idNorma=1016570

CNP. (2012). *Ley de Promoción de la Banda Ancha y Construcción de la red dorsal Nacional de Fibra Optica.* Peru: Biblioteca del Congreso de la Republica del Peru. Retrieved from http://www.congreso.gob.pe/ntley/Imagenes/Leyes/29904.pdf

CNP. (2013). *Ley que Establece Medidas para Fortalecer la Competencia en el Mercado de los Servicios, Sistema Peruano de Informacion Juridica.* Peru. Retrieved from http://transparencia.mtc.gob.pe/idm_docs/normas_legales/1_0_3239.pdf

Cortés, C. (2013). *La neutralidad de la red: la tensión entre la no discriminación y la gestión. Centro de Estudios en Libertad de Expresion y Acceso a la Informacion.* Retrieved from http://www.palermo.edu/cele/pdf/PaperNeutralidadFinal.pdf

CRC. (2011). Resolución 3502 por la cual se establecen las condiciones regulatorias relativas a la neutralidad en Internet, en cumplimiento de lo establecido en el artículo 56 de la Ley 1450 de 2011., Pub. L. No. 35. Colombia: Diario Oficial 48285 de diciembre 16 de 2011. Retrieved from http://www.alcaldiabogota.gov.co/sisjur/normas/Norma1.jsp?i=45061

Cullell-march, C. (2012). El futuro de la Web ante la neutralidad de la Red: estado de la cuestión en la Unión Europea. *El Profesional de La Informacion, 1*(1).

DG. (2010). Chile: Las dudas del proyecto de ley sobre neutralidad en la red Fundación Vía Libre. Retrieved July 7, 2014, from http://www.vialibre.org.ar/2010/07/28/chile-las-dudas-del-proyecto-de-ley-sobre-neutralidad-en-la-red/

EDPS. (2011). *European Political Strategy Centre. Opinion of the European Data Protection Supervisor*. Brussels. Retrieved from http://ec.europa.eu/bepa/european-group-ethics/docs/activities/peter_hustinx_presentation_(1)_15_rt_2011.pdf

FGV. (2014). *The Brazilian Civil Rights Framework for the Internet*. Retrieved July 1, 2014, from http://direitorio.fgv.br/noticia/the-brazilian-civil-rights-framework-for-the-internet

G1. (2010). *Barreto defende criação de "Constituição" da Internet*. Retrieved July 1, 2014, from http://g1.globo.com/brasil/noticia/2010/05/barreto-defende-criacao-de-constituicao-da-internet.html

Gutierrez, B. (2014). Brasil aprueba el Marco Civil de Internet, modelo para la Carta Magna de la Red. Retrieved June 26, 2014, from http://www.eldiario.es/turing/Brasil-marca-ritmo-neutralidad-Internet_0_243925947.html

Hahn, R. W., & Wallsten, S. (2006). The economics of net neutrality. *The Economists Voice, 3*(6), 1–7. Retrieved from http://www.bepress.com/ev/vol3/iss6/art8

Henriquez, S. (2015). *¿Te importa la Ley de Neutralidad de la Red en Chile?* Retrieved August 5, 2015, from https://gobiernoti.wordpress.com/2015/04/17/te-importa-la-ley-de-neutralidad-de-la-red-en-chile/

Horvitz, R. (2013). *Geo-Database Management of White Space vs. Open Spectrum*. Retrieved from http://papers.ssrn.com/abstract=2279099

ITU. (2007). *Decision regarding the complaint of Voissnet and the National Economic Prosecutor's Office against Telecomunicaciones de Chile for restrictive practices in the telecommunication market, and the counter-claim of Telecommunications de Chile against Voissnet*. Retrieved June 30, 2014, from http://www.ictdec.org/ictdec-web/en/regions/region_3/zone_63/database_33/decisions/118/es/index.html

Krämer, J., Wiewiorra, L., & Weinhardt, C. (2013). Net neutrality: A progress report. *Telecommunications Policy, 37*(9), 794–813.

La Rotta, S. (2011). La polémica "Ley Lleras." *El Espectador*. Retrieved from http://www.elespectador.com/noticias/actualidad/vivir/polemica-ley-lleras-articulo-261793

LAT. (2012). *Peru enforces net neutrality, looks to roll out fiber backbone*. Retrieved June 30, 2014, from http://bi.galegroup.com.libezproxy2.syr.edu/essentials/article/GALE|A307919839/0c1b38fd1bbbd0ea0b5e7c49074c03c1?u=nysl_ce_syr

Ledesma, L. (2011). Colombia adhiere a la neutralidad de red. Retrieved June 26, 2014, from http://www.telesemana.com/blog/2011/12/27/colombia-adhiere-a-la-neutralidad-de-red/

Lehman, S. (2014). Brazil's new Internet "Bill of Rights" protects privacy, ensures net neutrality|CTV News. *CTV News*. Retrieved from http://www.ctvnews.ca/sci-tech/brazil-s-new-internet-bill-of-rights-protects-privacy-ensures-net-neutrality-1.1789673

Mari, A. (2013). "Internet Constitution" becomes priority for Brazilian government. Retrieved July 1, 2014, from http://www.zdnet.com/internet-constitution-becomes-priority-for-brazilian-government-7000017839/

Morachimbo, M. (2012). Congreso peruano regula la Neutralidad de Red (nuevamente). Retrieved June 19, 2014, from http://www.blawyer.org/2012/06/18/congreso-peruano-regula-la-neutralidad-de-red-nuevamente/

MTC. (2013). Reglamento de la Ley 29904, Ley de Promoción dela Banda Ancha y Construcción de la Red Dorsal Nacional de Fibra Optica, Pub. L. No. 29904. Peru. Retrieved from http://www.mtc.gob.pe/portal/comunicacion/politicas/normaslegales/REGLAMENTO.pdf

MTT. (2011). Reglamento que regula las características y condiciones de la neutralidad de la red en el servicio de acceso a Internet, Biblioteca del Congreso Nacional de Chile. Santiago de Chile, Chile: Biblioteca del Congreso Nacional de Chile. Retrieved from http://www.leychile.cl/Navegar?idNorma=1023845

Mueller, M. (2007). Net neutrality as global norm for internet governance. In *2nd Annual Giganet Symposium*.

ONG Civico. (2013). *Pruebas concretas: Cómo VTR viola la ley de neutralidad de la red en dos ejemplos*. Retrieved July 7, 2014, from https://ongcivico.org/neutralidad-en-la-red/pruebas-concretas-como-vtr-viola-la-ley-de-neutralidad-de-la-red-en-dos-ejemplos/

OSIPTEL. (2005). Resolución de Consejo Directivo Directivo N° 040-2005-CD/OSIPTEL, Pub. L. No. 040-2005-CD/OSIPTEL. Peru. Retrieved from file:///E:/MisDocumentos/Downloads/res0402005CDOSIPTEL.pdf

Pautasio, L. (2014). Perú pone en consulta pública iniciativa para regular los MVNO. Retrieved August 20, 2015, from http://www.telesemana.com/blog/2014/12/09/peru-pone-en-consulta-publica-iniciativa-para-regular-los-mvno/

Pautasio, L. (2015). Perú aprueba regulación para MVNOs. Retrieved August 5, 2015, from http://www.telesemana.com/blog/2015/08/05/peru-aprueba-regulacion-para-mvnos/

Penarredonda, J. L. (2015). Neutralidad en la red: ¿en riesgo por el Plan de Desarrollo? Retrieved August 5, 2015, from http://www.enter.co/cultura-digital/colombia-digital/neutralidad-en-la-red-colombia-plan-de-desarrollo/

Rubio Correo, M. (2011). *El Sistema Juridico.- Introdución al Derecho* (10th ed.). Lima, Peru: Fondo Editorial. Pontificia Universidad Catolica del Peru. Retrieved from https://drive.google.com/file/d/0B7RnIpJ-DnLqb1dPcTFRcXpvdDQ/edit

Saltzer, J., Reed, D. & Clark, D. (1984). End-to-end arguments in system design. *ACM Transactions on Computer Systems (TOCS), 2*(4), 277–288.

Semana. (2015, February 12). Polémica por la neutralidad de internet en Colombia. *Semana.* Bogota, Colombia. Retrieved from http://www.semana.com/tecnologia/articulo/polemica-por-la-neutralidad-de-internet-en-colombia/417713-3

Silva, A. (2007). *Summary Voissnet vs. Telefonica (CTC – Chile) – Decision Issued by the Antitrust Court.* Retrieved from http://www.worldservicesgroup.com/publications.asp?action=article&artid=1779

Sturm, C. (2011). Chile: Gobierno publica reglamento de Neutralidad en la Red – FayerWayer. Retrieved August 8, 2014, from http://www.fayerwayer.com/2011/03/chile-gobierno-publica-reglamento-de-neutralidad-en-la-red/

Subtel. (2013). *Sector Telecomunicaciones Diciembre 2013.* Santiago de Chile. Retrieved from http://www.subtel.gob.cl/images/stories/apoyo_articulos/notas_prensa/06032014/Analisis_Sectorial_Diciembre_2013.pdf

TeamWork. (2011). *Plan Nacional de Desarrollo.* Retrieved August 7, 2014, from http://teamworksas.com/asesoria/377/plan-nacional-de-desarrollo-colombia-2010-2014.html

Wu, T. (2003). Network neutrality, broadband discrimination. *Journal on Telecommunications & High Technology Law, 2.* Retrieved from http://heinonline.org/HOL/Page?handle=hein.journals/jtelhtel2&id=145&div=&collection=

Chapter 11
Network Neutrality Debates in Telecommunications Reform: Actors, Incentives, Risks

Alejandro Pisanty

11.1 Network Neutrality in 2014

The term Network Neutrality (NN), as is well known, was coined by Prof. Tim Wu a few years ago, based mostly on hypotheticals, a reading of the end-to-end principle of Internet architecture, and a few concrete cases.

The term has become polysemic to the point of near meaninglessness so an exploration of what it means in each concrete case and use—and for each specific social actor uttering it—is necessary. Further, it is not uniformly championed by Internet-principles experts; one could even say that the more a person is related to the history and core design of the Internet, the less likely he/she is to even use the phrase "network neutrality" except possibly as a placeholder. Activists in favor of mandated network neutrality decry this as "the technical community wavers" or "the technical community gets lost in details".[1]

The means proposed to achieve and guarantee network neutrality, for any given definition, are a broad selection and vary significantly from country to country; this also signals that although there may be a relatively universal core to the meaning of network neutrality, many layers of its meaning are anchored in national language, technical and commercial history, and attitudes towards regulation and legislation, as well as power balances within the Internet and telecommunications industries and among sectors of both. A recent exposition of trends in Europe *vis-á-vis* the United States has been made by Scott Marcus.[2]

---

[1] A. Andersdottir, personal communication.

[2] Marcus (2014); see also comments by Robert Pepper and others in the same source.

A. Pisanty (✉)
National University of Mexico, Mexico City, Mexico

© Springer International Publishing Switzerland 2016   127
L. Belli, P. De Filippi (eds.), *Net Neutrality Compendium*,
DOI 10.1007/978-3-319-26425-7_11

The sections that follow present aspects of the network neutrality debate in a simplified form. A much better source is the paper by Bauer and Obar[3] on reconciling political and economic goals of network neutrality.

11.1.1   Meaning?

The first question to be asked in approaching network neutrality in 2014 is what each party means exactly by network neutrality. For this author, the etymology of "definition" is useful—to define is not only to express what is meant by a word or phrase but also to state what it is not. A clearer boundary between both may increase understanding.

Network neutrality can be defined as the condition in which a network operator, or, more precisely, an Internet Service Provider (ISP), in so far as providing access to the Internet (possibly physical connectivity; a public, routable IP address, and the ability of the user to access Internet services provided by other networks interconnected to the global Internet) delivers to his/its users all Internet traffic they request, inbound and outbound, regardless of protocol (as long as it is compatible with Internet standards), port number, contents, point of origin, or point of destination. We sometimes call this "the five alls" (all protocols, all ports, all contents, all origins, all destinations).

The opponents of network neutrality, especially in the telco/ISP camp, often twist this argument by replying that the converse of this condition would be the delivery of every single IP-protocol packet to the user, including malware, spam, port scans, and many other forms of Internet traffic that is undesirable, would overwhelm the user, and could damage seriously and permanently the user's capacity to communicate. They argue in favor of network management, traffic engineering, traffic shaping and similarly-named activities.

This is a fallacy.

The argument in favor of network neutrality is in favor of the possibility of access to the "five alls" as the user needs them, not a plea for the full stream in the firehose.

Traffic management is indispensable in today's Internet and has been so for many years. Avoidance of malware, attacks and even preparations for potential attacks; prioritization of different, and continuously evolving, types of messages; improvement of user experience; and many other reasons back this need. The plea for network neutrality rationally accepts reasonable network management; what it does reject is an abuse of this management in order to favor a commercial ally of the ISP or to disfavor its competitors unfairly. The poison is in the definitions of vague or subjective categories such as "reasonable" and "fair" in the absence of objective metrics and thresholds that can be applied equally in widely varying conditions.

---

[3] Bauer and Obar (2014), pp. 1–19.

With the above paragraph, we land in one the thickest parts of network neutrality arguments: what are the definitions of "abuse", "unfair" and "reasonable" for network management? Further questions are begged: who is responsible for the characteristics of traffic and the behavior of the services on the Internet of today? Are the definitions taking into account the much more complex environment of "OTT" (over-the-top) services, of interconnection, of OTT/OSP-ISP connections, of CDNs (content distribution networks), of the "last mile" to the user?

Can deterioration of Internet traffic behavior consistently and credibly be attributed to the specific cause originating it in each occasion? These causes may include violations of network neutrality but may also include network congestion, poor links and inadequate equipment and management in the "last mile" beyond the telco or ISP's control. Since all factors may be present at the same time, it may be particularly difficult to quantitatively distinguish them and attribute one specifically to deliberate action, and, further, identify this as malfeasance.

A further set of arguments often invoked in favor of network neutrality is the fear of or objection to DPI, deep packet inspection, a technique to read the contents of Internet traffic that has become widespread at least among larger operators (it requires improvements in active network equipment such as fast processing, large memory, and storage). The original design of the Internet assumes that the only information contained in the packets that is read by the active network equipment is in the headers, not in the payload; this is one formulation of the end-to-end principle, also summarized as "dumb network, smart edge". The network is agnostic with respect to the contents and intention of the messages contained in the packets. Knowing more than the protocol may allow the network operator to optimize the performance of the network for—or against—email, voice, video, etc. Accessing the contents of the packets may actually allow the operator to know the contents of the messages, with potentially serious consequences for privacy and therefore against freedom of speech and of association.

A definition of network neutrality today cannot be only technical. At best it is technically based, and susceptible to measurement; but it is commercial, and it relates to competition, to regulation, to legislation, and to rights—human, civil, social—and thus also becomes political.

To understand proposals to regulate network neutrality, recourse to the basic argument of the end-to-end principle on either side of the argument may be insufficient. As an example recently explained by Scott Marcus, European and developing-country fixed and mobile operators are much more aggressive in blocking Skype than those in the US, because Skype diminishes their revenue model far more than in the US. This in turn is related to economic statistics on the relative importance of fixed and mobile provision of Internet access.

The massive funding of lobbyists and of otherwise independent organizations, and alliances with the press and media (often in the same conglomerate as the ISPs) can further serve as a tool to dissect the origins of some actors' views and thus to address their real agendas.

For legislative and regulatory purposes a definition of network neutrality needs to be algorithmically unequivocal (it must be possible to clearly identify compliance and violations in an uncontrovertible way), yet open to evolution; legally anchored in the legislation and regulatory practice of the country in which it is used for legislation and regulation, in order to ensure the rule of law; and compatible with countries with which controversies may arise. Further it must be accepted and actionable.

11.1.2 Needed?

Is network neutrality needed? Does it have to be mandated?

There are two opposing streams of thought in this space. The first considers network neutrality a fundamental principle for the Internet, to be protected by all possible means. The other one refuses regulatory intervention, believes that competition, user demand and other market mechanisms will ensure access to the same benefits as the regulation is proposed to reach, and fears that mandating network neutrality will have the perverse effect of stifling the innovation it purports to promote and protect. There are further distinctions within each stream.

In the camp that sees network neutrality mandates as necessary there is further discussion about the means to achieve such mandates: telecommunications and related legislation, market regulation, competition regulation, consumer rights, or new Internet user rights are the approaches most usually discussed, with great geographical variation.

The legislative approach has been used in countries like The Netherlands, Belgium, Chile, Brazil and most recently Mexico. In the last two, recent legislation mandates network neutrality in general terms but cannot be fully acted upon until specific rules are written by the Presidency (in Brazil) and the regulator (in Mexico). In Mexico at the time of this writing, specific guidelines for network neutrality are yet to be published.

In Europe network-neutrality mandates (save for The Netherlands and Belgium where they are law already) are likely to occur in the telecommunications regulatory framework. BEREC and some of its members like the UK's OFCOM have taken a wait-and-see stance. The European Commission and the European Parliament are discussing starker measures. The discussion is ongoing and moving towards explicit mandates for network neutrality in the second half of 2015.

In the US, network neutrality has been subject to vigorous debate. Courts have found that the FCC doesn't have a solid enough legal basis to mandate network neutrality provisions, having undone the common-carriage provision for broadband a decade ago. Appeals are ongoing, for example in the search for a new basis, within existing legislation, to force the FCC to mandate network neutrality. A critique of these efforts points to the fact that this resource would actually mandate a much broader, well-nigh all-encompassing, regulation of the Internet by the FCC, the government, or the state, which would in turn have highly undesirable consequences. The discussion in the original edition of this study evolved to the adoption by the FCC of a body of law known as Title II of the Telecommunications Act, which regulates public-service providers, and limitations on what clauses the FCC will apply.

The key question for the US debate is whether the classification of ISPs as "common carriers" or public-service providers will have more negative consequences than the possible benefits it may bring. Further references to the Internet as a "common good" can also lead to highly inadequate regulatory regimes despite the best of intentions.

Classifications of the Internet or, the specific case in the US, broadband, such as "common carrier" or "common good" have well-established legal implications, at national and also international levels. An unexpected burden on the Internet may arise from them, with deleterious results such as opening up many new avenues for governmental intervention that are not at all necessary or useful. The intricacies of national law, in particular in the US, may be of huge global consequence. Other countries need be particularly helpful when they craft legislation in order to absorb the best that experience provides.

To state this in a different way: classifying Internet access or even broadband (at a lower layer only) as common carriage may bring in government regulatory powers to bear on much more than fairness—in the form of non-blocking and/or non-discrimination. Whether government intervention at this level can promote or stifle innovation is hotly debated.

The need for network neutrality mandates may turn out to be an illusion depending on the ultimate goals it is expected to serve. It may be an actual need in order to support and maintain fairness in commercial Internet access operations, but it may not lead to the availability of the actual full Internet. This will be explained later.

There is a trend among Internet pioneers and protocol engineers to avoid even the name "network neutrality", given the now-known complexities of the term, its almost meaninglessness, and the intricacies of network planning, operation and management. In these communities the terms "open networking" and "open Internet" tend to take the place of "network neutrality" with a large space for interpretation and nuance. For instance, the Internet Society has preferred to speak of Open Internet in the last few years.

In fact, some analysts consider network neutrality and the end-to-end principle fundamentally obsoleted or negated since the introduction of the MPLS protocol, NATs, and other network management procedures. In this view, the end-to-end principle strictly applied only during the first few years of the Internet, when all points connected to the network were in principle equal and all were both consumers and producers of content or services. Further in this view, as some of these points at the edge became exclusively consumers or clients of others (e-commerce comes to mind but even a student–school relationship embodies this view), the nature of the Internet as connecting peers was lost.

Internet access is formally defined above the physical layer and thus presumes the existence of the physical layer, provided by either private or public companies. These companies manage traffic in ways that inevitably preclude the pure end-to-end principle; they have to make decisions as to traffic prioritization, interconnection, traffic, etc. The managed telco network is not really "dumb" and has never been neutral. On the other hand, in the United States at least, some forms of telco service are subject to common-carriage rules and therefore have to be neutral.

The complexity of network management and the negation of the end-to-end principle have only increased in the later years. The introduction of ever more complex services and of ever more sophisticated techniques to manage (hopefully improve) the user experience, including performance, security, advertising, etc., has made claims of network neutrality all the more subtle and qualified. Some of the changes make the analysis of network neutrality particularly difficult: CDNs (content distribution networks), IXPs (Internet exchange points), interconnection cost settlements, the fact that OTTs may purchase their own communications links to points very close to the user, ISPs setting up their own OTTs, etc.

In this view, demands for network neutrality are demands for the suppliers to simulate the behavior of a rather idealistic primeval Internet while conserving the benefits of the non-end-to-end technologies. The telcos and ISPs thus arrive at the question whether the Internet users would really want to receive the raw stream of data that the network would be throwing at them. (That primeval past was also broken within a quite concrete act in the United States, namely the removal of common-carriage obligations for Internet traffic in the early 2000s.)

Also, the demand for more points of access (more users, more devices per user, a broader geographical distribution of users), for more services and for more capacity (at a time in the 1990s the capacity demanded per user increased 50 % per year in email only) requires more network resources at the physical and other levels. Most of the capacity growth requires investments which are capital-intensive and entail long times to materialize the return on the investment. These are made by telcos and ISPs, not necessarily by suppliers of services such as search, video, etc.

The economics of this field requires high levels of expertise with which most civil-society and even technical organizations are not endowed. Value generation occurs now in the upper layers and is decoupled from investment sources for the lower layers. While this situation may change, in the interim it has caused cries for change on the telco/ISP side that cannot be simply brushed away or wished out of existence. Further, these companies' influence on public opinion, governments, regulators, the press and media, and other industries is non-negligible.

11.1.3   Principles or Commerce?

There are many ways to view the network neutrality debate. It can be seen as a matter of principle or a controversy between commercial players.

The players involved would be the telcos/ISPs, especially the ones with larger scale, scope, spatial coverage and/or client bases (including but not limited to Tier 1 providers), on one side, and online-services providers (including but not limited to OTT or "over the top" services such as video-on-demand providers like Netflix).

The telcos and ISPs in this case demand payments from the OSP's that are based on higher unit prices than for ordinary users, arguing either:

that the OSP's force the infrastructure providers to make large investments in order to keep up with the demand of bandwidth, reduced latency and jitter, etc., in such a way that the investment is made by the infrastructure providers without a return on the investment, while at the same time the OSP's are reaping huge profits by "piggybacking" on someone else's expensive, long-term infrastructure business, or more blatantly, that the OSP's are making too much money out of their use of the network and the infrastructure providers should get a piece of it (this argument was articulated by César Alierta, CEO of Telefónica, with respect to Google, a few years ago, and was recovered, in a slightly finessed way, by ETNO, the European Telecommunications Network Organization, through its spokesman Luigi Gambardella—the formulation being that investment money is needed to expand the networks and it can only come from the users making the largest profits from their use of the network).

The Alierta/ETNO/Gambardella argument appears in many discussions at national levels; it attracted major attention and bitter controversy in 2013, in the run-up and during WCIT, the World Conference on International Telecommunications held by the ITU in Dubai.

The controversy between Comcast and Netflix is paradigmatic in exhibiting opportunities for both lines of analysis. The agreements between Google and Verizon of about a year earlier also represent both faces of the analysis. These controversies differ in the points and types of points in the network where interconnection is negotiated.

It is likely that in any given country or jurisdiction (including the European Union) a mixture of both the principles and the commercial controversy debates are taking place at any given time, with lobbyists for either commercial side taking up the cloak of principles against the other. It is very hard for civil society, technical and academic organizations to peel off the different layers in order to take informed part in the debate without involuntarily being hauled to support an undisclosed commercial party in a commercial dispute, and hard, as well, to stay out of the debate on grounds of this fear.

For many organizations in the civil society and academic spaces, no doubt, network neutrality remains a fundamental principle, and its defense is being stepped up as I write.

11.2 Where?

11.2.1 Network Neutrality in the Legislative Debate in Mexico

Network neutrality has been in debate in the legislative processes as well as in the regulatory sphere of Mexico for a few years now.

One of the most remarkable moments in this history took place in 2011/2012 when social pressure prompted a group of legislators to present a draft of network neutrality legislation; this was primarily written by a consultant with strong ties to industry. The draft, in summary, established a minimal definition of network neutrality, then reduced compliance to transparent information to the ISPs' clients.

In other words, the legislation was a blank check for ISPs to manage their networks as they pleased as long as they informed their clients. This was noticed immediately by consultants, the technically-informed public, and civil society organizations. Pressure on the Senate (chamber of origin of the draft) caused an almost immediate call by the Senate for a public consultation with a broad spectrum of stakeholders.

The consultation session was brief but rich in the debate. It was apparent from very early in the session that most Senators in the commissions that convened the consultation were eager to have arguments they could use against the legislation. Not the least in importance was the Senator who was the major signatory of the draft; he was already campaigning to be elected to the lower chamber of Congress and the negative light coming against him in social media was beginning to hurt his campaign. Other legislators saw clearly the wrongs in the draft. The legislation was dropped on the spot.

The telecommunications regulator until 2013 was COFETEL (Comisión Federal de Telecomunicaciones); at that time, its Consultative Council studied the issue of network neutrality (full disclosure: this author was a member of the Council and was designated Chair of the Working Group of Network Neutrality of the Council).

The Working Group held several internal discussion and analysis sessions and had contacts with members of industry as well. It studied the options before us as legislation, telecommunications regulation, competition law and regulation, and consumer rights. The Working Group followed continuously the concomitant developments in The Netherlands, Chile, the United Kingdom, France, Belgium and the European Union, in particular the discussions and documents of BEREC. It concluded that the options before it were to recommend measures in favor of Network Neutrality as legislation, competition regulation, or consumer rights; that the time for making this decision was not ripe; and that COFETEL should continue to watch major players' behavior before reconvening for a new round of analysis and recommendations.

COFETEL was later dissolved and reconstituted as Instituto Federal de Telecomunicaciones (IFT) in a major Telecommunications Reform, which includes changes to the Constitution and several other laws. The so-called "secondary laws" have been in discussion in the Legislative until way into the writing of the present text and were finalized and approved at the end of July 2014.

The laws contain provisions for network neutrality. The new Constitutional text has a broad provision of network neutrality; this one in turn is detailed in the new (2014) Federal Law on Telecommunications and Broadcasting. The debate about this law was heated and extensive, considering major issues such as the regulator's scope, antitrust proceedings against dominant or preponderant market actors, the creation of new television broadcasting chains, and others.

As pertains to the Internet, the main issues under discussion were:

1. Network neutrality

2. Collaboration with authorities (mostly law enforcement; includes aspects such as suspending telecommunications services—"kill switch"—as well as traffic data retention, communications interception, and geolocalization).
3. Internet users' rights. The new Telecommunications Law contains clauses that declare and presume to protect some telecommunications users' rights. Among these, there are some that are either specific or applicable to Internet access. Network neutrality arguments based on users' rights pick up on either or a combination of both human/citizens' rights or consumer rights as follows:

   a. The approach based on human rights starts with the threat that manipulation of Internet traffic may lead to incidental or deliberate interference with freedom of access to information, freedom of speech, or freedom of association.
   b. The approach based on consumer rights has as a starting point the commercial nature of most Internet access provisioning. In this framework, Internet access is based on a contract between private parties, *viz.* the consumer and the ISP. The contract can be made to include provisions for or akin to network neutrality (prohibition of blocking, prohibition of discriminatory behavior). Compliance with the contract can be enforced by regulators—the telecommunications market regulator, the consumer regulator, and/or the competition regulator. Contract breaches may be litigated by the consumer before the consumer-protection authority. Class actions are conceivable. In Mexico, class action is not direct; it has to be picked up by an authority such as the consumer protection attorney.

The discussions about network neutrality follow patterns already established elsewhere, with the leading telco association (CANIETI) voicing its Mexico-City chair's, at the time a representative of Telefonica of Spain's branch in Mexico, demand that investment capacity for infrastructure be preserved (an only slightly modified variation of the ETNO/Gambardella argument discussed earlier in this text). AMIPCI, the Internet industry trade association, has among its members both access providers and companies active in higher layers, such as search engines, advertisers, broadcasters, e-commerce, etc. and is more split about network neutrality mandates.

The demand for network neutrality took several different but intertwined forms; arguments have been in favor of freedom of speech, of all rights, of an expansive rights agenda, of consumer rights, of contract compliance, of innovation, of technical-standards compliance ("the five alls") and more. Activism, not all of it online but also in the form of demonstrations and blockades, engaged citizens through social media, the press, established collectives, and NGOs. Some organizations' arguments in other aspects of the telecommunications reform have been pointed by the press as almost entirely coincident with some of the telcos' agendas (mostly Telmex).

Civil-society campaigns in favor of mandated network neutrality have appeared together with those for other issues in the law, or almost alone. Among the first are organizations such as AMEDI (Asociación Mexicana para el Derecho a la

Información), which has a broad agenda that includes increased telecommunications and broadcasting competition, state control of broadcasting and mass media, television viewers' rights, and Internet-specific issues. Organizations like ContingenteMX and SocialTIC are more Internet-oriented. A loosely organized campaign called Libre Internet para Todos led an effective campaign to include Internet access as a right in the Constitutional change (allied with establishment politicians such as Senators, and an agenda that was already promised within the Presidential campaign) and later led public actions in favor of competition in the telecommunications and broadcast market and for network neutrality.

Geolocalization merits mention, even though it is not a network-neutrality issue, because it signals the complex civil-society environment for some key telecommunications and Internet issues. Geolocalization of communications has been written into the law with relatively low levels of authorization (agents of the Ministerio Público, roughly equivalent to US District Attorneys, part of the Executive branch in Mexico, can ask for geolocalization data without judicial controls); this is a combined response of law-enforcement interests within the government and civil society demands from sectors of society which have been hit with high-profile crimes, particularly kidnappings. At the time of this writing high-ranking officials of IFAI (Instituto Federal de Acceso a la Información, the FOIA authority of Mexico which is now also the DPA—Data Protection Authority) have made stark public expressions of opposition to the geolocalization measure; it is not unlikely that higher levels of judiciary control will be instituted, with a spillover effect for other measures in the law such as network neutrality.

The result of the legislative process for network neutrality has been the establishment of an article in the Federal Telecommunications and Broadcasting Law that mandates and partially defines Network Neutrality and requires that conditions for investment be preserved. The issue ended up unresolved, therefore only broadly defined in the Law, and open for a new round of debate and enhancement of the Law when the time comes to write the norms and bylaws that will be prescriptive.

11.2.2 The Use of Network Neutrality Arguments against Mobile Telephony/Social Media Packages ("Zero-Rating") in Chile

Chile is arguably the first country to have enacted mandated network neutrality obligations in national law, in 2010. At the time there were some qualms about the legislation from organizations concerned with the protection of privacy but otherwise it was broadly well received.

In July 2014, SUBTEL, the under-secretariat for telecommunications of the newly elected government of Chile, headed by under-secretary Pedro Huichalaf, ordered mobile telephony companies to stop offering social media bundles to their clients, on grounds that SUBTEL considers these bundles a violation of network neutrality.

As is well known, these bundles are common in many countries. The offering is access to the cellular network including a small amount of data traffic and access to Facebook and maybe other online social media services. The access to Facebook may be without cost or at a limited cost, plus possibly a data cap. All data above this cap and the cap on the data contract come at a high price. This type of bundle is most often offered in prepaid services, which are most used by low-income users.

The theory behind SUBTEL's interpretation is that these bundles are meant to entice consumers to start using the mobile telephony service at a low price until they become dependent on it and then move on to higher levels of consumption. Further, the bundle causes the user to choose the service that falsely appeals to lowest prices in a loss-leader type of offer, leads the users away from the whole Internet and only towards a small fraction of it (Facebook in this example) and is thus anticompetitive. This anticompetitive behavior triggers the network neutrality violation interpretation.

The reactions to the ruling have been—predictably—mixed. Some authors say that by this ruling the government of Chile is making access to the Internet more expensive and consequently "broadening the digital divide".[4] Lyons explains some further possible harms of this rule, which in his view include deterring innovation, and cites it as an example of the harms to be caused by rigid *ex-ante* regulation. His studies are presented in more detail in "Innovations in Mobile Broadband Pricing".[5]

Also, note that there is precedent for this case in MetroPCS (see the paper by Lyons cited in the previous paragraph).

11.2.3   Venezuela: Network Neutrality, Filtering, or Operational Incidents?

Network traffic in Venezuela is reported to have a very wide variation over time for any given place and user. This is partly attributed to electrical power outages and brownouts, lack of investment in the networks, and other reasons. There is also some suspicion of politically-motivated blocking and filtering.

During the particularly violent period of political protest at the beginning of 2014, there were reports from Venezuela with significant bandwidth losses, differential per provider, and the outright blocking of websites informing the exchange rates for foreign currency both in the legal and in reputedly existing parallel markets (with a large difference between both). The government officially acknowledged and justified this blocking by accusing the sites of purposely intending to damage the economy and taking sides with radical opposition to destabilize the country.

---

[4] Lyons (2014a).
[5] Lyons (2014b).

Some authors in Venezuela are exploring whether these instances of traffic management by the government's own ISP, CANTV, which has a dominant position in the country and is exempt from market rules by its governmental character, signal violations to network neutrality principles. Since there is no *ex ante* regulation or legislation for network neutrality in Venezuela, there is hardly any violation of existing law and violations of principles will be much harder to detect and confirm.

11.3 International Lobbying and Counterlobbying Patterns and Arguments: Fingerprints

Over the latest few years the debates about network neutrality have expanded in many countries and regions, and patterns are beginning to emerge.

In the United States network neutrality debates usually follow the position of Prof. Tim Wu or take a view opposite to his. The side that favors network neutrality mandates invokes common carriage, the power of carriers and ISPs, freedom of information, of speech following First Amendment lines, and to a lesser extent freedom of assembly. The basic premise is that most Internet access arrives at home via telcos' copper cable or optical fiber, and through cable television companies; a separate discussion focusses on wireless where provisioning is understood to be a scarce resource.

In Europe the debate focusses more on the power of telcos and ISPs to block applications such as Skype, which impinge on their revenue stream. Further, it teeters on a balance between the needs of economies of scale for the Internet economy (concomitantly then also the unified Continental telecommunications market) and a stronger regulatory, rights-based hand. While Executive and Legislative bodies tend to search for more regulation, paradoxically most regulators and their collective, BEREC, tend to favor a lighter hand with a wait-and-see approach. The risk for the regulators is to be late with *ex-post* regulation in a region where the rule of law is premised mostly as *ex-ante*.

The opponents of mandated network neutrality tend to invoke light-touch government or frank deregulation, the "invisible hand" of markets, the need for investment and attractive returns on it, the perceived unfairness that the infrastructure providers do not make quick profits while the businesses that run exploiting the infrastructure do, and the freedom to innovate. Hands-off government is invoked more often in the United States, government intervention to protect infrastructure investment is more often invoked in Europe.

Innovation is paradoxically a banner for both sides. Proponents of mandated network neutrality invoke permissionless or permission-free innovation as a result of network neutrality; opponents invoke permissionless innovation as the result of the government's non-intervention to regulate the network at all. Both sides have Internet-specific examples; pro-network neutrality activists have companies large and small on their side, from Google and eBay to Etsy; the anti-mandate speakers say Skype wouldn't have been possible if not for the deregulation of broadband as common carriage (Skype is in both sides' banners, but, now owned by Microsoft, we will never know what the original Skype says).

These patterns translate into other countries, with copies of each side everywhere network neutrality is discussed.

This we already have seen for a decade or two in CLEC–ILEC relations in the telecommunications market. ILEC or incumbent local exchange carriers are in a constant fight with Competitive local exchange carriers before the telecommunications regulators in most markets. In Latin America notoriously the row takes place mostly between the local instantiations of America Movil (property of the well-known Mexican entrepreneur Carlos Slim) and those of Telefonica (a careful study by Judith Mariscal and Hernan Galperin has shown that these two companies, considered at Continental level in Latin America, configure a duopoly). The CLEC–ILEC dynamic is such that the arguments are the same for the CLEC whether it be America Movil or Telefonica in each country; local variations due to the specifics of the law and the market are less determining of the discourse.

However, for network neutrality the analyst has to exert care. The arguments for or against mandated network neutrality are rarely fully adapted to the local situation. Commercial actors (mostly telco/ISPs as the OSC's and OTT's have less presence and influence locally) get the ear and sometimes the pen of legislators. The patterns described have to be deconstructed into a finer-grained filigree for other stakeholders to be able to act successfully towards their purposes.

References

Bauer, J. M., & Obar, J. A. (2014). Reconciling political and economic goals in the net neutrality debate. *The Information Society: An International Journal, 30*(1), 1–19. doi:10.1080/0197224 3.2013.856362.

Lyons, D. (2014a, June 2). In Chile, net neutrality widens the digital divide. *TechPolicyDaily*, 2014. http://www.techpolicydaily.com/communications/chile-net-neutrality-widens-digital--divide/, visited 9.8.2014.

Lyons, D. (2014b, March). *Innovations in mobile broadband pricing*. Working Paper 14-08, 2014. Mercatus Center, George Mason University. http://mercatus.org/sites/default/files/Lyons_BroadbandPricing_v1.pdf, visited 9.8.2014.

Marcus, S. (2014). Network neutrality in Europe – Lessons for the US, video. http://new.livestream.com/internetsociety/netneutrality-in-europe, retrieved 9.8.2014.

Chapter 12
Net Neutrality in Australia: The Debate Continues, But No Policy in Sight

Angela Daly

12.1 Introduction

Australia has been somewhat late to the debate on net neutrality: it has only emerged as a major issue in public discourse in the last few years,[1] and there are no plans to introduce any kind of further legislation or regulation beyond the existing regimes. This contribution will analyse the status of net neutrality in Australia, looking at how the debate has been playing out, the current law and regulation which may affect ISPs' conduct, and directions for reform if the *status quo* does not go far enough to advance Internet users' interests.

12.2 Net Neutrality and the Internet in Australia

12.2.1 Net Neutrality Explained

Net neutrality, although a contested term, can be said to be a principle proposed for user access to the Internet, which would prevent Internet Service Providers (ISPs) from discriminating between different kinds of Internet traffic (regardless of the amount of bandwidth the traffic takes up), and from restricting content, sites or platforms (at least those which are legal). Such 'non-net neutral' conduct might include blocking certain Internet traffic entirely from being sent or received by end-users, speeding up certain traffic when it is passing over the network and/or slowing down other types of traffic. Increasingly other forms of conduct are being considered as violations of the net neutrality principle, such as the deployment of content delivery

---

[1] Turner (2014).

A. Daly (✉)
Swinburne University of Technology, Melbourne, VIC, Australia

© Springer International Publishing Switzerland 2016
L. Belli, P. De Filippi (eds.), *Net Neutrality Compendium*,
DOI 10.1007/978-3-319-26425-7_12

141

networks by large content providers to deliver their data more quickly to end-users, and users being offered 'unmetered' or free access to a certain site or provider's content but not for sites or content from other sources, such as the Facebook Internet. org initiative in operation in mainly low and middle income countries.

The Internet was not originally set up like this. The design principle underpinning the Internet was 'end-to-end connectivity' which ensured that the network did not traditionally interfere with the packets of information passing through it (regardless of what this information actually was). In this way all information sent was 'equal'. This is described as being a position of 'net neutrality' which was the 'default' for the Internet prior to the development of deep packet inspection (DPI) which facilitated the real-time monitoring of the content of packets, and content delivery networks which permit players such as large content providers to bypass the once-hierarchical Internet backbone networks when sending their content to end-users, which can entail that content reaching users more quickly and more completely.

The debate around net neutrality has been triggered by these technological and commercial developments, and essentially involves the issue of the extent to which ISPs can manage their own networks and what information their customers send and receive and at what speed or priority this content is sent and received.

12.2.2 The Internet in Australia

The Internet in Australia is provided in various ways by various players. Historically, Australia has followed a similar path to European countries in terms of its privatisation of former state-owned telecoms monopoly Telstra, and the liberalisation of telecoms markets. Despite the introduction of competition, Telstra is still Australia's largest telecoms and media company. Among its many services, it owns the fixed line telecoms infrastructure (which is subject to local loop unbundling and infrastructure access by competitors), it provides retail fixed line services, it operates Australia's largest mobile telecoms network (in terms of both subscriptions and geographical coverage),[2] it provides wholesale and retail Internet services (via a variety of means, including fixed line, cable, satellite and mobile broadband), and owns undersea cables linking Australia's communications with the rest of the world. Telstra also has a 50 % share of Foxtel (the other 50 % is owned by Rupert Murdoch's News Corporation) a pay TV service provided over cable, satellite and IPTV which has the exclusive rights to much attractive premium content in Australia, such as live broadcasts of Australian Rules Football and National Rugby League sports matches, major films and hit TV series such as the currently popular Game of Thrones.

Telstra's rival Optus, which is Australia's second largest telecoms company and emerged into the marketplace in the early 1990s, has its own network infrastructure and so does not have to deal with Telstra to provide services. Optus provides Internet including via cable, fixed line and mobile services.

---

[2] Australia has a large proportion of its population concentrated in a few key, urban areas with large amount of the country sparsely populated.

Despite the high level of vertical integration comprised by Telstra, the situation in Australia overall is certainly more encouraging than in the US, with its more concentrated telecoms markets, and is more in line with the EU experience, in terms of encouraging retail competition via local loop unbundling allowing access to the incumbent's infrastructure. For instance, in June 2013, there were 419 ISPs operating in Australia, nine of which had more than 100,000 subscribers.[3] 1.2 million people were estimated to have changed their home ISP in the preceding 12 months.[4]

However, Australia has a highly concentrated media landscape, particularly around Rupert Murdoch and his holdings, which dominate newspaper ownership and newspaper sales as well as possessing the aforementioned 50 % share of Foxtel.[5]

The Internet in Australia has been mostly provided using a 'volumetric' pricing model, by which end-users pay ISPs for Internet access at a pre-determined speed and have a maximum download quota. If this quota is exceeded their either the user's speed is slowed down or the user faces additional charges on a per MB basis. While there is an argument that ISPs do not have an incentive to engage in non-net neutral conduct since the more the end-users consume, the more they must pay the ISP, Marsden has argued that all ISPs have an incentive to engage in traffic shaping i.e. blocking and throttling content, and particularly non-affiliated content i.e. not from a subsidiary content provider.[6]

12.2.3   The National Broadband Network

One of the major topics in Australian Internet matters in the last decade has been the National Broadband Network (NBN), which started life as an election pledge by the opposition Labor party at the 2007 federal election to build a super-fast national broadband network if elected, which indeed happened. After an initially unsuccessful request for proposals (RFPs), in 2009, the then-Government announced it would bypass the existing copper network and construct a new national network encompassing mainly fibre to the premises (FTTP) technology, along with some fixed wireless and satellite uses, and set up government-owned company NBN Co in 2009 with the task of designing, building and operating the NBN. In 2010, NBN Co reached agreements with Telstra and Optus regarding the migration of their customers from their legacy infrastructures once FTTP had been installed for those customers, and in the case of Telstra the efficient re-use of Telstra's existing infrastructure. It is arguable that the NBN in this initial incarnation as a super-fast twenty-first century broadband network may have made net neutrality concerns redundant as on such a network there would have been fewer problems with limited bandwidth or congestion.

The NBN itself is a publicly-owned wholesale-only network which offers its services on an open, equivalent access basis to wholesale and retail carriers and service

---

[3] Australian Communications and Media Authority (ACMA) (2013), p. 25.

[4] Ibid., p. 31.

[5] Dwyer (2014) and Noam (2011).

[6] Marsden (2007), pp. 407–435.

providers. At the time of writing over half a million premises have activated NBN services.[7]

Nevertheless, the 2013 federal election and change of government to the Liberal-National Coalition changed the course of the project's future. The Coalition government has controversially preferred a reduced speed Fibre to the Node (FTTN) model for the remaining NBN rollout which was supposed to reduce costs although this may not happen in practice, and be further detrimental in terms of resulting in a slower technology for a similar amount of money compared to the original FTTP model.[8]

12.3 Current Regulatory Framework

At the time of writing, there is no specific *ex ante* regulation to address net neutrality concerns in Australia, and instead the general competition regime administered by the Australian Competition and Consumer Commission (ACCC), and some sector-specific telecoms regulation are the only tools available.

The general competition regime in Australia is found principally in the *Competition and Consumer Act* 2010 (Cth) ('CCA') and is similar to that of many other developed jurisdictions such as the EU. The main elements of Australian competition law are a prohibition on collusive conduct (section 45), the misuse of market power i.e. abuse of a dominant position (section 46) and exclusive dealing (section 47).

There are also specific provisions relating to the telecoms industry contained in Parts XIB and XIC of the CCA providing the ACCC with additional powers which address anticompetitive conduct by telecoms companies (including anticompetitive conduct related to content being delivered) and network access regulation respectively. However, the Australian Government announced that these provisions would be reviewed in late 2015, in particular their relationship to the NBN.[9]

In addition, there is a specific regulatory scheme which governs the NBN in the form of a Special Access Undertaking which was finalised in late 2013.[10] This Undertaking provides the terms and conditions under which the NBN will operate, including an open access principle and regulated wholesale prices.

12.4 The Net Neutrality Debate Down Under

Developments in the EU and (more notably) the US have tended to influence debate on a number of aspects of life in Australia, with Internet matters being among them. These developments, in particular the FCC's net neutrality trajectory, have been

---

[7] NBN (2015).

[8] Tucker (2015).

[9] Australian Government (2014b).

[10] Australian Competition and Consumer Commission (2013).

reported in the Australian media, with technology journalists beginning to question the effect of any such regulation on the Australian Internet, and assessing what the current situation is here as well. While, as already mentioned, there is no net neutrality regulation in place or proposed in Australia, it is a topic which has been raised over the last few years by different stakeholders and often in the context of government consultations around the NBN, as the following sections will show.

12.4.1 2009 NBN Consultations

The initial flickering of net neutrality discussion in Australia can be traced back to 2009, and in particular the Australian Government's *National Broadband Network: Regulatory Reform for 21st Century Broadband* Discussion Paper which was published in April of that year.[11] Although the consultation itself did not mention 'net neutrality' or 'network neutrality', various stakeholder responses to the paper did. Industry stakeholder ninemsn (a major Australian online media company 50 % owned by Microsoft) in its submission noted the absence of net neutrality from the consultation and 'encourage[d] the Government to consult with all relevant stakeholders prior to the introduction of the NBN on the need to preserve the principle of net neutrality in any legislative reform agenda'.[12] ninemsn also proposed three net neutrality rules that it advocated be established before the NBN was set up, encompassing: (1) the prohibition of interference by ISPs with users' ability to access, use or offer content, applications and services over the Internet; (2) the obligation of ISPs to operate their networks in a non-discriminatory fashion; and (3) the prevention of the prioritisation of selected content, applications or services.

ninemsn was not alone in supporting a regulatory approach which would encompass binding net neutrality rules. Indeed, other industry stakeholders comprising major content players in the form of Free TV Australia, Seven Network, Google Australia and PBL Media also made submissions to the review along similar lines to ninemsn's, supporting net neutrality regulation.[13]

This can be contrasted, perhaps unsurprisingly, with the views of Australian telecommunications providers, which were dismissive of idea of net neutrality regulation. They disregarded the whole debate as around an 'American problem' which did not exist in Australia, since here a 'user pays' model has been adopted due to the geographical asymmetry in Internet traffic, with Australian users wanting to access more traffic from overseas than originating domestically.[14]

The little academic commentary that there is on net neutrality in Australia has generally accorded with the telecommunications industry's view, that there is no

---

[11] Australian Government Department of Broadband, Communications and the Digital Economy (2009).

[12] ninemsn (2009).

[13] Manwaring (2010), pp. 630–639 and 635.

[14] Hill (2008).

problem here that needs addressing. For Endres, Australian markets for Internet access are competitive (unlike the case in the US), and competition law can operate residually to address any problems that do arise.[15] Manwarning did not see any evidence that non-net neutral conduct by ISPs would be detrimental to the Australian market, and, again, competition law could deal with any problems that did occur.[16] Endres does concede however that greater transparency around ISPs' traffic management practices might be desirable, as well as more information on any commercial agreements which would affect the speed of Internet traffic including arrangements within vertically integrated players which resulted in the prioritisation of subsidiary content.

One dissenting academic stakeholder has been Johnson, who argued that broadband services in Australia including the NBN ought to operate on the principles of net neutrality for the Australian Internet to flourish, noting conditions such as the vertical integration between network and content providers in Australia, as well as warning of the increased barriers to entry for start-ups raised by a situation of non-neutrality, with the potential to dampen innovation.[17]

Interestingly, Johnson also broke out of the orthodox competition paradigm by raising the issue of what situation would be valuable for Australian society as a whole, rather than just what would be advantageous for ISPs, and questioning the wisdom in large corporate interests controlling end-users' access to Internet content as well as that content itself—with Telstra and its Foxtel interest being a case in point—which in extreme cases could result in end-users' access to certain content being blocked for ideological as well as economic reasons.

In 2010 the Australian government published a follow-up report, *National Broadband Network Implementation Study*.[18] This time 'net neutrality' was mentioned explicitly on two occasions The first was in a short comment acknowledging it as an 'emerging' issue, while concluding that there was 'no consensus on how the global network should, or will, evolve'.[19] The second mention seemed to define net neutrality as 'content non-discrimination' and recognised it as a regulatory issue 'beyond the NBN... [which] will also strongly influence the sustainability of competition in the content and application markets', along with local content laws, media ownership restrictions and broadcast licensing.[20]

Some responses to this consultation also discussed net neutrality. The Communications Law Centre at University of Technology, Sydney, while continuing to view net neutrality through the competition prism, did assert that *ex ante* 'regulation is needed to protect the consumer interest' since 'the competitive market may produce an outcome that may harm consumers' through the increased barriers

---

[15] Endres (2009), pp. 22.1–22.10.

[16] Manwaring (2010), *supra* note 13, pp. 635–636.

[17] Johnson (2009), pp. 19.1–19.16.

[18] Australian Government Department of Broadband, Communications and the Digital Economy (2010).

[19] *Ibid.*, p. 423.

[20] *Ibid.*, p. 430.

to entry for potential competitors and consumer adoption caused by permitting ISPs to discriminate between Internet traffic.[21] This suggests that the Communications Law Centre did not view pre-existing *ex post* competition laws, or the contemporary levels of competition among retail ISPs, as sufficient to protect consumers in the face of ISPs' ability and incentives to discriminate between different kinds of Internet traffic.

12.4.2   2012 Convergence Review

Net neutrality made its next Australian outing in the then-Government's (ultimately ill-fated) Convergence Review Final Report in 2012.[22] The Convergence Review was an independent review established by the Government to examine the policy and regulatory frameworks that applied to media and communications in Australia, particularly in light of the phenomenon of convergence. The Review's Final Report, released in April 2012, pointed to content-related competition issues as being one area where new policy and regulation should be implemented, since the current powers were viewed as being 'too narrow to address evolving content-specific issues, such as exclusive rights arrangements and bundling, and network neutrality issues that inhibit competition'.[23] Again, the Review frames net neutrality in terms of a problem regarding limited competition and reduced innovation at the hands of ISPs, which the proposed content-related competition regulation should, when implemented, address.

However, the Convergence Review and the majority of its recommendations, including that for *ex ante* net neutrality regulation, were effectively abandoned with the change of government brought about by the 2013 federal election, which was not supportive of any further reform in this area.[24]

12.4.3   2014 Competition Review

Finally, net neutrality has reared its head again in submissions to the Australian Government's Competition Policy Review Issues Paper.[25] This consultation is part of the Australian Government's first comprehensive review of competition law and policy in more than 20 years with the aim of 'build[ing] strong foundations for a

---

[21] Communications Law Centre, UTS (2010).

[22] Australian Government Department of Broadband, Communications and the Digital Economy (2012).

[23] *Ibid.*, p. 29.

[24] Bodley (2013).

[25] Australian Government (2014a).

more productive and competitive twenty-first century Australian economy'.[26] The Review has become known as the 'Harper Review' after the Chairman of the Review Panel, Professor Ian Harper.

While the Issues Paper (generic in its scope and not specific to the media, telecoms or Internet sectors) again did not mention net neutrality specifically, the Australian Communications Consumer Action Network (ACCAN) made a submission to the inquiry highlighting what it views as net neutrality concerns in Australia that ought to be addressed.[27] ACCAN, a consumer interest group, raised particular concerns regarding the conduct of Telstra, and its access to exclusive rights over premium content. Telstra also has the exclusive broadcast rights to major Australian sporting events, namely Australian Rules Football League and National Rugby League matches, and has provided access to this content on an unmetered basis for Telstra customers, whereas the customers of rival mobile ISPs only have access on a metered basis, which ACCAN views as being of concern for net neutrality. Indeed, before 2013, this content was not accessible via these competitors' mobile networks. This has also been the case for Telstra subsidiary Foxtel's video-on-demand content, which has been offered on an unmetered basis to Telstra home Internet customers.

The Pirate Party Australia, a political party which represents civil liberties and digital rights issues, also raised concerns about Telstra's activity which may not comply with net neutrality principles, in particular trials of throttling peer-to-peer Internet traffic ostensibly for reasons of addressing traffic congestion.[28] This practice prompted the ACCC to warn Telstra and other ISPs in 2013 that they may be subjected to investigation if they were slowing down filesharing services in order to favour their own video content reaching end-users.[29]

Nevertheless, other stakeholders such as Cisco have asserted that the current legislative and regulatory framework for competition in Australia is sufficient to deal with any problems that may arise, and that in any event, some network management is desirable in order to address 'congestion' in the network.[30]

In 2015 the Final Report was issued, which also did not mention net neutrality.[31] However, one of the Report's recommendations was that the Australian Government task the Productivity Commission to undertake an overreaching review of intellectual property in Australia which should focus on competition policy issues in intellectual property arising from new developments in technology and markets.[32] The Review Panel in particular thought it was appropriate that commercial transactions involving licensing or assigning intellectual property rights be subject to the CCA, which is not the case at the moment. If this is altered, anti-competitive terms in licensing agreements would be subjected to competition scrutiny, which might go

---

[26] The Hon Bruce Billson MP Minister for Small Business press release (2014).

[27] Australian Communications Consumer Action Network (2014).

[28] Pirate Party Australia (2013a, b).

[29] Hutchinson (2014).

[30] Taylor (2014).

[31] Australian Government (2015).

[32] *Ibid.*, p. 41.

some way to resolving the competition concerns, which are also net neutrality concerns, discussed above in relation to premium content in Australia.

12.4.4   2015 Developments

There have been a number of net neutrality developments in Australia during 2015.

Comments have been made from a representative of Australia's second largest ISP Optus that streaming services such as Netflix should pay ISPs extra to ensure a 'premium' quality of service, shortly after Netflix itself announced that it would not enter into unmetered data agreements with Australians ISPs.[33] Netflix entered the Australian market in early 2015,[34] and the ISP iiNet had offered its customers unmetered access to Netflix's offerings but its customers complained about slow network speeds. Another commentator has pointed out that many popular streaming services in Australia are actually owned by incumbent media companies or telecommunications providers, and that these vested interests are what will spark the net neutrality debate in this country.[35]

Another development has been the Trade in Services Agreement (TiSA), an international services-only trade agreement being negotiated among 25 countries worldwide including Australia, the USA and the European Union. The agreement covers various sectors, including telecommunications and e-commerce. Similar to the Trans Pacific Partnership in which Australia is also a negotiating party, TiSA is also being negotiated in secret, and the general public has only been able to access the negotiating texts via a series of leaks. A leak from December 2014 encompassed US proposals which could undermine TiSA countries from implementing strong net neutrality rules, particularly those banning zero-rating services and other forms of price discrimination.[36] A further draft of the text was then leaked in February 2015 which also caused concern for net neutrality.[37] In Australia, the Pirate Party has made public its concerns about the impact of the TiSA on the Australian Internet, including the net neutrality aspects.[38]

12.5   Competition, Public Policy and Digital Rights

As can be seen from the above, the Australian net neutrality debate has been predominantly framed in terms of competition and consumer issues with less emphasis on net neutrality as a public policy choice, and the digital rights aspect of net neutrality barely being addressed.

---

[33] Colley (2015).
[34] Barr (2015), pp. 12–26.
[35] Caruana (2015).
[36] Masse (2014).
[37] Malcolm (2015).
[38] Pirate Party Australia (2015b).

Australian competition law, enshrined in the CCA and enforced by the ACCC, is cited as a reason for not having *ex ante* net neutrality regulation in Australia. While it is true to say that at the retail level there is competition among ISPs at least in urban areas, two problems persist. Firstly, there is little to no information about whether and how ISPs are 'managing' the traffic flowing through their networks. Similar rhetoric was at play in the EU, proclaiming the situation there more competitive than in the US and with the competition laws able to take care of any damaging non-net neutral conduct. This view, especially from the European Commission, persisted until the publication by the Body of European Regulators for Electronic Communications (BEREC) of data which found that there was widespread interference with peer to peer networks and VoIP on fixed and mobile networks in the EU.[39] The author could not find any similar data for Australia, so perhaps if such information were available as well, the attitude to net neutrality as being adequately addressed by the *ex post* competition regime might change as well.

Secondly, and related to the first point, there is still little transparency around these network practices in Australia, which deprives end-users of the information that would be useful in permitting them to make an informed decision about different providers' offerings in the context of a competitive market. However, even if a user did become unhappy with her Internet service due to certain content or services being blocked or delayed, the fixed term contracts that are widespread here (of up to 24 months) may mean she would either have to pay a penalty fee to exit that contract before its end, or stay with the original provider even though she is unhappy with the service. Thus, end-users experience a certain amount of lock-in to the Internet services they purchase and cannot easily and/or cheaply switch provider if they are unhappy, impeding the mitigating operation of competition.

Furthermore, as mentioned above, while the Australian Internet access markets may be competitive, Telstra still poses problems in terms of its highly vertically integrated character, and in particular its ownership of exclusive rights to attractive content. As can be seen from the previous section, the few practical net neutrality issues that have arisen in Australia seem to concern Telstra and its subsidiaries, such as impeding access to this content for non-Telstra subscribers and possibly throttling peer to peer filesharing services in order to privilege its own content delivery system. Thus, Telstra given this vertical integration has at least the incentive to engage in such non-net neutral action. Nevertheless, the ACCC's warning above regarding the alleged throttling of peer to peer services suggested that other ISPs apart from Telstra were engaging in this conduct as well—unless this constituted collusive conduct, it is unlikely to be a misuse of market power (abuse of dominance) as these other ISPs are unlikely to have market power. Non-dominant ISPs acting in non-net neutral ways are unlikely to be sanctioned by competition law. It remains to be seen whether net neutrality will be addressed indirectly through the Productivity Commission's forthcoming review of intellectual property in Australia.

Aside from Johnson's comments mentioned in the previous section, net neutrality in Australia has not been framed as a public policy issue. Arguably this may be

---

[39] BEREC press release (2012).

due to much public policy discourse regarding the Internet being around firstly the NBN's design and rollout, and secondly discussions of media ownership and concentration involving the ubiquitous Foxtel and News Corporation media as opposed to retail ISPs' control over the last mile to end-users. However, a rhetoric of light touch regulation based on neoliberal principles has been apparent in Australia as well as in other parts of the developed West such as North America and the EU,[40] which would entail more invasive regulation of *e.g.* ISPs to enforce net neutrality only being warranted in the case of 'market failures'.

Absent a market failure, it is perceived that there is no need for regulation on the matter, even to pursue public policy goals, as the market should provide. It is true that regulation in Australia is more complex than simply reflecting neoliberal theories,[41] particularly in the media and communications sector,[42] and the NBN might suggest government intervention on a scale eschewed by neoliberalism. However it seems that the NBN 'corrects' a market failure and so is permitted under the logic of neoliberalism.[43] In addition, there are plans to consider the privatisation of the NBN once it has been set up fully. Net neutrality, though, may still be viewed as going too far to address a problem that is too 'remote' a 'market failure'.

While net neutrality can also be framed as a digital rights issue, this conception has been absent from the Australian debate, with only Pirate Party Australia providing a notable exception. The Party started developing a position on net neutrality from 2009 onwards, which became situated in its 'Digital Liberties' policy alongside other rights such as privacy, transparency and censorship.[44] Furthermore, the Party has also spoken out on the potential threat that TiSA poses to net neutrality in Australia, as mentioned in the previous section. Electronic Frontiers Australia, the main digital rights NGO in the country (as opposed to the Pirates who are a political party), does not have any formal policy on net neutrality but would likely be favourable towards the principle.[45]

Perhaps the lack of recognition of net neutrality as a rights issue can be explained at least in part by the generally weak significance given to fundamental rights in Australia. There is no comprehensive set of human rights guarantees in the Australian Constitution. While there is express protection for certain specific rights such as the right to vote and freedom of religion, a right to free speech had to be 'implied' into the Constitution by judges during the 1990s,[46] and this implied right is very limited in its application i.e. to political communication. Certainly it would provide scant if not no basis to force net neutrality regulation for the benefit of Australian citizens' freedom to receive and impart information.

---

[40] Quiggin (1999), pp. 240–259.

[41] Braithwaite (2005).

[42] Flew (2012), pp. 1–17.

[43] Johnson (2011), pp. 3–18.

[44] Pirate Party Australia (2015a).

[45] Correspondence between the author and Electronic Frontiers Australia, on file with the author.

[46] Starting in *Australian Capital Television Pty Ltd v Commonwealth* (1992) and *Nationwide News Pty Ltd v Wills* (1992).

Furthermore, there is no constitutional right, either express or implied, to privacy in Australia, in sharp contrast to 'similar' jurisdictions such as the UK. Privacy is incidentally affected through the use of DPI in facilitating non-net neutral conduct by ISPs.[47] While Australia has some legislative protection of privacy, it is very much a patchwork of different statutes protecting different aspects of privacy rather than an overarching enforceable principle. The *Lenah Game Meats* case left open the possibility of the judiciary introducing a tort of invasion of privacy given the right circumstances, but did not do so based on the facts at hand on which it was found that there had been no invasion of privacy.[48] It could be argued that the practical prospects of Australia moving to protect privacy rights have been greatly diminished with the introduction of mandatory data retention laws in early 2015 (despite similar laws being ruled invalid in the EU in 2014),[49] and revelations about the dearth of privacy impact assessments conducted before national security legislation is passed in Australia.[50]

At the state and territory level in Australia, the Australian Capital Territory (ACT) and the State of Victoria both have human rights legislation which introduces individual rights including free expression and privacy.[51] However these rights are only enforceable vis-à-vis public bodies and so would again provide scant or no basis to force net neutrality regulation in the ACT and Victoria.

12.6   Looking to the Future

While, as can be seen from above, net neutrality in Australia has been a topic of debate for some years, stimulated by a variety of government consultations, and despite the recommendation in the Convergence Review, Australia still does not have any *ex ante* net neutrality regulation.

It is disappointing that the Harper Review of competition law and policy did not specifically recommend the implementation of net neutrality in Australian law and regulation. While some indirect steps towards net neutrality may be taken as an outcome of the Productivity Commission's review into intellectual property, it will not result in comprehensive *ex ante* net neutrality rules by which all telecoms providers and content providers must abide regardless of whether or not they have market power. Furthermore, increased transparency regarding ISPs' traffic management practices would be useful in determining the extent to which net neutrality is a problem (or not) in Australia, and it is important to note the change in rhetoric in the EU once the consequence of a lack of net neutrality had been shown empirically in many Member States.

---

[47] Daly (2011).

[48] *ABC v Lenah Game Meats Pty Ltd* (2001).

[49] Greenleaf (2015), pp. 26–28.

[50] Australian Broadcasting Corporation (2015).

[51] Respectively: *Human Rights Act (ACT)* (2005), *Charter of Human Rights and Responsibilities Act (Vic)* (2006).

While the net neutrality debate in Australia has been primarily framed in terms of competition concerns, this only paints a partial picture of what is at stake when it comes to ISPs' network and traffic management practices and agreements with large content providers. Unlike similar public discussions in the EU or US, only a few Australian stakeholders have acknowledged the individual rights aspect of net neutrality for end-users' privacy, free expression and autonomy online. This may well be tied in with the general lack of legal and rhetorical prominence rights-based discourses have in Australia, yet is worrying for the preservation of users' ability to send and receive the information they wish (providing it is legal) over the Internet.

Nevertheless, with large vertically integrated corporations such as Telstra with incentives to manage traffic in certain ways, and the emergence of streaming services such as Netflix which encourage zero-rating or paid prioritisation deals with ISPs, a long shadow is cast over the Australian Internet landscape, and net neutrality seems to be a debate unlikely to recede from view in the near future.

References

ABC v Lenah Game Meats Pty Ltd. (2001). 185 ALR 1.

Australian Broadcasting Corporation. (2015, August 24). New security laws being introduced without proper impact assessments. http://www.abc.net.au/lateline/content/2015/s4299342.htm. Accessed 9 Sept 2015

Australian Capital Television Pty Ltd v Commonwealth. (1992). 177 CLR 106.

Australian Communications and Media Authority (ACMA). (2013). Communications report 2012–2013. http://www.acma.gov.au/theACMA/LibraryCorporate-library/Corporate-publications/communications-report-2012-13

Australian Communications Consumer Action Network. (2014). Competition policy review: Submission by the Australian Communications Consumer Action Network to the Harper Review. http://competitionpolicyreview.gov.au/files/2014/06/ACCAN.pdf. Accessed 9 Sept 2015

Australian Competition and Consumer Commission (2013). ACCC final decision on the SAU lodged by NBN Co on 19 November 2013. https://www.accc.gov.au/regulated-infrastructure/communications/national-broadband-network/nbn-co-special-access-undertaking-2013/final-decision

Australian Government Department of Broadband, Communications and the Digital Economy. (2009). National Broadband Network: Regulatory Reform for 21st Century Broadband Discussion Paper.

Australian Government Department of Broadband, Communications and the Digital Economy. (2010). National Broadband Network implementation study.

Australian Government Department of Broadband, Communications and the Digital Economy. (2012). Convergence Review Final Report.

Australian Government. (2014a). Competition Policy Review Issues Paper.

Australian Government. (2014b, December). Telecommunications Regulation and Structural Reform. https://www.communications.gov.au/sites/g/files/net301/f/Telecommunications%20Regulatory%20and%20Structural%20Reform%20Paper.pdf

Australian Government. (2015). Competition Policy Review Final Report.

Barr, T. (2015). Whither Netflix?'. Australian Journal of Telecommunications and the Digital Economy, 3(2), 12–26.

BEREC press release. (2012). BEREC preliminary findings on traffic management practices in Europe show that blocking of VoIP and P2P traffic is common, other practices vary widely.

Bodley, M. (2013, April 22). Convergence Review is unlikely to revive, The Australian. http://www.theaustralian.com.au/archive/media/convergence-review-is-unlikely-to-revive/story-fndfo21g-1226625364771. Accessed 3 Aug 2014

Braithwaite, J (2005). *Neoliberalism or Regulatory Capitalism?* ANU Regulatory Institutions Network, Occasional Paper 5

Caruana, A. (2015, April 21). Net neutrality debate stirs in Australia, Macworld. http://www.macworld.com.au/news/net-neutrality-debate-stirs-in-australia-137476/#.Ve-x1clurTp. Accessed 9 Sept 2015

Charter of Human Rights and Responsibilities Act (Vic) (2006).

Colley, A. (2015, April 20). Optus considers breaking net neutrality in Australia, IT News. http://www.itnews.com.au/news/optus-considers-breaking-net-neutrality-in-australia-402909. Accessed 9 Sept 2015

Communications Law Centre, UTS (2010). Submission to the Department of Broadband, Communications and the Digital Economy in response to the National Broadband Network Implementation Study.

Competition and Consumer Act (2010) (Cth)

Daly, A. (2011). The legality of deep packet inspection. *International Journal of Communications Law & Policy* (14).

Dwyer, T. (2014). Press freedom discourses after Leveson: Ethics, elections and media concentration in Australia. *The Political Economy of Communication, 2*(1), 49–59.

Endres, J. (2009). Net neutrality – how relevant is it to Australia? *Telecommunications Journal of Australia, 59*(2), 22.1–22.10.

Flew, T. (2012). Globalisation, media policy and regulatory design: Rethinking the Australian media classification system. *Australian Journal of Communication, 39*(2), 1–17.

Greenleaf, G. (2015). Going against the flow: Australia enacts a data retention law. *Privacy Laws & Business International Report, 134*, 26–28.

Hill, J. (2008, September 24). Net neutrality is an 'American problem, ZDNet. Viewed 3 Aug 2014. http://www.zdnet.com/net-neutrality-is-an-american-problem-1339292161/

Human Rights Act (ACT) (2005)

Hutchinson, J. (2014, February 12). ACCC takes aim at internet slowdowns, Australian Financial Review. http://www.afr.com/p/technology/accc_takes_aim_at_internet_slowdowns_DNxYfamGg7IZdqO1IcZC1L. Accessed 9 Sept 2015

Johnson, C. (2011). The politics of broadband: Labor and new information technology from Hawke to Gillard. *Australian Journal of Political Science, 46*(1), 3–18.

Johnson, K. (2009). The importance of net neutrality to the digital economy. *Telecommunications Journal of Australia, 59*(2), 19.1–19.16.

Malcolm, J. (2015, May 27). TISA: Yet another leaked treaty you've never heard of makes secret rules for the internet, Electronic Frontier Foundation. https://www.eff.org/deeplinks/2015/05/tisa-yet-another-leaked-treaty-youve-never-heard-makes-secret-rules-internet. Accessed 9 Sept 2015

Manwaring, K. (2010). Net neutrality: Issues for Australia. *Computer Law & Security Review, 26*(6), 630–639.

Marsden, C. (2007). Net neutrality and consumer access to content. *SCRIPTed, 4*(4), 407–435.

Masse, E. (2014). Leak: U.S. pushing to undermine net neutrality and privacy in major trade agreements. https://www.accessnow.org/blog/2014/12/18/leak-u.s.-pushing-to-undermine-net-neutrality-and-privacy-in-major-trade-ag. Accessed 18 Dec 2014, 9 Sept 2015

NBN. (2015). Progress Report for Week Ending 27 August 2015. http://www.nbnco.com.au/corporate-information/about-nbn-co/corporate-plan/weekly-progress-report.html

ninemsn (2009, June 4). Letter to the Assistant Secretary, Networks Competition Branch, Department of Broadband, Communications and the Digital Economy.

Noam, E. (2011). *International media concentration research project.* New York: Columbia Institute of Tele-Information.

Pirate Party Australia. (2013a, February 7). Telstra's plan to break net neutrality. http://pirateparty. org.au/2013/02/07/telstras-plan-to-break-net-neutrality/. Accessed 9 Sept 2015

Pirate Party Australia. (2013b, September 11). Telstra throttling an unacceptable solution for net- work congestion. http://pirateparty.org.au/2013/09/11/telstra-throttling-an-unacceptable- solution-for-network-congestion/. Accessed 9 Sept 2015

Pirate Party Australia. (2015). Draft platform: Net neutrality. http://pirateparty.org.au/oldwiki/ index.php/Draft_Platform#Net_Neutrality. Accessed 9 Sept 2015

Pirate Party Australia. (2015, May 29). Trade in services agreement: A threat looming on the hori- zon'. https://pirateparty.org.au/2015/05/29/trade-in-services-agreement-a-threat-looming-on- the-horizon/. Accessed 9 Sept 2015

Quiggin, J. (1999). Globalisation, neoliberalism and inequality in Australia. *The Economic and Labour Relations Review, 10*(2), 240–259.

Taylor, J. (2014, June 13). Australian competition watchdog will help net neutrality: Cisco, ZDNet. http://www.zdnet.com/au/australian-competition-watchdog-will-help-net-neutrality- cisco-7000030503/. Accessed 3 Aug 2014

The Hon Bruce Billson MP Minister for Small Business press release (2014, December 4). Review of competition policy with The Hon Tony Abbott MP Prime Minister. http://bfb.ministers. treasury.gov.au/media-release/014-2013/. Accessed 9 Sept 2015

Tucker, R. (2015, September 8). The NBN: why it's slow, expensive and obsolete, The Conversation. Viewed 8 Sept 2015. https://theconversation.com/the-nbn-why-its-slow-expensive-and -obsolete-47191

Turner, A. (2014, February 26). Net neutrality – a debate we can't afford to ignore, Sydney Morning Herald. http://www.smh.com.au/digital-life/computers/blog/gadgets-on-the-go/net- neutrality--a-debate-we-cant-afford-to-ignore-20140226-33hco.html. Viewed 9 Sept 2015

Nationwide News Pty Ltd v Wills (1992) 177 CLR 1.

Chapter 13
Test of the FCC's Virtuous Circle: Preliminary Results for Edge Provider Innovation and BIAS Provider Investment by Country with Hard Versus Soft Rules

Roslyn Layton

13.1 Introduction

The net neutrality movement, its leaders and acolytes, should take stock of its success. Barely a decade ago "network neutrality" was an academic concept,[1] but no longer. A recent blog[2] from Access Now shows a world map with some two dozen nations with net neutrality rules of some kind, 28 EU member nations on track with rules, and India, Pakistan and South Africa considering rules.

With regimes in place a number of countries for 5 years are more, it is appropriate to take stock of the expected benefits, namely that countries with net neutrality rules should experience more edge provider innovation and broadband internet access service (BIAS) provider investment in network infrastructure. The FCC, the US telecom regulator, calls this the virtuous circle, and codified it in its net neutrality rules[3] adopted in February 2015.

This paper reviews an empirical test of the virtuous circle, looking at the record of the countries with rules versus the countries with no rules at all. There is no doubt that mobile applications proliferate around the world, particularly with American and Chinese providers, *e.g.* the family of apps from Facebook (WhatsApp, Messenger, Instagram etc.); Google (Gmail, YouTube etc.); WeChat, QQ, and Twitter. However this paper investigates to what degree net neutrality supports the emergence of mobile applications from outside the USA, particularly that a specific country produces edge provider innovation from its own country for its own users.

---

[1] Wu (2003), p. 141, 39.

[2] Olukotun (2015).

[3] Net Neutrality Ruling by FCC (2015).

R. Layton (✉)
Center for Communication, Media and Information Technologies,
Aalborg University, Copenhagen, Denmark

© Springer International Publishing Switzerland 2016
L. Belli, P. De Filippi (eds.), *Net Neutrality Compendium*,
DOI 10.1007/978-3-319-26425-7_13

The investigation finds a significant and positive correlation for countries with soft forms of net neutrality rules (guidelines, codes of conduct, and multi-stakeholderism) and the incidence of local country edge provider innovation for mobile applications. No correlation was observed between net neutrality and increased BIAS provider investment. No benefits for edge provider innovation and investment were observed for countries with hard rules (legislation and regulation).

The paper reflects an ongoing investigation that continues to refine the analysis with more granular data. It offers a review of the various legal instruments of net neutrality and some observations for net neutrality policymaking.

13.2 Types of Net Neutrality Rules Around the World

A survey of rules from around the world shows that policymakers can—and do—tailor their approach to net neutrality. Not only is there significant variation in how the concept is defined and promulgated, but in how it is enforced and punished. Net neutrality rules are implemented via one of three legal instruments: legislation, telecom regulation, or soft law (guidelines, codes of conduct, and multi-stakeholderism).

13.2.1 Legislation

Legislation is accomplished by developing or updating the country's communications laws and clarifying the authority of the telecom regulator. In Europe, such net neutrality rules were created in the Netherlands in 2011[4] and Slovenia in 2012.[5] Building on a Parliamentary resolution in April 2014,[6] the European Commission and Council of Ministers concluded an agreement in June 2015, and assuming ratification, will come into force on April 30, 2016.[7]

Latin American countries have also adopted the legislative approach, including Chile in 2010[8] with an update to their telecommunications laws, Colombia in 2011[9] as part of the 4 year presidential development plan, Peru in 2012[10] as part of a

---

[4] Telecommunicatiewet (2015).

[5] O Razglasitvi Zakona O Elektronskih Komunikacijah (ZEKom-1) (2012).

[6] European Single Market for Electronic Communications (2014).

[7] Commission Welcomes Agreement to End Roaming Charges and to Guarantee an Open Internet (2015).

[8] Consagra El Principio de Neutralidad En La Red Para Los Consumidores Y Usuarios de Internet (2010).

[9] Por La Cual Se Expide El Plan Nacional de Desarrollo (2011).

[10] Ley de Promocion de La Banda Ancha Y Construccion de La Red Dorsal Nacional de Fibra Optica (2012).

national plan to construct a fiber backbone, Brazil in 2014[11] as part of the Civil Framework for the Internet, and Mexico in 2014[12] as part of the new constitution. The differing approaches reflect that there no standard process for implementing net neutrality laws.

The countries that have taken the legislative approach have also elected to include different provisions in their legal texts. While prohibitions against blocking and throttling are common, countries have appended other requirements, including parental controls, protection from malware and viruses, user-requested blocking, and requirements for privacy, data retention, network security, and notifications to users before taking action on congestion. It has been observed that rules may be contentious and idiosyncratic. For example advocates in Peru and Colombia claim that the regulator has undue power to define violations and that the statute only protects against "arbitrary" practices.[13]

Naturally the benefit of parliamentary legislation is that it is obstensibly democratic, and the law-making approach ostensibly includes the appropriate consultations with the public, edge providers, and operators. Such a process was conducted in Slovenia and Chile, but not the Netherlands. Ideally an official investigation of traffic practices would also be conducted, but this does not always happen. For example in the EU, the Body of European Regulators for Electronic Communications (BEREC) conducted a survey[14] of *contract disclosures* of traffic management practices by European operators. It found that about a quarter of operators had provisions in their contracts saying that they could conduct certain kinds of practices. However the survey of policies was never validated with a real world test to see whether the practices actually occured. Such a survey could be accomplished in 3–6 months with focused effort and would seem to provide the necessary evidence and due diligence as part effective rulemaking.

Real world data was collected, though not published, as part of a raid of three large operators by the European Commission's Antitrust section. No abuse of content or interconnection markets was found.[15] In any case, the EU took some important and necessary steps as part of its rulemaking that other governments have not.

As will be discussed in the next section, legislation is more sustainable legally than regulation because laws are enshrined and promulgated as part of a country's telecom statutes or even constitution.

---

[11] Estabelece Princípios, Garantias, Direitos E Deveres Para O Uso Da Internet No Brasil (2014).

[12] Expiden La Ley Federal de Telecomunicaciones Y Radiodifusion, Y La Ley Del Sistema Publico de Radiodifusion Del Mixcano; Y Se Reforman, Adicionan Y Derogan, Diversas Disposiciones En Materia de Telecomunicaciones Y Radiodifusion (2014).

[13] Vargas-Leon (2014).

[14] A View of Traffic Management and Other Practices Resulting in Restrictions to the Open Internet in Europe BEREC Findings on Traffic Management Practices in Europe - Traffic Management Investigation (2012).

[15] Antitrust: Commission Closes Investigation into Internet Connectivity Services but Will Continue to Monitor the Sector (2014).

13.2.2   Regulation

It is interesting that the United States[16] and Canada,[17] eschewing a democratic approach, have chosen the path of making net neutrality rules from telecom regulation. This is a risky approach for the telecom regulators as it can bring legal challenges that ultimately strike down rules all together. It was exactly this tactic which brought a lawsuit against the Chilean telecom regulator Subtel in which the operator claimed that the regulator did not have the authority to make net neutrality rules. The issue was litigated for years until the situation was resolved by the Chilean Congress updating the country's communications laws and vesting the proper authority within the telecom regulator to enforce net neutrality rules.

Canada's net neutrality rules, which apply only to wireline providers, consist of a set of Internet Traffic Management Principles (IMTP) adopted in 2009, are essentially ideological requirements, but not technical classifications as such. The Canadian rules have been relatively uncontroversial until a recent ruling over mobile video in which the operator challenged the regulator's decision as an unlawful attempt to regulate a broadcast service with telecommunications law.[18]

The issue of whether wireless telecom regulations can be applied to wireline is fraught with difficulty for regulators. It is one of a number of challenges facing the FCC, now in its third time in court for net neutrality rulemaking. The agency faces nine lawsuits, from both large and small telecom providers, trade associations, and entrepreneurs.[19] Other charges as elaborated by the petitioners and amici include that the rules violate the Constitution and Communications Act, exceed the FCC's statutory authority, fail to take account of relevant economic and legal evidence, will harm the environment for investment; will impose harm to poor and disadvantaged communities through increased prices and decreased network deployment; did not follow the rules of administrative procedure, contravene essential technical and engineering realities and constraints; and impair the environment for edge innovation.[20] It has been observed that is unlikely that the rules will emerge intact from so many legal challenges.[21] This is an important issue for other countries considering pegging their rules to the US model, as they may find that the US rules are overturned in the courts.

---

[16] Federal Communications Commission, Report and Order on Remand, Declaratory Ruling, and Order (2015).

[17] Telecom Regulatory Policy CRTC 2009-657 (2009).

[18] Broadcasting and Telecom Decision CRTC 2015-26 (2015).

[19] Petitioners' Join Proposed Briefing Format and Schedule (2015).

[20] Veigle (2015).

[21] Smith (2015).

13.2.3 Soft Law

Eight countries use forms of soft law to address net neutrality. The countries and their dates of rules are Sweden[22] and Norway[23] in 2009; France[24] and Japan[25] in 2010; Denmark,[26] South Korea[27] and the United Kingdom[28] in 2011; and Switzerland[29] in 2014. This approach uses co-regulation, codes of conduct, and multi-stakeholderism to address net neutrality concerns proactively and collaboratively.

France has had since 2010 perhaps the most comprehensive understanding of Internet regulation that contemplates not just Internet access but the totality of the user's experience online. Codified in "10 Principles" by the telecom regulator, it includes ensuring non-discriminatory access to content, applications and services; consumer rights to broadband with declared quality and capacity; transparency; the ability of operators to offer managed services; device neutrality; and the regulator's role to monitor interconnection, traffic practices and connection quality.

The French have been skeptical about net neutrality which they see as a policy which promotes American Internet companies' squatting on French government owned networks without paying taxes or contributing to local infrastructure costs. As French telecom regulator ARCEP chief Sébastien Soriano observed, "The EU is being colonized by American Internet companies. . . We need to examine the Internet giants who dominate and shape the rules . . . We don't want Net Neutrality to throttle innovation."[30] He indicated a desire to move toward general "neutrality" regulation with a rating system, for example Google's search engine would get a 5 out of possible 10.[31] Concerns about Google's market power have fueled the European Commission's antitrust investigation[32] into the company, and Tim Wu himself published a study on search neutrality,[33] describing Google's search practices as anticompetitive.

The United Kingdom and Switzerland have formal a Code of Conduct, a series of provisions which operators agree to uphold. The UK model has a blend of provisions to support the "best efforts" functioning of the Internet. While blocking is

---

[22] Nätneutralitet (2011).

[23] Nettnøytralitet: Retningslinjer for Nøytralitet På Internett (2009).

[24] Neutralité de l'Internet et Des Réseaux (2010).

[25] New Competition Promotion Program 2010 (2007).

[26] Samarbejde Om – Og Retningslinjer for "netneutralitet" (2011).

[27] "방송통신위원회, 망 중립성 및 인터넷 트래픽 관리에 관한 가이드라인 제정" (Seoul, SK: KCC, December 26, 2011), www.kcc.go.kr/download.do?fileSeq=33164.

[28] Ofcom's Approach to Net Neutrality (2011).

[29] Netzneutralität: Bericht Zur Arbeitsgruppe (2014).

[30] Sebastien Soriano: Speech ETNO-MLEX 2015 (2015).

[31] Ibid.

[32] Case Search – Competition – European Commission – Google (2015).

[33] Luca et al. (2015).

banned outright, operators are allowed to offer managed services, provided that they do not degrade the best efforts Internet. The regulator's role is to ensure transparency, monitor traffic management practices, and to issue a periodic Key Facts Indicator Report. The regulator Ofcom conducted a significant and time-consuming review of tools designed to detect discriminatory traffic management practices, but ultimately found that none of the prevailing tools were reliable.[34]

In light of the Switzerland's review of its Communications Act, the CEO of Swisscom requested the telecom regulator to convene a multi-stakeholder discussion. The results informed the country's code of conduct which includes an arbitration board.

The Nordic countries have perhaps the best and longest track record of deterring net neutrality violations. Sweden was a first-mover in net neutrality, establishing guidelines in 2009. After an extensive review of the telecommunications market, the Swedish telecom regulator (PTS) declared that Sweden did *not* have an Internet access problem that warranted legislative or regulatory action. From PTS's perspective, net neutrality is about ensuring transparency in pricing, service offerings, network quality, as well as upstream and downstream capacity so that consumers are clear in what they purchase and can easily switch providers. PTS claims its consumer-centric, light-touch approach is successful and has improved operating norms so much that adopting to the proposed EU parliamentary solution is a step backward.[35] Sweden is a rare instance where a review of the market and alleged harmful practices was actually conducted before net neutrality rulemaking.

Norway established its net neutrality rules only a month after Sweden. It provides a set of rules and dialogue via an annual stakeholder meeting to discuss the status of net neutrality. "The Norwegian guidelines can be seen as an approach that prevents the potential need to require net neutrality by law," notes the regulator.[36] A review of the Norwegian model is offered by Christopher Marsden.[37]

In Denmark broadband providers took action without the prodding of government authorities. The country's Telecom Industry Association convenes a Net Neutrality Forum which includes the nation's telecom operators, content providers, industry and consumers associations, and user representatives. At the time of Forum's founding, the telecom regulator was an observer. The Forum upholds four principles: users have the right to an Internet connection with declared capacity and quality; users have the right to access lawful content and to use applications and services of their choice, provided it does not affect the integrity of the network; users must have access to transparency measures (disclosure of an operator's traffic management principles); and operators must not discriminate in relation to specific service providers, content or applications.

---

[34] Traffic Management Detection Methods and Tools (2015).
[35] Bergström (2014).
[36] Sørensen (2013).
[37] Marsden (2015).

It is interesting to note the Danish telecom regulator was dismantled by the Center Left government in 2011,[38] though the country's telecom laws remain. Regulatory employees were re-assigned across four agencies and can discharge any statutory responsibilities as needed. The decision to decommission the agency was made for a number of reasons, but one of the most important was the belief that little value is added by a telecom authority micromanaging and monitoring networks. Instead, it is believed that professionals with telecom regulatory expertise add more value to society by assisting other agencies (health, education, transportation etc.) to enable broadband technologies.

Denmark is a key example of government as facilitator, not regulator, of broadband. This is considered a more evolved and effective approach of industrial policy[39] as the regulatory model appears increasingly ineffective to deliver high speed broadband networks. Denmark, just pushed South Korea of out of first place in the ICT Development Index (IDI) of the International Telecommunications Union for 2014.[40] The ranking reflects the country's performance for its high rate of broadband investment (incidentally there are almost no public subsidies for broadband), advanced networks and devices, high Internet adoption, and competitive prices.

The different legal instruments of net neutrality have benefits and costs. Legislation provides clarity and legitimacy, but simultaneously creates pressure on policymakers to find violations. It should be recognized that a law is working if no violations occur after a law is made. However, it can be embarrassing politically, for it may appear that the law was made too hastily or without evidence. As such, there can be political pressure to find a problem to justify the law ex post. This may have something to do with political reluctance to conduct official investigations before rulemaking, as the case for the rules may not be as strong as some policymakers desire.

For example Chile, Slovenia, and Netherlands were first movers in making net neutrality laws and subsequently toughened them to outlaw certain forms of zero rating. However investigations of those countries found that the bans have unduly harmed the 3rd and 4th tier operators which are trying to compete with incumbents; reduced welfare for consumers in forcing them to make phone calls instead of using mobile broadband connections to top up their mobile account balances; and reduced traffic to local content providers by half. Legal challenges against regulators are afoot in Slovenia. A detailed discussion of Netherlands, Chile, and Slovenia describes the outcome of hard law in these three countries.[41]

Legislation and regulation are not bullet proof, but they highlight some of the advantages of soft measures, including the absence of costly litigation. While it may seem on the surface that soft measures have less legitimacy, in practice they have been shown to encourage desirable behaviors and deter net neutrality violations.

---

[38] Henten and Falch (2014).

[39] Falch and Henten (2015).

[40] Measuring the Information Society Report 2014 (2014).

[41] Layton and Elaluf-Calderwood (2015).

Soft measures for net neutrality require attention and participation of stakeholders, something important for net neutrality advocates. More generally the ability to deliver desired outcomes without hard measures is the essence of soft power.[42] As such, a key accomplishment of the net neutrality movement is that it has changed social norms such that the "Open Internet" is a near inviolable political concept. Journalists and social media users have effective soft power to name and shame practices they don't like. Indeed such a collective ability may be more effective over the long run in the likely event that hard rules and regulations that can't survive in court.

Soft rules work because of the proverbial carrot and stick. Broadband providers have an incentive to do the right thing (carrot) while the threat of greater rulemaking is always in the background keeping them in check (stick). Perhaps most important, soft measures as associated with higher levels of edge innovation as the following discussion explains.

13.3 An Empirical Test of the FCC's Virtuous Circle

13.3.1 Theoretical Background

This section reviews an empirical test of the FCC's "virtuous circle", its notion underpinning net neutrality and its role to stimulate edge innovation and network investment. In its 2010 Open Internet Report & Order, the FCC presented the idea[43] and reiterated it in its 2015 rules,[44] noting that "Internet openness drives a 'virtuous circle' in which innovations at the edges of the network enhance consumer demand, leading to expanded investments in broadband infrastructure that, in turn, spark new innovations at the edge.[45]" The logic follows that countries with net neutrality rules should have both higher edge innovation and network infrastructure investment.

The virtuous circle defines three set of actors: broadband Internet access providers (BIAS, or what might typically be known as ISPs or Internet service providers); edge providers (those non-BIAS third party entities creating content, services and application, *e.g.* Internet companies such as YouTube, WhatsApp, Netflix); and end users or consumers. BIAS providers are said to occupy the core of the Internet while edge providers and consumers are at the ends.[46]

"BIAS" and "edge providers" are terms of art created by the FCC. They are legal, not engineering constructs. It is important to recognize that the goal of the FCC's

---

[42] Nye (2005).

[43] FCC Open Internet Report & Order 10-201, Paragraph 14 (2010).

[44] Verizon v. FCC, 740 F. 3d 623 (Court of Appeals, Dist. of Columbia Circuit 2014). FCC Releases Open Internet Order (2015).

[45] *Id.* at 659.

[46] Lemley and Lessig (2000).

rules is to *prioritize innovation by edge providers at the edge of the network* but not within the network itself. While it is possible to imagine that network innovations themselves could deliver major improvements for throughput, security, and user driven specifications (*e.g.* 5G mobile wireless standards), supporting those developments is not the goal of net neutrality as the FCC defines it. The FCC asserts that edge provider innovation is a function of net neutrality and thereby rejects a number of established theories of innovation that contradict its policy including the National Innovation System,[47] complementary assets,[48] disruptive innovation,[49] diffusion of innovation,[50] and creative destruction.[51]

Studying the effects on a country level is important from a policy perspective, particularly because net neutrality rules are pursued at the country level and involve nation state actors and nation state requirements. Therefore observing benefits at the nation state level is an expectation of the model. A key theoretical assumption of net neutrality is that it lowers barriers to entry for edge providers. Developers and engineers in poor countries have free or low cost tools and common protocols in which to innovate, putting them on equal footing with rich countries. Most, if not all, developing countries already have local content in the form of newspapers, television and radio, as well as a range of content creators, including government, businesses, individuals, and other entities.[52] As such, local content and applications, and services should proliferate for the given country in a state of net neutrality as those innovations have the same ease to get to users as any others. It follows that countries with net neutrality rules, developed or developing, should have a meaningful rate of local country innovation.

13.3.2 Model Design and Variable Selection

A random effects model was constructed with the dependent variables of edge provider innovation and capital expenditure. Fixed effects included the types of net neutrality rules (soft law, legislation, regulation, and no specific law), the country, and the year. Calculations were conducted three times with different data sets for capital expenditure, but each test produced roughly the same result. A dataset was constructed from publicly available sources so that others may replicate such tests. This paper reflects that dataset and is the third iteration of the model. A fourth iteration of the model is in progress.

---

[47] Freeman (1995), pp. 5–24.
[48] Teece (1986).
[49] Christiansen (1997).
[50] Rogers (2003).
[51] Schumpeter (1942).
[52] Kende and Rose (2015).

The preliminary design of the test and its limitations was outlined in last year's report.[53] Shortcomings include the heterogeneity of countries and the individualized rules they adopt; the fact that investment is cyclical and network equipment is subject to price change; and that there are not many global data sets to measure edge provider innovation.. The incidence of mobile wireless innovation requires some degree of advanced networks and smartphone penetration. The FCC does not discuss the role of devices in its virtuous circle, but it is significant for mobile wireless innovation. For example, the FCC states that net neutrality drives edge provider innovation, and the edge provider innovation happens *before* BIAS investment. But it is not clear how users can access mobile apps if the country does not have the requisite mobile network, and the users do not have the minimum standard smartphone.

From a statistical perspective, there is a problem with spuriousness of the data; variables may be statistically related to each other but have no causal relationship. The typical example is that ice cream sales and drownings tend to increase at the same time. It is faulty to presume that one causes the other, but putting the variables in context, that they both increase during the summer, explains the increase. For net neutrality, this means that while we want to attribute greater edge innovation and investment to the presence of rules, this may be the result of other factors that have nothing to do with net neutrality.

The test attempted to characterize edge provider innovation by using a number of datasets. There is an inherent bias in that innovation measurements cover formal and commercialized inventions. To be sure, net neutrality advocates like the notion of a hacker in the garage. As salient as that notion may be, it was not possible to collect information about those hackers for this study. As such innovation for this study can only be quantified by what can be measured and observed.

One dataset is the World Intellectual Property Organization's IP Statistics Data Center.[54] This database provides a list of patents by country and by year. There is no "Internet" category of patents as such so the patents from the areas of audio visual technology, telecommunications, digital communications, basic communications, computer technology, IT methods, and semiconductors were tallied. This sum gives only the number of patents, not the filer. It might be the case that WIPO categories commingle network and "edge" innovation. However the only way to select the quasi-Internet related patents that are disaggregated from all patents in the country was to choose from WIPO's pre-assigned categories.

There are many important Internet innovations that are not patented, but a database for those applications could not be found. Measuring open source innovation was attempted then rejected because attribution could not be accounted for by country. Moreover many open source innovations have proprietary elements, so it would create a problem of double-counting for patents. Additionally open source software is frequently a multinational project so it can't necessarily be attributed to a single country.

---

[53] Layton (2014).
[54] WIPO Intellectual Property Statistics Data Center (2015).

The statistical test discussed in this paper was performed on the R Project, an open source software package for statistics.[55]

For example a leading open source platform is Android, Google's operating system for mobile devices, found on at least 80 percent of the world's smartphones. Some 1 million applications have been developed for Android and have been downloaded more than 50 billion times.[56] While Android is based on the Linux open source technology, it includes a number of proprietary elements. Google offers the platform for free and recovers costs by advertising in the apps that are developed with it. In this way, Android and TCP/IP, are both open source, but Android might not be "neutral" because Google reserves some restrictions on the platform. For example developers can't develop a competitive email service to Gmail using Android.[57]

Given that the Internet increasingly transitions to mobile platforms, and the likelihood that the next two thirds of world who have yet to come online will do so via mobile broadband, it is important to understand edge provider innovation on mobile and wireless platforms. This also provides some balance to developing countries away from developing countries where desktop platforms predominate. Incidentally the mobile app data was regressed in two stages, once with mobile wireless capex only and again with all network capex. A similar step was taken for patents.

Data for edge provider innovation was obtained from the free version of AppAnnie. com, a leading market research tool for mobile applications which aggregates download and revenue data for app stores by country and app marketplace. Data was collected by country for both the Apple iOS AppStore beginning in 2010 and Google Play beginning 2012. The country origin of the application was noted as part of the data collection, as a number of edge providers are multinational companies.

There are other mobile app platforms such as Microsoft, Amazon, and a number of Chinese providers,[58] but given the combined market share of iOS and Apple, it was statistically significant to focus on just these two marketplaces. This predominance of just two app stores globally brings to attention an issue of market power and neutrality.[59]

The number of downloads per app is not given in AppAnnie.com, but appearance in the top ten of the app store indicates high level of downloads, approximately 10,000–25,000 per day. While it will depend on the country and the category, the top 100–200 apps are significant for the market, assuming the depth of the particular category. After position 200 the significance falls precipitously and below 300 ceases to matter. One can understand the phenomena from Google's search engine in that the first three results get the lion's share of clicks, followed by the remaining seven on the first page, but generally users never go past the first page.[60] Thus appearing in the top 10 for the category is important for adoption in app stores as it is in search engines.

---

[55] R: R Foundation Members and Supporters (2015).
[56] Facts on Android (2015).
[57] When It Comes to Net Neutrality, Why Don't People Talk about Operating Systems? (2013).
[58] O'connell (2013).
[59] Hestres (2013), p. 15.
[60] Ramos and Cota (2009).

AppAnnie.com offers more than a dozen categories for mobile apps including health, travel, kids, business and so on, but three key categories are particularly important: messaging/social networking apps (WhatsApp, Facebook Messenger, Line, KakaoTalk, WeChat); entertainment/video streaming (Netflix, YouTube, HBO, Hulu), and games (Clash of Clans, Candy Crush, Game of War). The platform also organizes the information for free and paid apps. This is significant because how an application earns revenue varies. For example, some apps earn a fee when a user downloads them in the store. In other cases, the app is free but revenue is earned inside the app either through advertising (a form of zero rating, as the advertising subsidizes the free distribution of the app) or in-app purchases, for example micro-transactions within game play. Popularity of an app does not necessarily translate to profitability.

While Google and Facebook dominate a number of app categories, games is one area where new players from a variety of countries have emerged with popular titles and sustainable business models. This includes of course publishers from the US, China, South Korea, and Japan, but a massive multiplayer game such as Agar.io from Miniclip in Switzerland has taken the world by storm, as have titles from Vietnam and France.

While the web has been and remains to a large extent an American phenomenon, as measured by the proliferation of American websites dominating traffic and revenue, the mobile Internet is driven in large part by China, a country with large base of broadband-connected smartphone users and world class application providers. In fact Apple's App Store has more downloads in China than in the US.[61] China has a number of powerhouse video streaming providers including Tencent, Baidu's iQIYI, Sohu TV, Youku Tudou, and LeTV.

It turns out that the biggest challenge for mobile application adoption is app discovery.[62] For example Apple's App Store lists just 200 apps for any country. Net neutrality holds that that consumers and edge providers blithely traverse the Internet without the need of marketing strategies or platforms to find what they are looking for.[63] On a more prosaic level, that edge providers must invest significant resources in the practices of SEO (search engine optimization) and ASO (app store optimization) to be findable calls into question the neutrality of intermediaries.[64]

The investment data was first modeled using information from the IHS Infonetics report[65] of private expenditure on capital equipment for communications networks and the Bank of America Merrill Lynch collection of publicly available capital expenditures for the world's mobile wireless providers. The ITU's World Telecommunication/ICT Indicators Database,[66] with data beginning from 1960 for wireline as well as wireless as soon as it was available, was also used.

[61] Report: China Surpasses United States by iOS Downloads (2015).

[62] Personal Interview with mobile application developer Babar Baig, creator of the WriteReader iPad application for educators, August 26, 2015.

[63] Yoo (2009), p. 77.

[64] Ramos (2014).

[65] IHS Infonetics Service Provider Capex and Subscribers, prepared semi-annually. "Infonetics Research," *Infonetics*, 2015, http://www.infonetics.com/research.asp?cvg=ServiceProviderCapex andSubscribers.

[66] World Telecommunication/ICT Indicators Database (2015).

13.3.3   Preliminary Results and Limitations

The results[67] highlight some important findings, but can still be improved with further research. The presence of net neutrality rules was not predictive for edge providers innovation as measured by patents or for investment in network infrastructure (capex). This outcome is important because the measures were calculated over a long period of time from 2000 onward and include observations both before and after net neutrality rules are imposed.

The measure of edge provider innovation with mobile applications only begins from 2010, when data became available. There is limited data before that date as mobile apps were just beginning. This creates a problem for assessing before and after changes in certain countries, so mobile apps were assessed both nominally as well as statistically within the model.

In any event there is a positive and significant correlation between countries with soft rules for net neutrality and the incidence of local country edge provider innovation as measured by rank and number mobile applications for the given country.

The calculations for edge provider mobile app innovation follow. The calculations for patents and capex were omitted in the interest of brevity.

Apple AppStore 2010–2015	Estimate	Standard error	t value
Level of mobile edge innovation (Intercept)	0.1278	0.2796	0.457
Countries with soft net neutrality rules	5.2503	0.9455	5.553
Countries with net neutrality legislation	1.5621	1.6327	0.957
Countries with net neutrality regulation (US, Canada)	0.61	2.5381	0.24
	0.5991	0.597	1.003

Google Play Store 2012–2015	Estimate	Standard error	t value
Level of mobile edge innovation (Intercept)	0.1643	0.2497	0.658
Countries with soft net neutrality rules	3.4599	0.914	3.785
Countries with net neutrality legislation	1.9788	1.5959	1.24
Countries with net neutrality regulation (US, Canada)	0.5986	2.304	0.26
	−0.7072	0.5879	1.203

Countries with soft net neutrality rules have a high level of edge provider mobile app innovation, especially Denmark, Sweden, Japan, and South Korea. Interestingly almost all of the countries with soft approaches appear consistently in the top 10 of the ITU's ICT Development Index[68] a composite measure covering 11 factors

---

[67] A complete study will be available from the Center for Communication, Media and Information Technologies at Aalborg University.

[68] Measuring the Information Society Report 2014 (2014).

related to Internet access, use, and skills for 215 countries since 2007. But this also suggests that net neutrality alone might not driving the trend in favor of edge providers.

It is interesting that Denmark and Sweden, two countries with small populations, have such high rates of edge provider innovation. The FCC does not discuss innovation as a function of population size or user base, but this would seem to be important. Normalizing innovation data for country size and economy might make the US and China seem less like outliers, but simultaneously, might make Denmark and Sweden greater performers.

It bears mention that the Danish government was key to stimulating Internet adoption through the digitization of the public sector, including a national digital signature program and record system which offers citizens a one-stop shop for all of their government information, health, tax, and social services. As such there is significant mobile traffic to government entities. Denmark's Kiloo is a leading game publisher. The mobile pay solution from Danske Bank is the world's most successful as measured by national adoption. Similarly, Sweden is known for Spotify, a leading mobile application for music streaming.

Both Japan and South Korea produce a number of edge applications. In contrast to the neutral platform philosophy of net neutrality which posits the need for structural separation of content and connectivity providers,[69] content and connectivity were integrated on purpose in those countries because there was not Korean or Japanese content outside the respective countries. Japan has a number of video game publishers including Nintendo, Square Enix, Sony, and Bandai Namco. It is also significant that China (WeChat, QQ), Japan (LINE) and South Korea (KaKao Talk) are essentially the only countries where WhatsApp and Facebook Messenger are not the dominant messaging applications.

Countries with hard rules, including Chile, Colombia, Peru, Slovenia, Brazil, and Mexico showed no relationship between net neutrality rules and an increase in local country edge provider innovation or investment.

Surprisingly, Dutch edge provider innovation is limited. It appears that Dutch edge provider innovation has declined since the promulgation of the country's net neutrality law. For the year to date in 2015 just two Dutch mobile applications emerge in the top 25 for the country. Countries with soft measures for net neutrality generally have at least 10 or more apps per year in the top ten for their respective countries.

One Dutch scholar has remarked that the Dutch net neutrality law that was supposed to be a "silver bullet" has created new problems. Instead of a flowering of local content and services, the Netherlands experiences the "Netflix effect"[70] in which a single American company consumes 20 percent of the country's bandwidth with a small subset of users.

It is interesting to note that Netflix is the most popular mobile entertainment app in the Netherlands, and it made comments in Dutch in a proceeding to support the country's

---

[69] Lemley and Lessig (2003), Wu (2003).

[70] Van Eijk (2014).

toughening of the net neutrality rule to outlaw zero rating and force operators to increase data caps on mobile broadband plans.[71] The policy supports Netflix's business (while it does make low volume users worse off) and appears to be one way to ensure that no competing video provider challenges its dominance. Subsequently the zero rating of HBO Go was deemed illegal, even though the app only had 3200 users and never reached a significant rank in the country. The €200,000 fine placed on Vodafone Netherlands is probably more than the broadband provider earned on the service.[72]

The study does not explain the strong performance for countries with no net neutrality rules at all, specifically China and Hong Kong. These countries have high and growing rates of edge provider innovation and capital investment. While it may be attributed to the large and growing market for Internet related goods and services, it bears mention that China is not considered to have an "open Internet". Its system is termed a government allowed "intranet" where government-sanctioned applications are delivered on government-owned networks.[73] Nevertheless there is no question that China's applications and services are innovative, and they are gaining increasing popularity outside of the country.

The US and Canada occupy their own category for their type of net neutrality rule and are difficult to characterize, particularly because the new US rules just came into effect this year. In the US, prior rules were challenged and subsequently overturned, so it's difficult to know to what degree that they were followed and enforced, and whether it had an impact on investment or innovation. It bears mention that net neutrality rules have been in place on certain US companies such as AT&T and Comcast at different times as part of mergers. However in other cases they have been expressly absent, such as the case of the FCC's 2010 rules which did not apply to wireless networks. It may be significant that there were no net neutrality rules on wireless in the US for the period studied suggesting that a lack of rules fosters edge provider innovation.

There is no doubt that the US and Canada have had historically high rates of network infrastructure investment, and the US an extraordinarily high rate of innovation. The US accounts for an overwhelming share of the world's innovation in both measures for this study, patents and edge innovation. Moreover for the last two decades the US has accounted for almost a quarter of the world's investment in telecommunications networks. These figures are staggering for a country with just 4 percent of the world's population. Because the level of investment and innovation is so high already, it is difficult to believe that a net neutrality rule could increase the performance of these metrics going forward. However a decline of 12 percent in investment in wireline infrastructure by BIAS providers has been observed in the first half of 2015 compared to the first half of 2014,[74] indicating that hard rules may have the opposite effect of the FCC's stated intention.

---

[71] Besluit van de Minister van Economische Zaken van 11 mei 2015, nr. WJZ/15062267, houdende beleidsregel inzake de toepassing door de Autoriteit Consument en Markt van artikel 7.4a van de Telecommunicatiewet (Beleidsregel netneutraliteit) (2015).

[72] Supra Layton and Elaluf-Calderwood (2015).

[73] Negro (2015).

[74] Singer (2015).

The US case is certainly worthy of more empirical investigation, and at the least, suggests that the FCC's virtuous circle while intuitively compelling, might not fully explain the complex interplay of factors that drive innovation and investment. It may be the case that ISPs actually support rather than deter Internet innovation. A case in point was the exclusive arrangement between AT&T and Apple to launch the iPhone in 2007, obliging users to some extent to Apple's walled garden. However the partnership succeeded to introduce the concept of the smartphone to users and provided a catalyst to mobile wireless innovation in devices, content, and applications. But such a partnership would probably not have been allowed if the FCC's 2015 hard rules were in place in 2007.

Consider that part of the FCC's new rules is a process to solicit new Internet business plans in advance so that "advisory opinions"[75] can be issued. In many instances parties don't know what to expect before they try their models. The seeming goal of the effort is to deter "discriminatory" business models before they happen. But how might the FCC advise on a business model such as Uber? Many users love Uber because it has significantly reduced the cost of taxi rides and improved the user experience dramatically. At the same time, many taxi drivers feel disenfranchised by Uber, and as a result a number of taxi commissions have restricted, if not banned it outright.[76] Will it be the case that a mobile application succeeds only if it can get the right political support in the respective location and at the FCC?[77]

In policy discussions, net neutrality is frequently billed as the sine qua non of edge provider innovation. However the ongoing studies of innovation and national rankings by a number of leading institutes never mention net neutrality. It would seem that if net neutrality rules are so necessary immediately, then this would be included in the indices published by organizations such as the Global Innovation Index (INSEAD, Cornell),[78] Bloomberg Innovation Index,[79] and the OECD Innovation Indicators,[80] but this is not the case.

13.4   Implications for Policy

13.4.1   Conflicting Policies for Broadband and Net Neutrality

The data are clear that among countries with rules, the countries with soft approaches have a higher rate of edge provider innovation in mobile applications. It is interesting that these countries—Denmark, Sweden, Japan, South Korea, France, and

---

[75] FCC Press Release (2015).

[76] Grant and Khosla (2015).

[77] Kelly (2014).

[78] The Global Innovation Index (2015).

[79] The Bloomberg Innovation Index (2015).

[80] Innovation Indicators (2015).

United Kingdom—have been praised[81] relentlessly by net neutrality advocates for their national broadband policies resulting in advanced networks, high speeds, high adoption, and competitive broadband prices. It is not logical that the policies that work so well to deliver broadband should not also work well to deliver net neutrality. In fact, it is a risk, as the Swedish regulator observed, to move to a hard approach because the dynamics that support the collaborative relationship between regulators, broadband providers and other community stakeholders that delivers the many broadband benefits could be compromised. Moreover the data suggests that countries with soft measures will suffer under hard rules, as the countries with hard rules do not produce significant edge provider innovation.

13.4.2 Hard Net Neutrality Disproportionately Serves American Edge Providers at Local Country Expense

It appears that net neutrality in countries with hard rules disproportionately serves US based edge providers. Given the importance of America's Internet companies to its economy, it is not surprising the net neutrality is part of the country's international trade policy. However an upset to the status quo that would allow a non-US company to displace the current leaders would not be desired by the US or its Internet companies.

It is counterintuitive, but bans on paid prioritization actually serve established American companies to the detriment of non-US entrants. Though such a case has never been observed, it is precisely an upstart that could benefit with a so-called fast lane to challenge the American giants. Because extreme difficulty for a startup to challenge YouTube or Netflix by building a base of content and servers from scratch, the ability to purchase improved quality delivery is a low cost way to enter the market. Thus prohibiting any company from doing it is a hedge that solidifies the market leaders' positions should those technologies become available in the future.

In any case startups access "fast lanes" today through the purchase of content delivery networks. This is a key reason that Akamai lobbied the FCC to have content delivery networks exempted from the final net neutrality rules.[82] Incidentally Akamai, Level 3 and Cogent have indicated they will offer "friend of the court" support in favor of the FCC in its lawsuits.[83] It is likely that if net neutrality were made law, these providers of peering and transit would be subject to net neutrality while they are not today. Protecting market position is the more likely motive for net neutrality than altruism on the part of American Internet companies.

---

[81] Examples of articles include Susan Crawford, Why Can't We Be Like South Korea? When Internet Access Is Slow or Just Nonexistent in the US, We Shrug Our Shoulders. But in That Small Asian Nation, Lousy Connections Are Not Tolerated. (2015), Kehl et al. (2014), Crawford (2013), Karr (2011), O'Brien (2014), Geoghegan (2013).

[82] FCC Open Internet Rules Paragraph 372, Page 171 (2015).

[83] Public Knowledge (2015).

To be sure, a smattering of startups formed the Internet Freedom Business Alliance[84] to lobby the FCC, but none of these are competitors to established Internet companies (Tumblr is owned by Yahoo for example). If anything, the media visibility of lobbying gives these companies notoriety to increase their prospective value for Initial Public Offerings (IPO).[85] Given that Google and Netflix have been longtime supporters of net neutrality,[86] it is important for advocates to check that their efforts are not a red carpet for the Internet giants.

An important issue that is overlooked in the discussion of net neutrality is an economic analysis of the disproportionately high level of traffic generated by the top 10 mobile applications and the aggregation of traffic at exchanges and backbones. Net neutrality wants to ensure equal access to sites and services for end users, but such performance can only be achieved by keeping good provision, upgrade, and maintenance of the telecom network, which implies costs and relationships between the pricing of services and expenditure.

How traffic is aggregated and the impact the transport cost of data through backbone networks is transferred to users is not clearly understood, nor is such vital information readily available. Not having the information or mischaracterizing the situation can lead to false conclusions. Some basic trends are known however and are helpful to review.[87]

Video is a huge and growing portion of the traffic delivered to mobile devices, comprising more than two-thirds of all traffic in some countries. Significantly, just two entities, Google/YouTube and Netflix take an overwhelming share of this traffic.

Data centers are integral to the way the Internet works, not only because of the prevalence of virtualization and cloud services, but also because they provide the means to structure traffic worldwide. This puts considerable power in the hands of a few big players, including Google, Facebook, and Amazon. Akamai, Level 3, and other content delivery providers are important, as are the data centers of banks and telecom providers.

The structure of the traffic flows differ significantly from the archetypal model of the three layered Internet (infrastructure, transport, service/data). Internet exchanges and private contracts for peering and transit re-draw routing worldwide. The structure today is more modular and "platformized." The idea of content/application providers passively accessing transport networks has given way to the reality of proactive approaches in which content provider develop individualized solutions and relationships for advanced, dynamic delivery and competitive differentiation. Content providers avail themselves to non-neutral pricing as a matter of course. Differential treatment of traffic is the norm, and this is what content providers want when they purchase traffic delivery solutions from a range of intermediary providers.

---

[84] Hattem (2014).

[85] Rogers (2015).

[86] Netflix Has Replaced Google as the Face of Net Neutrality Netflix Has Replaced Google as the Face of Net Neutrality (2014).

[87] Weller and Woodcock (2013), Liebenau et al. (2013), Liebenau (2012), pp. 248–272.

Decisions about transit and data centers by content/applications providers have material impacts to end users. For example, people in Latin America use global (American) platforms such as Google, Facebook and Twitter to talk with people around the corner. How those platforms are provisioned locally and regionally has technical, regulatory, and geopolitical implications. For example Google built a CDN in Chile, allowing traffic to be redistributed from the Miami Internet exchange. This improves the experience for its end users in Chile.

In Europe, the practical evidence shows that Europeans largely use American platforms to communicate with other Europeans. Unfortunately the Amsterdam Internet Exchange (AMIX) has not been forthcoming to allow academics to measure or test these traffic trends.[88]

13.4.3   Tie Performance Measures for Net Neutrality Advocacy to Socially Beneficial, Not Privately Beneficial, Measures

So if the data shows that soft rules are better, why do advocates pursue hard ones? It may be that net neutrality organizations are locked in to delivering "results" to their funders rather than being incentivized to perform to more meaningful and socially beneficial indicators such edge provider innovation per country, local country content development, and local country adoption for local content. Perhaps legislation is simply seen as a next step so that organizations can maintain and grow their operating budgets. It appears that simply driving the passage of laws and regulations does not necessarily sync to the measures that would indicate that users and innovators are served.

It may be the case that for some policymakers in some countries that a net neutrality rule is box to check and with luck, once a law is made, advocates will go away. It may be the case that countries could "check out" on net neutrality after a law is made, and regulators want to "move on" to other things. By contrast, through soft approaches, net neutrality organizations can maintain visibility in the public and "keep the heat on ISPs", thereby building a case for multiyear budgets from their funders.

In the case of soft measures, we see the telecom regulators in Sweden, Norway, Japan, South Korea, France, United Kingdom, and Switzerland convene stakeholders for a variety of activities related to net neutrality. The outcomes include developing formal guidelines and codes, official meetings, workshops, and reports. There is no doubt that net neutrality activists can have an important, influential, and demonstrable role in these proceedings. Staff and resources are needed to participate in the time-consuming and labor intensive process to maintain multi-stakeholder dialogues.

---

[88] Silvius (2011).

13.4.4   Differences between the EU and US in Net Neutrality Rulemaking and the Benefits of the Soft Approach

Presently there is an attempt to pressure EU policymakers into a hard approach, one in a Netflix funded study[89] and another in a study without relevant empirical evidence.[90] These studies point to the rules adopted in the US, but fail to mention that the American rules will likely be changed, if not struck down, by the courts. These studies fail to recognize the different political processes between the US and EU and why the EU approach is more inclusive and ultimately more sustainable.

The EU took its time in making the rules. For 18 months and through a number of leadership changes, the issue stayed credibly on top of the policy agenda. By placing net neutrality within the larger context of their Digital Single Market and Telecoms package, the EU offered a coherent framework and thoughtful portal[91] for the policy on its website. Furthermore, the fragmented nature of the EU forced the government to commission independent research and analysis,[92] thereby providing voters with a more developed view of the proposal. An additional official survey shows that EU consumers value net neutrality, but are willing to sacrifice some amount of it in exchange for lower prices.[93] In all, the EU's more thoughtful process fostered the buy-in of stakeholders and branches of government, increasing the likelihood that net neutrality endures in a meaningful way in the EU.

There was no formal evidence gathering or investigation in making the US rules, and the FCC issued no official report to support its proposed policy. In the EU, net neutrality has support from a broad coalition of parties, but in the US, it is clearly a Democrat vs. Republican issue. The Harvard University Berkman Center's assiduous analysis of coordinated media and advocacy concludes that net neutrality is a "conventionally defined partisan issue," as the media and journalists that support it follow party lines.[94]

While the spectacle of President Obama instructing the FCC to impose tough net neutrality rules[95] inspires advocates around the world, it presents a precarious legal future for net neutrality. That the FCC knowingly pursues a path that could result in net neutrality struck down forever begs the question of whether advocates are truly committed to net neutrality or driven primarily for the need to fundraise and therefore create a political theatre to portray the issue. Advocates are making a gamble

---

[89] Crawford and Scott (2015).

[90] Scott et al. (2015).

[91] European Commission (2015).

[92] Marcus (2014).

[93] "How Do Consumers Value Net Neutrality in an Evolving Internet Marketplace? A Report into Ecosystem Dynamics and Demand-Side Forces" (BEREC, June 2015), http://berec.europa.eu/eng/document_register/subject_matter/berec/download/0/5024-berec-report-on-how-consumers-value-net-_0.pdf.

[94] Faris (2015).

[95] Nagesh (2014).

not to seize the opportunity of the "high water mark" of support[96] for net neutrality and enshrine a law once and for all. The 2016 presidency can be a game changer in the mix of parties and political support. It is widely recognized that Obama had unprecedented support from Silicon Valley,[97] and it's not clear that the next candidate, even if she is a Democrat, will enjoy the same popularity.

This cynical view of the US will likely come as a surprise to advocates in other countries to whom net neutrality is synonymous with freedom of speech and something above such petty politicking. Indeed it is repugnant to those who wish to have evidence, not politics, to drive policy making.

Net neutrality advocates should take stock of their success, a growing global recognition of the value of an Open Internet. Advocates may equate hard rules with perfection, but the evidence clearly shows that there is no benefit to innovation or investment with the hard approach. The hard approach is overkill, and leads to litigation that may ultimately undo net neutrality rules all together.

The soft approach, on the other hand, has demonstrated success to deter violation and stimulate innovation. Moreover it offers net neutrality advocates an ongoing role to play in civil society.

The US even had its own multi-stakeholder model on net neutrality in 2011–2012,[98] and there is no reason why this dialogue can't be recreated. For the EU, the Nordic approach is proven to promote European companies and is more appropriate for Europe than that of the FCC which is aligned with American companies. Moreover a key first step to launch the European Digital Single Market is for the respective EU nations to digitize their public sectors and stimulate developers to create apps for their own countries. Denmark is a country which has used the public sector to drive Internet adoption. This is a path for other European countries, as lack of public sector digitization is a key area to be addressed.[99]

For the EU, US, and the rest of the world, the benefits of soft rules for net neutrality are clear. Soft is beautiful.

References

A View of Traffic Management and Other Practices Resulting in Restrictions to the Open Internet in Europe BEREC Findings on Traffic Management Practices in Europe – Traffic Management Investigation. (2012, May 29). http://ec.europa.eu/digital-agenda/sites/digital-agenda/files/Traffic%20Management%20Investigation%20BEREC_2.pdf

Antitrust: Commission Closes Investigation into Internet Connectivity Services but Will Continue to Monitor the Sector. (2014, October 3). *Europa.eu*, http://europa.eu/rapid/press-release_IP-14-1089_en.htm

---

[96] Brake (2015).

[97] Farivar (2012).

[98] "Open Internet Advisory Committee," FCC, (November 4, 2014), https://www.fcc.gov/encyclopedia/open-internet-advisory-committee.

[99] European Innovation Scoreboards (2015).

Bergström, O. Director at Swedish Post and Telecom Authority - PTS, Gives an Interview at ETNO-MLexSummit2014. viEUws(ETNO,2014,July7).www.vieuws.eu/etno/etno-etno-mlex-summit-2014-interview-with-ola-bergstrom-director-for-international-affairs-swedish-post-and-telecom-authority-pts/

Besluit van de Minister van Economische Zaken van 11 mei 2015, nr. WJZ/15062267, houdende beleidsregel inzake de toepassing door de Autoriteit Consument en Markt van artikel 7.4a van de Telecommunicatiewet (Beleidsregel netneutraliteit). (2015, May 15). officiële publicatie, *officielebekendmakingen*, https://zoek.officielebekendmakingen.nl/stcrt-2015-13478.html

Brake, D. (2015, August 14). Legal arguments take shape against title II. *The Innovation Files*, http://www.innovationfiles.org/legal-arguments-take-shape-against-title-ii/

Case Search – Competition – European Commission – Google. (2015, August 31). *Ec.europa.eu*, http://ec.europa.eu/competition/elojade/isef/case_details.cfm?proc_code=1_39740

Christiansen, C. (1997). The innovator's dilemma: When new technologies cause great firms to fail. *Harvard Business Review*.

Commission Welcomes Agreement to End Roaming Charges and to Guarantee an Open Internet. (2015, June 30). *Europa.eu*, http://europa.eu/rapid/press-release_IP-15-5265_en.htm

Consagra El Principio de Neutralidad En La Red Para Los Consumidores Y Usuarios de Internet. (Ley 20.45, 2010, August 26). http://www.leychile.cl/Navegar?idNorma=1016570&buscar=N EUTRALIDAD+DE+RED

Crawford, S. (2013, December 17). Stockholm and Leverett: Case studies in fiber deployment. *Scrawford.net*, http://scrawford.net/stockholm-and-leverett-case-studies-in-fiber-deployment/

Crawford, S., & Scott, B. (2015, June). Be careful what you wish for: Why Europe should avoid the mistakes of US internet access policy. *Stiftung-Nv*, http://www.stiftung-nv.de/sites/default/files/us-eu.internet.access.policy.pdf

Estabelece Princípios, Garantias, Direitos E Deveres Para O Uso Da Internet No Brasil. (Lei 12965, 2014, April 23). http://www.planalto.gov.br/ccivil_03/_ato2011-2014/2014/lei/l12965.htm

European Commission. (2015, June 10). Net neutrality challenges. *Digital Agenda for Europe*, http://digital-agenda/en/net-neutrality-challenges

European Innovation Scoreboards. (2015, July 8). *European Commission*, http://ec.europa.eu/growth/industry/innovation/facts-figures/scoreboards/index_en.htm

European Single Market for Electronic Communications. (2014, April 3). *Europeparl.europa.eu*, http://www.europarl.europa.eu/sides/getDoc.do?pubRef=-//EP//TEXT+TA+P7-TA-2014-0281+0+DOC+XML+V0//EN

Facts on Android. (2015, August 31). www.statista.com, http://www.statista.com/topics/876/android/

Falch, M., & Henten, A. (2015). European Broadband Policy – Regulation vs. Facilitation, Aalborg University, Denmark. doi:10.13140/RG.2.1.4728.0484.

Faris, R. (2015, February 10). Score another one for the Internet? The role of the networked public sphere in the U.S. net neutrality policy debate|Berkman Center. Harvard University, *Berkman Center for Internet and Society*. https://cyber.law.harvard.edu/publications/2015/score_another_one_for_the_internet

Farivar, C. (2012, May 30). Silicon valley donations to Obama reach record levels. *Ars Technica*, http://arstechnica.com/business/2012/05/silicon-valley-donations-to-obama-reach-record-levels/

FCC. (2015, March 12). Net neutrality ruling by FCC. https://apps.fcc.gov/edocs_public/attach-match/FCC-15-24A1.doc

FCC Open Internet Report & Order 10-201, Paragraph 14 (FCC, 2010, December 21), https://apps.fcc.gov/edocs_public/attachmatch/FCC-10-201A1_Rcd.pdf

FCC Open Internet Rules Paragraph 372 (p. 171). Retrieved August 20, 2015. https://apps.fcc.gov/edocs_public/attachmatch/FCC-15-24A1.doc

FCC Press Release. (2015, July 2). Public notice: Open internet advisory opinion procedures. https://www.fcc.gov/document/public-notice-open-internet-advisory-opinions

FCC Releases Open Internet Order. (2015, March 12). *FCC*, https://www.fcc.gov/document/fcc-releases-open-internet-order

Federal Communications Commission. (2015, March 12). Report and order on remand, declaratory ruling, and order. Washington DC: FCC. https://apps.fcc.gov/edocs_public/attachmatch/FCC-15-24A1.pdf

Freeman, C. (1995). The national system of innovation in historical perspective. *Cambridge Journal of Economics* (19), 5–24. http://www.degruyter.com/view/j/fman.2009.1.issue-2/v10238-012-0017-8/v10238-012-0017-8.xml

Geoghegan, T. (2013, October 28). Why is broadband more expensive in the US? *BBC News*. Washington. http://www.bbc.com/news/magazine-24528383

Grant, E., & Khosla, S. (2015, April 8). Here's everywhere Uber is banned around the world. *Business Insider*, http://www.businessinsider.com/heres-everywhere-uber-is-banned-around-the-world-2015-4?IR=T

Hattem, J. (2014, October 10). New net neutrality coalition gets first lobbyists. *The Hill*, http://thehill.com/policy/technology/220378-new-net-neutrality-coalition-gets-first-lobbyists

Henten, A., & Falch, M. (2014, June). The future of telecom regulation: The case of Denmark. http://vbn.aau.dk/en/publications/the-future-of-telecom-regulation(87df5174-0a28-4865-b5a4-5f4bf2c758f5).html

Hestres, L. E. (June 30, 2013). App neutrality: Apple's app store and freedom of expression online. *International Journal of Communication*, 7(0), 15.

How Do Consumers Value Net Neutrality in an Evolving Internet Marketplace? A Report into Ecosystem Dynamics and Demand-Side Forces. (2015, June). BEREC, http://berec.europa.eu/eng/document_register/subject_matter/berec/download/0/5024-berec-report-on-how--consumers-value-net-_0.pdf

Innovation Indicators. (2015, August 31). *OECD.org*, https://stats.oecd.org/Index.aspx?DataSetCode=REG_INNO_TL2

Karr, R. (2011, June 28). Why is European broadband faster and cheaper? Blame the government. *Engadget*, http://www.engadget.com/2011/06/28/why-is-european-broadband-faster-and-cheaper-blame-the-governme/

Kehl, D., Morgus, R., & Morris, S. (2014, October 30). The cost of connectivity 2014 – data and analysis on broadband offerings in 24 cities across the world. *New America*, http://www.newamerica.org/oti/the-cost-of-connectivity-2014/

Kelly, W. (2014, August 25). How Rahm Emanuel profits from brother Ari's Uber Payday. *Communities Digital News*, http://www.commdiginews.com/business-2/ari-emanuels-billion-dollar-uber-payday-and-what-it-means-for-rahm-24532/

Kende, M., & Rose, K. (2015, January 12). The content side of the access equation. Internet Society, http://www.internetsociety.org/blog/public-policy/2015/01/content-side-access-equation

Layton, R. (2014, September). Net neutrality regulation and broadband infrastructure investment: How to make an empirical assessment. *Network Neutrality: An Ongoing Regulatory Debate, Second Report of the Dynamic Coalition on Network Neutrality*. https://docs.google.com/file/d/0B4CMvT0NORh9RHhKa2IybThhR0U/edit?pli=1

Layton, R., & Elaluf-Calderwood, S. M. (2015, August 15). *Zero rating: Do hard rules protect or harm consumers and competition? Evidence from Chile, Netherlands and Slovenia*. SSRN Scholarly Paper. Rochester, NY: Social Science Research Network. http://papers.ssrn.com/abstract=2587542

Lemley, M. A., & Lessig, L. (2000, October 1). *The end of end-to-end: Preserving the architecture of the internet in the broadband era*. SSRN Scholarly Paper. Rochester, NY: Social Science Research Network. http://papers.ssrn.com/abstract=247737

Lemley, M. A., & Lessig, L. (2003, June 5). *The end of end-to-end: Preserving the architecture of the internet in the broadband era*. SSRN Scholarly Paper. Rochester, NY: Social Science Research Network. http://papers.ssrn.com/abstract=247737

Ley de Promocion de La Banda Ancha Y Construccion de La Red Dorsal Nacional de Fibra Optica. (Ley 29904, 2012, July 20). http://www.leyes.congreso.gob.pe/Documentos/Leyes/29904.pdf

Liebenau, J. (2012). Strategic challenges for the European telecom sector: The consequences of imbalances in internet traffic. *Journal of Information Policy*, 2, 248–272.

Liebenau, J., Elaluf-Calderwood, S., & Kärrberg, P. (2013, June). European internet traffic: Problems and prospects of growth and competition. Monograph, http://www.lse.ac.uk/management/research/initiatives/lseTech/home.aspx

Luca, M., Wu, T., & Yelp Data Science Team. (2015, June 28). Is Google degrading search? Consumer harm from universal search. http://www.slideshare.net/lutherlowe/wu-1

Marcus, J. S. (2014, December). Network neutrality revisited: Challenges and responses in the EU and in the USA. European Parliament, *IMCO Committee*. http://www.europarl.europa.eu/RegData/etudes/STUD/2014/518751/IPOL_STU(2014)518751_EN.pdf

Marsden, C. (2015, March 31). *Comparative case studies in implementing net neutrality: A critical analysis*. SSRN Scholarly Paper. Rochester, NY: Social Science Research Network. http://papers.ssrn.com/abstract=2587920

Measuring the Information Society Report 2014. (2014). ITU, http://www.itu.int/en/ITU-D/Statistics/Documents/publications/mis2014/MIS2014_without_Annex_4.pdf

Nagesh, G. (2014, November 10). Obama calls on FCC to issue rules protecting 'Net Neutrality. *Wall Street Journal*, sec. Tech. http://www.wsj.com/articles/obama-calls-on-fcc-to-issue-rules-protecting-net-neutrality-1415633678

Nätneutralitet.(2011).Post-ochTelestyrelsen(PTS),http://www.pts.se/sv/Bransch/Internet/Oppenhet-till-Internet/

Negro, G. (2015, June 11). Opinion: U.S. follows China's example on internet regulation. *InsideSources*, http://www.insidesources.com/u-s-follows-chinas-example-on-internet-regulation/

When It Comes to Net Neutrality, Why Don't People Talk about Operating Systems? (2013, June). *Strand Consult*, http://www.strandconsult.dk/sw5548.asp

Netflix Has Replaced Google as the Face of Net Neutrality Netflix Has Replaced Google as the Face of Net Neutrality. (2014, September 14). *National Journal*, http://www.nationaljournal.com/tech/netflix-has-replaced-google-as-the-face-of-net-neutrality-20140915

Nettnøytralitet: Retningslinjer for Nøytralitet På Internett. Oslo, NO: Post-og Teletilsynet (PT), February 24, 2009. http://www.nkom.no/teknisk/Internett/nettnøytralitet/nettnøytralitet/attachment/972?_ts=13837548973

Netzneutralität: Bericht Zur Arbeitsgruppe. Bern, SUI: Bundesamt für Kommunikation (BAKOM), October 23, 2014. http://www.bakom.admin.ch/themen/Internet/04810/index.html?lang=en%20Code%20of%20conduct

Neutralité de l'Internet et Des Réseaux. Paris, FR: Autorité de Régulation des Communications électroniques et des Postes (ARCEP), September 2010. http://www.arcep.fr/uploads/tx_gspublication/net-neutralite-orientations-sept2010.pdf

New Competition Promotion Program 2010. (2007, October 23). Ministry of Internal Affairs and Communications (MIC) Japan, *Soumu*, http://www.soumu.go.jp/main_sosiki/joho_tsusin/eng/Releases/Telecommunications/pdf/news071023_2_ap.pdf

Nye Jr., J. S. (2005). *Soft power: The means to success in world politics* (New Ed). New York: PublicAffairs.

O Razglasitvi Zakona O Elektronskih Komunikacijah (ZEKom-1). (2012, December 21). *Uradni*, http://www.uradni-list.si/1/content?id=111442

O'Brien, C. (2014, November 12). What France has taught me: Americans are suckers who have themselves to blame for Crappy broadband. *VentureBeat*, http://venturebeat.com/2014/11/12/what-france-has-taught-me-americans-are-suckers-who-have-themselves-to-blame-for-crappy-broadband/

O'connell, R. (2013, May 8). 10 app stores in China you really ought to be on, *Appflood*, http://appflood.com/blog/top-10-alternative-app-stores-from-china-2013

Ofcom's approach to net neutrality. London, UK: Ofcom, November 24, 2011. http://stakeholders.ofcom.org.uk/consultations/net-neutrality/statement/

Olukotun, D. (2015, August 11). Status of net neutrality around the world. *Blog|Access*, https://www.accessnow.org/blog/2015/08/11/hows-your-country-on-net-neutrality

Open Internet Advisory Committee. (November 4, 2014). FCC, https://www.fcc.gov/encyclopedia/open-internet-advisory-committee

Petitioners' Join Proposed Briefing Format and Schedule. (2015). United States Telecom Association, et al., v Federal Communications Commission, and United States of America. http://vcxc.org/documents/briefing_schedule.pdf

Por La Cual Se Expide El Plan Nacional de Desarrollo. (Ley 1450, 2011, June 16). http://www.wipo.int/wipolex/en/text.jsp?file_id=226358

Public Knowledge. (2015, May 15). Amicus Brief on behalf of FCC in US Telecom et al v. FCC. https://www.publicknowledge.org/assets/uploads/blog/CoCMotionForLeave.pdf

R: R Foundation Members & Supporters. (2015, September 7). https://www.r-project.org/foundation/donors.html

Expiden La Ley Federal de Telecomunicaciones Y Radiodifusion, Y La Ley Del Sistema Publico de Radiodifusion Del Mixcano; Y Se Reforman, Adicionan Y Derogan, Diversas Disposiciones En Materia de Telecomunicaciones Y Radiodifusion. (2014, July 14). http://www.diputados.gob.mx/LeyesBiblio/pdf/LFTR_140714.pdf

Ramos, A. (2014, October). The ASO book: App store optimization by Andreas Ramos. *Andreas.com*, http://andreas.com/book-aso.html

Ramos, A., & Cota, S. (2009). Search engine marketing. McGraw-Hill. http://andreas.com/book-search-engine-marketing.html

Report: China Surpasses United States by iOS Downloads. (2015, April 28). *App Annie Blog*, http://blog.appannie.com/china-surpasses-united-states-ios-downloads/

Rogers, E. M. (2003). *Diffusion of innovations* (5th ed.). New York: Free Press

Rogers, K. (2015, April 16). Meet six-figure entrepreneurs behind the Etsy IPO. *CNBC*, http://www.cnbc.com/2015/04/16/etsy-ipo-debuts-at-31share-as-some-sellers-make-six-figures.html

Samarbejde Om – Og Retningslinjer for "netneutralitet". Copenhagen, DK: Tele Industrien (TI), September 20, 2011. http://teleindu.dk/wp-content/uploads/2012/05/netneutralitetprincipper-20-09-2011.docx

Schumpeter, J. A. (1942) *Capitalism, socialism, and democracy*. New York: Harper.

Scott, B., Heumann, S., & Kleinhans, J-P. (2015, July 30). Landmark EU and US net neutrality decisions: How might pending decisions impact internet fragmentation? *Cigionline*, https://www.cigionline.org/publications/landmark-eu-and-us-net-neutrality-decisions-how-might-pending-decisions-impact-internet

Sebastien Soriano: Speech ETNO-MLEX 2015. (2015). European Telecommunications Network Operators' Association, https://www.etno.eu/home/news-room/pictures-videos/etno-mlex-regulatory-summit-2015-videos/sebastien-soriano-speech-etno-mlex-2015.

Silvius, S. (2011). Internet exchange points: A closer look at the differences between Continental Europe and the rest of the world. Amsterdam: EURO-IX. https://www.euro-ix.net/documents/894-ix

Singer, H. (2015, August 26). Does the tumble in broadband investment spell doom for the FCC's open internet order? Forbes, http://www.forbes.com/sites/halsinger/2015/08/25/does-the-tumble-in-broadband-investment-spell-doom-for-the-fccs-open-internet-order/

Smith, J. (2015, August 25). The net neutrality report: Where we are now, what happens next, and why mobile is central to the debate. *Business Insider*, http://uk.businessinsider.com/what-net-neutrality-means-for-mobiles-biggest-stakeholders-clone-2015-08

Sørensen, F. (2013). The Norwegian model for net neutrality. Norwegian Post and Telecommunications Authority. http://www.nkom.no/aktuelt/nyheter/_attachment/6472?_ts=13d3aeda9cc

Teece, D. (1986, June). Profiting from technological innovation: Implications for integration, collaboration, licensing and public policy. School of Business Administration, University of California, Berkeley, CA 94720, U.S.A. http://www4.lu.se/upload/CIRCLE/INN005/Teece_Reflections.pdf

Broadcasting and Telecom Decision CRTC 2015-26. Ottawa, CA: Canadian Radio-television and TelecommunicationsCommission,January29,2015.http://www.crtc.gc.ca/eng/archive/2015/2015-26.htm

Telecom Regulatory Policy CRTC 2009-657. Ottawa, CA: Canadian Radio-television and Telecommunications Commission, October 21, 2009. http://www.crtc.gc.ca/eng/archive/2009/2009-657.htm

Telecommunicatiewet. (2015, September 8). http://wetten.overheid.nl/BWBR0009950/Hoofdstuk7/Artikel74a/geldigheidsdatum_10-02-2014

The Bloomberg Innovation Index. (2015). *Bloomberg.com,* http://www.bloomberg.com/graphics/2015-innovative-countries/

The Global Innovation Index. (2015, September 17). *Global Innovation Index,* https://www.globalinnovationindex.org/content.aspx?page=GII-Home

Traffic Management Detection Methods & Tools. (2015). *Stakeholders.ofcom.org.uk,* http://stakeholders.ofcom.org.uk/market-data-research/other/technology-research/2015-reports/traffic-management

Van Eijk, N. (2014, August 2). The proof of the pudding is in the eating: Net neutrality in practice, the Dutch example. SSRN Scholarly Paper. Rochester, NY: Social Science Research Network. http://papers.ssrn.com/abstract=2417933

Vargas-Leon, P. (2014, September). Network neutrality: An ongoing regulatory debate, Chapter 2. *2nd Report for Dynamic Coalition of Net Neutrality.* https://docs.google.com/file/d/0B4CMvT0NORh9RHhKa2IybThhR0U/edit?pli=1

Veigle, A. (2015, July 8). Amicus briefs show open internet order illegalities. *USTelecom,* http://www.ustelecom.org/blog/amicus-briefs-show-open-internet-order-illegalities

Weller, D., & Woodcock, B. (2013, January 29). *Internet Traffic Exchange.* OECD Digital Economy Papers. Paris: Organisation for Economic Co-operation and Development. http://www.oecd-ilibrary.org/content/workingpaper/5k918gpt130q-en

Why Can't We Be Like South Korea? When Internet Access Is Slow or Just Nonexistent in the US, We Shrug Our Shoulders. But in That Small Asian Nation, Lousy Connections Are Not Tolerated.(2015,July23).*Medium,*https://medium.com/backchannel/why-can-t-we-be-like-south-korea-58d8d702030d

WIPO Intellectual Property Statistics Data Center. (2015, July 24). *Ipstats.wipo.int,* http://ipstats.wipo.int/ipstatv2/index.htm?tab=patent

World Telecommunication/ICT Indicators Database. (2015, June). *ITU,* http://www.itu.int/en/ITU-D/Statistics/Pages/publications/wtid.aspx

Wu, T. (2003). Network neutrality, broadband discrimination. *Journal of Telecommunications and High Technology Law, 2*(1), 141–176. http://papers.ssrn.com/abstract=388863

Yoo, C. (2009, September). Free speech and the myth of the internet as an unintermediated experience. *George Washington Law Review, Vol. 78, Pg. 697, 2010 University of Pennsylvania, Inst for Law & Econ Research Paper No. 09-33 University of Pennsylvania Law School, Public Law Research Paper No. 09-26 TPRC 2009,* 77.

Chapter 14
Net Neutrality: An Analysis of the European Union's Trialogue Compromise

Joe McNamee and Maryant Fernández Pérez

In September 2013, the European Commission launched its "Telecommunications Single Market" Regulation. This was a heavily political proposal, which needlessly squeezed fully and partially unrelated issues such as roaming, spectrum, net neutrality and users' rights into the same instrument. After ignoring three Parliament resolutions calling for net neutrality proposals in the previous 4 years, the Commission finally issued its (deeply flawed) proposal, with just 9 months to go before the May 2014 European Parliament elections.

In this paper, we provide an analysis and background of the political compromise reached in July 2015, after intense political negotiations between the European Commission, the European Parliament and the Council of the European Union, the so-called "trialogue" negotiations.[1] In the autumn 2015, the Parliament is going to approve, amend or reject the net neutrality text put forward by the trialogue compromise.

14.1 A Brief History

14.1.1 Introduction

In September 2013, the European Commission launched its "Telecommunications Single Market" Regulation. This was a heavily political proposal, which needlessly squeezed fully and partially unrelated issues such as roaming, spectrum, net neutrality and users' rights into the same instrument. After ignoring three Parliament

---

[1] Trialogues are informal, closed-door meetings between the three institutions, with a limited number of participants to work towards an agreement. The process is regulated by Parliament's "rules of procedure".

J. McNamee (✉) • M.F. Pérez
European Digital Rights, Brussels, Belgium

© Springer International Publishing Switzerland 2016
L. Belli, P. De Filippi (eds.), *Net Neutrality Compendium*,
DOI 10.1007/978-3-319-26425-7_14

resolutions calling for net neutrality proposals in the previous 4 years,[2] the Commission finally issued its (deeply flawed) proposal, with just 9 months to go before the May 2014 European Parliament elections.

14.1.2 Initial Commission Proposal (September 2013)

While claiming to support net neutrality and written in a way which sought to give this impression, the Commission's proposal was peppered with loopholes that would have profoundly undermined the neutral, innovative internet in Europe.

A perfect example of this misleading drafting was Article 23.5 of the initial proposal. While appearing to ban blocking and other forms of discrimination, this was limited to situations where (potentially very low) agreed data volumes and speeds were implemented. Outside of any such agreed data volumes and speeds, the rules would not have applied.

> 23.5. *Within the limits of any contractually agreed data volumes or speeds* for internet access services, providers of internet access services shall not restrict the freedoms provided for in paragraph 1 by blocking, slowing down, degrading or discriminating against specific content, applications or services, or specific classes thereof, except in cases where it is necessary to apply reasonable traffic management measures. (emphasis added)

The proposal limited the scope of the ban on discriminatory treatment to discrimination that fell within "any data volumes or speeds", thus severely limiting the range of the ban on discriminatory traffic management. Laws should be designed to clearly achieve their policy goal, rather than creating legislative loopholes, as in this case. As regards net neutrality legislation, the goal is to avoid discriminatory conducts, which are motivated by economic interests and can harm users' rights and interests.

14.1.3 Parliament First Reading (April 2014)

Racing against time, with the elections coming in May 2014, the European Parliament worked hard to close the many obvious and not-so-obvious loopholes in the Commission's chaotic, contradictory net neutrality provisions, at the same time as assessing and amending the chaotic proposals in this four-regulations-in-one-text proposal.

---

[2] On 17 November 2011, on 26 October 2012 and on 11 December 2012, cf. EDRi and Access (2015)

The Parliament did a solid job in fixing the loopholes. For example, the above text was amended to say:

> 23.5. Providers of internet access services and end-users may agree to set limits on data volumes or speeds for internet access services. Providers of internet access services shall not restrict the freedoms provided for in paragraph 1 *by blocking, slowing down, altering, degrading or discriminating against specific content, applications or services*, or specific classes thereof, except in cases where it is necessary to apply traffic management measures. (emphasis added)

Similarly, the Parliament changed the definition of "specialised services" to make it clear that these could not be "functionally equivalent" to online services.

14.1.4   Council Agreement (March 2015)

The Member States of the EU, in the Council, pulled the European Commission's proposal to pieces. It deleted the sections on radio spectrum management and end-user rights, severely watered down the provisions on roaming and produced an entirely destructive, loophole-ridden text on the "open internet". Indeed, the Council refused to mention, either in debates or in written documents, the words "net neutrality".

As proposed by the Council, the Regulation would have been vastly worse than useless, with all of the relevant provisions totally annihilated by gaping loopholes. Recital 7 is just one of many egregious examples:

> End-users, including providers of content, applications and services, should **therefore remain free to conclude agreements** with providers of electronic communications to the public, **which require** specific levels of quality of service. (emphasis added)

In short, the "safeguard" suggested by the Council to ensure that anti-competitive fast-lanes are not created on the internet was that there needed to be an agreement between either the online service or the "end-user" and the access provider! Again, this is the very essence of bad regulation—the text added confusion, sent a needless political message and permitted exactly what it claimed to prevent.

14.1.5   Informal Trialogue Negotiations (March–June 2015)

After the adoption of the Council political agreement in March 2015, the informal "trialogue" negotiations started. For the entire 4 months of the negotiations, the Council put intense pressure on the Parliament to compromise. At each step, the Parliament compromised and the response of the Council was to say "we welcome your compromise, now please give in on everything"[3] and to make public statements complaining about the Parliament's unwillingness to compromise.[4] Due to the abusive, undemocratic posture of the Council for the entire period of the negotiations, it always seemed that the best outcome available would be a very bad agreement or no agreement at all.

14.2   Need for Improvement

At the beginning of July 2015, a political compromise[5] was reached. In the final stage of the negotiations, the Parliament persuaded the Council to move a little from its initial position. We congratulate the Parliament for this achievement. However, there are five points for which the text needs important clarifications on private law enforcement, congestion, traffic management, price discrimination and "specialised services".

14.2.1   Private Law Enforcement and Other Censorship

It is essential to remember that the Charter of Fundamental Rights is applicable to issues regulated by the EU legal framework.[6]

Article 2.2 of the compromise clearly states that connections should be available to all technically available end points. The recital dealing with illegal content (recital 9) makes it clear that the obligations of the Charter of Fundamental Rights apply to any restrictions, such as blocking, that may be applied by internet providers:

> (…) The requirement to comply with Union law relates, among others, to the compliance with the requirements of the Charter of Fundamental rights of the European Union in relation to limitations of fundamental rights and freedoms. (…)

---

[3] That can be extracted from the different "compromises" proposed by the Latvian Presidency (the presidency which led the discussions during the trialogue negotiations) on behalf the Council, accessible at EDRi, Net Neutrality: document pool II, available at https://edri.org/net-neutrality-document-pool-2/.

[4] See, for instance, statements at the Ministerial meeting on 12 June 2015, cf. EDRi, Council confirms it wants to trade net neutrality for end of roaming charges, available at https://edri.org/council-confirms-it-wants-to-trade-net-neutrality-for-end-of-roaming-charges/.

[5] The text is accessible at www.consilium.europa.eu/en/press/press-releases/2015/07/pdf/st10409-re01_en15_pdf/.

[6] See European Parliament (2014).

One of the requirements of the Charter is that restrictions must be provided for by law. However, in Article 3.3.a the Regulation states that blocking of content is possible by "measures giving effect to such Union or national legislation, in compliance with Union law, **including** with orders by courts **or public authorities vested with relevant powers**" (emphasis added). Here, the Regulation appears to contradict itself, as it is not possible to comply with the requirements of the Charter in relation to limitations of fundamental rights and freedoms and, implicitly, permit blocking (by measures other than court orders or orders of legally empowered authorities) that is not provided for by a (specific, predictable) law.

There is likely to be a huge amount of argument about the Regulation "banning" the voluntary blocking of *alleged* child abuse websites. However, the inclusion of blocking in the 2011 Child Exploitation Directive (2011/92/EC) meant that blocking was already part of the EU legal framework and, therefore, the provisions of the Charter with regard to restrictions needing to be provided for by law already apply, regardless of the recital which claims the contrary.

"Parental controls" are a service that can be added to an internet access service that allow a parent to block or filter certain content based on various criteria that they choose, such as pornography or violence or the length of time the child is allowed to be online. In at least one EU country, internet providers have such controls turned on by default. Sometimes these are difficult to turn off and sometimes services are "dumb", offering no "control" to parents to adjust the filters to suit the educational needs and development of children.

Under the compromise text, it will, of course, continue to be possible for both internet providers and software providers to offer such services. However, it will not be possible for internet companies to arbitrarily block content by default and without request, under the name of "parental controls". The compromise gives the control back to parents.

The removal of proposals on "parental controls" is a clear improvement as compared with the Council text agreed in March (the text that started the trialogue negotiations). However, it may be argued that the aforementioned provisions are contradictory and particularly unclear, and may lead to breaches of the Charter of Fundamental Rights. The relevant recital seems also to be exceptionally badly drafted and includes text that has no agreed meaning.

14.2.2   Congestion

The European Commission initially foresaw open-ended rights for internet companies to "manage" their traffic for reasons of "congestion", with very few restrictions on how this provision could be (ab)used. The final text is weak in that it includes a provision on preventing "impending" network congestion, with few safeguards on how this can be interpreted.

However, the text does require the congestion to be either "temporary" or "exceptional" and, at the request of the Parliament, this is now explained in a much more comprehensive way. While it remains difficult to interpret "impending" congestion, the exception appears tight enough to ensure that it cannot easily be used indefinitely as a strategy for hiding anti-competitive behaviour.

In sum, thanks to the provisions of the recital on the "temporary" or "exceptional" nature of the implementation of this exception, the compromise text is probably workable, although the provision on "impending" congestion is unnecessary and adds a degree of doubt.

14.2.3 *"Traffic Management" Without Congestion*

The basis for network neutrality is the "best effort" principle. Network management should be limited to times of congestion and be as application agnostic[7] as possible, in order to preserve the neutral character and innovative capacity of the network. Deviations from this principle have to be limited and justified. Rather than emphasising the "best effort" principle and recognising its contribution to the success of the internet, Article 3.3 and Recital 8 allow for deviations which are not limited to the exceptions provided for in Article 3. Consequently, the potential justifications for such traffic management are not clear. The "right" to manage traffic in this way is clearly not meant to be open-ended, as it can only be maintained for as long as "necessary", with no clarification at all as regards what this might mean.

That relevant recital states that network management outside of congestion is possible if it is based on "objectively different technical quality of service requirements of specific categories of traffic". These categories cannot be based on commercial considerations, but are nonetheless established by the Internet Service Provider (ISP) and allow for discrimination against a whole category of applications (video streaming, file uploads, etc). It also could imply a degree of surveillance of data traffic to assess the kinds of content they contain (but not the specific content), to the potential detriment of protocols such as FTP, P2P, protocols not recognised by the network and even to the detriment of encrypted data, whose requirements cannot be read and risk being assumed to have lower priority. This can lead to traffic management which appear to be neutral as defined by Recital 8, but is nonetheless arbitrary from the point of view of end-users and content/application providers, and ultimately to the detriment of end-user choice. The disadvantages of this type of traffic management are likely to outweigh the advantages in many cases, particularly for users relying on de-prioritised categories of data, such as businesses that exchange large files using protocols such as FTP or peer-to-peer or data which is encrypted and whose priority may, therefore, not be known to the internet access provider.

The first and last lines of Recital 8 on "traffic management" appear to convey opposite messages. The first sentence suggests that the "traffic management" being referred to is a standard practice for maintaining an efficient network. The final sentence says, however, that it should only be "maintained for as long as is necessary",

---

[7] As opposed to application-specific. See Van Schwick (2010).

suggesting that it is an exceptional activity. It should be clarified that traffic management under Recital 8 is not meant to be a permanent activity, as appears to be the intention behind the final sentence of the recital.

In order to preserve a user-centric internet, the aforementioned provisions should be amended to limit "traffic management" to times of congestion and give priority to application agnostic resolution strategies, which are the strategies that have the internet has successfully used until now.

14.2.4   Price Discrimination (Zero-Rating)

Price discrimination schemes allow internet users to pay for a certain volume of download capacity and get unlimited access to some websites but not all the internet. Such schemes are controversial because they limit users' fundamental right to send and receive information—the very opposite of net neutrality. Price discrimination achieves the same goal (from the side of the telecoms operator) as any other form of net neutrality violation, as it allows the operator to demand payment from online companies for privileged access to their customers. It may be argued that the consequences of this practice are as harmful as other forms of net neutrality violations, as it splits the online population between those who can pay for "full" internet access, those who cannot pay for such access and between those who can pay for the privilege of an unlimited freedom to communicate information and ideas and those who cannot.

This is the point where the Regulation is the most unclear. The Commission and Council tried very hard to add wording to the legislation that would clearly allow price discrimination.[8] The Parliament's first reading text did not permit price discrimination, but did not make this point explicitly. In the end, negotiators agreed not to legislate on this point.

However, the agreed text could be argued to permit price discrimination, as it allows agreements on data volumes and commercial practices that do not completely remove the right of end-users to use and provide content, services and applications of their choice. It could also be read as prohibiting price discrimination, on the basis that this would amount to a discrimination on the basis of the services being used and that it would limit the right to distribute information. Parliament negotiators were assured that the issue was NOT covered by the Regulation. This was confirmed at the press conference involving the Parliament's Rapporteur (Ms Del Castillo) and Commissioner Oettinger (among others), where Ms Del Castillo made it clear that she believed that zero rating was not covered and was not contradicted by the Commissioner.[9] Now, however, the European Commission has produced a grossly inaccurate analysis of what zero-rating is, how it works and, implicitly, that it is regulated by the agreed text.[10]

---

[8] Cf. Recital 47 and Article 23(5) of the Commission's proposal and recitals 6 and 8 of the Council's March text.

[9] Press conference of 30 June 2015, available at http://www.europarl.europa.eu/ep-live/en/other-events/video?event=20150630-1415-SPECIAL&utm_campaign=engagor&utm_content=engagor_MzgyOTE2MQ%3D%3D&utm_medium=social&utm_source=twitter&ms=1435673400.

[10] European Commission (2015).

It is important to note that if zero-rating is considered by courts as being allowed by the Regulation, then national decisions to ban zero rating (such as in the Netherlands) would be overturned. The easiest way to resolve this problem is for the Parliament at least to add an amendment to confirm that zero rating is not regulated in the legislation. At best, the Parliament should add an amendment definitively banning price discrimination, a practice that is an affront to competition and freedom of communication.

14.2.5 "Specialised Services"

In the Commission's initial proposal, such "fast lane" services were (badly) defined by the Regulation. The Parliament suggested a narrower, clearer definition. The final agreement sets a number of criteria, but these are very subjective. These are:

– optimisation is necessary in order to meet requirements of the content, applications or services for a specific level of quality;
– that the quality of service levels cannot be "assured" (the meaning of which is very unclear) by an internet access service;
– optimisation is objectively necessary to ensure one or more specific and key features of the content, application or service and to enable a corresponding quality assurance to be given to end-users; and
– that the optimisation is not simply granting general priority over comparable content, applications or services available via the internet access service and thereby circumventing the provisions regarding traffic management applicable to the internet access service.

The abovementioned criteria would be good enough for a good regulator to implement efficiently, without fear of being successfully sued. However, those criteria are weak enough to discourage politically and economically weak national regulators from implementing them correctly. As the Body of European Regulators for Electronic Communications (BEREC) Guidelines will severely limit the interpretation and application scope of these provisions, the outcome cannot be foreseen.

14.3 Conclusion: The Parliament's Second Reading

In autumn 2015, the Parliament will need to approve, amend or reject the net neutrality text which, due to the chaotic initial Commission proposal, is still attached to the "roaming surcharge ban" (that does not, incidentally, ban roaming surcharges).[11]

---

[11] See, for instance, BEUC (2015).

As the compromise currently stands, the EU institutions have avoided making a choice. It has left it up to courts and unelected regulators to seek to give meaning to some of the key elements of the Regulation.

The Parliament has a choice, therefore. It either has to table amendments to give meaning to the provisions, or it, can decide not to decide. To this extent, the Rapporteur and Shadow Rapporteurs should urgently consider the preparation and adoption of amendments to the compromise text in order to:

– remove unverifiable "impending" congestion exception for traffic management or at least narrow the contexts in which it can be used in a way that would make this meaningful;
– confirm that "traffic management" does not go beyond the basic, best-effort principle that is the essence of the internet's success;
– either clearly prohibit "price discrimination" or make it clear that Member States who wish to protect competition by banning such discrimination remain free to do so;
– revert to a clearer definition of "specialised service", to give regulators the tools to do their job more effectively.

Alternatively, a regulation meant to foster harmonisation may *de facto* foster regulatory fragmentation and European citizens and online businesses will have to wait to find out how courts and regulatory authorities decide to interpret the regulation.

References

BEUC. (2015, June 30). EU reaches unambitious deal on roaming charges and net neutrality. Available at http://www.beuc.eu/publications/beuc-pr-2015-012_telecom_single_market.pdf
EDRi and Access. (2015, June 1). Net Neutrality—building on success. Available at https://edri.org/net-neutrality-non-compromises/
EDRi. Council confirms it wants to trade net neutrality for end of roaming charges, available at https://edri.org/council-confirms-it-wants-to-trade-net-neutrality-for-end-of-roaming-charges/
European Commission. (2015, June 30). Roaming charges and open Internet: Questions and answers. Available at http://europa.eu/rapid/press-release_MEMO-15-5275_en.htm
European Parliament. (2014). Fundamental rights in the European Union: The role of the charter after the Lisbon Treaty. Available at http://www.europarl.europa.eu/RegData/etudes/IDAN/2015/554168/EPRS_IDA%282015%29554168_EN.pdf
Van Schwick, B. (2010). Network neutrality: What a non-discrimination rule should look like. Stanford Public Law Working Paper No. 1684677, 2010. Available at http://papers.ssrn.com/sol3/papers.cfm?abstract_id=1684677

Part III
Network Neutrality in Action: Challenges and Implementations

This final part analyses the most recent challenges to the network neutrality debate as well as the implementation of net neutrality regulations in different jurisdictions. The contributions contained in this Part critically analyse the most recent regulatory approaches to net neutrality, suggesting elements that should be taken into account in order to develop solid national approaches. Emerging challenges are explored, nurturing a reflection on the implementation of net neutrality policies to zero-rating schemes, Internet access provision through drones and grassroots community networks. To conclude, a legally interoperable approach to net neutrality is proposed, identifying the core elements of net neutrality policies and distilling them in a Policy Statement to be discussed at the 10th United Nations Internet Governance Forum.

The preservation of openness, the protection of end-users rights and the maximisation of consumers' welfare may be seen as some of the core objectives of net neutrality policies. The regulatory intervention aimed at preserving network neutrality is not only motivated by the existence of market failures, but also on the need to preserve users' fundamental rights. As such, net neutrality regulations should carefully consider the impact of market practices on end-users' fundamental rights and consumers' expectations.

Arnold et al. argue that, at the European level, little effort has been made to date by policymakers to understand properly consumers' preferences, values or motivations. Notably, the authors note that, despite the European Commission's attempt to frame its 2012 Public Consultation on network neutrality around the actual needs and preferences of consumers, the results of the consultations are not always reliable, and often do not properly reflect the actual values and motivations of consumers. To emphasize this point, the authors compare the views expressed in the European Commission's public consultation with the results of a representative study on the value of network neutrality to European consumers, undertaken by the authors in 2014. Based on this empirical study, the authors show that the views expressed by citizens in the public consultation differ significantly from representative consumer's preferences and values. While consumers generally tend to favor an open and neutral Internet, their preferences towards network neutrality are in fact much more nuanced than it appears from the public consultation. As such, the authors argue that a more widespread use of representative consumer's insights, based on objectively unbiased sampling, should be used to support policy making and regulation.

The elaboration of sound net neutrality frameworks may also require the further consideration of some elements that have not been duly considered over the past decade. In this regard, Konstantinos Stylianou argues that in most jurisdictions a sustainable net neutrality regime has not yet emerged, despite persistent regulatory efforts. According to the author, in the US, Europe and Latin America, net neutrality rules are either frequently changed or frequently challenged or impossible to adopt in the first place. Three main reasons may be found at the origin of such difficulties. First, regulators as well as involved stakeholders frequently push for black-and-white solutions, disregarding the nuances of the implicated issues, thus tending to be either overinclusive or under-inclusive. A solution to this problem may be offered by flexible framework clauses, like those used in antitrust, which may be capable of filtering out harmful practices while allowing non-harmful ones. Further integration of antitrust-like analysis and principles into telecommunications regulation would indeed offer regulatory tools that can accommodate the arguments of both sides. Second, the author criticise the insistence on traditional principles of the Internet architecture, arguing that they may not be fully applicable or beneficial today as when the Internet was first conceived and commercialised. As an instance Stylianou argues that mobile cellular networks, which are more managed and more complex than fix ones, may not benefit from the imposition of the original Internet design principles that should be reconsidered in order to allow free technological evolution. Lastly, the author suggests that regulators need to focus further on the competitive conditions in the market, which includes the identification of potential bottlenecks and the power interrelations among them. Current practice seems to pay insufficient attention to modern power interrelations and may fail to identify which players are favourably positioned in the value chain. Hence, further analysis of the relevant players their mutual interrelations may be very beneficial.

The first semester of 2015 has been characterised by the attempt to define sustainable net neutrality approaches, sparking intense debate and substantial novelties as regards net neutrality regulation. In February the U.S. Federal Communications Commission published its new net neutrality rules; on 1 July a political agreement about the European net neutrality rules was reached between the European Commission, the Parliament, and the Council; and heated discussions have emerged, as regards the compatibility of zero-rating schemes with the non-discriminatory treatment mandated by net neutrality policies and regulations. Regulators have been very active, proposing and implementing net neutrality rules around the globe. In this regard, Frode Sørensen explores the most recent European and US approaches to net neutrality through his article on "A Norwegian perspective on European regulation of net neutrality". The author highlights that the two approaches have similarities and differences. Similarities may be easily understood due to cross-Atlantic influence while the interpretation of the differences requires further reflection. Frode Sørensen discusses some key elements that have characterised net neutrality debates both in the U.S. and EU, such as application-agnosticism, reasonable traffic management, specialised services and, finally, zero-rating. The author's analysis seems instrumental to understand current as well as future net neutrality discussions, clarifying that the goal of net neutrality is not to treat all traffic identically but rather to preserve the Internet as an open platform for communication and avoid discrimination between applications or fragmentation.

Analysing the concept of application-agnosticism, Sorensen stresses that this is not only a technical characteristic regarding traffic management practices but also reveals economic implications on charging models, leading to conclusions on zero-rating. A major criticism that has been raised regarding the political compromise on European net neutrality rules is that it hardly addresses zero-rating practices on which net neutrality discussions are increasingly concentrating. In this regard, the author explains that the goal of non-discrimination should be kept in mind when analysing charging models that, due to the commercial incentive to select specific applications, leads to favour specific traffic above other traffic. As Sørensen points out, this is exactly the type of situation that net neutrality policies should aim to avoid.

The growing trend towards the provision of sponsored data plans in mobile services seems one of the most important challenges that Network Neutrality is currently facing. In many developing countries, where broadband connection is not or hardly present on the territory, mobile phones are the main source of Internet connectivity. Yet, in order to optimise Internet traffic management, most mobile operators introduced specific data plans to cap the amount of Internet traffic that can be achieved through the telephone subscription, with the exception of the traffic stemming from affiliate partners, so-called sponsored content. In his article on Zero Rating and Mobile Net Neutrality, Chris Marsden considers whether sponsored data plans pose an actual challenge to Internet openness and the extent to which zero rating may or may not infringe the network neutrality principle. In particular, the author suggests two regulatory actions to encourage the correct use of zero rating: treating zero rating as a short-term exception to net neutrality, and ensuring that any such short-term exception is not exclusive.

Subsequently, the report investigates the potential implications of network neutrality regulations in a variety of new and innovative contexts, ranging from community mesh networks to civilian drones. Primavera De Filippi and Félix Tréguer analyse the question through the lenses of the network commons, by investigating how public policy could help promote the deployment of open and non-discriminatory community networks. The authors first provide a historical overview of the Internet access market in Europe, to subsequently focus on the rise of Wireless Community Networks (WCN) as a communitarian reaction to the growing centralization of the Internet network, combined with the advent of draconian regulations encouraging the surveillance and control of online communi-cation. De Filippi and Tréguer highlight the new power dynamics emerging in today's telecom infrastructures, by describing the interplay that subsists between telecom operators and grassroots community networks. While WCNs potentially constitute an important counter-power that could limit the abuses that commercial operators have the capability to inflict on their user-base, the authors bring attention to the fact that current telecom regulations creates significant hurdles that might significantly restrain the deployment of large-scale WCNs. The chapter concludes with a series of policy recommendations to support the deployment of community networks and promote the development of the network commons.

Similar reasons motivate the deployment of unmanned aircraft systems (UAS)—commonly known as drones—for novel applications such as the delivery of broadband connectivity to remote areas with no Internet or telephone coverage. As explained by Leonidas Kanellos, in some developing countries, companies such as Google and Facebook are already undertaking these activities with solar-powered drones and high-altitude balloons, while at the U.S. level they have already obtained relevant testing licenses from the FCC. Yet, to ensure coverage across wider regions, inter-drone communication needs to be established and maintained. In his article on the 'Network Neutrality Aspects of Civilian Drones', Kanellos explores emergent policy questions related to the use of civilian drones to provide Internet access to underserved areas. Specifically, the article investigates the opportunities that these aerial devices provide in terms of extended broadband connectivity, as well as the implications of traditional platforms such as Google and Facebook progressively turning into access providers. The article concludes with an illustration of the potential negative impacts of drones on the privacy and security of users, stressing the need for a coherent regulation of drones at the global level.

As a conclusion of this book, Luca Belli and Nathalia Foditsch analyse net neutrality under the lenses of legal interoperability, identifying the basic elements that a net neutrality policy statement should include. A network of networks based on a globally interoperable architecture may be considered as difficulty reconcilable with an international system based on mutually excluding legal frameworks. Indeed, while the technical Internet standards allow heterogeneous networks to communicate and cooperate, legislations and regulations are essentially based on national sovereignty, whose inherent purpose is to establish different domestic approaches. As technical interoperability aims at making networks work together, legal interoperability aims at making national rules compatible across jurisdictions, thus avoiding legal fragmentation. Luca Belli and Nathalia Foditsch analyse the importance of fostering legal interoperability, in order to allow legal systems to frame common problems in a compatible fashion, as technical standards do. Shared principles and compatible rules amongst various juridical systems have, indeed, the potential to decrease transaction costs, reduce barriers to cross-border trade, and introduce important non-monetizable benefits, by fostering individual empowerment and ensuring the protection of fundamental rights.

Net neutrality policy focuses on Internet traffic management, an issue virtually affecting every electronic network composing the Internet. To date, national legislators and regulators have been adopting different approaches for the promotion of net neutrality, although many similarities and common features can nonetheless be identified. To this extent, it seems both possible and useful to analyse existing regulatory frameworks in order to synthesise best practices within a principle statement, which may be used to foster a shared level net neutrality protection. Indeed, due to the transnational nature of the Internet, the development of legally interoperable net neutrality frameworks may prove beneficial in order to preserve the open, distributed and general-purpose nature of the Internet, while simultaneously setting shared standards for protection of end-users' rights. Luca Belli and Nathalia Foditsch scrutinise the network neutrality concept and stress its importance for maintaining the original architecture of the Internet, by preserving technical interoperability and fostering global connectivity on a non-discriminatory basis. After having identified common features shared by existing net neutrality frameworks, the authors propose a common principle-based approach that may be used to develop legally-interoperable net neutrality regulations, fostering legal certainty without introducing excessive legal fragmentation. Such principle-based approach has been elaborated through an open and multi-stakeholder process, organised through the IGF Dynamic Coalition on Network Neutrality and presented as an outcome of the Coalition at the 10th Internet Governance Forum.

Chapter 15
All But Neutral: Citizen Responses to the European Commission's Public Consultation on Network Neutrality

René C.G. Arnold, J. Scott Marcus, Martin Waldburger, Anna Schneider, Bastian Morasch, and Frieder Schmid

Network neutrality is a complex and multi-faceted subject. Not surprisingly, consumer views toward network neutrality appear to be correspondingly complex and nuanced.

Our paper highlights the relevance of objective, representative consumer research for regulatory and policy decisions regarding the European network neutrality debate. Despite its immediate impact on consumers, little effort has been made to date by policymakers to understand consumers' preferences, values or motivations. Moreover, much of the assessment of such consumer preference data as is available tends to be simplistic and/or misleading. To emphasize this point, we compare views expressed in the public consultation on network neutrality that was conducted by the European Commission in 2012 and comprehensively reported on in a 2014 study by the authors for the European Parliament, with those from a representative study of the value of network neutrality to European consumers undertaken in 2014, also led by the authors.

We find that the views expressed in the public consultation differ significantly from representative consumer preferences and values. For instance, consumer opinions about traffic management were largely negative among citizens in the public consultation, while the unbiased survey results demonstrate that there is in fact a substantial segment of consumers who are interested in purchasing prioritized services. More generally, our results shed some doubts on the reliability of public consultations and other surveys where respondents are self-selected as a sole means to understand consumers' preferences, values and motivations. We argue for a more widespread use of representative consumer insights based on objectively unbiased sampling to support policy making and regulation.

R.C.G. Arnold (✉) • J. Scott Marcus • M. Waldburger
WIK-consult GmbH, Bad Honnef, Germany
e-mail: r.arnold@wik-consult.com

A. Schneider • B. Morasch • F. Schmid
YouGov Deutschland AG Cologne, Cologne, Germany

© Springer International Publishing Switzerland 2016
L. Belli, P. De Filippi (eds.), *Net Neutrality Compendium*,
DOI 10.1007/978-3-319-26425-7_15

15.1 Introduction

Network neutrality is a complex and multi-faceted subject. Not surprisingly, consumer views toward network neutrality appear to be correspondingly complex and nuanced. We question whether the public debate about network neutrality to date has properly captured the richness and complexity of consumer views.

Potential concerns involve:

- The relative paucity of serious, objective studies of consumer attitudes and preferences toward network neutrality; and
- The risk that there might be a minority of consumers who hold strong and polarized views, and that because they are vocal they might be far more visible than large numbers of consumers whose views are more complex.

This possible risk of a distorted view of consumer preferences is the main focus of this paper. The risk is linked to the well-known statistical phenomenon of *self-selection bias*—when respondents to a survey or consultation select themselves, those who feel most strongly about the issue are disproportionately likely to respond. Those who conduct serious surveys of consumer (or voter) behavior typically invest a great deal of effort in ensuring that their samples are *representative*.

There is good reason to worry about possible self-selection bias in surveys and consultations relating to network neutrality. First, one might well wonder what fraction of citizens are, in the normal course of events, even aware of public consultations on network neutrality conducted by the European Commission, or BEREC, or Member State governments. Second, one might wonder what fraction of the public has sufficient awareness and knowledge to motivate them to take the trouble to comment.

In this paper, we aim to shed light on the degree of self-selection bias by comparing (1) the responses of self-selected citizens from the public consultation conducted by the European Commission on network neutrality in 2012 to (2) those of a representative sample used in a study on behalf of BEREC (the European Board of Regulators of Electronic Communications) on the value of network neutrality to European consumers. To this end, we draw on two studies conducted by the authors of this paper for the European Parliament[1] and BEREC[2] in 2014.

The remainder of the paper is structured as follows. First, we briefly summarize the existing literature on consumers' attitudes to and preferences for network neutrality as well as network neutrality-related product attributes for Internet Access Services (IAS). Second, the methodology used for the two studies is reported. Third, we compare the results of the public consultation and the representative consumers survey on network neutrality. The paper closes with concluding remarks.

---

[1] Reference not inserted here to preserve authors' anonymity.
[2] Reference not inserted here to preserve authors' anonymity.

15.2   Literature Review

Whilst for some policy and regulatory decisions there may be ample existing insights on consumer preferences, values and motivations available, this is not the case for network neutrality. In this part of the paper, we present the few relevant published insights. First, we review qualitative insights into the issue. Second, quantitative studies focusing on consumers' willingness-to-pay for network neutrality are reviewed. The literature review culminates in a short summary and implications section.

15.2.1   Qualitative Studies on Consumers and Network Neutrality

One of the most relevant studies in this area is that of Lawford et al. (2009), who conducted six focus group discussions in various Canadian cities. The participants were heavy Internet users, yet one major finding was that their "awareness and recognition of the term 'network neutrality' was very limited". The majority of them were unfamiliar with it, and those who had heard the term before still lacked a clear idea of its meaning; suggestions ranged from a lack of online censorship to an Internet where business interests have no influence. They often blamed their lack of awareness on being complacent about their own ISP's service. All participants had previously experienced disruptions, but they did not usually blame their ISP for these and instead thought the problem lay with their own hardware and/or software, or another server. These views can also be seen in Kenny and Dennis (2013). Once participants were made aware of network neutrality, they showed great interest in it. Many were concerned about what they had learned about traffic management practices, and opposed the idea of the unnecessary throttling or prioritization of certain content. Almost all of them saw ISPs' interest in profit as an insufficient reason for traffic management.

Quail and Larabie (2010) presented similar findings from a single focus group discussion with communication studies students at a Canadian university. Their participants were also largely unaware of network neutrality, despite the fact that they studied communications. When provided with information about it, they understood the concept and engaged more in the focus group discussion than before. Generally, they also seemed concerned about the influence that business interests might have on the Internet, which they thought of as a public utility.

15.2.2   Quantitative Studies on Consumers and Network Neutrality

Another stream of literature addresses consumers' willingness-to-pay for specific product attributes as part of an Internet Access Service (IAS). These studies commonly rely on conjoint analysis to determine this willingness-to-pay. Among the numerous studies investigating this topic, only two could be identified that included network neutrality-related product attribute in their choice experiments.

Huck and Wallace (2011) conducted a choice experiment with 156 students at the University College London, in which they focused on the influence of color as compared to numerical coding of information about broadband speed and network neutrality in fictitious ISPs' offerings. The subjects were asked to make appropriate decisions for given individual or multi-user scenarios based on usage pattern descriptions. Subjects received an incentive for correct answers.

The fictitious packages were developed around their access speed (up to 10, 20 and 50 Mbit/s). For each of these levels, there was a distribution of typically tested choice criteria such as price, and one attribute capturing traffic management. This attribute covered (1) data consistency during peak time, (2) none, (3) download slowdown at peak times, (4) download slowdown of P2P at peak times and (5) prioritization of real time services such as VoIP or video streaming.

Subjects in Huck and Wallace's study made right choices in less than half of the cases (i.e. they performed worse than had they picked offers at random which would have led to 50 % correct choices). Subjects who received the numerical information performed significantly better. They chose the right option in 50.7 % of the exercises. Personal characteristics such as intelligence quotient (IQ) did not have a statistically significant effect on subjects' performance. Due to the limitations of the specific method used, Huck and Wallace did not publish part-worth utilities for the product attributes tested. Thus, a specific willingness-to-pay for the traffic management attribute cannot be inferred.

Nam et al. (2011) address this issue. Their conjoint choice experiment conducted with 1049 consumers features four attributes: (1) Price (low 28US$, medium 34US$, high 40US$); (2) Access speed in Mbit/s (guaranteed minimum speed/ maximum advertised speed: 1/10, 5/50, 10/100); (3) Content Availability (free access to all content, access except for some content); (4) Quality of the Public (Low-Tier) Network (access speed of public network is guaranteed, access speed of public network can be reduced). Respondents considered price to be the most important attribute in their broadband choice, followed by access speed. Taken together, these two attributes add up to more than 60 % of part-worth-utilities. The relative importance of the two attributes directly linked to network neutrality were considerably lower in end-users' choices. The quality of the public network scored 19 % and content availability scored 14 %. The latter seems especially surprising given that unblocked access to all content is one of the characteristics of the Internet commonly referred to by consumers as highly desirable in the qualitative studies described in the above.

Nam et al.'s (2011) research seems somewhat limited in comparison to the other conjoint experiments reviewed in that the number of attributes tested is low. Therefore it seems likely that the relative importance of network neutrality is identified unreliably and would likely change significantly if other important attributes such as bundling with TV or the brand of the ISP had been introduced to the experimental setting.

15.2.3   Summary and Implications of the Literature Review

The reviewed studies, however, concur that consumers were concerned about these issues as soon as they have learned about network neutrality and traffic management practices. On this backdrop, it appears important that citizens' views are heard in the public consultation on network neutrality.

However, all studies also found that consumers lack awareness of the term "network neutrality" and have great difficulty grasping its meaning. An Ofcom study further supports this point. They found that only around one in ten UK consumers are aware of the term "traffic management", and even these consumers do not think that ISPs in the UK use it (Ofcom 2013). This insight clearly indicates that a simplistic open forum procedure to capture citizens' views is unlikely to result in a holistic and representative picture of the value of network neutrality to consumers. In fact, it calls for an approach that can explore in-depth the issue with a broad sample of consumers and hence verify as well as further investigate the value of network neutrality quantitatively using a representative sample. This is further supported by the fact that each of the reviewed studies covers only a small part of the issue. Although only one of the relevant studies reviewed here refers to the European context and none of them has been published after 2011, some fundamental insights may be gained from them that can critically guide the development of such a holistic and representative study.

Qualitative exploration should focus on generating insights that can critically guide the development of a quantitative research approach that can overcome the shortcomings of the two papers described in the above. For instance, doubts exist on whether the terminology applied to describe network neutrality-related product attributes and general information actually meets consumers' understanding and conceptualization of the issues. Qualitative exploration can shed light on the terminology used by consumers and their conceptualization of network neutrality. Quantitative research has to investigate the value of network neutrality to consumers in conjuncture with the full breadth of typically tested attributes. The lack of critical attributes such as product bundling with TV or mobile contracts in the two quantitative studies reviewed is likely to have adversely affected the results on network neutrality.

The following part of the paper describes how we have addressed these implications in our methodology for the representative consumer study discussed here.

15.3   Methodology

In this paper, we compare the results of two studies. We describe in some detail the methodologies employed in these two studies in the following sections.

15.3.1 Public Consultation Study

Late in 2012, the European Commission conducted a public consultation on network with an eye to a legislative initiative in 2013. For whatever reason, the Commission never published a comprehensive analysis of the results of that public consultation. In a study in 2014,[3] we went back to the Commission's public available source data and effectively completed the consultation that the Commission had begun. The source data included more than 400 multiple choice citizen responses from the public consultation that had been collected using a web-based tool.

We separately assessed the views of on a fourth of the 131 organizational stakeholders based on their detailed non-confidential text responses.

15.3.2 Representative Study on the Value of Network Neutrality to European Consumers

For the pan-European study on the value of network neutrality to consumers, we used a mixed-methods approach. The research was conducted in four carefully selected test areas: Croatia, the Czech Republic, Greece and Sweden. The qualitative part of the research consisted of 12 offline focus groups (three per country). The quantitative part comprised an online survey including a conjoint experiment. In each test area, at least 1000 usable questionnaires were obtained. Within the online survey, we performed a test as regards the impact of additional information about network neutrality in each country. Respondents were randomly assigned to the test group (with additional information) and control group (without additional information). The effect of the additional information on respondents' knowledge about network neutrality was confirmed as part of the questionnaire.

Focus group discussions were chosen for the present research as their characteristics echo our research objectives. The stimulation of ideas and concepts through interaction supported us in exploring significant cultural differences between countries and generate insights into consumers' conceptualization of and attitudes towards different aspects of network neutrality. Our search for the drivers of these attitudes has been aided by the candor, spontaneity and potential to retrieve new ideas typical for focus groups. Equally, we were able to learn more about the attributes of ISP choice in less time as compared to individual interviews, which considerably helped to keep the tight schedule of the project.

The most relevant methodological choice as regards the quantitative part of the research was to prefer ACA to CBC in the conjoint experiment. This choice was based directly on the results of the literature review indicating that network neutrality-related attributes had to be tested within a broad set of typically tested product attributes for IAS and that their impact may be relatively small. ACA is better suited than more popular CBC for exactly this kind of task. First, ACA forces

---

[3] Reference not inserted here to preserve authors' anonymity.

the respondent to perform choices, in conjunction with the information at prior stages of the questionnaire, this provides reliable insights on each product attributes regardless of whether it is a primary decision driver or not. ACA can test more attributes at once. Finally, this type of conjoint questionnaire is more engaging for respondents as the method "adapts" to the answers a respondent gives and forces increasingly difficult trade-offs.

Those advantages came at the cost that ACA requires more space in the questionnaire as it combines decision tasks between possible offers with additional questions regarding attractiveness and decision importance. Also, price effects are underestimated in ACAs, limiting the applicability to pricing research and predicting market shares. An analysis of respondents' willingness-to-pay was still possible in ACA nonetheless.

15.4 Findings

From a first inspection of the citizen responses in the public consultation, one can observe that they appear to reflect a high degree of concern over traffic management. Interestingly, this degree of concern is more often than not even higher than that expressed by consumer advocacy groups, and also higher than that expressed by content and application providers (who are presumably the parties who would be most directly impacted by anticompetitive forms of traffic management). This can be taken as a first indication of a strong underlying self-selection bias. This is supported further by comparing the consultation responses of self-selected individuals to the results of individuals in our balanced and representative survey on behalf of BEREC.

15.4.1 Views on Traffic Management Measures to Deliver Specialized Services

For the item referring to ensuring of a guaranteed quality of service for a specific content or application, citizens in the public consultation expressed a significant degree of concern. Two thirds of them found traffic management measures applied to deliver special services problematic. Around one fourth felt they were appropriate, while 9.2 % see them as a necessity.

The representative consumer survey shows a much more nuanced picture as regards such services. To contextualize consumers' views, we have benchmarked them against BEREC's four assessment criteria for traffic management measures.

(1) Non-discrimination between players: The practice is done on a non-discriminatory basis among all content and *application* providers.
    This first criterion identified by BEREC reflects consumers' concept of fairness as regards traffic management quite well. The focus group and survey results

reflect clearly that consumers care about fairness if traffic management measures are used. For instance, around 75 % of respondents across all four test areas agreed with the statement "If prioritizing one user means that someone else gets slower access to the Internet, I find this unfair". Thus, one might even argue that consumers go beyond the idea that all content and application providers have to be treated equally by also considering the impact that their potential choice for a prioritized content/application service might have on the quality of experience for other users.

In essence, consumers subscribe to the idea that some data can or, in some cases, even should be prioritized, either for extra payment or due to reasons of urgency. On the other hand, consumers do not want prioritization to take place at the expense of anybody else's access and in particular not their own quality of Internet access. As they consider potential effects of traffic management not only on themselves but also on others, consumers exhibit a pronounced sensitivity for fairness when it comes to network neutrality. In this context, consumers also consider to some extent greater societal effects. For instance, Swedish focus group participants were concerned about potentially harmful effects of deviations from network neutrality on innovation.

(2) End-user control: It is an important indicator of reasonableness when the practice is applied on the request of users at the edge, who can control and deactivate it. The level of control is deemed higher when the user does not incur costs for removing a restriction

The role and control of the end-user are reflected clearly in our results. If consumers opt for prioritized services, they want to make the choice themselves about which particular content or applications are prioritized and are reluctant to accept any predefined selection that their ISP may offer. In fact, in the focus group discussions, many participants voiced doubts that ISPs could actually anticipate their specific needs and create bespoke products. This is also reflected in the low agreement with the item in the survey that asks if ISPs should make the choice of which content and applications are prioritized and which ones are not. Similarly, respondents showed relatively little agreement with the item referring to ISPs prioritizing their own content such as IPTV over other (third-party) content.

(3) Efficiency and proportionality: The measures should be limited to what is necessary to fulfill the objective, in order to minimize possible side effects. The intensity of the practice, such as frequency and reach, is also important when assessing its impact.

First and foremost, the focus group discussions highlighted that consumers would like to be as free and uncontrolled as possible when they are online. On the other hand, many participants also voiced their wish for a sort of anticipatory filtering of content that they deem offensive, fraudulent or dangerous. Some participants did subscribe to the idea of a "guardian angel" in the background and intended to perform this task themselves, probably severely underestimating its magnitude.

As hard as it might be (if possible at all) to achieve this consumer ideal, the only institution that most of the participants would have faith in performing it is their own government. The actual fulfillment of the task is further impeded by consumers' clear wish that their personal data remain untouched (as far as possible). While this suggests that they adhere to the principle put forward by BEREC quoted above, in fact neither ISPs nor the government or an NRA could possibly fulfill the task of filtering without analyzing user data.

(4) Application agnosticism: As long they are able to achieve a similar effect, BEREC expresses a general preference for 'application-agnostic' practices. This reflects the fact that the decoupling of the network and application layers is a characteristic feature of the open Internet, and has enabled innovation and growth.

The results of our study show that consumers by and large are unaware of the technical underpinnings of the Internet, nor of the specific role that ISPs play within it. They care mostly about their own quality of experience and have a strong preference for open, unrestricted and reliable access to the content and applications they want. In addition, ideas about the wider effects of potential prioritization of content and applications on the competition and innovation also register to some extent with consumers. Overall, we found stable and clear-cut attitudes towards network neutrality as described in detail above.

Citizens in the public consultation found application-agnostic practices the least problematic. Only 36.7 % felt that measures 'affecting all applications and content providers in the same way (application-agnostic)' were problematic. Around a quarter felt that it was necessary to treat all applications/content providers in the same way.

15.4.2   Views on Traffic Management Measures to Ensure Quality of Experience

The second set of items analyzed more closely by us from the public consultation refers to traffic management measures that are used to 'take into account the sensitivity of the service to delay or packet loss'. The majority of citizen respondents found this problematic (53.8 %). Around one third felt they were necessary while 13.4 % consider them necessary. Similarly, a significant majority of citizens opposed measures 'applied during busy times and places, when and where congestion occurs'—67.7 % found them problematic. An even more negative picture is found for measures referring to 'targeting types/classes of traffic contributing most to congestions'. In total, 82.8 % of citizen respondents found this problematic.

The representative consumer survey results underline that consumers in fact show little concern for the technical details of data transport; however, they are concerned about their quality of experience. Thus, it is not surprising that consistently more than 60 % of respondents agree with that traffic management for technical reasons such as the ones cited above should be conducted. Greek consumers showed the lowest share of agreement (62 %), while 78 % of consumers in the Czech Republic agreed with the corresponding statement. In this context, it should be noted that consumers by and large were satisfied with the quality of their IAS at home and experienced only occasional disruptions of their service. The focus groups indicated a comparatively poor quality of experience in the Czech Republic, which may contribute to the high agreement with the idea of traffic management being used to ensure the quality of service.

15.4.3   Views on Traffic Management Measures for Blocking Specific Applications or Contents

The results referring to the use of traffic management to manage compliance with explicit contractual restrictions for instance as regards blocking of VoIP or P2P traffic concur across the two sources we compare. In the public consultation, 85.9 % found such practices problematic. Only 2.4 % felt that such practices were necessary.

The results of representative consumer study concur with this finding. In essence, they highlight that consumers care about free, unrestricted, reliable access to and high quality of content and communication. For them, that is the essence of quality of experience. The relevance of free and unrestricted access becomes obvious when one considers the role that the Internet plays in their lives today. Around 90 % of respondents use the Internet every day at home. Interestingly, the focus group discussions in particular were able to shed some light on differences in the role that the Internet plays in people's lives. For instance, in Sweden the Internet is woven into consumers' lives and they often use it almost without realizing, such as when streaming music or videos on a smart stereo system or TV. Thus, it is not surprising that we observed much higher expectations as regards the reliability of respondents' Internet connection in Sweden than in any other test area. Independent from where they are, even in rural areas, Swedes simply expect their access to the Internet to work. On the other hand, Czech consumers noted that they are very conscious of their Internet use and do not use it all of the time. They use it predominantly for organizational purposes, such as arranging to meet friends.

15.4.4   Views on Traffic Management Measures to Manage Access to and Usage of the ISPs' Own Infrastructure

The final set of items reviewed in detail for our analysis of the European public consultation refers broadly to the idea of fairness. The first item in this set looked at 'targeting heavy users whose use is excessive to the extent that it impacts on other users'. Three quarters of citizen respondents found such a practice problematic.

Around one fifth agreed that it was appropriate and 5.2 % found it necessary. Traffic management used by ISPs to limit competition for their own services was frowned upon even more strongly. In total, 96.2 % saw this practice as being problematic. Correspondingly, only a marginal share of respondents felt traffic management was appropriate or even necessary under these circumstances.

While the first item is largely covered by the strong sensitivity for fairness by consumers in the representative survey when traffic management is done by ISPs as outlined previously, the second item was covered in our survey by the item "It is fine if Internet providers prioritize applications that are offered directly by them (*e.g.* IPTV from the provider)". The responses to this item conflict somewhat with the concept of fairness. In three out of the four test areas, a majority of respondents agreed with this statement. The highest agreement was found in Croatia. Here, 60 % of respondents had no concerns with this sort of traffic management practice (CZ 52 %; ET 54 %). In Sweden, however, only 40 % agreed with the statement. This results is unsurprising as Swedes also were the ones who expressed strong concerns in the focus group discussions that commercially driven deviations from network neutrality could harm the competitive environment.

15.5   Discussion and Conclusion

In the introduction to this paper, we expressed the general concern that European policy might not be sufficiently informed regarding the views of citizens in regard to network neutrality, and the specific concern that citizens with strong views (but not necessarily typical or representative views) might be over-represented in the materials available to policymakers.

These concerns appear to be valid. The responses of self-selected citizens to the public consultation on network neutrality conducted by the European Commission in 2012 differ dramatically from those obtained based on a representative and holistic mixed-methods study on the value of network neutrality that we conducted in 2014 on BEREC's behalf. This tends to supports our expectation that a strong self-selection bias underlies the citizen responses.

The literature review for the present paper suggests that information about consumer views on network neutrality is in fact vital to the decision process; however, reliable publicly available information on consumer preferences regarding network neutrality continues to be limited. Our representative study was able to shed light at the issue from various angles of consumer perception, however, it seems to have raised at least as many questions as it was able to answer. For instance, initial tests of selected attitude questions in Germany, the UK and the US showed marked differences compared to the four test areas. Also, we could only cover the at home usage situation, while many network neutrality concerns are strongly linked to out of home i.e. mostly mobile usage of broadband connections. This indicates that significantly more work is needed in the area.

More generally, and looking beyond the network neutrality debate, our findings shed doubt on the reliability of public consultations and other surveys where respondents are self-selected as a sole means to understand consumers' preferences, values and motivations.

Acknowledgment　We gratefully acknowledge the Commission's prompt and helpful assistance in processing the multiple choice responses.

References

EC. (2013). Answers from the public consultation on specific aspects of transparency, traffic management and switching in an Open Internet. Available at: http://ec.europa.eu/digital-agenda/en/news/answers-public-consultation-specific-aspects-transparency-traffic-management-and-switching-open

Huck, S., & Wallace, B. (2011). *Consumer information on broadband speed and net neutrality experiment*. London Economics.

Kenny, R., & Dennis, A. (2013). Consumer lock-in for fixed broadband. Communications Chambers.

Lawford, J., Lo, J., & De Santis, M. (2009). *Staying neutral: Canadian consumers and the fight for network neutrality* (p. 17). Ottawa: Public Interest Advocacy Centre. Available at: http://tinyurl.com/6fnbu73.

Nam, C., Lee, H., Kim, S., & Kim, T. (2011). Network neutrality: an end-user's perspective. *International Telecommunications Policy Review, 18*(1), 1–15.

Ofcom. (2013). Consumer research into the transparency of traffic management information provided by ISPs. Available at: http://stakeholders.ofcom.org.uk/binaries/research/broadband-research/1145655/traffic-research.pdf

Quail, C., & Larabie, C. (2010). Network neutrality: Media discourses and public perception. *Global Media Journal – Canadian Edition, 3*(1), 31–50.

Chapter 16
The Persistent Problems of Net Neutrality or Why Are We Still Lacking Stable Net Neutrality Regulation

Konstantinos Stylianou

16.1 Introduction

The debate on net neutrality has been around long enough to allow its various aspects to emerge and develop sufficiently. Indeed, after years of scholarly and policy attention we now have a deep understanding of the industrial economics behind net neutrality regulation,[1] the dynamic competition and innovation aspects to it,[2] the technical infrastructure of the networks and actors that are subject to the relevant rules,[3] and the human rights and plurality considerations surrounding the rules.[4]

And yet we are still far from reaching a resolution that garners multi-stakeholder support and offers some guarantees of stability. The volatility of net neutrality regulation is evidenced by the failure of various jurisdictions to enact stable rules, even after years of persistent efforts. The Federal Communications Commission (FCC) in the United States was recently sued again over the latest regulations it passed in February 2015, which marks the third challenge of relevant rules over the past decade.[5] In Europe, the Council and the European Parliament are sharply divided over the projected rules that are pushed as part of the Digital Agenda, and that date back to the updated telecom package of 2010.[6] And in countries where net

---

[1] Yoo (2005), Hahn and Wallsten (2006), Sidak (2006), Speta (2000), SCF Associates (2012), ITU (2012), and Institute for Policy Integrity (2010). See generally In the Matter of Protecting and Promoting the Open Internet, GN Docket No. 14–28 (2015) (Report and Order on Remand, Declaratory Ruling, and Order).

[2] Lee and Wu (2009) and Lemley and Lessig (2000).

[3] Crowcroft (2007) and Faratin et al.(2007).

[4] CoE Steering Committee on Media and Information Society (2013).

[5] Fung (2015).

[6] See Geere (2015) and McNamee (2014).

K. Stylianou (✉)
University of Leeds, Leeds, UK
e-mail: k.stylianou@leeds.ac.uk

© Springer International Publishing Switzerland 2016
L. Belli, P. De Filippi (eds.), *Net Neutrality Compendium*,
DOI 10.1007/978-3-319-26425-7_16

neutrality only recently became a policy issue, like Latin America countries, the relevant adoption and implementation process has not gone smoothly either.[7] These recent developments and the unresolved situation they leave behind foreshadow a protracted regulatory battle.

One could reasonably inquire as to what might explain this never-ending net neutrality saga. Could it be the lack of political will to resolve the issue, because in fact net neutrality is of little importance to consumers and regulators alike, despite the academic obsession with it? Probably not, considering the intense public participation (the FCC for example collected four million comments in the latest round of public consultation),[8] the repeated presidential interventions in the US debate,[9] the numerous front-page headlines in the media, and the overall engagement of high-level stakeholders with the issue. Or maybe is it because net neutrality regulation is a highly complex issue? As just mentioned there are several stakeholders involved and various conflicting interests to reconcile (economic, technological, social). But isn't all (or most of) regulation complex and an attempt to strike a sustainable balance between opposing interests? Moreover—and this comes with a pinch of arbitrariness—no major new issues have arisen in the net neutrality debate recently, as evidenced by the largely recycled questions that regulators are still grappling with.[10] On the other hand, it could be the case that net neutrality regulations have failed because of contextual reasons. For example in the United States the highly litigious environment has made FCC's work extremely difficult, while in Europe the peculiarities of the European Union decision-making process results in complexities that are not common in non-supranational systems.

There is some truth to all of those reasons. Yes, some policy-makers consider net neutrality an unimportant topic, net neutrality does indeed present hard questions that combine law, economics and technology which do not avail themselves to easy solutions, and contextual factors do create obstacles. But, besides the fact that these reasons do not explain fully why progress has stalled, there is little that can be done about them, because fixing them would require an overhaul of the context in which net neutrality is being discussed.

On the contrary, what this paper suggests is that there are also persistent problems with the net neutrality debate that are specific to the *way* the debate is conducted, not its *context*, and therefore, hopefully, easier to fix. The identified problems are irrespective of whether one supports or opposes net neutrality; they rather focus on the factors that have precluded a stable policy outcome to arise.

---

[7] See, *e.g.* for Open Society Foundations et al. (2013), Nathalia Foditsch et al. (2015).

[8] Kastranakes (2014).

[9] Obama Says Unequivocally Committed to 'Net Neutrality', New York Times, October 9, 2014; White House (2014).

[10] Compare, for example, the discussion and issues in FCC's 2010 and 2015 Open Internet Orders: In the Matter of Preserving the Open Internet, Broadband Industry Practices, GN Docket No. 09-191 (Report and Order) (2010) and the 2015 Open Internet Order, supra note 1. Even if the resolutions adopted in the two Orders are different the main themes remain the same: blocking, discrimination, paid prioritization, specialized services, neutrality in wireless, scope of the rules, legal basis for the rules.

In that direction I discuss three issues. The first has to do with the persistence of policy-makers to adopt either the full arsenal of net neutrality protections (*e.g.* U.S., Brazil, Mexico, Chile, Netherlands, Slovenia), or no rules at all. This black-and-white approach disregards the nuances of the implicated issues and tends to be over-inclusive or under-inclusive. Instead, regulators could choose a flexible framework clause, like those used in antitrust, which is capable of filtering out harmful practices while allowing the rest. The FCC came close to this solution in April 2014 but decided otherwise in the end.

The second problem concerns the fixation of stakeholders with certain historical features of the Internet, which are seen as immutable axioms that should define today's Internet the same way they did decades ago (*e.g.* end to end, neutrality, openness). This clinging is impractical because the Internet and the marketplace around it have evolved and the continuing application of historical principles without justifying their modern relevance obscures rather than illuminates the debate. To set the discussion on the proper base, it is therefore advised that the starting point for the debate is not how to ensure neutrality, openness, non-discrimination and the end to end principle, but whether those characteristics apply with the same force today as when the Internet was first conceived and commercialized. Once there is agreement as to which principles serve the Internet better, the discussion can continue on how to safeguard them.

Third, and on a related topic, to determine whether regulation is needed to safeguard the Internet's desired features (as per above), regulators need to determine the competitive conditions in the market, which includes the identification of potential bottlenecks and the power interrelations among them. Current practice seems to ignore a prevalent form of competitive pressure in telecommunications, namely vertical competition, which, if taken into account, should affect the way regulators view the necessity or type of appropriate regulation. These three issues are examined in sequence below.

16.2 The Three Plagues of the Net Neutrality Debate and How to Overcome Them

16.2.1 Polarization and the Pursuit of Categorical Regulation

One thing that is fairly obvious to anyone that has followed the net neutrality debate over the past decade is that there are two clearly defined camps to it and that regulatory choices have by and large sided with one of them. In particular, countries have either opted to not adopt rules at all, or where net neutrality rules have been adopted, they contain clear no-blocking, no-discrimination, no-paid prioritization provisions with an exception only for reasonable network management.[11] Such rules are almost

---

[11] Such is the case, for example, in the U.S., Brazil, Chile, Mexico, Netherlands and Slovenia. These countries represent the majority of those that have enacted net neutrality rules. For the U.S. see 2015 Open Internet Order, supra note 1; for Latin America see Ferraz et al. (2012 Content Filtering in Latin America: Reasons and Impacts on Freedom of Expression, available at http://www.palermo.edu/cele/pdf/english/Internet-Free-of-Censorship/Content-Filtering-Latin-America.pdf; on the Netherlands see Art. 7.4(a), Telecommunicatiewet—BWBR0009950; on Slovenia see Art. 203, Zakon o elektronskih komunicijah (ZEKom-1), Stran 12069.

in complete consonance with the pro-net neutrality camp, and, conversely, they leave little to no room to accommodate the concerns of net neutrality skeptics, who don't see the need for such pervasive regulation for a variety of reasons that have been fleshed out in detail in the relevant literature.[12] This regulatory bipolarity leaves the issue unresolved, whereas greater regulatory flexibility could provide a middle road solution receptive to the priorities of both sides.

Normally, clear-cut regulation is desirable, because it creates legal certainty by specifying ex ante which behavior is allowed and which is banned. As a result, market actors can safely develop their business plans and investment strategies. For instance, when carriers know that, if they want to offer some kind of video service with assured quality, their only option is to package it as a specialized service and not through a fast lane, because regulation bans fast lanes, they can plan accordingly without wastefully investing (time, capital, human resources etc) in a business arrangement that regulators will seek to block.

But in reality, clear-cut regulation and legal certainty are only desirable if they advance good rules; otherwise one should hope for a change, and the continuing effort to get there will negate the very benefits clear-cut regulation seeks to advance (i.e. certainty). So the question is whether the rules currently in place are good and stable. I believe the answer is negative, but not because they support net neutrality (in my view, complete absence of regulation would be also wrong). Rather, because they are one-sidedly in favor of net neutrality, and the issues raised by net neutrality are such that no black and white regulation — in favor or against — can address them properly. Therefore, to the extent that stakeholders advocate for rules that uniformly allow or ban blocking, discrimination, prioritization, zero-rating and other practices that fall within the ambit of net neutrality, and to the extent that regulators adopt such rules, the problem will persist unless one side decides to give up.

The reason is simple: there are provenly valid and powerful arguments on both sides, and rules that prioritize simplicity over accuracy by picking one side will necessarily be so detached from the interests of the other side that the rules will not reflect the current state of scientific knowledge, and will be out of touch with reality.[13] It is neither practical nor essential to attempt a full discussion of the pros and cons of net neutrality here. That the communications industry, in all its peculiarities and our expectations from it, cannot be trusted to be fully unsupervised, but that at the same time absolute bans on blocking, discrimination and differentiation are not necessary are points already proven by existing literature, and it is indeed odd that regulators still fail to see that.[14]

I say this with a certain degree of confidence because it is backed by decades of scholarly work in the fields of antitrust and industrial economics, both of which, much like telecommunications regulation, are concerned with the efficient operation

---

[12] See Yoo (2005), Spulber and Yoo (2012).

[13] On the problem of treating dissimilar situations (*e.g.* discrimination, blocking etc.) the same, see Speta (2014), p. 491, Verizon v. Federal Communications Commission (2014).

[14] On the arguments for both sides see supra notes 1–4. On the necessity for regulation that adapts to circumstances see Weiser (2003), pp. 60–63, Yoo (2007), pp. 504–409.

and organization of the industry, and which have routinely been called into use in the telecommunications area.[15] Indeed, many of the arguments in the net neutrality debate can be traced back to economic and industrial organization theory. What this body of literature tells us is that both an absolute ban and a blank check on discriminatory practices are misplaced, and it also provides us with the tools to differentiate between good and bad instances of discriminatory practices.[16]

This makes the integration of antitrust-like analysis and principles into telecommunications regulation useful and appropriate as regulatory tools that can accommodate the arguments of both sides. By doing so, regulation can move away from fixed predefined rules that are bound to be over-inclusive or under-inclusive, and instead rely on flexible clauses that leave room for different treatment of harmful and beneficial practices. This approach could be a good way out of the current net neutrality deadlock.

In antitrust theory, net neutrality is, to a large extend, an issue of vertical exclusion, namely the practice by which a market actor blocks or discriminates against another actor upstream or downstream along the value chain, most commonly with the view to extend or maintain power to the upstream or downstream market or to raise entry barriers by making entry efficient only if it occurs in two levels at the same time.[17] Industrial economics and antitrust have sufficiently defined the circumstances under which such practices should invite scrutiny[18]: actors must have an incentive to discriminate or block.[19] Incentives cannot be taken for granted because it is well-established that conduit and content exist in a coöpetitive and not simply competitive relationship, but also because conduit providers have alternative ways to recuperate lost surplus from vertical competition than to resort to aggressive

---

[15] See, *e.g.* United States v. AT&T Co. (1982), pp. 135–36; Verizon Communications, Inc. v. Law Offices of Curtis V. Trinko (2004); Verizon, 740 F.3d 623.

[16] Tirole, as early as (1988), p. 193; stated that "few topics in industrial organization are as controversial as market foreclosure." Tirole (1990).

[17] Rey and Tirole (2007), pp. 2145, 2145, 2148–50; Areeda and Hovenkamp (2006), ¶ 756b7; Viscusi et al. (2005). EU Guidelines on the Assessment of Non-horizontal Mergers Under the Council Regulation on the Control of Concentrations Between Undertakings, 2008/C 265/07, at ¶ 29–30; Sullivan and Grimes (2000), p. 638; Carlton and Waldman. The Strategic Use of Tying to Create and Preserve Market Power in Evolving Industries, 33 RAND Journal of Economics 194, 194; Tirole (1990), p. 185 (with internal references).

[18] Sullivan and Grimes (2000), pp. 415–418, 667–670; See also EU Guidelines on the Assessment of Non-horizontal Mergers, supra note 17, at ¶ 32; Horizontal Merger Guidelines, passim (2010); 2010 Open Internet Order, supra note 10, at ¶ 20–35, 80–93; Geradin and Sidak (2003), p. 519.

[19] See, *e.g.* FCC (1999) (where the Commission highlighted the need to "analyze the incentive and ability to discriminate ... with respect to competitors providing advanced services, interexchange services, and local exchange services in the SBC and Ameritech regions."); Parker (1999) (where Parker commenting on the canceled vertical merger between Barnes & Noble and Ingram explained the emphasis the FTC placed on the incentives to raise rivals' cost: "As I already suggested, the question we ask is whether the newly vertically-integrated company will have an incentive (and, of course, the ability) to raise the costs of its rivals.").

strategies like discrimination or blocking.[20] Second, the discriminatory practice must have a harmful effect on the competitive conditions of the industry.[21] If the institutional structure of competition remains intact, isolated problems are self-correcting and there is no need for an over-inclusive generalized regulatory response. Third, if there is good justification or countervailing efficiencies that flow from discriminatory practices they must be weighed against the harms.[22] Evidently, some discriminatory practices can be pernicious to the industry while others not so much, or they may even be beneficial if the countervailing efficiencies offset whatever harm is caused.

Current rules are not receptive to this possibility, and instead outlaw virtually all blocking and discrimination. As a result, none of the concerns of the anti-net neutrality camp seem to have been taken into account, which perpetuates the problem. The FCC came very close to adopting the model advocated for here, namely a antitrust-like standard, in April 2014 when it released a Notice for Proposed Rulemaking (NPRM).[23] In the 2014 NPRM the FCC proposed the adoption of a flexible standard by which it would assess the effect of discriminatory practices on the market. In particular the proposed rule "would prohibit as commercially unreasonable those broadband providers' practices that, based on the totality of the circumstances, threaten to harm Internet openness and all that it protects.[24] At the same time, it could permit "broadband providers to serve customers and carry traffic on an individually negotiated basis, 'without having to hold themselves out to serve all comers indiscriminately on the same or standardized terms,' so long as such conduct is commercially reasonable."[25]

---

[20] See Bengtsson and Kock (1999) (where the authors analyze the spectrum of relationships between firms in coexistence, cooperation, co-opetition, and competition); Zineldin (2004), pp. 780–781 (where the author suggests that industry cooperation is based on "a value net of involved actors—suppliers, distributors, subcontractors, "complementors", competitors–who collectively add value to one another's organisations." at 781). For the so called "one monopoly rent" theorem see, among others, Bork (1978), Viscusi et al (2005), p. 249.

[21] Areeda and Hovenkamp (2006), ¶ 335.2f (1986 Supp.) ("the foreclosure argument has grave weaknesses; only where foreclosures reach monopolistic proportions—or threaten to do so—does a vertical merger become troublesome"); Page (1980), p. 467, 495. See also, *e.g.* United States v. Brown University, 5 F.3d 658, p. 668 (1993) ("The rule of reason requires the fact-finder to weigh all of the circumstances of a case in deciding whether a restrictive practice should be prohibited as imposing an unreasonable restraint on competition. The plaintiff bears an initial burden under the rule of reason of showing that the alleged combination or agreement produced adverse, anti-competitive effects within the relevant product and geographic markets.").

[22] See Guidance on the Commission's Enforcement Priorities in Applying Art. 82, ¶ 46 et seq. See also In re IBM Peripheral EDP Devices Antitrust Litigation, 481 F. Supp. 965, 1005 (N.D. Cal. 1979) (holding that IBM did not violate section 2 by tying its computer central processing unit to its peripheral devices, because the combination resulted in an improved design), affd sub nom. Transamerica Computer Co. v. International Business Machines Corp., 698 F.2d 1377 (1983).

[23] In the Matter of Protecting and Promoting the Open Internet, GN Docket No. 14-28 (2014) (Notice of Proposed Rulemaking).

[24] Id., ¶ 128.

[25] Id., ¶ 116.

The genius of this rule is twofold: first, it is flexible in the sense that it requires the showing of particular harm and allows for a margin of appreciation. Second, while it is inspired by antitrust, it does not merely replicate the antitrust standard of "restraint of trade or commerce" but adapts it to the particular needs of the telecommunications industry, namely the threat "to harm Internet openness and all that it protects." By means of such a rule regulators are in the position to customize their treatment of dissimilar situations, and respect and uphold the special characteristics and features of the communications ecosystem (*e.g.* in the Internet ecosystem, pluralistic participatory innovation seems to play a more prominent role than in other industries). This is an important point of departure from those who claim that antitrust law alone is sufficient to safeguard the industry from anticompetitive practices.[26] An antitrust-inspired customized rule for the communications industry is more responsive to its needs and peculiarities and has greater chances of success.

Unfortunately, the NPRM was superseded by the rules the FCC passed in February 2015, which take the familiar road of a full ban on blocking, discrimination and prioritization (save the reasonable network management exception). Other jurisdictions in Europe and Latin America, whose countries are lately seen as pioneers of Internet legislation also opted for black and white rules that leave little room for the reconciliation of opposing interests.[27] It is hard to see how these choices can conclusively resolve the debate in a way that the various considerations are justly balanced against each other. The EU has recently shown some encouraging flexibility by orientating towards explicitly allowing specialized services, but this doesn't fully solve the problem, because innocuous discriminatory practices outside of the specialized services exception are still banned. Regulatory flexibility along the lines of antitrust clauses seems like the only Pareto efficient solution.

16.2.2   Clinging to Historical Principles of the Internet

Another factor that obfuscates the debate and prevents a mutually accepted solution from emerging is that stakeholders often invoke historical principles they assign to the Internet without justifying their continuing relevance to today's ecosystem. Citing a principle without explaining why one should abide by it or whether there are limitations that may be pertinent today but were not when the principle was first conceived, is not helpful because it stalls the debate.

This phenomenon is common with what are considered the foundational principles of the Internet, such as end-to-end, openness, decentralized control and innovation, and the Internet as a unified whole. These features are often used as axioms from which one is not supposed to deviate, because they account for much

---

[26] See, *e.g.* Huber (1997).

[27] See supra note 11.

of the indisputable success and contribution of the Internet as we know it today.[28] I don't mean to say that these features have not been crucial to the development of the Internet or that they are no longer valuable today. To the contrary, they are backed by rich theoretical and empirical literature and they are still instrumental to the Internet ecosystem.

However, at the same time, the Internet is not what it used to be when it was first conceived as a scientific project, or when it was first commercialized. It has evolved, matured, and it serves different needs and consists of different actors.[29] Market players such as content delivery networks (CDN) or IP inter-exchange providers (IPX) were not in operation or common, and business practices like secondary peering, and multihoming only recently became widespread too. These developments change the shape and nature of the network in a way that historical principles may still be relevant, but one should at least consider whether there are limitations and exceptions to them that make them less applicable or absolute than in the past.[30] We may very well discover that full adherence to the traditional nature of the Internet is the optimal solution today as well, but before we get there the various stakeholders need to engage in a discussion on its merits. Unfortunately, this discussion is largely missing making compromise impossible.

In the limited space here, I can only anecdotally attempt to explain the kind of limitations and qualifications historical principles may be subject to today as opposed to earlier phases of the Internet's evolution. Taking into account these limitations and qualifications can result in enriching the traditional values of the Internet that net neutrality seeks to safeguard with those elements that would make them more relevant and appropriate for today's Internet.

---

[28] Lemley and Lessig (2000) ("allowing such bundling [:cable companies integrating to the ISP market] will compromise an important architectural principle that has governed the Internet since its inception: the principle of "end-to-end" design ("e2e"). Nothing less than the structure of the Internet itself is at stake in this debate."; Lemley and Lessig (2000), p. 925; Wu and Lee (2009). Subsidizing Creativity Through Network Design: Zero Pricing and Net Neutrality, 23.3 Journal of Economic Perspectives, 61, p. 63 ("The overall network does not, by its own design, distinguish between content providers and users. Consequently, content providers — who may also be users — are also able to reach an audience consisting of every single Internet user. These norms and expectations, which have created a de facto ban on termination fees, stands in sharp contrast to what is standard practice on other important information networks, like the telephone and cable networks. One reason for the differences between networks is rooted in history. The Internet was conceived by various visionaries, particularly the Department of Defense researchers J. C. R. Licklider and Robert W. Taylor, as a "network of networks" or an "intergalatic network" that would make it possible for users of any single computer network to reach users on any other network (Licklider and Taylor, 1968)."; The FCC also, on several occasions has reiterated its strong faith that the openness flowing from network neutrality "promotes competition ... [and] enables a self-reinforcing cycle of investment and innovation in which new uses of the network lead to increased adoption of broadband, which drives investment and improvements in the network itself." 2010 Open Internet Order, supra note 10, ¶ 3.

[29] See, generally, Yoo (2012).

[30] Many engineers have explained how the original design of the Internet poses limitations and may not serve modern needs any more. See Handley (2006), p. 119; Huston (2008).

For instance, one of the most revered characteristics of the Internet is the end-to-end principle, which limits the core of the Internet to the simple function of transmitting data in order to achieve maximum interoperability, and additional functions are added in the layers above and below the slim waist of the IP layer.[31] The resulting "inherent" neutrality (since all the core does is route packets) has accounted for much of the innovation and entry that has occurred in the Internet ecosystem.

Assuming that this depiction accurately characterizes the nature of the Internet,[32] we need to acknowledge that, at the same time, the insistence on a bare-bones core has resulted in some limitations and has prevented some efficient implementations of quality of service, security, and congestion management.[33] All three issues are good candidates to be dealt with at the network level because the coordinated cooperation of network operators instead of the independent response of the edges can be a more effective way to deploy or resolve them.

Indeed, networks that perform better in terms of quality of service, security and congestion incorporate those functions in the network design rather than rely solely on the intelligence of the edges. A good example is mobile cellular networks, which are heavily managed and more complex.[34] To achieve the above-stated goals they employ (virtual) circuits, encapsulation, and elaborate architectures for QoS, user verification and mobility management, all of which rely on core functionality.

One might say that mobile cellular networks are more specialized than the public Internet and that this is why they are built on specialized architectures with additional features, but convergence is quickly eroding this argument. The Internet is supplanting uses cellular networks were traditionally associated with, and cellular networks are carrying more and more Internet traffic. Inevitably, the interaction between the two networks will result in some cross-transplantation of features. Artificially sticking to the original design of the Internet (whatever that might be) would impose a technological freeze to an evolving socioeconomic and technological environment.[35]

Consider now another feature that most policy-makers associate with the modern Internet, namely that it is universal and undivided. There seems to be long-standing agreement that the success of the Internet was partly driven by the fact that every public address (device or host) is reachable from every other public address under

---

[31] Saltzer et al. (1984), p. 277. See also Clark. Interoperation, Open Interfaces and Protocol Architecture, in The Unpredictable Certainty: White Papers on Information Infrastructure Through 2000 133, pp. 133–134 (NII 2000 Steering Committee, Computer Science and Telecommunications Board, Commission on Physical Sciences, Mathematics, and Applications, National Research Council, 1998).

[32] Despite the popular belief, the Internet has never been completely egalitarian—technically or as a marketplace. See Hass (2007), p. 1565; Sasso (2014).

[33] See, *e.g.* Yoo (2004), p. 23.

[34] On the different philosophies of the telephone network and the Internet, see Wu (2007). A Tale of Two Platforms, available at http://ssrn.com/abstract=993288.

[35] David Clark, a prominent Internet engineer, has nice described how networks should be designed as a playing field where different interests and priorities compete, rather than with a specific outcome in mind. This means that as needs change the network should change with them. See Clark (2005).

the same terms and conditions, making the Internet a unified whole, and resulting in fast scaling up and powerful network effects.[36] Vint Cerf recently stated that "fragmentation is destructive of the basic functioning of the Internet. ... Fragmentation would be a terrible outcome [and] destroy value."[37]

There is no denying that the universality of the Internet has added enormous value to it and drove its initial and ongoing expansion. But here is precisely the crucial point: the Internet is no longer an emerging product/market; it is a mature well-developed and highly evolved one, and the fact that it is now in a different phase in its life-cycle should inform us about its current characteristics and not only the historical ones.[38] Young markets are characterized by fluidity, uncertainty, high experimentation and fast growth.[39] In this context a platform that is not designed for any specific use and at the same time does not serve any specific purpose seems ideal. But in mature markets, demand diversifies, various preferences and sub-markets emerge and market actors try to deliver greater value to consumers by meeting their (by now crystallized) needs.[40] What this tells us is that in the current state of the Internet, "forking" part of it and assigning to it properties that go against neutrality will not only not be catastrophic but it may actually serve niche specialized demand. Therefore, re-evaluating the need for and purpose of an undivided universal Internet seems like a necessary step to be performed by regulators, which will affect their stance towards fast lanes and specialized services.

Moreover, in the years from the Internet's early age to today's maturity, we have gained valuable insight into how market fragmentation and differentiation can be welfare enhancing and desirable. Niche or incompatible sub-markets have the potential to better address specialized consumer demand, they can operate more efficiently by adopting forms and mechanisms that may be ill-suited for the entire market, they can attract entry by averting too fierce competition that results from uniformity, and they encourage innovation and experimentation because they are able to adopt novel and differentiated practices.[41]

In the Internet context, this type of fragmentation (and accompanying pros and cons) has come up in various forms, including free or subsidized access to only a subpart of the Internet, walled gardens, and blocking off parts of the Internet for a variety of reasons (*e.g.* national security, intellectual property etc). These are all practices that are in tension with net neutrality. I don't mean to say that such practices should be lightheartedly accepted, but their scientific merits as mentioned above and elaborated on in the relevant literature seem to be missing from the debate too.

The general point of criticism here, and the advice that flows for policy-makers is that the fixation on perceived traditional, established, and foundational principles of the Internet may today hinder good policy-making as the conditions have changed and with them the value, meaning and relevancy of said principles. When contested,

---

[36] On the risk of Internet balkanization see Lessig (2009).

[37] Rosenbush (2015).

[38] See Yoo (2010).

[39] Porter (1980), pp. 159–161. Utterback and Abernathy (1975), p. 639, 643.

[40] Porter, id.; Kotler and Keller (2008), p. 288; Grant (2008), p. 271.

[41] See, *e.g.* Church and Gandal (2005), p. 117; Spence (1976), p. 407; Dickson and Ginter (1987), p. 1.

as they often are, those principles must be proven, much like any other position that aspires to become policy, not simply assumed.

16.2.3   Not Up-to-Date Competition Analysis

Two of the most fundamental underpinnings of net neutrality regulation is that the broadband access market is not adequately competitive, and that as a result of that but also because of their bottleneck position in the value chain broadband providers have the power to discriminate against service, application and content providers if so they wish.[42] In this context, the idea is that regulation becomes necessary to prevent such anticompetitive discrimination.

Logically, if any of the conditions mentioned above is not fulfilled the rationale for net neutrality regulation is undermined. Therefore appropriately defining the competitive interrelations between broadband access providers and service, application and content providers (or other involved actors for that matter) is key to good policy-making. This task has presented great difficulties for regulatory authorities leaving them unable to assess the true competitive conditions in the market and accordingly devise appropriate regulation.

More specifically, the assessment of competitive conditions in the market has focused too much on existing competition and not enough on entry potentials, and it has maintained a somewhat antiquated understanding of power allocation between broadband access providers, and other actors in the value chain (notable service, application and content providers), namely that broadband access providers are the defining bottleneck in the Internet value chain.[43] These two weaknesses prevent stakeholders from agreeing on what metrics they need to look at in determining competitiveness levels, market power and consequently the need for and type of regulation. The reason why I identify these two instances of competitive analysis as obsolete is that technological developments have altered how easy it is for market players to jump from one layer or role in the value chain to another (*e.g.* content/application providers becoming conduits), which is known as vertical entry and which creates additional competitive pressure, and to amass power vis-a-vis other players in the value chain, thusly building bargaining power.[44] Any competition

---

[42] I conventionally focus here on broadband access providers and service, application and content providers as the most representatives sides in the net neutrality debate, but as we can see from the recent expansion of the scope of the rules in some jurisdictions, including the U.S. (Open Internet Order) and Brazil (Marco Civil), other actors may be implicated, *e.g.* interconnection providers.

[43] See infra notes 45, 46 and accompanying text.

[44] Vertical entry and competition are generally not considered as factors in the mainstream competition analysis because successive steps in the value chain are seen as complements, not as competitors. See Steiner (2008). Vertical Competition, Horizontal Competition, and Market Power, 53 The Antitrust Bulletin 251; Non-Horizontal Merger Guidelines (Originally issued as part of "U.S. Department of Justice Merger Guidelines," June 14, 1984), ¶ 4.0 ("By definition, nonhorizontal mergers involve firms that do not operate in the same market."); Lianos (2009).

analysis has to take this fluidity in mind. Otherwise regulators and stakeholders are bound to rely on a non-realistic perception of the industry.

The relevant analyses performed in the US and in the EU do just that. In the 2015 Open Internet Order—much like in the 2010 Open Internet Order—the FCC based its justification for the need for regulation on the fact that broadband access providers are uniquely positioned to pressure service, application and content providers, and that the US broadband access market is an oligopoly (at best) because there is a limited number of ISPs available to most consumers.[45] In other words, it performed a horizontal competition analysis. At the EU level, while the new Connected Continent Regulation gives deference to national regulatory authorities and so there is no overarching principle, BEREC in a recent report on interconnection, which was used as input for the European rules on the Open Internet, similarly treats service, application and content providers as mere customers of broadband providers, who have the ability and incentive to exercise market power over them.[46] This, again, preconceives both the position of power of broadband access providers and their complementary rather than co-opetitive relationship with the other actors in the value chain (i.e. "customer" relationship). The result is that both jurisdictions (and others) see a need to protect service, application and content providers from potentially abusive practices of broadband providers.

The problem with this treatment is that it presents only half the picture or a version of the picture that may have been accurate in the past but not today. The technological structure of today's broadband industry is such that it makes vertical entry and substitution much easier than in the past, and it also allows value to flow from one layer to another in a way that doesn't a priori allow the conclusion that one type of actor holds more power in the value chain than another (as it is assumed, for example, for broadband access providers).

For these reasons, regulators and stakeholders need to move away from the cozy *presumption* that a certain type of actors (notably access providers, but it can be others, like interconnection providers) is favorably positioned in the value chain and instead rebuild the list of relevant actors and their inter-relations and then decide whether, where, and what type of regulation is needed.[47] It is entirely possible that regulators and stakeholders, even after responding to the call above, will conclude that broadband access providers still deserve to be regulated. This is acceptable. But in this case, first, the conclusion will have been based on a sounder assessment of the industry's state, and second, it might result in more flexible regulation in recognition of the fluid nature of the industry as described supra, as opposed to black and white regulation of the kind we have today.

---

[45] 2015 Open Internet Order, supra note 1, ¶ 78–85.

[46] BEREC (2012). An assessment of IP interconnection in the context of Net Neutrality, BoR (12) 130, pp. 9–15.

[47] BEREC attempted this assessment in the interconnection report but omitted the vertical dynamics.

To go into more detail, entry is an important parameter in the analysis of competitive conditions because it tells us how easily competition can be created even in situations that it is underdeveloped.[48] In fact, entry does not necessarily have to actually occur; the threat of it can be enough to discourage market players from resorting to practices that will harm consumers, which rivals can see as an opportunity to join the market to fill in for the unsatisfied demand.

In high technology industries, like the communications industry, entry (or threat thereof) into one layer from existing players in adjacent layers is facilitated by the technological proximity between layers.[49] Technological proximity is the ability of neighboring market actors to amass the necessary know-how and assets to enter similar/adjacent markets.[50] This is because there are *no exogenous boundaries* to layers and so actors do not have to be confined to one specific role,[51] because the transferability of technical know how allows greater *absorptive capacity* which is useful for firms to expand,[52] and because the *natural boundaries* of layers change as the industry evolves thereby allowing or forcing actors to expand up and down the value chain.[53]

We see the result of this in the emergence of new sources of competition in various layers. Google, for example, started off as an application provider (search) and, aided by the technical nature of the industry, expanded gradually to operating systems (Android), devices (Nexus) and infrastructure (Google Fiber, Google Wi-Fi, Project Fi). Another example is the transformation of CDNs from providers of a service (local caching) to providers of backbone connectivity infrastructure and of service and application platforms. Moreover, traditional access providers (notably mobile carriers) are now morphing into service and application platform providers by upgrading their networks to general-purpose IP-based architectures (*e.g.* IMS), and by virtualizing the

---

[48] EU Guidance on the Commission's Enforcement Priorities in Applying Art. 82, ¶ 30, where the European Commission stresses that "where there is no residual competition and no foreseeable threat of entry, the protection of rivalry and the competitive process outweighs possible efficiency gains."; U.S. Department of Justice & Federal Trade Commission, Horizontal Merger Guidelines (2010), p.¶ 5.1, 5.2 and 9 (where it is proposed that the response by competitors should be assessed inter alia based on timeliness, likelihood and sufficiency). Sullivan and Grimes (2000), pp. 603–608. See also R. J. Reynolds Tobacco Co. v. Philip Morris, 199 F. Supp. 2D 362, p. 383 ("[a] mere showing of substantial or even dominant market share alone cannot establish market power sufficient to carry out [an anticompetitive pricing] scheme. The plaintiff must show that new rivals are barred from entering the market and show that existing competitors lack the capacity to expand their output to challenge the [defendant's] high price.").

[49] See Bresnahan and Greenstein (1999), p. 1.

[50] Id. pp. 20–21.

[51] Bresnahan (1999), p. 155.

[52] Cohen and Levinthal (1990), p. 128. See also Knoben and Oerlemans (2006), pp. 71, 77–78.

[53] Baldwin and Clark (2000), p. 64. See also Boudreau (2006), pp. 2–3; Gawer and Henderson (2007), pp. 3–6.

network functions so that they can serve as generative hubs for other providers to build upon without relying exclusively on the Internet.[54]

In all these cases players assume more than one functions and occupy positions in more than one segments of the industry creating competitive pressure that has been unaccounted for and continues to be largely ignored. In the recent net neutrality proceedings this kind of "*divided technical leadership*" to use the words of Bresnahan and Greenstein,[55] that has traditionally characterized the computer and communications industry and forcefully continues to do today, seems to be absent from the analysis. Again, while even if this type of vertical competitive pressure is not enough to change the conclusion that regulation is needed, it should at least play a role in moving regulation away from absolutist black and white solutions that trap the industry in a static state of what is allowed and what not, and instead adopt a flexible framework as advocated above, that has the ability to take into account the new forms of competitive pressure mentioned here, when and to the extend they apply.

Further, as mentioned, entry/expansion doesn't necessarily have to occur; along with technological proximity, the technical interdependence between layers creates a bi-directional bond and consequently limits the independent exercise of market power of each actor in the various layers.[56] In this context, it is unclear a priori which layer/actor has more power and more value, and in fact the allocation is fluid.[57] The much-publicized case of Comcast's interconnection battle with Netflix (operating in different markets) shows that Comcast needed Netflix as much as

---

[54] See, *e.g.* TATA Communications (2011). Infrastructure-as-a-Service: Fulfilling the Promise of Cloud Computing, White Paper, available at http://www.tatadocomo.com/business/download/WhitePaper-Infrastructure-as-a-Service.pdf; Interoute, What is IaaS, available at http://www.interoute.com/what-iaas; Hoffmann and Staufer (2011); Ashiq Khan et al., Network Sharing in the Next Mobile Network: TCO Reduction, Management Flexibility, and Operational Independence; 2011 IEEECommunications Magazine 134 (2011); Press Release, Fujitsu Unveils 'Network as a Service Concept,' available at http://www.fujitsu.com/global/about/resources/news/press-releases/2007/0516-02.htm; NokiaSiemens Networks, Network Virtualization Enabling Novel Business Models in a Dynamic Market, available at http://networks.nokia.com/system/files/document/nsn-noo-2012_networkvirtualization_v01.pdf; Hao et al. (2009), p. 33; Mishra (2010), pp. 206–208; Fogliata and Mussini (2008). Intelligence-Ready Network Infrastructure: An Ecosystem to Control Third-Party Intelligence Distribution Close to Nomadic Users, 13 Bell Labs Technical Journal 105, 107 (" A network operator running an 'open platform' for network-distributed computing (OPNDC) may offer several competing service providers an opportunity to deploy their software modules, loading the desired service logic directly onto network equipment or network management system nodes. Such a separation of roles allows both the network operator and the service provider to focus on its respective core mission and makes it faster and easier to deploy new network-intensive services packaged as plug-ins independent of network infrastructure upgrades. ... The resulting secondary market of value-added services, provided by a constellation of smaller and dynamic partner companies through the deployment of plug-in software for the standard platform of network machines, can expand the offer of new value-added services, relying on network-based information to create a common user context across the services.").

[55] Bresnahan and Greenstein (1999), p. 3.

[56] Fransman (2010) pp. 41–42.

[57] See, *e.g.* Sabat (2002), p. 505; Peppard et al. (2006), p. 128; Ballon (2009), p. 4; Gawer and Henderson (2007), pp. 1–3.

Netflix needed Comcast, and that it took many years of Netflix straining broadband access providers' capacity until they successfully pushed back, a testament to the vertical power Netflix holds vis-a-vis broadband access providers on account of its tremendous value in the ecosystem.[58] Similarly, the power balance between mobile device manufacturers and mobile carriers is constantly changing too: in the US the major national carriers were traditionally considered the most powerful player in the value chain, but along came Apple to disturb this power allocation, while in Europe giants like Ericsson and Nokia commanded great power due to the fragmented national carrier scene, but when they lost market share to Apple and Samsung, their position vis-a-vis national operators worsened dramatically.[59]

What these examples and the underlying theories show is that the peculiarities of the technology-intensive environment of the modern communications sector does not lend itself to the kind of competition analysis that we have applied so far. Recognizing and factoring in the parameters of technological proximity, technical interdependence and the resulting vertical entry, pressures and value flow between layers will allow regulators and stakeholders to more accurately assess the competitive state of the industry and devise appropriate regulation. Even if the regulatory result is the same (which it shouldn't—at a minimum a more flexible approach as described above should emerge), it will have been based on an up-to-date analysis, hopefully one that is more future-proof than the current.

16.3 Concluding Remarks

I have attempted to briefly present in this article the three main reasons why, I think, regulators around the world are not closer to a solution that shows signs of stability. These do not depend on one's position on net neutrality. Even after taking them into account, regulators can very well choose to support or oppose net neutrality, although the factors considered here point to a middle road.

Of the three reasons, the first one concerns regulatory rigidity, the second fixations on historical principles of the Internet, and the third the reliance on a not up-to-date competition analysis. These problems may seem disparate and high-level, and it is perhaps why they haven't been collectively addressed, but in essence they all have a common underlying cause: path dependence. Net neutrality rules (perhaps unavoidably) are building upon past regulations (*e.g.* common carrier regulation, essential facilities), historical practices and state of affairs (*e.g.* the belief that the Internet is not owned or controlled by anyone), and extant scientific knowledge (*e.g.* on industrial economics and organization).

If we could restart from zero and had to identify the relevant players and markets, see how they relate to each other, determine a desirable outcome based on industrial

[58] See Bode (2014) and Raybum (2014). See also Zeidler (2010).
[59] A good illustration about this power balance can be found in the case studies on i-mode in Takeshi Natsun, The i-Mode Wireless Ecosystem pp. 1–20 (2003); Tee and Gawer (2009), p. 217.

organization analysis and other socioeconomic considerations and devise regulation that can take into account the resulting conflicting interests, we could come up a solid piece of legislation with multi-stakeholder support. Hopefully, the factors discussed here and the relevant literature will help overcome the influence of the past and devise stable regulation for the future.

References

Areeda, P. E., & Hovenkamp, H. (2006). *Antitrust law: An analysis of antitrust principles and their Application*. Kluwer.

Baldwin, C., & Clark, K. (2000). *Design rules: The power of modularity* (vol. 1, p. 64). MIT Press, Cambridge, MA.

Ballon, P. (2009). *Platform types and gatekeeper roles: The case of the mobile communications industry* (p. 4). Paper presented at the Druid Summer Conference 2009. Available at http://www2.druid.dk/conferences/viewpaper.php?id=5952&cf=32

Bengtsson, M., & Kock, S. (1999). Cooperation and competition in relationships between competitors in business networks. *Journal of Business and Industrial Marketing, 14*, 178, 180–182

BEREC. (2012). An assessment of IP interconnection in the context of Net Neutrality. BoR (12), 130.

Bode, K. (2014, February 24). No, netflix's new deal with comcast probably won't destroy the internet. Yet., T ECHDIRT.

Bork, R. (1978). *The antitrust paradox: A policy at war with itself* (pp. 372–374, 225). New York: Basic Books.

Boudreau, K. (2006). *The boundaries of the platform: Vertical integration and economics incentives in mobile computing* (pp. 2–3). MIT Sloal Working Paper.

Bresnahan, T. (1999). New modes of competition. In J. Eisenach & T. M. Lenard (Eds.), *Competition, innovation, and the Microsoft monopoly: Antitrust in the digital marketplace* (p. 155).

Bresnahan, T. F., & Greenstein, S. (1999). Technological competition and the structure of the computer industry. *The Journal of Industrial Economics, 47*, 1.

Carlton, D., & Waldman, M. The strategic use of tying to create and preserve market power in evolving industries. *RAND Journal of Economics, 33*, 194

Church, J., & Gandal, N. (2005). Platform competition in telecommunications. In S. K. Majumdar et al. (Eds.), *Handbook of telecommunications economics*. North Holland (Vol. II, p. 117).

Clark, D. D. (2000). Interoperation, open interfaces and protocol architecture. In *The unpredictable certainty: White papers on information infrastructure through 2000* (Vol. 133, pp. 133–134).

Clark, D. D. (2005). Tussle in cyberspace: Defining tomorrow's internet. *IEEE/ACM Transactions on Networking, 13*, 462.

CoE Steering Committee on Media and Information Society, Protecting Human Rights Through Network Neutrality: Furthering Internet Users' Interest, Modernising Human Rights and Safeguarding the Open Internet, CDMSI (2013) misc 19E (2013, December).

Cohen, W. M., & Levinthal, D. A. (1990). Absorptive capacity: A new perspective on learning and innovation. *Administrative Science Quarterly, 35*, 128.

Crowcroft, J. (2007). Net neutrality: the technical side of the debate: A white paper. *ACM SIGCOMM Computer Communication Review, 31*(7), 49.

Dickson, P. R., & Ginter, J. L. (1987). Market segmentation, product differentiation, and marketing strategy. *Journal of Marketing, 24*(1), 1–10.

Faratin, P., Clark, D. D., Bauer, S., & Lehr, W. (2007). Complexity of internet interconnections: Technology, incentives and implications for policy.

FCC. (1999, October 6). In re applications of Ameritech Corp. and SBC Communications Inc. for Consent to Transfer Control of Corporations Holding Commission Licenses, Memorandum Opinion and Order, CC Docket No 98-141.

Ferraz, J. V., Souza C.A., Magrani, B. and Britto, W. (2012) *Content Filtering in Latin America: Reasons and Impacts on Freedom of Expression*. Available at http://www.palermo.edu/cele/pdf/english/Internet-Free-of-Censorship/Content-Filtering-Latin-America.pdf

Foditsch, N., et al. (2015, November 30–December 3). Shedding light on net neutrality: Towards possible solutions for the Brazilian Case. 20th ITS Biennial Conference, Rio de Janeiro, Brazil.

Fogliata, P., & Mussini, M. T. (2008). Intelligence-ready network infrastructure: An ecosystem to control third-party intelligence distribution close to nomadic users. *Bell Labs Technical Journal, 13*, 105, 107

Fransman, M. (2010). *The new ICT ecosystem: Implications for policy and regulation* (pp. 9–10, 41–42). Cambridge: Cambridge University Press.

Fung, B. (2015, April 14). The real net neutrality lawsuits are finally here. *Washington Post*.

Gawer, A., & Henderson, R. (2007). Platform owner entry and innovation in complementary markets: Evidence from Intel. *Journal of Economic and Management Strategy, 16*(1), 3–6.

Geere, D. (2015, March 6). Europe reverses course on net neutrality legislation. *Wired*.

Geradin, D., & Sidak, J. G. (2003). European and American approaches to antitrust remedies and the institutional design of regulation in telecommunications. In S. K. Majumdar et al., (Eds.), *Handbook of telecommunications economics*. North Holland (Vol. II, p. 517, 519).

Grant, R. (2008). *Contemporary strategy analysis*. John Wiley & Sons (6th ed) (p. 271).

Hahn, R. W., & Wallsten, S. (2006). The economics of net neutrality. *The Economists' Voice, 3*(6), 1–7.

Handley, M. (2006, June). Why the internet only just works. *BT Technology Journal, 24*, 119

Hao, F. et al. (2009). Enhancing dynamic cloud-based services using network virtualization. *Proceedings of the 1st ACM Workshop on Virtualized Infrastructure Systems and Architectures* (p. 33).

Hass, D. A. (2007). The never-was-neutral net and why informed end users can end the net neutrality debates. *Berkeley Technology Law Journal, 22*, 1565.

Hoffmann, M., & Staufer, M. (2011). Network virtualization for future mobile networks: General architecture and applications. *IEEE International Conference on Communications Workshops* (p. 1).

Huber, P. W. (1997). *Law and disorder in cyberspace: abolish the FCC and let common law rule the telecosm*. Oxford University Press, USA

Huston, G. (2008, June) The internet – 10 years later, The ISP Column. Available at http://www.internetsociety.org/sites/default/files/10years.pdf

Institute for Policy Integrity. (2010). *Free to Invest: The Economic Benefits of Preserving Net Neutrality*. Report No. 4.

ITU. (2012). *Exploring the Value and Economic Valuation of Spectrum*. Broadband Series Report.

Kastranakes, J. (2014, September 16). FCC received a total of 3.7 million comments on net neutrality. The Verge.

Knoben, J., & Oerlemans, L. A. G. (2006). Proximity and inter-organizational collaboration: A literature review. *International Journal of Management Reviews, 8*, 71, 77–78.

Kotler, P., & Keller, K. L. (2008). Marketing Management 288. Pearson (6th ed).

Lee, R. S., & Wu, T. (2009). Subsidizing creativity through network design: Zero-pricing and net neutrality. *The Journal of Economic Perspectives*, 61.

Lemley, M., & Lessig, L. (2000). Open access to cable modems. *Whittier Law Review, 22*(3), 9.

Lemley, M., & Lessig, L. (2000). The end of end-to-end: Preserving the architecture of the internet in the broadband era. *UCLA Law Review, 48*, 925.

Lessig, L. (2009, November 16). The internet under siege. Foreign Policy.

Lianos, I. (2009). The vertical/horizontal dichotomy in competition law: Some reflections with regard to dual distribution and private labels. In A. Ezrachi & U. Bernitz (Eds.), *Private Labels, Brands and Competition Policy* (p. 161).

McNamee, J. (2014, November 24). European Parliament fights back hard on net neutrality. EDRi.

Mishra, A. R. (2010). *Cellular technologies for emerging markets: 2G, 3G and beyond*. John Wiley & Sons.

Open Society Foundations, Mizukami, P., Reia, J., & Varon, J. (2013). *Mapping digital media: Brazil*. Open Society Foundations.

Page, W. H. (1980). Antitrust damages and economic efficiency: An approach to antitrust injury. *University of Chicago Law Review, 47,* 467, 495.

Parker, R. G. (1999, September 28). Senior Deputy Director, Bureau of Competition, Federal Trade Commission, Address Before the International Bar Association.

Peppard, J., et al. (2006). From value chain to value network: insights for mobile operators. *European Management Journal, 24,* 128.

Porter, M. (1980). *Competitive strategy* (pp. 159–161). New York: Free Press.

Raybum, D. (2014, February 23). Inside the netflix/comcast deal and what the media is getting very wrong. Streaming Media Blog

Rey, P., & Tirole, J. (2007). A primer on foreclosure. In M. Armstrong & R. H. Porter (Eds.), *Handbook of industrial organization.* Elsevier (Vol. III, pp. 2148–2150, 2145).

Rosenbush, S. (2015, May 14). Google's Vint Cerf warns against fragmentation of internet. *Wall Street Journal.*

Sabat, H. K. (2002). The evolving mobile wireless value chain and market structure. *Telecommunications Policy, 26.9,* 505.

Saltzer, J. et al. (1984). End-to-end arguments in system design. *ACM Transactions of Computer Systems, 2,* 277.

Sasso, B. (2014, May 13). The net has never been 'neutral'. *National Journal.*

SCF Associates. (2012). *Perspectives on the Value of Shared Spectrum Access.* Final Report for the European Commission.

Sidak, G. (2006). A consumer-welfare approach to network neutrality regulation of the internet. *Journal of Competition Law and Economics, 2,* 349.

Spence, M. (1976). Product differentiation and welfare. *American Economic Review, 66,* 407.

Speta, J. (2000). Handicapping the race for the last mile: A critique of open access rules for broadband platforms. *Yale Journal on Regulation, 17,* 39.

Speta, J. B. (2014). Unintentional antitrust: The FCC's only (and better) way forward with net neutrality after the mess of Verizon v. FCC. *Federal Communications Law Journal, 66,* 491.

Spulber, D., & Yoo, C. (2012). *Networks in telecommunications: Economics and law,* passim. Cambridge, UK.

Steiner, R. L. (2008). Vertical competition, horizontal competition, and market power. *The Antitrust Bulletin, 53,* 251.

Sullivan, L. A., & Grimes, W. (2000). *The law of antitrust: An integrated handbook* (p. 638). St Paul: West Publishing.

TATA Communications (2011). *Infrastructure-as-a-Service: Fulfilling the Promise of Cloud Computing,* White Paper. Available at http://www.tatadocomo.com/business/download/WhitePaper-Infrastructure-as-a-Service.pdf

Tee, R., & Gawer, A. (2009). Industry architecture as a determinant of successful platform strategies: A case study of the i-mode mobile internet service. *European Management Review, 6,* 217.

Tirole, J. (4th reprint 1990). The theory of industrial organization, 193. MIT Press.

United States v. AT&T Co. (1982). 552 F. Supp. 131, 135–36.

Utterback, J. M., & Abernathy, W. J. (1975). A dynamic model of process and product innovation. *Omega: The International Journal of Marketing Management 3,* 639, 643.

Verizon v. Federal Communications Commission. (2014). 740 F.3d 623, 633

Verizon Communications, Inc. v. Law Offices of Curtis V. Trinko. (2004). 540 U.S. 398.

Viscusi, W. K. et al. (2005). *Economics of regulation and antitrust* (pp. 248–253). Cambridge: MIT Press.

Weiser, P. J. (2003). Towards a next generation regulatory strategy. *Loyola University Chicago Law Journal, 35,* 60–63, 41.

White House. (2014, November 14). The president's message on net neutrality. Available at https://www.whitehouse.gov/net-neutrality

Wu, T., & Lee, R. (2009). Subsidizing creativity through network design: Zero pricing and net neutrality. *Journal of Economic Perspectives, 23*(3), 61, 63.

Wu, T. (2007). A tale of two platforms. Available at http://ssrn.com/abstract=993288

Yoo, C. (2004). Would mandating broadband network neutrality help or hurt competition? A comment on the end-to-end debate. *Journal of Telecommunications and High Technology Law, 3*, 23.

Yoo, C. S. (2005). Beyond network neutrality. *Harvard Journal of Law and Technology. 19*(1), 1–77.

Yoo, C. S. (2007). What can antitrust contribute to the network neutrality debate. *International Journal of Communication, 1*, 504–409, 493.

Yoo, C. (2010). Product life cycle theory and the maturation of the internet. *Northwester University Law Review, 104*, 641.

Yoo, C. (2012). *The dynamic Internet: How technology, users, and businesses are transforming the network.* AEI Press.

Zeidler, S. (2010, December 1). Netflix scrambles future of TV and films. Reuters.

Zineldin, M. (2004). Co-opetition: The organisation of the future. *Marketing Intelligence and Planning, 22*, 780, 780–781.

Chapter 17
A Norwegian Perspective on European Regulation of Net Neutrality

Frode Sørensen

17.1   Introduction

An agreement about European net neutrality rules was reached between the Commission, the Parliament and the Council in Brussels 30 June 2015. The FCC published the US net neutrality rules 26 February 2015, a step ahead of the European developments.

The first part of this paper presents some thoughts regarding comparison between the two approaches to net neutrality on the different sides of the Atlantic, as seen from a Norwegian perspective.

And the second part of the paper discusses the relationship between net neutrality and traffic handling, and the relationship between net neutrality and charging models, including zero-rating, from a Norwegian perspective.

First, a quick walk along the Norwegian historical milestones related to Internet, net neutrality and democracy:

- **Norway has the longest running net neutrality regime in Europe**
  In 2009 Norwegian net neutrality guidelines were adopted based on a co-regulatory approach, with clear rules against blocking and throttling of applications (not to be compared to self-regulation which typically only covers transparency, while allowing throttling and blocking).[1]
- **Norway was the first country outside US that was connected to the Internet**
  In 1973 Norway established the first non-US node on ARPANET, the predecessor of the Internet. In the beginning, the connection was primarily used for seismic data exchange, subsequently giving access to additional Norwegian research institutions.[2]
- **Norway has one of the oldest constitutions in the world which is still in use**

---

[1] http://eng.nkom.no/technical/internet/net-neutrality/net-neutrality.

[2] http://www.norsar.no/norsar/about-us/History/Internet/.

F. Sørensen (✉)
Norwegian Communications Authority, Lillesand, Norway

© Springer International Publishing Switzerland 2016
L. Belli, P. De Filippi (eds.), *Net Neutrality Compendium*,
DOI 10.1007/978-3-319-26425-7_17

There is a strong democratic tradition in Norway. Inspired by the US Declaration of Independence 1776 and the French revolution 1789, the Norwegian Constitution from 1814 was at the time considered one of the most liberal and radically democratic in the world.[3]

This may be mere coincidence, and I will not speculate, although it is a fascinating constellation of historical facts. Anyway, Norwegians are today enjoying an open Internet!

17.2   A Comparison between European and US Attitude to Net Neutrality[4]

Europe is a large continent with varying cultures, as well as different approaches to net neutrality. And how do Europe compare with US regarding attitude to net neutrality? There are several significant differences which I would like to address.

17.2.1   Can Regulated Local Loop Unbundling Ensure Net Neutrality in Europe?

It has often been speculated whether local loop unbundling in Europe would lead to a significant difference in the need to regulate net neutrality.[5] Unbundling stimulates the establishment of competing providers of Internet access services. This increases users' possibility to choose a neutral Internet access service.

However, Internet access is not like any other service, since an Internet user is (of course) not communicating with himself. Users need to communicate with *other* users in the other end, and these users may not be switching to a neutral Internet access service.

And restrictions on Internet access services for some users fragments the Internet, the possibility for user-to-user communication becomes lower, and the size of the market for content and application providers becomes smaller. The network effect is reduced.

---

[3] http://en.wikipedia.org/wiki/Constitution_of_Norway.

[4] These considerations were elaborated for the Net Neutrality panel of the SMART Workshop which was organized on 22 April 2015 in Barcelona (ref. http://internet-monitoring-study.eu/), where these two approaches were discussed between Scott Jordan (FCC) and Frode Sørensen (Nkom). The considerations were subsequently updated after the 1 July agreement to reflect latest European developments in the area.

[5] Marsden (2009).

17.2.2   Significant Level of Restrictions of Internet Access in the European Market

An investigation of the actual level of restrictions on Internet access in the European market, conducted by BEREC in 2012, showed that every fifth fixed Internet connection and every third mobile Internet connection experienced blocking or throttling of applications.[6]

It is interesting to read the analysis by van Schewick in The Atlantic in 2014: "Unlike Internet users in Europe, many of whom are on restricted Internet service plans that ban the use of specific applications on mobile networks, U.S. users have experienced the power of an open Internet—and they are not willing to give it up."

The amount of restrictions was one of the major reasons presented by the European Commission when they in September 2013 proposed a net neutrality regulation.

17.2.3   Europe, despite the European Union, Still Consists of Many Strong National States

Furthermore, different national approaches to net neutrality have developed over time. Norway has its co-regulatory approach, while the Netherlands and Slovenia have adopted net neutrality laws. Several member states were considering net neutrality rules before the European Commission proposed the regulation of net neutrality.[7]

After the European Parliament in April 2014 strengthened the proposed net neutrality regulation, the national interests within the Council of EU discussed significantly weaker proposals which were presented during the trilogue meetings between the Commission, the Parliament and the Council in Brussels. And finally, on 30 June 2015 an agreement between the three was announced.

17.2.4   The Most Successful Content and Application Providers (CAPs) Are US-Based

ISPs express worries about increasing power of CAPs, and many major successful CAPs are US-based. This may have given an impression that there is a particular need to protect European ISPs against US CAPs. However, blocking and throttling

---

[6] BEREC (2012).

[7] European Commission, 2014 Report on Implementation of the EU regulatory framework for electronic communications, https://ec.europa.eu/digital-agenda/en/news/2014-report-implementation-eu-regulatory-framework-electronic-communications: *"Belgium and Luxemburg were considering legislating and have opened a debate on net neutrality; however the process is pending the co-legislative process on the Connected Continent initiative. In Germany the draft decree on net neutrality of June 2013 was not further pursued. In January 2014 the Finnish Government submitted its proposal to the Parliament on the 'Information Society Code', a telecoms legislative package scheduled for 2015 that includes provisions on net neutrality."*

of content and applications would not lead to any stimulation of European CAPs! And CAPs are essential since it is the demand for content which drives the demand for bandwidth.

The ISPs have a gatekeeper role towards their subscribers. And the termination monopoly problems leading to sector specific regulation of traditional telecoms may revive in new fashions for providers of Internet access services due to the powerful deep packet inspection techniques. Therefore, net neutrality is important for innovation among European CAPs that can compete with US-based CAPs.

17.2.5 European Telecom Technology Has Shown Major Success in Mobile Communications

The European Telecommunications Standards Institute (ETSI) developed the GSM mobile telephony system, which became widespread over the world. Furthermore, its successor the 3G-system UMTS, standardized by 3GPP, has also taken over as a prevailing technology for the previous US-dominated 3GPP2 standards, while being succeeded by LTE ("4G").

US on the other hand, have a stronger tradition in IP technology, being "the cradle" of the Internet. This may have led to a better position in the communication technology development where IP has become "the winner", as well as a better understanding of how to adapt to this new paradigm which is replacing traditional telecommunications.

17.2.6 How Come US Citizens Show Such Enthusiasm in Protecting Net Neutrality?

What is the reason for the strong engagement of the US population in the public net neutrality discourse? There seems to be a more relaxed attitude to net neutrality in Europe, although there are some strong advocates on this side of the Atlantic as well.

Can this be understood in the context of the First Amendment to the US Constitution and the strong position of freedom of speech in the US society? Is the "Internet freedom" simply highly valued by US citizens as a prolongation of this well-established constitutional principle?

17.3 Fundamental Elements of Net Neutrality Regulation

How does this difference in background between Europe and US influence the proposed net neutrality regulations on the different continents? This may be difficult to prove, but the differences in the regulations are anyway interesting to investigate.

17.3.1   Application-Agnosticism

Equal treatment of traffic from different applications, so-called application-agnosticism, is the essence of net neutrality, and therefore it should be expected that this is safeguarded in such regulation. Non-blocking and non-throttling are obvious characteristics of both proposed regulations reflecting this.

The rules from FCC are even clearer and add non-prioritization to these characteristics. Regarding the European proposed rules, they announce: "Providers of internet access services shall treat all traffic equally, when providing internet access services".[8] However, the effect of this depends on the implementation of the rules for exceptions.

17.3.2   Reasonable Traffic Management

Net neutrality is of course not regulated to give obstacles to efficient operation of networks or protection of citizens, even though stakeholders sometimes present such travesty. To accommodate such measures, reasonable traffic management is allowed. A typical example is preservation of network integrity and security.

The proposed European rules have fairly well designed exceptions for reasonable traffic management. Unfortunately, the rule for handling of network congestion does not prescribe that the exception should only be granted when application-agnostic methods are not usable. Traffic overload can in many cases be fully handled by application-agnostic methods.

17.3.3   Specialised Services (Non-internet Access Services)

Specialised services, also referred to as "non-Internet access services", provide extensive exceptions from net neutrality. Therefore there must be clear rules regarding which services that can be approved as specialised services. First, the traffic from such services should be isolated from the traffic on the Internet, and second, specialised services should not be provided at the expense of Internet access services.

Regarding the former, the proposed European rules remain unclear, while the US rules say that "these services use some form of network management to isolate the capacity used by these services from that used by broadband Internet access services". Regarding the latter, the European rules say that such services may be offered "only if the network capacity is sufficient to provide them in addition to any internet access services provided". But the implementation of this rule is still pending.

---

[8] Council of the European Union, 2015, Roaming and open internet draft regulation, http://data.consilium.europa.eu/doc/document/ST-10409-2015-REV-1/en/pdf.

17.3.4   Zero-Rating and Price Discrimination

Recently, there has been much attention to data caps and zero-rating, in particular for mobile Internet access services. Simple data caps can be application-agnostic and would then not lead to concerns regarding net neutrality. However, in case of exempting particular applications from charging, so-called zero-rating, would obviously not be application-agnostic.

In the legislative net neutrality initiatives on both sides of the Atlantic, this question is not fully resolved yet. However, the US net neutrality rules seem to acknowledge that this will need particular regulatory attention, and such matters will be scrutinized on a case-by-case basis.

In Europe, a few national initiatives have tackled the issue. In the Netherlands and in Slovenia, the regulators have taken concrete decisions against zero-rating based on the national laws. In Norway as well, it has been clarified that zero-rating would be regarded as a breach of the national net neutrality guidelines. However, proposed European rules, has not resolved this issue explicitly. And it remains to be seen how "commercial practices which by reason of their scale, lead to situations where end-users' choice is materially reduced in practice" will be interpreted.

Net neutrality has been an important regulatory question in Nkom's work for many years, and it is interesting to see how the relevance of net neutrality has grown in Europe lately. But the public debate never reached the same temperature as in the US, while FCC has taken a clear position to strengthen net neutrality through its new rules. The question is; has Europe really taken a strong stance regarding net neutrality to achieve similar safeguards for an open Internet, or will we be lagging behind the US?

17.4   Net Neutrality and Charging Models[9]

Lately we've seen a change in the European net neutrality discussion where charging models have become more central. In this part of the paper we discuss how the relationship between net neutrality and traffic handling has implications regarding the relationship between net neutrality and charging models. The clues to this discussion are application-agnosticism and user-control. But this still allows rich possibilities for ISPs to perform traffic management and product differentiation, as described below.

In simple terms, net neutrality means that the Internet works the same for different users of the net, regardless of who you are. Norway has had guidelines on net neutrality since 2009, and these seem to be working well as a regulatory tool to preserve net neutrality for the citizens. Through the EEA Agreement, the new regulation of net neutrality in Europe will also apply to Norway when it enters into force.

---

[9]This paper was originally published at Nkom's web site (http://eng.nkom.no/), but has subsequently been updated to reflect latest developments.

17.4.1   Net Neutrality: Equality and Variation

Some people argue against net neutrality on the grounds that the Internet has never worked the same for all users, or for all types of usage, which is in itself true. However, the goal of net neutrality is not that all traffic should be handled identically—which would never be possible in practice. The aim is rather to preserve the Internet as an open platform for communication and avoid discrimination between applications or fragmentation of the Internet.

A commonly used analogy for Internet communication is the road network. In this analogy net neutrality means that we want the same rules for all traffic on the "road network". But, as for the road network, there are various ways of accessing the Internet. Different technologies such as telephony networks, cable TV networks, fibre networks and mobile networks all have varying qualities and provide varying access speeds. It is also common practice for a single technology to operate at different speeds for various types of subscription. However, with regard to net neutrality, the point is that it is the users of the Internet access who decides what their access is to be used for.

Following the analogy, inside the Internet too, the various "highways" have different capacities. The capacity is typically deployed by the Internet service provider, based on how much traffic there is to the various destinations. As users of Internet communications, we can observe this by running speed tests via our own Internet access. In some cases disputes arise when the interconnection between the different providers' networks need upgrading. Until such disputes are settled, this can lead to short-term reduced speed when users communicate via these interconnections. But as long as all the different applications are treated equally, this is not a direct violation of net neutrality.

17.4.2   Charging Models for Internet Access Services

Internet service providers use differentiation of Internet access services as a natural element of their business model. We all benefit from well-functioning businesses that can offer a wide range of well-functioning, affordable communication services to the population. Today it is common for providers to charge users on the basis of capacity (speed) and/or volume, depending on the technological platform.

According to economic theory, offers of different qualities at different prices can help to ensure that people with lower willingness to pay are also able to obtain a product.[10] Product differentiation can be fully compatible with net neutrality, since different speed classes mean that the different products have varying quality. Differentiation based on other quality parameters such as time delay or service availability can also be used similarly. By contrast, services that provide access to selected sets of content or applications would be typical examples of differentiation that would violate net neutrality.

---

[10] https://en.wikipedia.org/wiki/Price_elasticity_of_demand.

Nowadays it has also become common practice for subscriptions to be differentiated on the basis of volume limits. Again, as long as this is done independent of the traffic type, this does not provide grounds for concern in respect of net neutrality. However, in recent years providers in some countries have launched service offers where specific applications are exempted from charging.[11]

17.4.3   What About Zero-Rating?

The Norwegian guidelines on net neutrality state quite clearly that "Internet users are entitled to an Internet connection that is free of discrimination with regard to type of application, service or content or based on sender or receiver address." This means that in the Norwegian market zero-rating would constitute a violation of the guidelines. At first glance it may appear that all traffic is handled equally in this charging model, but once you have used your quota, the traffic that is exempted will usually be allowed to continue, while all other traffic will be throttled or blocked. This is clearly a case of discrimination between different types of traffic.

Also for data plans where users can upgrade their basic data cap with an additional quota, there is discrimination between different traffic types. For any given total quota bought by a user, consider a user pumping exempted traffic, such traffic would always run at full speed since it never reaches the limit of the total quota, compared with a user pumping non-exempted traffic which would eventually become blocked when it reaches the limit of the quota.

Another way to consider this would be to assess the average speed provided to the users, which would become application-specific. Again, for a given total quota bought by a user, consider a user pumping exempted traffic, such traffic would achieve a considerably higher average speed, compared with a user pumping non-exempted traffic which would eventually reach the limit of the total quota and thereby achieve a lower average speed.

Furthermore, in the heads of the users there would probably be a "traffic filter" choosing which application(s) to prefer, based on a decision taken by the Internet service provider. Thereby we can understand that also for data plans with continuous volume charging without explicit quotas, such personal "traffic filters" would still have effect due to the incentive to select specific applications to avoid high bills by the end of the month.

There are of course arguments in favour of zero-rating that make the method seem quite fair. As consumers, we may find it advantageous that we do not have to pay for a particular type of traffic. Nevertheless, zero-rating lead to selected traffic from the Internet service provider itself or affiliated providers being favoured above other traffic. And this is exactly the kind of situation net neutrality aims to avoid—allowing the Internet service provider to decide how we use the Internet. Instead, the Internet should remain an open, neutral platform for all types of communication.

---

[11] Digital Fuel Monitor (2014).

The Norwegian Communications Authority (Nkom) has long been working actively for net neutrality for the benefit of Norwegian consumers, organisations and businesses. The Internet is important to economy, cultural diversity, social life and democracy, and Nkom therefore works to preserve the Internet as an open platform. Internet service providers should instead use other methods than discrimination of content and/or applications to differentiate their products, *e.g.* based on access speed.

References

BEREC. (2012). BoR (12) 30, A view of traffic management and other practices resulting in restrictions to the open Internet in Europe. https://ec.europa.eu/digital-agenda/sites/digital-agenda/files/Traffic%20Management%20Investigation%20BEREC_2.pdf

Digital Fuel Monitor. (2014). List of 75 zero-rated, potentially anti-competitive mobile applications/ services, violating net neutrality, in EU28. http://dfmonitor.eu/insights/2014_oct_zerorate/

Marsden, C. (2009). Net neutrality 'Lite': Regulatory responses to broadband internet discrimination. http://papers.ssrn.com/sol3/papers.cfm?abstract_id=1330747

Chapter 18
Zero Rating and Mobile Net Neutrality

Christopher T. Marsden

18.1 Introduction: Net Neutrality and Walled Gardens

Several developed countries have recently legislated for or regulated for net neutrality, the principle that Internet Service Providers (ISPs) should not discriminate between different applications, services and content accessed by their users. This came after 20 years of attempted discrimination between content streams within the walled gardens of both fixed and mobile ISPs,[1] such as AOL in the 1990s, BT Openworld (sic) around 2000[2] and Vodafone Live/360 in 2002-11, which was intended to challenge the Apple AppStore and Android/GooglePlay.[3] Alongside their walled gardens, these ISPs enforced monthly data caps preventing their customers having unlimited use of the Internet.

Fixed line walled gardens failed in view of the easy access at increasingly low cost offered by broadband access, though in the earlier dial-up analogue era, walled gardens had been assumed to predominate or at least offer the first "landing page" on the Internet. By 2003, it had become obvious that users preferred a landing page that represented their search engine of preference (and increasingly their browser of choice), in which competition Google rapidly won against Yahoo! and Microsoft. Continued attempts to maintain walled gardens throughout the past 10 years have focussed on both 'negative' and 'positive' net neutrality, as I have previously explained in depth.[4] I explain both in turn.

---

[1] Lemley and Lessig (1999) and Marsden (1999, 2010b).

[2] BT Openworld (known internally as 'OpenWoe') was merged with BT's joint venture BT-Yahoo! in 2002. Timms (2003).

[3] Wray (2009).

[4] Marsden (2010a).

C.T. Marsden (✉)
University of Sussex, Brighton, UK

© Springer International Publishing Switzerland 2016   241
L. Belli, P. De Filippi (eds.), *Net Neutrality Compendium*,
DOI 10.1007/978-3-319-26425-7_18

Negative neutrality is the blocking and throttling of content that threatens the business model of the ISP. This can be relatively benign when it is spam email and viruses that are blocked. It can also be self-serving and anti-competitive when it is unjustified and unreasonable restrictions on user's preferred content that is affected—for instance peer-to-peer file sharing or video streaming. It is this 'negative' net neutrality which is the target of most legislation in the area, based on the generic regulatory principle of "first, do no harm", in this case eliminating the harms caused by unreasonable negative blocking, or discrimination. Cases in the US such as Madison River and Comcast were about blocking,[5] and is it this that rouses much consumer anger and political action.

'Positive' net neutrality violations involve not blocking, but treating some content better than general Internet traffic. As cable TV provides High Definition and standard video and television channels at high fees in a separate logical pathway to the general Internet traffic on its cable, some telecoms companies hope to partition its Internet traffic to replicate this business model. Several ISPs attempted this practice over lengthy periods, notably by excluding television channels from monthly data caps for users, positively discriminating in favour of their affiliated content and against other video providers (such as YouTube). In this way, 'walled gardens' reappear with much more specialized walls—restrictions that affect only certain non-affiliated types of Internet traffic, such as social networks or video.

This use of excluding preferred content from data caps is described as "zero rating" because all that downloading costs precisely zero in terms of counting towards their monthly bill.[6] Note that many fixed ISPs have virtually unlimited data use as part of their offer, made possible because maximum speeds and user profiles mean that the cumulative download burden does not over-strain the network (a dial-up network would be an excellent candidate for "unlimited" service as users would find it very hard to download very much). An infamous example was Deutsche Telekom's 2013 announcement that its video service would be excluded from data caps and that users who downloaded in excess of their monthly limit would in the rest of the month find their speeds throttled back to 256 kpbs. It was both the positive discrimination in favour of Telekom's own service and the threat to users' service that caused the pre-election political outcry that led to Telekom deciding on 2 Mbps as the (rather more generous) throttled speed.

Data caps have been controversial throughout the consumer Internet's history,[7] especially in the United States where dial-up Internet was virtually free to the end-user (simply the cost of a local telephone call). The US Open Internet Advisory Committee noted the move towards capping data especially for mobile users and worried "whether caps or thresholds that are set too low could lead to a world where the average user carefully monitors her bandwidth use" given uncertainty over data

---

[5] Marsden (2013).

[6] Eisenach (2015) and Maillé and Tuffin (2014), pp. 89–90.

[7] ERMERT, MONIKA (2013) Managed services – a net neutrality trap? Internet Policy Review 03 MAY 2013 at http://policyreview.info/articles/news/managed-services-%E2%80%93-net-neutrality-trap/125.

caps as a "transitory or permanent concern"[8] which appears to be the case in developing (and many developed) nations' mobile data access. While data caps apply in many nations applied by many ISPs, the user often has little or no idea that they are approaching their monthly limit until informed by the ISP, and such warnings are often inaccurate. It is at best a blunt weapon for handling congestion, though there is little argument that data caps per se infringe net neutrality, as long as the cap gradually increases over time.

Politicians and telecoms executives who now claim to be in favour of net neutrality are in fact conceding that blocking and throttling users is no longer acceptable to politicians, and therefore regulators (even if the latter protest their independence). They largely only concede 'negative' net neutrality. 'Positive' net neutrality is a much more contested topic, and where download limits apply or ill-defined specialized services carry the zero-rated content, this concept of zero rating will be heavily contested. That is more the case with mobile than fixed networks, and more the case with developing nations' mobile ISPs than developed.

18.2   Towards the Mobile Internet

In the mobile Internet, speeds were so low and costs so high initially that a dial-up analogue type experience was all that users could expect. Smartphones were initially business-enabled Nokia and then Blackberry e-mail devices. The stark choice of price collapse for networks otherwise lacking any significant data use, or limited bandwidth offers faced the developed world in 2007, but two astonishing developments occurred together: smartphones and app stores, and social networking via mobiles.[9]

Prior to 2007, few Internet users accessed the Internet via their 2G or 3G mobile devices, as bandwidth was expensive, network build-out limited and mobile data was very expensive. First, the Apple iPhone was launched, offering a full Internet experience on mobile alongside its App Store which offered low bandwidth experiences that could be downloaded and used later: particularly useful for underground Metro journeys and in 3G "not-spots". It was the invention of the iPhone, and the networks' decision to move towards unmetered or more generous pricing to encourage use of the hitherto little-used 3G mobile networks, that led to the explosion of smartphone Internet use.

The number of active 'smartphone' users rapidly increased following the iPhone launch in 2007, especially when the Google Android operating system and Android (now Google Play) Store began to compete against Apple for lower cost and lower income users—whose interest lay mainly in entry price smartphones and free apps. Prices also collapsed due to use of 3G 'dongles' (USB-linked laptop antennae for 3G) as well as the ubiquitous use of WiFi within broadband-enabled homes, offices and coffee shops. This went alongside the expectation that users would download apps

[8] Open Internet Advisory Committee (2013), p. 13.
[9] Wu (2007).

over WiFi rather than eating into their expensive data plans, with the iTunes Store only accepting 3G purchases from autumn 2009, 2 years after the iPhone launch.[10]

Note that WiFi became widely available in laptops in 2001-4 with a lag of about 5 years in public 'hotspots', the number of public access hotspots increasing from 1 million in 2010 to 70 million by 2015.[11] There were over 3 billion WiFi chipsets shipped in 2015, in smartphones, laptops, tablets and other devices, including 166 million consumer WiFi terminals (as used in the home connected to a fixed broadband Ethernet connection).[12] Because WiFi 'piggybacks' on fixed connections, its essential role in mobile Internet access over the past decade is much overlooked and under-estimated, with a recent study for the European Commission estimating as much as 80–90 % of "mobile" traffic is actually carried by WiFi connections to the fixed network—i.e. only 20 % is truly mobile traffic: "as much as 80–90 % of Android smart phone and tablet mobile traffic is already being off-loaded to private Wi-Fi".[13] The conclusion is that the more WiFi and other hand-off to the fixed network, the cheaper mobile data becomes, with the most ubiquitously WiFi-enabled nations being South Korea and the United Kingdom.

The iPhone itself was tethered or "locked" exclusively into a single network at launch in 2007, a model started in the US with AT&T and continued with O2 in the UK and T-Mobile in Germany. These networks imposed severe cost penalties on customers who tried to leave before the end of their contract, and Apple's contracts made it a warranty violation to unlock the phone for use on other networks. Customers brought a class action law suit against AT&T, which backfired spectacularly resulting in the loss of customer rights to bring law suits if contracts contain compulsory arbitration clauses.[14] The iPhone, despite high costs and the App Store's aggressive filtering of applications considered technically or ethically unsound, rapidly outsold the Nokia and Blackberry competition. Android devices began to sell in volume with the Samsung and HTC families of phones, and at no point did Apple actually outsell its competitors (first Nokia until 2011, then Samsung thereafter became top selling global competitors in smartphones). The mass adoption of smartphones depended on driving a lower price point than Apple was willing to compete at, and the wealthy technologically literate early adopters are now far outnumbered by Android mass users (by 50 % to 25 % in the UK in 2015, for instance): about 1 in 7 smartphone sales worldwide are iPhones.[15]

Social networking using Web2.0 software expanded from a very low base at the start of the smartphone era. Brown and Marsden explain that "Facebook grew from nothing in 2004 to become the second most popular destination Web site in the

---

[10] About.com (2009).

[11] Lemstra et al. (2010). WiFi is the brand name for the IEEE802.11 family of standards, protocol released 1997, trademark adopted 1999.

[12] ABI Research (2015).

[13] Marcus and Burns (2013).

[14] *AT&T Mobility v. Concepcion*, 563 U.S. 321 (2011).

[15] Neal (2015).

world by 2012".[16] It grew to 100 million users by autumn 2008, surpassed 1 billion monthly active users (MAUs) in 2012 and 1.5 billion in 2015, which included 210 million in the US/Canada and 112 million in its second largest market, India, in autumn 2014. Facebook was floated on the stock market in 2012, warning investors in its prospectus that "There is no guarantee that popular mobile devices will continue to feature Facebook, or that mobile device users will continue to use Facebook rather than competing products."[17] It was thus a matter of great priority for Facebook to expand its mobile network partnerships rapidly internationally in the face of a decline in youth MAUs in its home US market from 2013.

18.3   Zero Rating and Internet.Org

I now examine the developing nation zero rating controversy, before considering the extent to which zero rating may infringe or support net neutrality and Internet access. The future controversy for net neutrality is mobile in the developing world, and specialised services in the developed world. That is the stark conclusion after the United States and Canada[18] implemented net neutrality in 2015, and the European Union legislated to provide net neutrality. This paper does not examine these developments in depth, but a complete analysis will be found in Marsden (2016).

While net neutrality law is coming into effect in those 30 countries and their European Economic Area neighbours (for instance Norway has implemented net neutrality since 2009, and Switzerland recently introduced industry-led co-regulation), outside East Asia most citizens in developing countries depend on expensive mobile access to the Internet. Odlyzko notes that the zero-rating debate exists in one Asian country, but does not explore in depth,[19] while monthly caps were important before zero rating had become commonly identified.[20] Just as net neutrality dates to the 1990s so zero rating dates to the same decade even if the term of art came much later.

There are ten times more mobile (5.6 billion) than fixed line connections (572 million) in developing countries, whereas the developed world ratio is 3:1. There are five times more mobile broadband subscriptions in the developing world with 2.37 billion to only 429 million fixed subscriptions (developed world 1.09 billion mobile to 365 million fixed at a ratio of 3:1). 70 % of Internet users totalling over 2 billion people are outside the EU/US, and total Internet penetration in 2014 was only 39 % of the population.[21] With similar GDP per capita to Brazil, it is only 50 % more expensive for Bulgarian or Romanians to access mobile data than Germans, but at least 600 % more for Brazilians (only €1 per GB for prepay data in

---

[16] Brown and Marsden (2013), p. xii.

[17] Cited in Brown and Marsden (2013), p. 123.

[18] CRTC (2015).

[19] Odlyzko et al. (2012), p. 15.

[20] Fierce Wireless (2011), p. 18.

[21] Source: International Telecommunications Union (2015).

Romania[22] but 200 MB per day for 3.29R in Brazil[23] maximum 6 GB per month for 100R = €26 or at least €4.3 per GB). Romania and Bulgaria may be smaller countries than Brazil but they have equivalent wealth. Something is seriously wrong with the Brazilian mobile competitors' data pricing.

If these 2 billion users are to get online as quickly as in developed nations, prices need to fall exponentially—extremely unlikely given the geography of interconnection.[24] Note also that stable oligopoly conditions are prevalent in mobile,[25] and the corrupt manner in which mobile licences are awarded by many developing nation governments.[26] Absent price competition, consumers seeking low cost messaging and calling need a limited Internet offer. In the developing world, which rapidly caught up in mobile phone subscription, achieving the same conditions of neutrality as in the developed world will need to focus on mobile ISP regulation. Mobile ISPs introduced walled gardens which are so-called 'sponsored data plans' or 'zero rating' of their affiliates' content. A particular business model for this practice is that of dominant social network Facebook, which from 2009 introduced Facebook Zero with mobile ISP partners, later called Facebook Lite in 2011, and in 2015 introduced a wider walled garden called "Internet.org" (which despite its name is an Intranet for 30–40 affiliates).

18.3.1 The Internet.Org Model

Internet.org has in September 2015 strict guidelines for applicants, no third party audit of scrutiny procedures and no appeal against its veto of new applications, while "submission and/or approval by Facebook does not guarantee that your site(s) will be made available through the Internet.org."[27] Internet.org was so closed that it did not even issue specifications for those applications seeking to join: "After global criticism to the closed and allegedly net-neutrality violating nature of Internet.org, Zuckerberg opened up the platform to any developer whose website meets the technical guidelines; and the set of technical guidelines was also published. Not only did this open the platform up, but, via the technical guidelines, it gave us a glimpse into what Facebook considers to be mobile-friendly".[28] This includes "emphasis on efficiency: infrastructure and data must be efficient so that operators can sustain infrastructure. This means high-bandwidth, VOIP, video and even image-heavy sites

---

[22] 12.5 GB for €12, see Orange Romania (2015).

[23] See TIM Brazil (2015).

[24] Telegeography (2015).

[25] A major policy challenge for the attempts to consolidate and reduce competition in mobile telecoms came with the EC veto of TeliaSonera's attempt to buy a Danish mobile network in 2015. See Europa (2015).

[26] Sutherland (2012), pp. 4–19.

[27] See Facebook (2015).

[28] Ruadhan (2015).

won't be included… this list reads as if it was straight out of the W3C mobile web best practices (MWBP)" written in 2006!

Internet.org was set up in August 2013 to extend far beyond the initial closed Facebook Zero model which dates to Facebook's original forays into mobile in 2009-10 and which inspired Wikimedia to follow suit. Facebook Lite was a version of the website optimised for low bandwidth users, launched in 2009 and closed in 2010 in favour of lightweight Facebook applications. It has been revived in June 2015 as a 300Kb apk file.[29] But Mobiforge explains that still means Facebook is gatekeeper: "Although Facebook has bowed to pressure and 'opened' up the platform, it's still not truly open, or universal. There are technical guidelines, but Facebook is the sole arbiter in respect of approving sites…the Internet.org proposition violates decentralization too, because of its approval process and proxy setup."

As an open letter to Mark Zuckerberg posted on Facebook by 67 rights groups point out, Internet.org is "misleadingly marketed as providing access to the full Internet, when in fact it only provides access to a limited number of Internet-connected services that are approved by Facebook and local ISPs. In its present conception, Internet.org thereby violates the principles of net neutrality, threatening freedom of expression, equality of opportunity, security, privacy and innovation."[30]

Zuckerberg claimed: "Some may argue for an extreme definition of net neutrality that says that it's somehow wrong to offer any more services to support the unconnected, but a reasonable definition of net neutrality is more inclusive. Access equals opportunity. Net neutrality should not prevent access." Bode argues this is: "simply disingenuous and obnoxious. Nothing about opposing zero rating 'prevents access'." He claims that "Zuckerberg's basically cementing his company's gatekeeper authority over developing nations for generations to come under the bright banner of selfless altruism, then taking offense when told that these countries might just be better off with un-apertured, subsidized access to the real Internet."[31]

Facebook claims that Internet.Org is succeeding, with 800,000 new Indian users: "20 %… did not previously access mobile data… Only 7 % of the data used by Internet.org subscribers came through the initiative's free, zero-rated offerings; other paid services accounted for the remaining 93 %."[32] If it does work as promised, it may drive down prohibitive data plan costs, which are highest in Brazil and Mexico compared to minimum wages.

Zero rating is practised by Facebook, Internet.org with their mobile ISPs partners, but also many other content providers. Wikipedia Zero, which is the Wikimedia Foundation's response since 2011 to the desire to spread Wikipedia to new territories, audiences and languages, operates in almost 60 countries.[33] MCent also operates with far more users than Internet.Org. Digital Fuel Monitor has collected evidence of more

---

[29] Brinkmann (2015).

[30] Access Now (2015).

[31] Bode (2015).

[32] Smith (2015).

[33] Marsden (2015b), http://www.slideshare.net/EXCCELessex/fgv-law-marsden-gringo-net contains many graphic illustrations of zero rating strategies by Facebook and Wikimedia.

than 90 zero rating schemes operating in over 60 nations: clearly this is a practice which has grown enormously in the last 2–3 years.[34] What have regulators done about it?

18.4   Zero Rating Regulation

In this section, I focus on three developing countries that are early movers in both zero rating and the net neutrality debate: India, Brazil and Chile. The methodology used was both literature review and empirical interview based. Research into comparative net neutrality law has recently been carried out by several Non Governmental Organisations (NGOs) and is well reported in the specialist media.[35] Additionally many regulatory documents are available in Spanish, Portuguese and English on regulator websites. The consultation process for net neutrality regulation was very well publicised in both Brazil and India, while Chile's 2010 law was well noted but little researched in academia outside Latin America. India has zero rating in practice but no effective regulation in mid-2015, Brazil the same despite a law passed with great fanfare in April 2014.

The practice of zero rating has been outlawed by several developed nation regulators, notably those of Netherlands,[36] Slovenia, Norway,[37] Canada,[38] all developed nations with ubiquitous fixed Internet access as well as relatively affordable mobile data. The Norwegian regulator stated that zero rating is "exactly the kind of situation net neutrality aims to avoid – allowing the [ISP] to decide how we use the Internet". Zero rating must be discriminatory to other apps not included, and therefore was ruled illegal without a case being brought. I briefly explore the Netherlands and Slovenia before turning to potential precedents for developing countries.

18.4.1   *Netherlands Zero Rating*

The new Netherlands rules only affect mobile ISPs in practice: "The new neutrality rules had no effect on the fixed market." The four issues dealt with by the Netherlands regulator once its net neutrality law came into effect in 2013 have caused academic

---

[34] Drossos (2015).

[35] Rossini and Moore (2015). See also Marques et al. (2015).

[36] Department of Economic Affairs (2015). In summary: "Pursuant to the Act, providers of internet access services may not block or obstruct services and applications on the Internet (with limited strict exceptions). Furthermore, providers may not differentiate between tariffs for internet access services, and services and applications provided or used through these services."

[37] Sørensen (2014).

[38] Canada has had a chequered record on net neutrality until 2015, with rules proclaimed by the regulator in 2009 but not enforced until this year. In 2011, the regulator explicitly supported capacity-based billing (rate caps) in Telecom Regulatory Policy CRTC 2011-703, Billing practices for wholesale residential high-speed access services (TRP 2011-703), which led the main ISPs to stop throttling video and other high bandwidth content as they had admitted so doing since 2008. It then adopted greater enforcement practices for net neutrality in 2014. Marsden (2015a).

expert van Eijk to caution that 'hard cases make bad laws' including for zero rating: "the new net neutrality rules… led to a new subscription structure, with a substantially increased emphasis on data traffic. Data bundles are priced more specifically, and existing packages with unlimited data access have been replaced by packages with a specific size (data caps) and specific speeds."[39] He cautions that "it is too early to tell whether net neutrality has had an effect on the overall costs for mobile broadband." He explains: "In two cases, the Authority investigated the bundling of data packages with free services (i.e. a mobile subscription with 'free' access to Spotify). To deal with these cases, a new guideline has been drafted by the ministry involved."[40] This clarifies that zero rating is illegal in the Netherlands, though it may not be a ruling that is compatible with the new draft European law which may be implemented in 2015/16.

18.4.2   Slovenia Zero Rating

Due to the language, limited size and resources of the regulator, and the peripheral nature of Slovenian (population 2 million), Slovenia's very strict net neutrality law has been analysed very little by non-Slovenes. The net neutrality law is Article 203 of the wider Electronic Communications Law 2012 (ZEKOM), drafted as an innovation measure in response to hostility by the dominant ISP and trades unions towards competition in Internet supply. The regulator is the Communications Networks and Services Agency of the Republic of Slovenia (AKOS). The law's author when Minister for Communications, Professor Ziga Turk, has examined its genesis and implementation in a publication for the European Commission (I declare an interest as co-author).[41] His main conclusion was that implementing net neutrality in a nation with such a weak regulator would prove very difficult. Drossos agreed with this analysis arguing that AKOS "led by a former industry executive, has not been an advocate of net neutrality. Instead, it has taken a pro-industry stance on net neutrality and has not opposed attempts to weaken or even remove net neutrality provisions from the law."[42]

While the ZEKOM law dates to the start of 2013, its regulation by AKOS was slow to arrive, with the main 4 rulings those of 24 January and 20 February 2015 against zero rating. AKOS confounded its critics with a strong zero rating decision when forced to investigate by the Electronic Communications Council (SEK), which filed a complaint in July 2014 alleging Telekom Slovenije violated net neutrality with zero-rated products. Telekom Slovenije from 2013 provided free

---

[39] van Eijk (2014).

[40] The other two cases in 2013/14 concerned public Wifi and mobile ISP throttling: "The regulator in charge – the Authority for Consumers and Markets – took a first decision on applying the new rules in a case where Internet access in trains was blocked for congestion reasons. In another case, a service similar to WhatsApp was inaccessible via wireless networks" (van Eijk 2014).

[41] Turk (2015).

[42] Caf (2014).

data for HBO and UEFA Champions League football, then later the music streaming service Deezer. AKOS also found against Si.mobil (the largest mobile ISP) for zero-rating cloud storage service Hanger Mapa. TS and Si.mobil were instructed to stop zero rating. In the second pair, bans were imposed against a zero-rated mobile TV service and web portal provided by AMIS (Mobia TV) and Tušmobil (Tuškamra), respectively. That completes rulings against all major ISPs in Slovenia, all of whom had zero rated affiliated content, and were given 60 days to comply. The issue was fought for by AKOS against substantial industry lobbying and the huge asymmetry in personnel between the ISPs and the very small regulator. A remaining issue is that football and cloud storage on Telecom Slovenije remains zero rated, though it stopped the practice with video channel HBO, whereas AMIS and Si.mobil were banned from video and cloud zero rating. It is difficult to convey to non-Europeans the importance of Champions League football, and it may be that politically to deprive viewers of that stream by capping downloads would be impossible.

The results of bans have been "Telekom Slovenije and Si.mobile have both come up with special offers and packages with larger data caps or inexpensive data cap options" to expand the cap, presumably to try to include their formerly zero-rated services. Just as in the US, Slovenian operators and the regulator are highly litigious and a final judicial decision was awaited in all cases.[43]

18.4.3   Chile and Zero Rating

Chile has the earliest known net neutrality law (from 18 August 2010)[44] and an implementation of regulation permitting zero rating from 2014. Ley 20.453 includes a provision which adds Article 24(h-j) to Ley N° 18.168 'General de Telecomunicaciones'. Article 24H expressly forbids ISP practices that "arbitrarily distinguish content, applications or services based on the source or ownership thereof." This would be relied upon by those opposed to zero rating. The original law required ISPs to self-report on any violations, resulting in infringement only for failure to report. Cerda reports that there were "allegations of negligent supervision of the law by public authority" in failing to enforce consumer rights.[45]

In Chile,[46] all four mobile ISPs (Claro, Entel, Telefonica and VTR) were notified to cease zero rating in 2014.[47] The regulator's (sub-secretary of communications: Subtel) conclusion was misreported in the developed nations' media as banning all

---

[43] Caf (2015).

[44] The Chilean 'Law 20.453 Which enshrines the principle of net neutrality for consumers and Internet users', of 18 August 2010 at http://www.leychile.cl/Navegar?idNorma=1016570&buscar =NEUTRALIDAD+DE+RED which is implemented by Decree 368 of 15 December 2010: http://www.subtel.gob.cl/images/stories/articles/subtel/asocfile/10d_0368.pdf.

[45] Cerda (2013).

[46] Huichalaf Roa (2015), p. 20.

[47] In Chile, a total of 40 cases may sound substantial, but 25 were in the first 2 years, and fully 29 relate to those four major ISPs. Most were for infringement of transparency rules or network self-measurement. Zero rating in 2014 was considered by many observers as the first true test.

zero rating from 1 June 2014, when it applied to social networks, notably Facebook and therefore Internet.Org. Wikipedia Zero was also excepted from the ban, though the reasons why are not declared by the government.[48]

Subtel stated: "las empresas que entregan algunas redes sociales gratis, lo que hacen es privilegiar el uso de estos servicios, mediante el acceso a una Internet bloqueada, excluyendo las redes sociales privilegiadas"—social networking apps received positive discrimination ('privilegiadas') when included in the zero rated offer. In fact, Claro (subsidiary of Mexican operator America Movil, also active in Brazil, Columbia and other Latin American nations) was permitted by the Chilean regulator to continue zero rating as long as it formed part of a wider data plan that customers could choose.[49] This was because data plans were included in the new zero rating offer, removing the part of the complaint relating to "cuando los usuarios salen a través de un enlace externo, las empresas piden pagar"—that non-zero rated websites have to pay for users to exit zero rating onto the wider Internet.

18.4.4   India and Zero Rating

In India, two zero-rated options have been offered in 2015, by both Internet.Org, owned by Facebook which has 1.5 billion monthly active users (MAUs), and Bharti Airtel (the largest mobile ISP in India with 226 million customers at April 2015, and over 300 million customers including its 19 subsidiaries in other markets[50]). An Indian Parliamentary committee in July 2015 suggested that the locally based Airtel's zero-rated option should be permitted but foreign-controlled Facebook's Internet.Org prohibited. In response to concerns most vociferously raised in India but also in Brazil, the US and other nations, Facebook made the terms of Internet. Org more transparent in May 2015, effectively opening access in principle to any app developer who could meet its terms.[51] Nevertheless, Facebook's privacy policies continue to apply and it is not possible to use Internet.Org without also being a Facebook user, while Facebook accesses all your tracking behaviour while logged in to any partner sites and can share that with mobile ISPs. Facebook's privacy and IP policies have been robustly analysed and critiqued for several years and are somewhat regulated in a light touch manner in the European Union and US (Brown and Marsden 2013: xvii–xviii, 19). It is also worth noting that many mobile ISPs use IMSI and other parsing methods to track everything you do on the Internet—in developed and developing countries.[52]

---

[48] See Rossini and Moore (2015) explaining the exchange of letters between Wikimedia Foundation and Subtel in 2014.

[49] The draft Direction of May 2014 apparently banned all zero rating, but the final decision of August 2014 permitted those plans offered only in addition to a data plan—i.e. where users had purchased wider access to escape the walled garden.

[50] For Airtel's collaboration with Internet.Org in Zambia, see Airtel Africa (2015).

[51] Pahwa (2015).

[52] Vallina-Rodriguez et al. (2015). The paper describes privacy violations and header enrichment practices performed by mobile operators (perma-cookies, x-forwarded-for, IMEI, IMSI,…).

Self-imposed FRAND may be the result of strong public and political pressure together with the threat of regulatory action as expressed by the Joint Secretary of the Department of Telecommunications, V. Umashankar: "if the need arises, the government and the regulator may step in to restore balance to ensure that the internet continues to remain an open and neutral platform for expression and innovation with no [ISP], or for that matter any content or application provider, having the potential or exercising the ability to determine user choice, distort consumer markets or significantly controlling preferences based on either market dominance or gatekeeping roles".[53] While the Indian government has not yet finally decided on its neutrality policy pending a final report from the regulator TRAI, its Joint Secretary explained that the Telecoms Committee report delivered in July 2015 proposed ex ante regulation: "a licensee has to file the tariff plan with TRAI prior to the launch. TRAI would examine each such tariff filing carefully to see if it conforms to the principles of net neutrality and that it is not anti-competitive by distorting consumer markets." Should zero-rating have already begun, as with Internet.org and Airtel, "penalties will be levied if there is a violation".[54]

18.4.5 Brazil and Zero Rating

Brazil has had zero rating since prior to 2014, a common practice by several mobile ISPs. Like Chile, Brazil has a bicameral constitution with a powerful directly elected executive president. Brazil had discussed net neutrality since the mid-2000s, with its formal advisory committee on Internet governance passing a resolution known as the 'Decalogue' in 2009 which in part stated: "Filtering or traffic privileges must meet ethical and technical criteria only, excluding any political, commercial, religious and cultural factors or any other form of discrimination or preferential treatment" (Resolução 2009/03 do CGI.br). This led to a period of public consultation led by the Ministry of Justice in 2009 (29 October–17 December) over a potential new legal framework. In 2011, the Chamber of Deputies (lower house of parliament) began to negotiate a law on privacy and net neutrality led by Deputy Alessandro Molon, which stalled in 2012/13. In late 2013 the political process was accelerated due to President Roussef's concerns over foreign surveillance of telecoms and Internet traffic (specifically her own communications), resulting in the Senate ratifying the Chamber of Deputies' proposed law in a single month.[55] Law No. 12/965 (the "Marco Civil da Internet") was signed by the President at the opening ceremony of the Net Mundial conference in Sao Paolo in April 2014.[56] The relevant section is Article 9 which states: "The party responsible for the transmission,

---

[53] Doval (2015).

[54] Quotation from Doval (2015).

[55] Wohlers et al. (2014).

[56] Law No. 12.965, April 23 2014 by the Presidency of the Republic, Civil House Legal Affairs Subsection.

switching or routing has the duty to process, on an isonomic [equality before the law] basis, any data packages, regardless of content, origin and destination, service, terminal or application." Moreover, according to Article 9(3) ISPs must "act with proportionality, transparency and isonomy" and "offer services in non-discriminatory commercial conditions and refrain from anti-competition practices". The question for regulators implementing zero rating is whether it is **proportional, transparent and non-discriminatory**.

Unsurprisingly for such a rushed final law, the consequent implementation has proved controversial, not least because it is not clear which of two consultative bodies and the Ministry of Justice should be in charge of the drafting and enforcement of the subsequent rules.[57] Article 9(1) states that it: "shall be regulated in accordance with the private attributions granted to the President…upon consultation with the Internet Steering Committee [CGI] and the National Telecommunications Agency [Anatel]". In 2015, both the regulator and the Ministry issued consultations, the latter organised together with the CGI in the period 28 January–30 April.[58] The results of the consultation are to be made public in an Executive Order expected in the latter part of 2015.

It is unclear whether zero rating or specialized services will be effectively regulated at the time of writing. At the 2015 Summit of the Americas in Panama on 10th April, President Rousseff met Mark Zuckerberg and was photographed with him,[59] he in a suit, she in a Facebook hoodie.[60] Her pronouncements in favour of Facebook's work in Brazil with poorer communities, and by inference Internet.Org, were a public scandal in view of the open consultations then ongoing. However, it is not clear what benefit such public lobbying achieved for Facebook/Internet.Org.

In practice, Anatel in 2014 chose not to regulate zero rating. TIM (the Brazilian subsidiary of Telecom Italia Mobile), in partnership with WhatsApp, released a zero rating plan that allowed subscribers to use the app in zero rating. Marcelo Bechara, counsellor of ANATEL, refused to regulate in the absence of specific prohibitions "If there is no prioritized traffic, I do not see why it breaks the Marco Civil. This is the free market. It's free business".[61]

In 2015, Claro abandoned a previous offer that offered zero rating only, and adopted its Chilean approach with free WhatsApp, Facebook and Twitter offered only to users who also subscribed to data plans (pre or post-pay).[62] Claro CEO Carlos Zenteno had said in April that zero-rating plans were no longer part of the carrier's strategy as less than 1 % of customers used only Facebook or Twitter, and in June added: "It's an evolution. We realized that it has no purpose only to offer zero-rating access to one site." Claro argues that zero-rating on top of existing data plans represents a positive discrimination that the consumer chooses. Anatel's decision on this issue will be critical to the future of Brazilian zero rating.

---

[57] Cruz et al. (2015).

[58] Ministerio da Justicia (2015) and Chilvarquer (2015).

[59] http://www2.planalto.gov.br/centrais-de-conteudos/imagens/encontro-com-presidente-do-facebook.

[60] Antunes (2015).

[61] Marques et al. (2015), pp. 66–67.

[62] Prescott (2015).

18.5 Conclusion: Regulating the Fair Reasonable and Non-discriminatory (FRAND) Mobile Internet?

I suggest two regulatory actions to encourage the correct use of zero rating: treating zero rating as a short term exception to net neutrality, and ensuring any such short term exception is not exclusive, by subjecting such contracts to Fair Reasonable and Non-Discriminatory (FRAND) conditions. (I have explained these interventions in depth in a previous book, referring to the policy toolkit recommendation as representing the first footsteps into **'prosumer law'**: those looking for the definitive full explanation should refer to that work.)[63]

These conditions are not dis-similar to the principles by which the Wikimedia Foundation permits Wikipedia Zero to be offered by mobile ISPs, in that it: "allows other public interest websites to ride onto its own scheme, eschews any exclusive rights or exchange of payment between itself and mobile carriers, and forbids carriers from selling the service as part of a limited bundle".[64] It is also similar to concerns expressed to Facebook by the 67 NGOs in their letter, by Public Knowledge in their recent study, by the Centre for Internet Studies in India,[65] and others. As it summarises my perspective since the 2010 book,[66] I make some claim to prior knowledge. I consider exceptions, non-exclusivity and FRAND in turn.

Short term exceptions to net neutrality are likely given the post hoc nature of regulation: regulators lay out ground rules then respond to complaints regarding infringing practices. Difficult marginal cases can require extensive investigation. Such processes can take several months in the case of effective regulators, requiring both technical and economic analysis, a call for evidence, hearings and enforcement notices. In the case of litigious market actors, appeals against decisions can take months, years or longer to reach constitutional courts as final appeal court. There is nothing in zero rating to suggest it is anything but a straightforward case of discrimination, which should not be subject to such long appeal processes. As explained earlier, walled gardens are nothing new, represent obvious discrimination and have been outlawed by those countries with effective net neutrality regulation. Any attempt to offer a time-limited zero rated offer as an introduction to mobile data use could be flagged as such and limited by regulation to perhaps 3 or 6 months. This would be subject to FRAND conditions and regulatory enforcement.

FRAND conditions could be applied to two areas depending on national regulatory powers: to mobile ISP contracts with Internet.org and other affiliated content providers, including the ISPs' own subsidiaries, and to the conditions under which the content providers offer access to their own portals. This would need to be applied to each mobile network as the stable oligopoly in each nation examined means no

---

[63] Brown and Marsden (2013).

[64] De Guzman (2014); Asia Pacific Bureau (2014).

[65] Jain et al. (2015), pp. 11, 17–18.

[66] Marsden (2010a), to be revisited in full length monograph in Marsden (2016).

one network is dominant, and in any case this is in legal terms an access-utility problem, not a generic competition problem.[67] The former is relatively straightforward to implement in theory, as it is basically vertical unbundling of the mobile ISP's business unit arrangements, following examples such as those of the local access monopoly Openreach within British Telecom in the UK, or similar arrangements in Italy and Sweden. In practice, regulatory independence and strength is needed to successfully carry through such a course. One could also compare it to the regulatory treatment under EU antitrust law of competitors to Microsoft's applications interoperating with their dominant Windows operating system. However, not all regulators are capable of equal treatment of subsidiaries with competitors, especially in the resource-challenged developing world where independence and regulatory commitment are less easily maintained.

An alternative form of FRAND may therefore be to regulate de facto at a regional or global level, in establishing the ground rules for access to the zero-rated platform which mobile ISPs will offer. Regional rules (such as those in the EU) or those of a very persuasive regulator (FCC) can provide a strong policy lead to neighbour regulators. In this case, the regulated actor is the 'host' platform for those applications that will be offered. If applications to join such a platform offer—such as Internet. Org or Wikipedia Zero's offer—are established under FRAND terms that can be examined and monitored independently, then the platform which is established for one developing market may, with few modifications, prove to be that offered in many others.

Jurisdiction will be the greatest challenge to any attempt to regulate the platform rather than the mobile ISP offering zero rating. There are three obvious routes to enforcement: via the telecoms regulator's enforcement of platform neutrality on the mobile ISP and therefore into the contractual terms of its agreement with the platform; via the antitrust route as a merger condition for any platform that choses to expand into this area; or by a considered coordinated response by a network of net neutrality enforcement agencies at regional level, such as in BEREC.[68] The first has the same resource constraints as with OpenReach-type regulation except that the better resourced early mover regulators may establish ground rules that can be 'copy and pasted' by later acting, less motivated regulators. The second is the type of net neutrality regulation that was adopted in the United States from 2005 onwards as an antitrust 'default' rule against large ISPs that wished to merge. In the global view of such mergers, a net neutrality undertaking for a limited time period was considered by the merger partners to be a small price to pay. The third is similar to the first, in that the larger well-resourced regulators acting in concert with their smaller cousins can issue a decision or opinion that will help other regulators to take similar or identical action to enforce neutrality. Given the networks of regulators,

---

[67] See Coates (2011), Ungerer (2005), pp. 52–60, Maniadaki (2015).

[68] In practice BEREC has an increasingly effective coordinator role for its members, which may be reflected in the final version of the ConnectedContinent Regulation still pending in September 2015. See for example Sorensen (2015) cited in Marsden (2015a).

consultants, civil society actors, academics and law firms that have exported and shared "best" (sic) practice in telecom regulation since the first liberalisations in the 1980s (in Japan, US, Sweden and UK), such networks can be expected to actively engage in spreading such practices internationally.

I now further consider whether zero rating poses a serious challenge to open Internet use and suggest areas for further independent research into the effectiveness of net neutrality regulation. I can be accused of the assumption based on neocolonial comparison, that zero rating is a short term problem whose significance can be overstated. I would argue that my belief that zero rating is a relatively minor short term problem is based on the technological development of alternative forms of hardware-supported mobile data, which drives consumer adoption of mobile Internet access. This is not technologically but price determinist as I now explain. Too many analysts of mobile Internet access fail to fully consider the role of free or low-cost hardware and Wifi in its growth. The majority of "mobile" data traffic is actually downloaded to devices via Wifi in home, office or hotspot location. It is not the cost of mobile data plans that is the dominant price driver, but that of hardware and prevalence of Wifi. There can never be as much Wifi in developing countries as developed, but open Wifi can be accessed relatively widely in countries where Internet policy is not dominated by the copyright maximalist lobby and morality (anti-pornography) cybercrime lobby. Hardware for mobile data is much cheaper than at its introduction a decade or more ago in the developed world, whether that be smartphones, laptops or tablets. Whereas the first iPhone was priced at $599 with 8 MB memory in June 2007 (equivalent to $689 in 2015), and an equivalent WiFi-enabled laptop in 2000 cost $1000 or more (equivalent to $1386 in 2015), consumers in developing countries can buy an 8 Gigabyte Android or Linux smartphone or tablet for $50,[69] or a Raspberry Pi mini computer for $30. Each is many times more powerful than those early equivalents. Combining the huge advances in technology pricing/performance with the prevalence of Wifi hotspots in 2015, it is clear that the environment for late adopter nations in mobile Internet access is far better than for developed countries in 2007. This applies despite the extremely high prices for mobile ISP data, which only forms a small part of the adoptive environment required to access the mobile Internet (arguably, no mobile ISP access is required at all given that schools, cafes, universities and other public areas offer free Wifi). Only 57 % of Indian and 43 % of Brazilian smartphone users actually use data plans at all, and the average amongst those Indians who do was 80 MB a month in 2015 (3–5 % of developed nation average usage).[70]

It is perhaps facile to argue that net neutrality regulation may be a somewhat blunt telecom regulatory instrument for a multi-faceted problem such as mobile Internet access, which also includes such policy issues as privacy and free expression as well as universal access and many Millenium Development Goals. The

---

[69] Freischlad (2015) states "Even in China, which is a more mature market [than Indonesia] by most measures and smartphone penetration is higher, data usage itself remains low. This tells us either Chinese smartphone users are not interested in using their phones on the go, or they are simply being thrifty."

[70] Olsen (2015).

wider issue of how Internet users of 'free' apps such as Facebook and others are being monetized by advertisers is associated with the net neutrality and zero-rated debates, and in particular the correct policy responses. In countries such as Indonesia where monthly Average Revenue Per User (ARPU) is only $2.20 for calls, texts and data, it is unsurprising that advertising is attractive as a further revenue partnership with zero rated apps. Next to such a pervasive Internet policy problem, neutrality in itself may be a sideshow. In most developed countries, neutrality developed from privacy concerns, a dynamic which needs further empirical comparative research in the developing nation context, which should be a subject for future research.

References

ABI Research. (2015). 802.11ac Wi-Fi CPE shipments to accelerate in 2015 to reach 71 million units,22Aprilathttps://www.abiresearch.com/press/80211ac-wi-fi-cpe-shipments-to-accelerate-in-2015-/

About.com. (2009). Apple Ditches iTunes DRM, Adds Variable Prices, 3G Downloads.

Access Now. (2015). Open Letter to Mark Zuckerberg Regarding Internet.org, Net Neutrality, Privacy, and Security May 18, 2015 at https://www.facebook.com/notes/accessnoworg/open-letter-to-mark-zuckerberg-regarding-internetorg-net-neutrality-privacy-and-/935857379791271

Airtel Africa. (2015). Internet.org apps, at http://africa.airtel.com/wps/wcm/connect/africarevamp/zambia/home/personal/internet/internet-org/internet_org/faqs

Antunes, A. (2015). Mark Zuckerberg Meets With Brazil's President At the 7th Summit of the Americas, In Panama, Forbes, April 11, at http://www.forbes.com/sites/andersonantunes/2015/04/11/mark-zuckerberg-meets-with-brazils-president-at-the-7th-summit-of-the-americas-in-panama/

Asia Pacific Bureau: Internet Society, 24 September, at http://www.internetsociety.org/blog/asia-pacific-bureau/2014/09/zero-rating-enabling-or-restricting-internet-access

AT&T Mobility v. Concepcion, 563 U.S. 321 (2011).

Bode, K. (2015). Tone Deaf Zuckerberg Declares Opposition To Zero Rated Apps An 'Extremist' Position That Hurts The Poor, from the new-AOL,-brought-to-you-by-Mother-Teresa dept, Tech Dirt: Broadband May 5th at https://www.techdirt.com/blog/netneutrality/articles/20150504/08341730885/tone-deaf-zuckerberg-declares-opposition-to-zero-rated-apps-extremist-position-that-hurts-poor.shtml

Brinkmann, M. (2015). Facebook Lite makes a return as a mobile application, Ghacks, January 26, 2015, http://www.ghacks.net/2015/01/26/facebook-lite-makes-a-return-as-a-mobile-application/

Brown, I., & Marsden, C. (2013). Regulating code. Cambridge, MA: MIT Press.

Caf, D. (2014). Zero-Rating Violates Slovenian Net Neutrality Law, Competitive Analysis & Foresight: Policy, Regulation and Strategy in Network Industries, Media and Technology 5 December at http://blog.caf.si/2014/12/zero-rating-violates-slovenian-net-neutrality-law.html

Caf, D. (2015). Another win for net neutrality advocates in Slovenia: AKOS issues new decisions limiting zero-rating, Competitive Analysis & Foresight: Policy, Regulation and Strategy in Network Industries, Media and Technology 22 February at http://blog.caf.si/2015/02/another-win-for-net-neutrality-advocates-in-slovenia-akos-issues-new-decisions-limiting-zero-rating.html

Cerda, A. (2013). An evaluation of the net neutrality law in Chile, Digital Rights LAC on July 17, at http://www.digitalrightslac.net/en/una-evaluacion-de-la-ley-de-neutralidad-de-la-red-en-chile/

Chilvarquer, M. (2015). Debate Público Regulamentação do Marco Civil da Internet, Secretaria de Legislativos Assuntos, Ministeria da Justicia, paper presented at Conferência Internacional sobre a Elaboração de Regras de Neutralidade de Rede, FGV Rio de Janeiro, 8 June 2015:

http://direitorio.fgv.br/eventos/Conferencia-Internacional-sobre-a-Elaboracao-de-Regras-de-
Neutralidade-de-Rede
Coates, K. (2011). *Competition law and regulation of technology markets*. Oxford: Oxford
University Press.
CRTC. (2011). Telecom Regulatory Policy 2011-703, Billing practices for wholesale residential
high-speed access services.
CRTC. (2015). Broadcasting and Telecom Decision CRTC 2015/M26, January 29, at http://www.
crtc.gc.ca/eng/archive/2015/2015726.htm
Cruz, F. C. d. B., Marchezan, J. C., & dos Santos, M. W. (2015). What is at stake in the regulation
of the Marco Civil Da Internet? Final Report on the Public Debate Sponsored by Ministry of
Justice on Regulation of Law 12.965/2014, Internet Lab, Rua Augusta, 2690, Galeria Ouro
Fino,Loja326athttp://www.internetlab.org.br/en/news/what-is-at-stake-in-the-regulation-of-the-
marco-civil/
De Guzman, N. F. (2014). Zero rating: enabling or restricting Internet access?
Decree 368 of 15 December 2010, Chile: http://www.subtel.gob.cl/images/stories/articles/subtel/
asocfile/10d_0368.pdf
Department of Economic Affairs. (2015). Net Neutrality Guidelines May 15th, for the Authority
for Consumers and Markets (ACM) for the enforcement by ACM of Article 7.4a of the
Netherlands Telecommunications Act 2012: "Besluit van de Minister van Economische Zaken
van 11 mei 2015, nr. WJZ/15062267, houdende beleidsregel inzake de toepassing door de
Autoriteit Consument en Markt van artikel 7.4a van de Telecommunicatiewet (Beleidsregel
netneutraliteit)" at https://zoek.officielebekendmakingen.nl/stcrt-2015-13478.html?zoekcriteri
a=%3fzkt%3dUitgebreid%26pst%3dTractatenblad%257CStaatsblad%257CStaatscourant%2
57CGemeenteblad%257CProvinciaalblad%257CWaterschapsblad%257CBladGemeenschapp
elijkeRegeling%257CParlementaireDocumenten%26vrt%3dnetneutraliteit%26zkd%3dInDe
GeheleText%26dpr%3dAlle%26spd%3d20150519%26epd%3d20150519%26sdt%3dDatumP
ublicatie%26ap%3d%26pnr%3d1%26rpp%3d10&resultIndex=0&sorttype=1&sortorder=4
Doval, P. (2015). Zero-rating plans must be open to all users: DoT panel member, Times of India
July 20, 2015, at http://timesofindia.indiatimes.com/tech/tech-news/Zero-rating-plans-must-
be-open-to-all-users-DoT-panel-member/articleshow/48138850.cms
Drossos, A. (2015). Guest blog: the real threat to the open Internet is zero-rated content, Web
Foundation, 17 February at http://webfoundation.org/guest-blog-the-real-threat-to-the-open-
internet-is-zero-rated-content/ via
Eisenach, J. (2015). Economics of Zero Rating, National Economic Research Associates, March,
at http://www.nera.com/content/dam/nera/publications/2015/EconomicsofZeroRating.pdf
Europa. (2015). Statement by Commissioner Vestager on announcement by Telenor and
TeliaSonera to withdraw from proposed merger, 11 September, at http://europa.eu/rapid/
press-release_STATEMENT-15-5627_en.htm
Facebook. (2015). Participation Guidelines for Internet.Org, undated, at https://developers.face-
book.com/docs/internet-org/participation-guidelines
Fierce Wireless. (2011). Do Usage-Based Pricing Models Work? (September, e-book) at p. 18, see
http://www.fiercewireless.com/offer/pricing_models
Freischlad, N. (2015). Soon everyone will be able to afford a smartphone. But what about data?
TechInAsia,Jul24,2015athttps://www.techinasia.com/smartphones-are-getting-cheaper-but-what-
about-data/
Huichalaf Roa, P. M. (2015). La Neutralidad de la Red: El Caso Chileno, Barcelona 3 July,
Subsecretario de Telecomunicaciones, Chile, p. 20 at http://berec.europa.eu/files/doc/2015-
07-13_10_00_01_4.%20Neutralidad%20de%20la%20red%20versi+%7Cn%20final.%20(3).pdf
International Telecommunications Union. (2015). World Telecommunication/ICT Indicators
Database, ITU: Geneva 19th edition released 1 July at http://www.itu.int/en/ITU-D/Statistics/
Pages/publications/wtid.aspx
Jain, R., Prof., Ravattu, R., Dara, R., & Prakash, P. (2015). Response to TRAI Consultation Paper
on Regulatory Framework for Over-the-top (OTT) Services 27th March, Centre for Internet
Studies, pp. 11, 17–18.

Law 20.453 of the Republic of Chile, which enshrines the principle of net neutrality for consumers and Internet users', of 18 August 2010 at http://www.leychile.cl/Navegar?idNorma=1016570& buscar=NEUTRALIDAD+DE+RED

Law No. 12.965, April 23 2014 by the Presidency of the Republic of Brazil, Civil House Legal Affairs Subsection.

Lemley, M. A., & Lessig, L. (1999). Ex Parte Declaration Of Professor Mark A. Lemley And Professor Lawrence Lessig In The Matter Of: Application For Consent To The Transfer Of Control Of Licenses of MediaOne Group, Inc. To AT&T Corp CS Docket No. 99-251 Before The Federal Communications Commission, Washington, D.C. 20554.

Lemstra, W., Hayes, V., & Groenewegen, J. P. M. (Eds.). (2010). *The innovation journey of Wi-Fi the road to global success*. Cambridge University Press.

Maillé, P., & Tuffin, B. (2014). *Telecommunication network economics: From theory to applications*. Cambridge University Press.

Maniadaki, K. (2015). EU Competition Law, Regulation and the Internet: The Case of Net Neutrality, Kluwer, on the interaction between communications and competition law.

Marcus, J. S., & Burns, J. (2013). Study on Impact of traffic off-loading and related technological trends on the demand for wireless broadband spectrum, prepared for the European Commission Project number: 2013.5370 ISBN 978-92-79-30575-7, doi:10.2759/19531 at http://bookshop.europa.eu/en/study-on-impact-of-traffic-off-loading-and-related-technological-trends-on-the-demand-for-wireless-broadband-spectrum-pbKK0113239/

Marques, C., Tresca, L., Filho, L. A. P., Rielli, M., & Iorio, P. (2015). Marco Civil da Internet: seis meses depois, em que pé que estamos? Article 19, 28 January at http://artigo19.org/blog/analise-marco-civil-da-internet-seis-meses-depois-em-que-pe-que-estamos/

Marsden, C. (1999). Pluralism In The Multi-Channel Market: Suggestions For Regulatory Scrutiny Council of Europe Human Rights Commission, Mass Media Directorate, MM-S-PL [99] 12 Def 2.

Marsden, C. (2010a). *Network neutrality: Towards a co-regulatory solution*. London: Bloomsbury Academic.

Marsden, C. (2010b). European law and regulation of mobile net neutrality. *European Journal of Law and Technology, 1*, 2 at http://ejlt.org//article/view/32

Marsden, C. (2013). *Net neutrality law: Past policy, present proposals, future regulation?* Proceedings of the United Nations Internet Governance Forum: Dynamic Coalition on Network Neutrality, Nusa Dua Bali, Indonesia, 25 October 2013. Available at SSRN: http://ssrn.com/abstract=2335359

Marsden, C. (2015a). *Comparative case studies in implementing net neutrality: A critical analysis*. Paper presented to 43rd TPRC, 26 September. Available at SSRN: http://ssrn.com/abstract=2587920 or http://dx.doi.org/10.2139/ssrn.2587920

Marsden, C. (2015b). *Gringo Net: Zero Rating in Brazil*. Paper presented June 08 to Conferência Internacional sobre a Elaboração de Regras de Neutralidade de Rede, FGV Rio de Janeiro.

Marsden, C. (2016). *Network neutrality*. Manchester University Press, forthcoming.

Ministerio da Justicia. (2015). Civil Rights Framework for the Internet in Brazil: Information in EnglishAbouttheConsultationathttp://pensando.mj.gov.br/marcocivil/civil-rights-framework-for-the-internet-in-brazil/

Neal, D. (2015). Apple and Samsung dominate smartphone sales, but new entrants snap at their heels,V3.co.uk24Julyathttp://www.v3.co.uk/v3-uk/news/2419132/apple-and-samsung-dominate-smartphone-sales-but-new-entrants-snap-at-their-heels

Odlyzko, A., St. Arnaud, B., Stallman, E., & Weinberg, M. (2012). Know Your Limits: Considering the Role of Data Caps and Usage Based Billing in Internet Access Service, Public Knowledge, April 23, p. 15 at https://www.publicknowledge.org/documents/know-your-limits-considering-the-role-of-data-caps-and-usage-based-billing

Olsen, P. (2015). This App Is Cashing In On Giving The World Free Data, Forbes, Jul 29, at http://www.forbes.com/sites/parmyolson/2015/07/29/jana-mobile-data-facebook-internet-org/

Open Internet Advisory Committee. (2013). Policy Issues in Data Caps and Usage-Based Pricing, Economic Impacts of Open Internet Frameworks Working Group; Open Internet Advisory

Committee of the Federal Communications Commission: Washington D.C. at https://transition. fcc.gov/cgb/oiac/Economic-Impacts.pdf at p. 13.

Orange Romania. (2015). No Limit Internet, at http://www.orange.ro/nelimitat/index.html

Pahwa, N. (2015). Facebook's Internet.org platform is a privacy nightmare: tracks users on partner sites, allows telcos to track, Medianama May 4, at http://www.medianama.com/2015/05/223-facebooks-internet-org-privacy/

Prescott, R. (2015). LatAm: Claro Brazil resumes zero-rating plans, RC Wireless on June 18, at http://www.rcrwireless.com/20150618/americas/latam-claro-brazil-resumes-zero-rating-plans

Rossini, C., & Moore, T. (2015). Exploring Zero-Rating Challenges: Views from Five Countries, Public Knowledge, 28 July at https://www.publicknowledge.org/press-release/public-knowledge-publishes-net-neutrality-paper-investigating-zero-rating-practices

Ruadhan. (2015). Internet.org: it's got 99 problems but mobile-friendliness ain't one, Mobiforge, 27 May 2015 at http://mobiforge.com/news-comment/internet-org-its-got-99-problems-mobile-friendliness-aint-one

Smith, J. (2015). Facebook's free internet initiative is working, Business Insider Intelligence Jun. 5, 2015, at www.businessinsider.com/facebooks-internetorg-is-doing-its-job-2015-6?IR=T

Sørensen, F. (2014). Net neutrality and charging models, Norwegian Post and Telecommunications Authority NKOM, 11 November at http://eng.nkom.no/topical-issues/news/net-neutrality-and-charging-models

Sutherland, E. (2012). Corruption in telecommunications: Problems and remedies. *Info, 14*(1), 4–19. Available at SSRN: http://ssrn.com/abstract=1937556

Telegeography. (2015). IP Transit Prices Continue Falling, Major Discrepancies Remain September 09, at https://www.telegeography.com/press/press-releases/2015/09/09/ip-transit-prices-continue-falling-major-discrepancies-remain/index.html

TIM Brazil. (2015). Infinity Offer daily Plan at http://www.tim.com.br/sp/para-voce/internet/simulador-de-dados

Timms, D. (2003). BT folds Openworld into Yahoo! venture, The Guardian, 16 June at http://www.theguardian.com/technology/2003/jun/16/newmedia.bt

Turk, Z. (2015). Case Study 3: Net neutrality legislation – the case of Slovenia, Annex: pp. 23–31 in Marsden, C. Zevenbergen, B., Marzouki, M., Bygrave, L., Morando, F., Powell, A., Turk, Z., and Salamatian, K. [2015] "Deliverable 4.3: Final Report" Internet Science EINS Project FP7-288021, at http://www.internet-science.eu/publication/1149

Ungerer, H. (2005). Competition in the media sector – How long can the future be delayed? *Info, 7*(5), 52–60.

Vallina-Rodriguez, N., Sundaresan, S., Kreibich, C., & Paxson, V. (2015). Header Enrichment or ISP Enrichment? Emerging Privacy Threats in Mobile Networks, paper presented at HotMiddlebox'15 (co-located with ACM SIGCOMM) 21 August 2015, at http://www1.icsi.berkeley.edu/~narseo/papers/hotmiddlebox2015.pdf and http://conferences.sigcomm.org/sigcomm/2015/hotmiddlebox.php

van Eijk, N. (2014). The Proof of the Pudding is in the Eating: Net Neutrality in Practice, the Dutch Example, August 2. Paper presented to the TPRC Conference 2014. Available at SSRN: http://ssrn.com/abstract=2417933 or http://dx.doi.org/10.2139/ssrn.2417933

Wohlers, M., Giansante, M., Carlos, A., & Fodich, N. (2014). *Shedding light on net neutrality: Towards possible solutions for the Brazilian case.* Conference Paper presented to International Telecommunications Society 20th Conference, Rio, 1 December 2014, at http://www.researchgate.net/publication/274310761_Shedding_light_on_net_neutrality_towards_possible_solutions_for_the_Brazilian_case

Wray, R. (2009). Vodafone 360: mobile provider launches new applications service – The social network-based set of apps is designed to rival the iPhone and any handsets using Google's Android software, The Observer, 20 September 2009, at http://www.theguardian.com/business/2009/sep/20/vodafonegroup-telecoms

Wu, T. (2007). Wireless Carterfone. *International Journal of Communication, 1*, 389, Columbia Public Law Research Paper No. 07-154. Available at SSRN: http://ssrn.com/abstract=962027

Chapter 19
Wireless Community Networks: Towards a Public Policy for the Network Commons?

Primavera De Filippi and Félix Tréguer

The history of communication technologies is populated with conflicts between centralization and decentralization. While many of these technologies started or have existed at some point of their development as a decentralized structure, often replacing older technological paradigms, nearly all progressively evolved into concentrated clusters of power as a result of industrialization and of the reaffirmation of state sovereignty, following a Schumpeterian process of "creative-destruction" (Wu 2010). However, when the needs of citizens turn out to be systematically overlooked in existing power dynamics, decentralized initiatives may emerge as an attempt to disrupt the dominant hegemony and allow for the democratic re-appropriation of technology—a process that the philosopher Andrew Feenberg calls "subversive rationalization" (Feenberg 1995).

In this paper, we focus on an ongoing—though too often neglected—phenomenon of decentralization in telecommunications networks. We show that current telecoms regulation significantly overlooks the contribution of community networks in fostering political and socio-economic objectives associated with broadband policy and we propose a number of policy recommendations to overcome this gap.

19.1 A Short History of the Internet Access Market in Europe

Since its early days, the Internet has followed a trend of emancipation. Already throughout the 1970s and 1980s, engineers and early hackers were experimenting with computers and exploring the potential of these new machines as communications

P. De Filippi (✉)
CERSA/CNRS/Université Paris II, Paris, France

Berkman Center for Internet & Society at Harvard, Cambridge, MA, USA
e-mail: pdefilippi@gmail.com

F. Tréguer
School for Advanced Studies in Social Sciences (CRH/EHESS), Paris, France

© Springer International Publishing Switzerland 2016
L. Belli, P. De Filippi (eds.), *Net Neutrality Compendium*,
DOI 10.1007/978-3-319-26425-7_19

devices. But it is only in the following years, as personal computing boomed and the computer networks spread, that efforts from civil society to democratize the use of these revolutionary technologies went viral. The creation of the World Wide Web in 1989 finally opened the door to widespread Internet use.

In the mid-1990s, the Internet access market boomed in Europe, partly because incumbent network operators had to open up the infrastructure rolled-out by state monopolies to small and innovative ISPs. In a context of rapid privatization, regulation promoted facility-based competition[1] and new companies began laying down their own network infrastructure. This, along with the explosion of mobile telephony and the democratization of Internet access, made liberalization look like a success story: innovation in telecom services was dynamic and fast-paced, prices were low, and the number of subscribers surged.

Today, the EU regulatory framework is still often praised when compared to the situation in the US, where local Internet access markets are generally under a duopoly. Regulatory policies have indeed ensured some level of competition in European markets. But more in more, the two markets have a similar outlook: EU telecom policy has been unable to prevent the growing concentration of power in the telecommunications sector. Ex ante merger control by the EU Commission has typically been loose (Thatcher 2014; Stoyanova 2008), leading to de facto oligopolies in national or regional markets. Meanwhile, abuses of dominant positions by incumbent network operators are fairly common.

Overall, in the EU, policy targets in terms of broadband penetration and quality of service remain a distant reality: more than a third of European households still have no broadband access (39 %) and, in a country such as Greece, broadband penetration is as low a 56 % (EU Commission 2013). A fifth of EU citizens with no Internet access say they are deterred by the sheer cost of it (EU Commission 2013): the cheapest available broadband offer can be as high as €46.20 in Cyprus, €38.70 in Spain or €31.40 in Ireland (EU Commission 2014a). Meanwhile, users are not provided with the service they paid for: on average, they only get 75 % of the broadband speed they signed up for; 63 % when they get it through ADSL rather than cable or fiber lines (SamKnows 2013). The situation is usually much worse in rural areas. Meanwhile, telecom operators also have the technical ability and economic or regulatory incentives to hinder the autonomy of Internet users, for instance by violating the principle of Net neutrality.

The trend towards centralization, combined with economic incentives and regulations encouraging surveillance and control has led to the revival of more decentralized, citizen-centric network architectures. This is illustrated, in recent years, by the deployment of Wireless Community Networks (WCN)—grassroots community networks, deployed at the local or regional level, managed *by* the community and *for* the community.

---

[1] Facility-based competition, or infrastructure-based competition, refers to the regulatory focus on creating competition between telecom firms that each have their own distinct network infrastructure for delivering end-user services, such as Internet access provision.

All across Europe, and beyond, there are currently a large number of grassroots community networks seeking to provide a decentralized alternative and more commons-based approach to the current Internet infrastructure. Rather than being driven by profits like most of the large, highly capitalized Internet Service Providers (ISPs), WCN focus on the actual needs of its participants. While most of them are very limited in scope—and are therefore not widely heard of—, the most popular ones enjoy more than dozens of thousands of users.[2]

19.2   Community Networks and New Power Dynamics in Telecom Infrastructures

Given the considerable investments required to set up an independent network infrastructure, and given the costs of purchasing wholesale access to last-mile landline networks from commercial operators, many grassroots community networks have decided to operate via wireless technologies, setting up network of peers sharing radio signals. Most of their network infrastructure consists of wireless radio equipment: Wi-Fi routers and antennas strategically distributed at different locations so as to maximize coverage. As a result, they can often provide a service of better quality than that which is generally available from commercial alternatives.

At the operational level, almost every grassroots community network tries to promote users' autonomy and fundamental rights to communication and privacy. As opposed to commercial ISPs blocking certain ports and censoring websites or content, community networks ardently protects Net neutrality. In several countries, small community networks are usually not bound by censorship orders issued by courts against illegal online content. In this regard, user autonomy and self-reliance is maximal when WCN are apprehended not just as part of the wider Internet but as autonomous local networks (or Intranets), allowing users to share information with other users connected to the same community network. Local networks also enable users to escape from the ubiquitous and pervasive surveillance that is occurring on the global Internet, as a result of privacy-intrusive practices undertaken by traditional online operators. In particular, given the lack of a central authority regulating access to the network, it is in theory more difficult for anyone to assess the real identity of users connected to these networks.

Accordingly, WCN constitute, essentially, a political choice: by establishing a mix of social and relational ties between participants involved in the provision of the network infrastructure, they promote a more democratic and cooperative political system, with a more symmetrical and participatory governance structure

---

[2] For the purpose of this paper, we focused on a handful of groups, and in particular FreiFunk (Germany), Wlan Slovenija (Slovenia), Guifi.net (Spain) and Tetaneutral.net in Toulouse (France)—the latter is also a member of the FFDN, a federation of French grassroots networks initially spearheaded by the landline community network FDN. Other European WCN include Ninux (Italy), Funfeuer (Austria), the Athens Wireless Metropolitan Network (Greece), Djurslands. net (Denmark) and Czfree.net (Czech Republic).

(Bauwens 2005). Besides, most of these grassroots community networks experiment with novel models of distributed governance relying on cooperation and sharing among a community of peers (from a dozen to tens of thousands participants), and that are reminiscent of commons-based peer production schemes (Benkler 2006).

From a political standpoint, WCN can be regarded as a counter-power to currently established power structures or incumbents. Following the typology of social movements drawn by Stefania Milan in her analysis of "emancipatory communication practices", we can infer three ways by which community networks could counteract existing power dynamics in the telecom sector.

One way is to address the issue from within the political system, as *insiders*, formally interacting with the power holders in order to make them support the deployment of community networks. Another solution is to fight the problem as *outsiders*, pressuring both regulators and incumbents from outside the political system, by means of protests, demonstrations and other campaigning tactics aimed at voicing dissent against the practices of commercial ISPs and against the lack of appropriate regulation for community networks.

Yet, most community networks do not properly qualify as what social movement scholars define as "insiders" (although they sometimes do interact with policy-makers), and much less as outsiders. Mostly, they fall within the third category — what Milan identifies as "*beyonders*". They acknowledge that law and regulation will always be late compared to practice and private ordering, and purport to influence the networked ecosystem by remaining beyond the political system. This objective is achieved by building self-organized, decentralized and citizen-owned communications networks and setting up alternative socio-political and technical arrangements as a substitute for the traditional top-down power dynamics typical of traditional institutions.

WCN can also be regarded as a potential source of competition to mainstream commercial ISPs. As we have seen, not only can WCN provide better services than commercial alternatives, they also adhere to specific ethical commitments and governance structures. As opposed to commercial providers, which often go counter to the interests of consumers by engaging in anti-competitive behaviors, WCN promote open and democratic values, such as Net neutrality and consumer protection. While they do not directly wage competition against traditional ISP, these nonprofit, community networks serve to increase diversity in the market for Internet access — thereby opening up the range of options available to citizens. In this sense, WCN constitute a form of grassroots, bottom-up regulation of established players that simply emerges from there being a viable (and more attractive) alternative to the dominant, commercial system.[3]

At this point in time, however, WCN cannot totally emancipate from traditional incumbents. Although they can be completely autonomous when they operate as closed local networks, most community networks eventually need to connect with

---

[3] In Berlin, for instance, Freifunk's popularity actually brought incumbent telecom operators to update their service agreements enabling subscribers to share their DSL connection to contribute bandwidth to the network.

the global Internet network. Uplink Internet access is achieved by linking the local network to one or several "Internet gateways" in charge of routing the traffic from and to global backbones.[4] Here, potential bottlenecks resurface.

To obtain such an uplink to the Internet, community networks currently choose from a number of strategies. The first is to use upstream through traditional mainstream last-mile ISPs. Some WCN, like Freifunk in Berlin, prefers not to build any formal relationship with third party ISPs, and simply rely on the goodwill of community members (who are also subscribers of commercial ISPs) to share their commercial Internet connection so as to provide bandwidth and connectivity to the rest of the network.

When relying exclusively on the uplink connections of mainstream ISPs to provide a gateway to the Internet is not possible, or perhaps simply not reliable enough, WCN must establish a commercial relationship with transit ISPs. The transit market is generally much more competitive than the mainstream last-mile Internet access markets. Lesser concentration creates a more diverse ecosystem where multinational firms, such as Cogent or Level 3, compete with smaller, local companies. Diversity drives both competition and cooperation, and allows grassroots community networks to escape the risk of abusive behaviors on the part of incumbent operators. For instance, in New York, the RedHook initiative is getting support from both medium-sized ISPs (such as Brooklyn Fiber) and a number of even smaller ones established in the area.

That being said, one cannot rule out the possibility of a transit operator exerting control over, and even disconnecting, a community network. To the extent that in some markets (in both urban and rural areas) a few large telecom operators retain the ability to filter, censor, monitor, discriminate online communications, or simply refuse to interconnect, the need for uplink leads to the emergence of new bottlenecks that replicate the problems that community networks aimed to address in the first place.

To meet that challenge, some activists have begun to organize: the goal is for community networks to collectively acquire more independence and more bargaining power in the various markets in which they operate, and promote their philosophy in the face of the conflicting value systems of commercial telecom operators who might engage in predatory practices. A first experiment of this kind was carried on in 2012, when community networks FunkFeuer from Austria, NEDWireless from Croatia, and Wlan Slovenija established a wireless backbone spanning across geographical borders to create a direct link between them. As the number of mesh networks deployed over the world grow, the potential for establishing a global and independent network infrastructure that abides to the founding principles of the Internet network will also increase.

---

[4] An Internet gateway is all that is required to connect a particular network to an existing Internet connection. The gateway router will share bandwidth with other devices on the network from that connection. Multiple gateways can be deployed on the same network to provide additional bandwidth, as does for instance Tetaneutral.net.

19.3 Regulatory Framework Favoring Commercial Players at the Expense of WCN

Despite their potential in fostering public interest goals in telecom policy, regulators have so far failed to support the efforts of community networks. More often than not, public policy actually puts important hurdles on their way.

The most striking example of such hurdles relates is that several community networks have been precluded from using public broadband networks funded with taxpayers' money. In France for instance, many local governments invested in rolling-out fiber networks in both urban and rural areas. These networks are built and managed by a private company contracted by the public authority, which leases access to traditional access providers that sell Internet access offers to subscribers. Yet, the fee charged to access the network is designed for big commercial ISPs, and is often prohibitive for nonprofit grassroots community networks.

Another other major problem of current telecom policies for WCN is the issue of spectrum management. Again, regulatory capture by commercial interests leads to regulatory choices that systematically overlook the potential of more flexible and citizen-centric policies. The recent allocations so-called "digital dividend" (i.e. the frequencies left vacant by the switch from analog to digital television) is a textbook case. In France, for instance, it was proposed to use part of the spectrum dividend to create new digital TV channels and develop mobile television as well as digital radio (neither of these two technologies has taken off thus far). The remaining half of these frequencies for the lower UHF bands (sought-after because of their long-range propagation) was then auctioned off to telecom operators for their 4G mobile Internet access.

In the process, one option has, however, never been considered: extending "unlicensed" access to some of these frequencies, effectively turning them into a commons open for all to use. Long thought to be unreasonable because of the risk of radio interferences, opening up the spectrum to multiple, non-coordinated radio users has actually been experimented on a worldwide basis more than a decade ago for the Wi-Fi frequencies. Needless to say, it has proved to be a very wise policy choice.

Against the backdrop of traditional economic theory, open spectrum policies suggest that commons-based approach to many-to-many communication infrastructure can actually work in practice. Through packet switching, best-effort delivery, as well as innovative radio transmission and bandwidth management's techniques, Wi-Fi has successfully verified Ostrom's claim that users themselves and ad hoc technical standards can create and enforce rules that mitigate the over-exploitation of the commons (Ostrom 1990). In many regards, though property-based allocations of spectrum and exclusive licensing still have the upper hand, they have often come short of fostering public interest goals, for instance by causing a very significant underutilization of this public resource.[5] Moreover, not only does the regulatory focus on exclusive licensing create an enormous opportunity cost by favoring established players over innovative new-entrants (such as community networks), it has even been argued by human rights NGOs that it may actually breach the international law on freedom of expression (Article 19 2005).

Meanwhile, despite the successes of Wi-Fi, unlicensed access to spectrum remains marginal and regulators have a tendency to ignore WCN's spectrum needs. Guifi.net and Freifunk, for instance, report having a hard time maintaining the quality of their network because of the saturation of the 5 GHz frequency bands.[6] Another issue for WCN is linked to the topography of their environment: Wi-Fi bands have some important technical limitations, in particular in terms of propagation, and signals are easily blocked by buildings or trees. WCN are thus faced with the choice of either renouncing to create a new radio link in a given location, or push the emission power levels beyond the legal limits to overcome these obstacles.

19.4   Towards a New Public Policy for the Network Commons

Much can be done at the regulatory level not only to lift the technical, legal and policy hurdles that community networks run into, but also to actively support them. Several elements presented in the course of this paper—from regulatory capture to the impressive results achieved by these small nonprofit citizen groups—show that this is both an urgent and sound policy move.

First, there is a range of regulations that make WCN's very existence significantly and often unnecessarily difficult. In a country such as Belgium for instance, the registration fee that telecom operators must pay to the NRA is relatively high,

---

[5] First, exclusive licensing have led to anti-competitive behaviors by spectrum owners, or favored certain technologies over potentially more promising ones. For example, several countries grant exclusive licenses to established commercial players providing Internet access through WiMAX or satellite, and even subsidize them. Second, such schemes have proved to encourage underutilization of the resource in the name of avoiding congestion, thus creating artificial scarcity of frequency bands. Many spectrum owners, be they the military or commercial operators (again, satellite or WiMAX come to mind) own important portions of spectrum but do not actually make full use of it, thus crowding out other technologies and potential uses of social value. TV and radio broadcasters also leave significant gaps between their respective channels (these so-called "white spaces") acting as buffers to avoid interference—thereby leaving many frequencies unused in the valuable UHF bands. Combined together, these phenomena bring underutilization to stunning levels: a recent study conducted for the EU Commission finds that, in Paris, the average spectrum use is as low as 7.7 % of the 400 MHz–3 GHz bands, while the average spectrum utilization rate in Europe is under 10 %.

[6] WCN theoretically could be allowed to use the other portion of spectrum by NRAs. Yet, they also refrain from doing so. Except for the 2.4 and 5 GHz license-exempt bands were high demand has driven prices down, radio networking remains a niche market for manufacturers of radio transmitters, and the gear necessary to deploy wireless networks in other bands is costly. Community networks generally cannot afford the price.

whereas in France, Spain or Germany, it is free—which may explain why the movement is much more dynamic in these countries. It is, therefore, all the more important that registration processes be harmonized at the EU level, and, in particular, that they remain free for nonprofit networks.

Second, several laws seek to prevent the sharing of Internet connections amongst several users by making people responsible (and potentially liable) for all communications made through their Wi-Fi connection. This is the case in France, for instance, where the 2009 three-strikes copyright law against peer-to-peer file-sharing also introduced a tort for improperly securing one's Internet connection against unlawful activity on the part of a third party. As a result, many community networks willing to establish open Wi-Fi networks in public spaces, such as parks and streets, refrain from doing so out of legal insecurity. It is our view that, even though connection sharing might sometimes make law enforcement more difficult by allowing many unrelated users to share the same IP address, this drawback is more than compensated by the benefits brought about by the deployment of open wireless networks.

Third, it is not just Internet wireless access points that can be shared, but also the intangible infrastructure on which radio signals travel. As we have seen, unlicensed spectrum is a key asset for community networks to set up affordable and flexible last-mile infrastructure, but it is currently very limited. In the US, the FCC has initiated promising policies in that field.[7] But for the moment, the EU has shied away from similar moves. In 2012, the EU adopted its first Radio Spectrum Policy Programme (RSPP). During the legislative process, the EU Parliament voted in favor of ambitious amendments aimed at opening more spectrum to unlicensed uses.[8] Even if some of these amendments were later scrapped by national governments, the final text still calls for member states and the European Commission to "assess" the "need for and feasibility of extending the allocations of unlicensed spectrum" in the Wi-Fi bands, while also voicing tepid support for mesh networks by stressing their potential to foster access to the global Internet. As EU lawmakers were working on the RSPP, a study commissioned by the EU Commission also called for a new 100 MHz of license-exempt bands as well as for higher power output limits in rural areas to reduce the cost of broadband Internet access deployment.[9]

---

[7] For the past years, through several regulatory moves, the FCC has been opening UHF "white spaces" to unlicensed uses. It has also started expanding the so-called "Unlicensed National Information Infrastructure" by adding 195 MHz of spectrum in the 5 GHz band and increase the permissible power for radio transmitters in these bands. See Farivar (2014).

[8] La Quadrature du Net (2011).

[9] For giving unlicensed access to another 100 MHz of spectrum bands, the report suggested that half of these should be in the 1 GHz bands and the other one at 1.4 GHz. To avoid underutilization, the report also calls on policy-makers to suspend exclusive use of specific channels whenever the use of that spectrum is consistently below a level justifying any form of exclusivity. In France, where WiMAX roll-out has been so slow that the NRA eventually notified the corresponding licensees that they were in breach of their obligations, such a measure could lead to many more channels being opened up for shared or even unlicensed use, for instance to community networks.

Since then, however, EU work on unlicensed spectrum and on flexible authorization schemes that would be more accessible to community networks has stalled. In a communication released in September 2012, the EU Commission failed to announce any concrete action to expand unlicensed use of the spectrum (European Commission 2012). At the national level too, there is unfortunately no policy change in sight.

Fourth, networks built with taxpayers' money could also be treated as a commons, and as such should remain free from corporate capture. Regulators should ensure that nonprofit community networks can access publicly-funded and subsidized physical infrastructures without unnecessary financial or administrative hurdles. Accordingly, they should review existing policies and current practices in this field, providing transparent information to map publicly funded networks, and mandate rules to allow community networks to use these on a preferential basis.[10]

Of course, countless other policy initiatives can help support grassroots networks, such as small grants and subsidies to help these groups buy servers and radio equipment, communicate around their initiative, but also support their research on radio transmission, routing methods, software or encryption (Shaffer 2013).

Yet, all these proposed policies point to an overarching issue, namely the need to democratize telecom policy and establish procedures that can institutionalize existing and potential grassroots community networks. In many countries, such as Spain or Italy, even though city councils may occasionally actively support these organizations to the extent that they provide better Internet access to their citizens, regional governments and national regulators have so far largely neglected them.

Given the revival of community networks in the past years, it is not enough for regulatory authorities to treat citizens as mere consumers by occasionally inviting consumer organizations at the table. Regulators and policy-makers need to recognize that the Internet architecture is a contested site, and that citizen groups across Europe and beyond are showing that for the provision of Internet access, commons-based forms of governance are not only possible but that they also represent effective and viable alternatives to the most powerful telecom operators. Their participants have both the expertise and legitimacy to take an integral part in technical and legal debates over broadband policy in which traditional, commercial ISPs are over-represented. They can bring informed and dissenting views to these debates, and eventually help alleviate regulatory capture.

But democratizing telecom policy is not the sole responsibility of institutional actors. If regulators are not ready to listen, community networks must organize politically and pressure them to do so. Indeed, many community networks are working to form a more cohesive and powerful group to discuss legislative issues and advocate regulatory reforms. Of course, a potential problem for sustaining political engagement is the fact that community networks are often run by volunteers whose

---

[10] On very-fast broadband roll-out, our interviewees also pointed to the need to reorient both public and private investments in fiber-optic last-mile networks where they are most needed, that is in rural communities where decent broadband is crucially lacking, rather than in already well-connected urban areas where there is usually less demand for higher speeds. They also called on regulators to better coordinate so that any public work being carried to roll-out fiber-optic cables that can then be used to expand and improve Internet access.

lack of time and resources may sometimes make it difficult form them to participate as actively as the full-time and well-resourced lobbyists of incumbent actors. But overtime, as the movement grows, it may be able sustain its engagement with public authorities, especially if the latter adapts and establish ad hoc contact channels and remote participation mechanisms. Going back to the typology of political action, direct engagement with policy-makers constitutes a more "insider" strategy that might well be worth pursuing.

References

Article 19. (2005). The legitimacy of license requirements for the use of wireless communications devices. Retrieved April 16, 2014, from http://www.wsis-community.org/pg/file/read/1674/the-legitimacy-of-licence-requirements-for-the-use-of-wireless-communications-devices

Bauwens, M. (2005). P2P and human evolution: Peer to peer as the premise of a new mode of civilization. *Ensaio, rascunho, 1*.

Benkler, Y. (2006). *The wealth of networks*. New Haven, CT: Yale University Press.

European Commission. (2012). *Communication on promoting the shared use of radio spectrum resources in the internal market*. Brussels.

European Commission. (2013). *e-Communications Household Survey* (Special Eurobarometer No. 396). Brussels: EU Commission. Retrieved from http://ec.europa.eu/digital-agenda/en/news/special-eurobarometer-396-e-communications-household-survey

European Commission. (2014a). *Broadband access in the EU: Situation at 1 July 2013*. Retrieved from http://ec.europa.eu//digital-agenda/en/news/broadband-access-eu-situation-1-july-2013

Farivar, C. (2014, March 31). More Wi-Fi is better: FCC expands use of 5GHz spectrum. *Ars Technica*. Retrieved May 11, 2014, from http://arstechnica.com/information-technology/2014/03/more-wi-fi-is-better-fcc-expands-use-of-5-GHz-spectrum/

Feenberg, A. (1995). Subversive rationalization: Technology, power and democracy. In A. Hannay & A. Feenberg (Eds.), *Technology and the politics of knowledge* (pp. 3–22). Indiana University Press.

La Quadrature du Net. (2011, May 11). EU Parliament Adopts Open Wireless Communications Policy. *LaQuadrature.net*. Retrieved May 12, 2014, from http://www.laquadrature.net/en/eu-parliament-adopts-open-wireless-communications-policy

Ostrom, E. (1990). *Governing the commons: The evolution of institutions for collective action*. Cambridge: Cambridge university press.

SamKnows. (2013). *SamKnows study on Internet speeds*. Retrieved from https://ec.europa.eu/digital-agenda/en/news/quality-broadband-services-eu-samknows-study-internet-speeds

Shaffer, G. (2013). Lessons learned from grassroots wireless networks in Europe. In A. Abdelaal (Ed.), *Social and economic effects of community wireless networks and infrastructures* (pp. 236–254). IGI Global.

Stoyanova, M. (2008). *Competition problems in liberalized telecommunications: Regulatory solutions to promote effective competition*. The Netherlands: Kluwer Law International.

Thatcher, M. (2014). European Commission merger control: Combining competition and the creation of larger European firms. *European Journal of Political Research, 53*(3), 443–464.

Wu, T. (2010). *The master switch: The rise and fall of information empires*. New York: Knopf.

Chapter 20
Safety, Privacy and Net Neutrality Aspects of Civilian Drones

Leonidas Kanellos

Unmanned aircraft systems (UAS) have a tremendous number of potential applications, particularly for industry and enterprises, such as delivery of broadband connectivity, speedy delivery of goods, parcels, geo-mapping, filming, as well as for government operations including surveillance, public safety, coastal security and disaster recovery.

Today drones monitor illegal fishing off Libya, Japan and the Galapagos Islands, count sea lions in Alaska and patrol oil and gas pipelines in Angola, Nigeria, Kuwait and Saudi Arabia. Archeologists in Russia are using small unmanned systems with infrared cameras to construct a 3-D model of ancient burial mounds. Researchers in Costa Rica fly small aircrafts through volcanic clouds to try to predict major eruptions. In Brazil, drones are being used by farmers to spot crop blights and apply pesticides with more accuracy. Conservationists in Nepal plan to use UAVs to help save endangered tigers and rhinos from poachers.

Civilian drones shall also be used by companies such as Google or Facebook)[1] to provide drone-enabled Internet access to remote areas that need capacity. On this purpose, Google aims at using solar-powered drones (Project Titan) combined with high-altitude balloons (Project Loon).[2] Said company is reported to have already obtained relevant testing licenses from the FCC.[3] Facebook plans to launch a lightweight drone with a wingspan similar to a Boeing 767 using solar power to deliver internet access via laser to people 60,000–90,000 feet below (Project

---

[1] http://www.techtimes.com/articles/36674/20150302/publish-mwc2015-google-titan-drones-loon-balloons-bringing-wireless-everywhere.htm.

[2] Google announce at the Mobile World Congress 2015 in Barcelona is available at https://www.youtube.com/watch?v=lKHDJs-zc1g.

[3] http://www.computerworld.com/article/2896581/googles-solar-drone-internet-tests-about-to-go-airborne.html.

L. Kanellos (✉)
University of Piraeus, Athens, Greece

© Springer International Publishing Switzerland 2016   271
L. Belli, P. De Filippi (eds.), *Net Neutrality Compendium*,
DOI 10.1007/978-3-319-26425-7_20

Aquila).[4] To ensure coverage across wider areas communications between drones need to be established and maintained.

The benefits of a supportive regulatory framework for the creation of an all-wireless network in the sky are clear. Such networks would be far less expensive, far less disruptive and take far less time to build than implementing a wired land-based infrastructure over very large swaths of the earth where no communications infrastructure currently exists. However, the commercial operation of such airborne networks worldwide still faces important technical constraints (reliability of the connection, weather conditions, capacity, etc.)[5] and legal uncertainties.[6]

20.1 The International Drones' Industry

From an industry perspective, a recent report,[7] submitted or vote to the European Parliament in July 2015, notes that the US is considered as the leading market for the use of RPAS, albeit for military operations while Europe is the leader in the civilian sector with 2500 operators compared to 2342 operators in the rest of the world (with 50 countries including Japan Australia, Brazil, China, Japan and South Africa currently developing RPAS).

The drone industry is estimated by ABI research[8] to climb to $8.4 billion by 2019. An IDATE industry forecast[9] covering 2014–2020 for commercial and consumer drones predicts that once a suitable regulatory framework is introduced and no significant disruption takes place, nearly 170,000 commercial drones will be operating across the globe by the end of 2020, alongside about 12 million hobby drones.

According to US industry analysts,[10] the economic impact of the integration of UAS into the US National Aviation System will total more than $13.6 billion in the

---

[4] A description of the Facebook Project Aquila is available at https://www.youtube.com/watch?v=PdxRa-nBtV4.

[5] Will internet access via drones ever fly? article published at http://www.wired.com/insights/2014/11/internet-access-drones/

[6] Kanellos (2015).

[7] The Draft Report (Rapporteur: Jacqueline Foster) on the safe use of remotely piloted aircraft systems (RPAS), commonly known as unmanned aerial vehicles (UAVs), in the field of civil aviation (2014/2243(INI)) Committee on Transport and Tourism can be accessed at http://www.europarl.europa.eu/sides/getDoc.do?pubRef=-//EP//NONSGML+COMPARL+PE-554.997+01+DOC+PDF+V0//EN.

[8] See Cadie Thomson's article entitled " Here is where the real money is in drones" at http://www.cnbc.com/2015/05/13/heres-where-the-real-money-is-in-drones.html.

[9] This report is on sale at http://www.idate.org/en/Research-store/Collection/Market-report_23/Commercial-and-consumer-drones_1005.html.

[10] The AUVSI Report on "The economic impact of unmanned aircraft systems integration in the United States" can be downloaded at https://higherlogicdownload.s3.amazonaws.com/AUVSI/958c920a-7f9b-4ad2-9807-f9a4e95d1ef1/UploadedImages/New_Economic%20Report%202013%20Full.pdf.

first 3 years of integration and will grow sustainably for the foreseeable future, cumulating to more than \$82.1 billion between 2015 and 2025. Moreover, the Integration into the NAS will create more than 34,000 manufacturing jobs and more than 70,000 new jobs in the first 3 years.

20.2   The Applicable Rules in Europe and the US

Despite notable divergences among various industry forecasts, they all agree that a suitable regulatory framework is critical for the take off of the drone industry worldwide.

In Europe, so far there is no legislation on civil drone use. In 2014, the European Commission requested a draft regulation from the European Aviation Safety Agency (EASA). EC Regulation No 216/2008[11] mandates the Agency to regulate Unmanned Aircraft Systems (UAS) and in particular Remotely Piloted Aircraft Systems (RPAS), when used for civil applications and with an operating mass of 150 kg or more. Experimental or amateur build RPAS, military and non-military governmental RPAS flights, civil RPAS below 150 kg as well as model aircraft are regulated by individual Member States of the European Union.[12] EASA is supported by two other agencies, EUROCONTROL, which coordinates the air traffic management services across Europe and the European Organisation for Civil Aviation Equipment (EUROCAE) which drafts the airworthiness and operational standards for aircraft.

In this direction, on 31 July 2015, the EASA launched a consultation process on a new regulatory framework for drones.[13] According to this approach, flight safety requirements are in relation to the risk an activity poses to the operator and to third parties such as the general public. On 24 August 2015, EASA made available a summary of its Proposals a for the Introduction of a Regulatory Framework for the Operation of Drones.[14]

---

[11] Regulation (EC) No 216/2008 of the European Parliament and the Council of 20 February 2008 on common rules in the field of civil aviation and establishing a European Aviation Safety Agency, and repealing Council Directive 91/670/EEC, Regulation (EC) No 1592/2002 and Directive 2004/36/EC was published at http://eur-lex.europa.eu/LexUriServ/LexUriServ.do?uri=OJ:L:2008:079:0001:0049:EN:PDF.

[12] A summary of national laws on drones in Europe can be found at http://epthinktank.eu/2015/03/12/civil-drones-in-the-eu/.

[13] The EASA Concept of Operations for Drones A risk based approach to regulation of unmanned aircraft can be accessed at http://www.easa.europa.eu/system/files/dfu/204696_EASA_concept_drone_brochure_web.pdf.

[14] Press release on the EASA proposals can be accessed at http://www.easa.europa.eu/newsroom-and-events/news/short-summary-easa%E2%80%99s-proposals-new-rules-drones.

Following the Riga Conference (March 2015) on remotely piloted aircraft systems entitled "the future of flying" a Declaration was issued on remotely piloted aircrafts.[15]

This policy document sets out five essential principles for future EU focus: (a) RPAS need to be treated as new types of aircraft with proportionate rules based on the risk of each operation; (b) EU rules for the safe provision of RPAS services need to be developed to enable the industry to invest; (c) technology and standards need to be developed to enable full integration of RPAS into the European airspace; (d) public acceptance is key to the growth of RPAS services; (e) the operator of an RPAS shall be responsible for its use. In July 2015, a Report outlining legislation plans on AUS was introduced in Parliament's Transport and Tourism Committee.[16] Such legislation is expected to be voted by the end of December 2015.

In the US, the 2012 US Drone Act (FAA Modernization and Reform Act) [17] contains provisions requiring the Federal Aviation Administration (FAA) to integrate fully unmanned aircraft into the National Airspace System by September 2015. Additionally, the Drone Act allows law enforcement agencies, including local police forces, to buy and use unmanned aircraft for evidence gathering and surveillance.

Recently, the FAA has released a Notice of proposed Rulemaking (NPRM) for small, unmanned aircraft,[18] which opened the door for public comments and the beginning of the rulemaking process. The main goal of this process is to allow routine use of certain small unmanned aircraft systems (UAS) in today's aviation system while maintaining flexibility to accommodate future technological innovations.

The FAA proposal offers safety rules for small UAS (under 55 lb) conducting non-recreational operations. The rule would limit flights to daylight and visual-line-of-sight operations. It also addresses height restrictions, operator certification, optional use of a visual observer, aircraft registration and marking, as well as and operational limits. Such rulemaking initiative is supported by an industry-led educational ("know before you fly") campaign.

Moreover, the public dialogue in the US focuses on matter such as regarding privacy, data protection, law enforcement and access to sensitive information collected by commercial drones, such as location data, safety regulations, licensing, airworthiness process and technical standardization. A Presidential Memorandum was issued on 15 February 2015 with the title "Promoting Economic Competitiveness

---

[15] The Riga Declaration on remotely piloted aircraft (drones) "Framing the future of aviation", of 6 March 2015 is available at http://ec.europa.eu/transport/modes/air/news/doc/2015-03-06-drones/2015-03-06-riga-declaration-drones.pdf.

[16] The Draft Report (Rapporteur: Jacqueline Foster) on safe use of remotely piloted aircraft systems (RPAS), commonly known as unmanned aerial vehicles (UAVs), in the field of civil aviation (2014/2243(INI)) Committee on Transport and Tourism can be accessed at http://www.europarl. europa.eu/sides/getDoc.do?pubRef=-//EP//NONSGML+COMPARL+PE-554.997+01+DOC+PDF+V0//EN.

[17] The Drone Act is accessible at https://www.congress.gov/bill/112th-congress/house-bill/658.

[18] The FAA Notice can be retrieved at http://www.gpo.gov/fdsys/pkg/FR-2015-02-23/pdf/2015-03544.pdf.

While Safeguarding Privacy, Civil Rights, and Civil Liberties in Domestic Use of Unmanned Aircraft Systems".[19]

20.3   Towards a Comprehensive Legal Framework for UAS

Except for flight safety rules, the commercial and private use of UAS also raises concerns over privacy, transparency, insurance for third party liability and accountability. Following many years of public consultation,[20] the European Commission has developed a strategy to support the progressive development of the RPAS market in Europe, while also addressing concerns about safety, security, privacy, liability and public acceptance.

The European Commission strategy was presented in a Communication, adopted in April 2014 and entitled "**A new era for aviation:** Opening the aviation market to the civil use of RPAS in a safe and sustainable manner".[21]

The European strategy focuses on Remotely Piloted Aircraft Systems (RPAS), a sub-set of Unmanned Aircraft Systems (UAS), which excludes fully autonomous systems. It aims to ensure the **safe and secure integration of RPAS into the European aviation system**, from 2016 onwards, through the development of: (a) A **common safety regulatory framework**, proportionate to risks for drones of all classes in order to promote the creation of a single European market for civil drones applications; (b) the **necessary enabling technologies** ('sense and avoid', 'comment and control communication link' etc.); (c) measures to ensure the protection of citizens (privacy, insurance, etc.); (d) measures to support market development and European industries.

20.4   Privacy Aspects of Drones

The progressive integration of drones into the European civil airspace combined with a large-scale deployment of drone and sensor technology creates privacy risks arise for the individuals' privacy and civil and political liberties. Drones process personal data such as images, sound and geolocation relating to an identified or identifiable natural person under non-transparent conditions as to for what purposes

---

[19] The Presidential Memorandum is published on the White House website https://www.white-house.gov/the-press-office/2015/02/15/presidential-memorandum-promoting-economic-competitiveness-while-safegua.

[20] See the UK Government's Response to the House of Lords European Union Committee's Seventh Report of Session 2014/15: Civilian Use of Drones in the EU http://www.publications.parliament.uk/pa/ld201415/ldselect/ldeucom/122/122.pdf.

[21] COM/2014/027 **"A new era for aviation Opening the aviation market to the civil use of remotely piloted aircraft systems in a safe and sustainable manner"** http://eur-lex.europa.eu/legal-content/EN/TXT/?uri=CELEX%3A52014DC0207.

personal data are being collected (bulk data collection) and by whom (law enforcement, private data collectors for possible unlawful multipurpose uses). Furthermore,
the dexterity of drones and the possibility to interconnect multiple drones further
facilitates their ability to avoid obstacles or not to be constrained by barriers, walls
or fences, so to easily enable the collection of a wide variety of information even
without the need for a direct line of sight, for long periods of time and across large
area without intermission.

To tackle privacy concerns under the European data protection principles (transparency, proportionality, anonymisation etc. under Directive 95/46/EC and the
forthcoming data Protection Regulation the European Data Protection supervisor
published), on 26 November 2014 his opinion on the above RPAS communication.[22]
On 16 June 2015, the Article 29 Data Protection Working Party adopted an opinion[23]
on privacy and data protection issues relating to the utilisation of drones. On 20
May 2014, the European Group of Ethics in Science and New Technologies issued
an opinion[24] which addresses the use of drones for surveillance missions.

20.5   Net Neutrality Aspects of Drones

One other important aspect of a coherent regulatory framework is the relation
between the provision of Internet access via drones and net neutrality. In 2013,
Facebook founded Internet.org, a partnership between the company and seven
mobile companies[25] to bring Internet access to users in developing countries by
subsidizing their data plans. Such initiative appears like a win-win situation for both
Internet.org partners and mobile users in developing nations. As pointed out in a
white paper for Internet.org[26] approximately 80–90 % of the world's population
lives today in areas already covered by 2G or 3G networks. In the remaining non-
connected areas, connectivity may be reached by combining all available technologies such as drones, satellites, mesh networks, radios and free space optics.

However, this initiative has been strongly criticized to constitute a violation of
net neutrality rules. In India, telecom companies fought against Internet.org, claiming the service gave web-based apps like Facebook's WhatsApp and Microsoft's
Skype an unfair edge over their own phone-based apps, which consume paid data.

---

[22]The European Data Protection supervisor's opinion is published at https://secure.edps.europa.eu/
EDPSWEB/webdav/site/mySite/shared/Documents/Consultation/Opinions/2014/14-11-26_
Opinion_RPAS_EN.pdf.

[23]The Article 29 Data Protection Working Party opinion is available at http://ec.europa.eu/
DocsRoom/documents/11481.

[24]The European Group of Ethics in Science and New Technologies opinion is published at http://
ec.europa.eu/DocsRoom/documents/11493.

[25]Samsung, Ericsson, MediaTek, Opera Software and Qualcomm.

[26]The White paper "Connecting the World form the Sky" can be retrieved at https://fbcdn-dragon-
a.akamaihd.net/hphotos-ak-ash3/t39.2365-6/851574_611544752265540_1262758947_n.pdf.

That pressure led travel site Cleartrip, one of Internet.org partners in India to withdraw from the alliance. In response to those net neutrality concerns Facebook opened the Internet.org platform to all developers meeting its criteria.[27]

It remains to be seen how attractive this offer will be compared to alternative platforms. In this respect, it has to be noted that the Internet.org technical guidelines exclude the use of various protocols such as HTTP. In order for a website to display properly within the Internet.org platform and be accessible to people on all types of phones and data plans, the mobile websites must meet certain technical conditions created by the Internet.org proxy.[28] If websites are found to contain any of the above post-implementation, they are blocked until the content has been removed.

20.6 Minimizing the Risk of New Gatekeepers

From an infrastructure viewpoint, it is true that using drones as an internet platform in remote areas, without network competition, could incentivize access providers to prioritize their own services to the detriment of others. Access providers might also allow access to selected services and not all internet content by violating the principle of net neutrality. Such trend could progressively lead to an increasing data monopoly through the commercial presence of certain companies in the unconnected regions of the planet.

For instance, in some parts of the world covered by the Internet.org initiative Facebook users and specific applications promoted by the access provider are reported to be a significant part of the open internet users. For instance, Facebook hit 100 million active users in Africa last September, and it had registered 112 million active users in India at the end of 2014. Those figures represent nearly half of all Internet users in both regions. A recent Geopoll survey revealed that 11 % of Indonesians and 9 % of Nigerians used Facebook, but yet had no idea they were connected to the Internet.[29] Those findings support the argument that Facebook's Internet.org is an attempt to establish a solid commercial presence by redefining the Internet under its own banner in emerging markets.

In the same vein, Google's Project Loon using high-altitude balloons placed in the stratosphere to create an aerial wireless network with up to 3G-like speeds could also raise similar net neutrality concerns. This is obvious to the extent infrastructure cost recovery for Google as an access provider will rely on profit maximization for the company as a service provider through the granting of higher speed access to its associated sites like youtube compared to other sites.

---

[27] "Facebook Opens Internet.Org To All Developers In Response To Net Neutrality Concerns". *TechCrunch*. May 4, 2015. Retrieved on 10 September 2015.

[28] Specifically, mobile websites should work in the absence of, JavaScript, SVG images and WOFF font types, HTTPS support, iframes, video and large images, flash and Java applets.

[29] Mirani. "Millions of facebook users have no idea they are using the Internet". Retrieved on 10 September 2015 at http://qz.com/333313/milliions-of-facebook-users-have-no-idea-theyre-using-the-internet/.

20.7   Open Questions

In this context, two sets of questions arise: on the one hand, are those allegations founded or do they neglect the positive effect of a big, innovative and costly effort to connect more users to the internet? Do those critics constitute an overreaction to the extent internet.org (and potentially similar activities by other manufacturers) neither blocks or throttles any other services nor creates fast lanes by remaining open to all developers and web publishers?

On the other hand, can Internet.org or in the near future Google Loon be considered as a "gatekeeper" for delivering select apps to poorer users? Can such drone-enabled access providers progressively turn into significant technical and content—monitoring bottlenecks for the unconnected?

It is obvious that companies powering such initiatives gain commercial advantages from tethering and locking users in developing markets to their ecosystems. The user lock-in effect emerges in terms of guaranteed user growth and more eyeballs for their display ads together with more search—and browsing activities by their subsidized clients. Under those conditions, can the subsidization of the user data plans be considered as a purely charitable act or as a smooth new market entry strategy?

20.8   How Drone-Enabled Data Traffic Be Regulated?

Furthermore, from a regulatory perspective, should drone-enabled data traffic be regulated differently from regular Internet access? For instance, in the U.S., should it be regulated under the common carriage rules of Title II of the Communications Act? How can European net neutrality rules[30] which, upon their adoption, will guarantee that "users will be free to access the content of their choice, they will not be unfairly blocked or slowed down any more, and paid prioritisation will not be allowed" be compatible with drone-enabled connectivity?

On which grounds and for how long could sponsored data activities and paid prioritization through drone-enabled internet access be treated differently in comparison to other communications platforms? More generally, should quality of service and equal access obligations be extended to cover "subsidized access" to basic services via UAS?

In conclusion, policy makers and regulators around the world considering how best to incorporate drones into existing airspace also including their role as internet access infrastructures will need to balance the many positive contributions they can make, as well as the obvious negative externalities they can inflict. Drones should be integrated into the existing aviation system and the communications infrastructures across the globe in a safe, proportionate and non-discriminatory manner. This integration should foster an innovative and competitive drone industry, creating jobs

---

[30] Commission welcomes agreement to end roaming charges and to guarantee an open Internet, Brussels 30 June 2015, Press release http://europa.eu/rapid/press-release_IP-15-5265_en.htm.

and growth but without compromising user privacy, data protection and secrecy of communications. From a policy viewpoint, it is also important to avoid over-regulation that could kill the global drones industry. Parliaments should recognize the significant financial, technical, legal and other constraints of infrastructure deployment in remote areas. Political support for the industry is a key factor to fulfill the vision of making available RPAS networks for underserved segments of the earth's population.

References

Facebook Opens Internet.Org To All Developers In Response To Net Neutrality Concerns (2015, May 4). *TechCrunch*. Retrieved on 10 September 2015.

Kanellos, L. (2015, June). *Regulatory challenges of drones : The sky is a limit*(Vol. 43, Issue 2). London: InterMEDIA. www.iicom.org

Mirani, L. Millions of Facebook users have no idea they are using the Internet. Retrieved on 10 September2015athttp://qz.com/333313/milliions-of-facebook-users-have-no-idea-theyre-using-the-internet/

Chapter 21
Network Neutrality: An Empirical Approach to Legal Interoperability

Luca Belli and Nathalia Foditsch

21.1 Introduction

The Internet is grounded in an open and interoperable architecture, giving rise to a quintessentially transnational environment. This global network of networks is, however, in natural tension with an international legal system based on mutually excluding legal frameworks. Differently from electronic networks, which are based on shared technical standards whose main objective is to make different systems compatible, national juridical system are based on essentially domestic rules, whose application to the online environment has the potential to fragment the Internet. The implementation of divergent domestic laws and regulation has indeed the potential to balkanise the global Internet creating separated national intranets and potentially conflicting cyberspaces. It seems important, therefore, to encourage the development of harmonious rules across jurisdictions, thus fostering the compatibility of the legal systems penetrated by the Internet. Promoting a "legally interoperable" environment may be considered as an instrumental step to achieving a better-functioning Internet ecosystem, in which new technologies can spur, and the free flow of information is not hindered by diverging national laws.

Although the promotion of legal interoperability should be seen an important policy objective, it must be recognised that advancing legal interoperability of issues of systemic importance is not an easy task. A promising approach in this regard consists in analysing existing regulatory frameworks in order to identify best practices and synthesise them within a policy model. As open standards, policy

L. Belli (✉)
Fundação Getúlio Vargas Law School, Rio de Janeiro, Brazil
e-mail: luca.belli@fgv.br

N. Foditsch
American University, Washington, DC, USA

© Springer International Publishing Switzerland 2016
L. Belli, P. De Filippi (eds.), *Net Neutrality Compendium*,
DOI 10.1007/978-3-319-26425-7_21

models should be freely accessible and usable by any interested stakeholder, so that policymakers, regulators or market actors could use them in order to shape legally interoperable frameworks.

One particular topic that lends itself well to be analysed from a legal interoperability perspective is net neutrality. Net neutrality policy focus on Internet traffic management, which is an issue virtually affecting every electronic network composing the Internet and, for this reason, it has already been addressed by several jurisdictions through different approaches.[1] Furthermore, the definition of legally interoperable net neutrality rules and principles may be particularly beneficial to address a shared problem that, over the past years, has gained great political momentum at the global level. In the U.S., the FCC consultation on net neutrality rules triggered nearly 4 million comments (White House 2015), in India, Internet users sent more than 150 thousand emails over one weekend to the telecom regulator asking to protect network neutrality in the country, as part of one of the biggest online protests in Indian history (Jayadevan 2015), while the European Union is putting forward new net neutrality rules (Ansip 2015) and national efforts have being undertaken in order to guarantee constitutional status to the net neutrality principle (Senato 2014).

At the same time, a Model Framework on Network Neutrality (Belli et al. 2015), aimed at fostering legal interoperability on this matter, has already been elaborated by the IGF Dynamic Coalition on Network neutrality (DCNN)[2] and has inspired more than one organisation, such as the European Parliament[3] and the Council of Europe.[4] In this paper we elucidate the importance of addressing net neutrality from a legally interoperable perspective in order to foster shared rules safeguarding the originally open and distributed nature of the Internet. Whereas it might be seen as a domestic matter, exclusively impinging upon how Internet traffic is managed by network operators at the national level, the protection of network neutrality determines immediate consequences on the Internet users' capability to freely seek, impart and receive information regardless of frontier. For this reason, legally interoperable tools fostering shared principles or providing compatible regulatory indications should be welcome in order to foster universal connectivity on a non-discriminatory basis.

---

[1] See Belli and De Filippi (2014).

[2] Dynamic coalitions are structural components of the UN-convened Internet Governance Forum (IGF). These multistakeholder groups are aimed at analysing and fostering debate with regard to specific topics and can be used as working groups in order to produce concrete outcomes. See http://www.intgovforum.org/cms/dynamiccoalitions.

[3] Compare the network neutrality principle's definition and the provisions regarding traffic management of the Model Framework on Network neutrality, available at http://www.networkneutrality.info/sources.html and of the European Parliament legislative resolution of 3 April 2014 on the proposal for a regulation of the European Parliament and of the Council laying down measures concerning the European single market for electronic communications and to achieve a Connected Continent.

[4] Compare Belli and van Bergan (2013); CDMSI (2015).

After providing a brief analyses of the concept of interoperability and its potential transposition from the technical to the regulatory level (Sect. 21.2), this paper examines the relevance of network neutrality in order to maintain the original end-user-empowering architecture of the Internet (Sect. 21.3). Lastly, after having identified common elements within the existing net neutrality frameworks, we suggest a common principle basis that may be used to develop future legally-interoperable approaches, avoiding fragmentation and fostering legal certainty while diminishing transaction costs for businesses (Sect. 21.4).

21.2 The Techno-Legal Nature of Interoperability

Interoperability is usually described as "the ability to transfer and render useful data and other information across systems, applications, or components" (ITU 2015). This concept is increasingly important as interconnected technologies, continuously receiving and transmitting data, are becoming the norm. Communication among interconnected devices, cars, engines, phones is only possible if they are interoperable and therefore, interoperability plays an instrumental role in furthering the sustainable evolution of the Internet, as a global ecosystem. In the sections below, we concisely analyse the concept of interoperability and its potential application to legal and regulatory systems rather than being merely confined to the technical domain.

21.2.1 What Is Interoperability and How to Foster It

Interoperability plays a key role in facilitating the free flow of information. Indeed, the purpose of interoperability is to fostering the ability to transfer and use data across heterogeneous technologies and systems. Conspicuously, this means having the possibility to create new applications and services and being able to use them to exchange information across technically different but compatible networks. This is indeed the quintessential purpose of the Internet, whose original Catenet model for internetworking aimed at establishing "a model and a set of rules which will allow data networks of widely varying internal operation to be interconnected, permitting users to access remote resources and to permit intercomputer communication across the connected networks" (Cerf 1987). From a technical perspective, such "models and sets of rules" are defined by the technical standards and protocols that allow all Internet users to exchange information and to utilise services in a cross-border fashion on a daily basis. Hence, technical interoperability plays an instrumental role in fostering openness, innovation and competition, while providing the user with wider choice amongst a greater diversity of content and services (Gasser and Palfrey 2007).

Interoperability is also one of the main purposes of the ITU's International Telecommunication Regulations, which "are established with a view to facilitating global interconnection and interoperability of telecommunication facilities and to promoting the harmonious development and efficient operation of technical facilities, as well as the efficiency, usefulness and availability to the public of international telecommunication services."[5] Such goals can be fostered through the actions of private as well as public actors, which can operate on a unilateral basis or via joint multistakeholder efforts. Hence, it is important to note that there is a spectrum of possibilities for public–private collaboration aimed at developing tools that may advance interoperability.

On the one hand, private actors unilaterally choose the design of products and services and can grant licenses to others, thus establishing rights and limitations to the use of technologies in a top-down fashion. Private actors can also foster interoperability trough technical collaboration. Technical collaboration has a broader level of cooperation that goes beyond the mere granting of IP licenses. Palfrey and Gasser (2012) cite mobile payments as an example to illustrate such broader level of cooperation, as they rely on licensing schemes but also require technical cooperation between retailers, manufacturers, payment processors and banks. Standards are the third way through which private actors collaborate towards higher levels of interoperability. Although standards have a great potential for achieving high degrees of interoperability their effectiveness might be limited (Palfrey and Gasser 2012). At the same time, both the elaboration and adoption of open standards is based on voluntary efforts which might suffer from the over-representation of those players having the financial capability necessary to continuously participate in voluntary but still resource-consuming efforts.

On the other hand, regulatory decisions influencing interoperability might also range from more unilateral actions to more collaborative actions. Regulators might mandate the adoption of interoperable standards, which might be an effective approach. However, governments might have difficulties to adapt rules to new realities once the standards become exceeded. Moreover, governments might lack sufficient expertise to choose the most efficient standards. Lastly, interoperability might be fostered through competition law, an ex-post type of intervention. Nonetheless, the limitations of such intervention are easy to infer, particularly due to its ex-post nature and procedural delays.

The concept of interoperability has been considered as beneficial for competition and innovation, increasing efficiency in the provision of services by Governments. Interoperability is also associated with reductions in the cost of technologies, as it promotes scalability (Palfrey and Gasser 2012). The benefits of technical interoperability tend to outweigh the possible challenges related to it and, for this reason, it seems important to enquire whether similar benefits may be achieved through the promotion of interoperability from a regulatory perspective rather than from an exclusively technical one. Particularly, shared principles and compatible rules amongst various juridical systems have the potential to reduce transaction costs, deflating barriers to cross-border trade and significantly lowering costs related to adaptation to different regulatory frameworks, but can also foster important

---

[5] See art. 1.3, ITR.

non-monetisable benefits, such as individual empowerment and the protection of fundamental rights. In the following section, we analyse the concept of legal interoperability in order to subsequently apply it to the concrete example of net neutrality regulation.

21.2.2   Can Juridical Systems Be Interoperable?

Legal systems can be considered as interoperable when the cost of regulatory fragmentation is low enough for people, goods and services subject to regulation to easily move between them (Tréguer 2012). Legal interoperability fosters compatibility of rules concerning the same topic within different jurisdictions or different administrative levels within a state, thus reducing regulatory fragmentation (Weber 2014). Like technical interoperability, legal interoperability stimulates the exchange of information within different systems. As such, interoperability of both technical and legal systems allows individuals—and, particularly, Internet users—to access and provide services in a cross-border fashion and to enjoy equal right-protection within different systems thanks to compatible (or, preferably, common) rules, principles, and procedures.

Models and sets of rules aimed at facilitating legal interoperability may be elaborated by players on an equal footing, in the context of harmonisation efforts; may be unilaterally imposed, in a top-down fashion, by a player enjoying an asymmetric power relationship with the other players; or may be fostered through transnational diffusion (Jörgens 2003; Belli 2015). Harmonisation relies on the cooperative effort of a group of—usually governmental—actors to elaborate a suitable solution to a shared and frequently transnational problem. To this end, public actors may define common regulatory tools aimed at fostering the free flow of information or, more generally, the free movement of people, goods, services and capital. Harmonisation usually backs legal interoperability via intergovernmental processes taking place within bilateral, plurilateral or multilateral fora. Harmonisation relies on the formulation of multilateral agreements, such as conventions, and subsequent implementation of policies consistent with such agreements by the entities that participated in the formulation process.

Legal interoperability through imposition occurs when a single actor—be it private or (inter)governmental—has the capacity to define unilaterally and enact policies that will affect other actors. For instance "business enterprises"[6] can unilaterally define the standard contractual agreements—or licenses—according to which they will provide a service and, subsequently, implement the contractual provision via

---

[6]The expression "business enterprise" should be considered as including "any business entity, regardless of the international or domestic nature of its activities, including a transnational corporation, contractor, subcontractor, supplier, licensee or distributor; the corporate, partnership, or other legal form used to establish the business entity; and the nature of the ownership of the entity." See: Sub-Commission on the Promotion and Protection of Human Rights 2003, § 21.

technical means (Schultz 2005; Belli 2015). One example in this regard is the use of Digital Rights Management techniques, allowing private actors to control both access and use of digital material (Palfrey and Gasser 2012).

Transnational diffusion, differently from the two former cases, is grounded on a process of voluntary adoption and reproduction of rules and procedures, by reason of their efficiency and reliability. Hence, contrary to harmonisation and imposition, transnational diffusion may occur in the absence of any institutional agreements. To this extent, international fora and NGOs may be the vehicle of transnational diffusion, facilitating policy development and offering breeding ground for policy cross-fertilisation (Béland and Orenstein 2009).

When considering the autonomous networks composing the Internet, it is spontaneous to remark that their technical interoperability is guaranteed by the use of shared standards that are voluntarily adopted by operators and service providers by reason of their proven efficiency. Indeed, the day-to-day operation of the Internet is based on the "voluntary adherence to open protocols and procedures defined by Internet Standard" (Bradner 1996) that enable end-to-end communication taking place via "a loosely-organized international collaboration of autonomous, interconnected networks" (Bradner 1996). Likewise, policy models framing shared regulatory problems may be a useful source of inspiration for national regulators and legislators—or even for self-regulatory efforts by market player—thus fostering legal interoperability through the adoption of compatible rules and procedures. Policy models may not only inspire legislative efforts but also be used as basis on which develop co-regulatory frameworks by national regulators in partnership with national stakeholders or even by private-sector actors themselves that may find it more convenient to craft their self-regulatory codes of conduct on the basis of existing policy models.

Globally shared regulatory issues such as net neutrality, data privacy or copyright regulation lend themselves very well to be the object of policy models that may subsequently be used by various stakeholders to transnationally diffuse legally interoperable rules. As we will discuss in the next sections, the net neutrality principle aims at guaranteeing a non-discriminatory treatment of Internet traffic in order maintain the Internet's open, interoperable and general-purpose nature. Such non-discriminatory treatment can be promoted by national policies but, given the global nature of the Internet, a more suitable approach may be to experiment the development of open policy-standards or open model-frameworks aimed at fostering the protection of net neutrality in a legally interoperable fashion. In light of the fact that open technical standards facilitate the development of interoperable technology, it seems reasonable to posit that open policy standards may be instrumental to the development of legally interoperable policies and regulations. The next section will emphasize the endogenously neutral character of the Internet architecture and will identify some elements that should be considered in order to define legally-interoperable net neutrality approaches.

21.3   From Endogenous Neutrality to Exogenous Net Neutrality

Network neutrality is the principle according to which Internet traffic shall be treated without discrimination, restriction or interference regardless of its sender, recipient, type or content so that Internet users' freedom is not restricted. The concept of network neutrality prescribes a non-discriminatory management of Internet traffic in order to guarantee that all Internet users enjoy universal access to all online resources, thus maintaining their power to decide autonomously how to use the network rather than being subject to the usage decisions imposed by network operators. To this extent it is important to bear in mind that the Internet has been conceived as a general purpose internetwork whose end-to-end architecture and layered structure were precisely aimed at decentralising the intelligence of the network in its applications (run by end-users), rather than keeping it within the control of the networks' operators (Saltzer et al. 1984).

This decentralised approach is mirrored in the TCP/IP protocol suite, the "technical constitution of the Internet" (Belli 2015) that structures the network in different layers to which distinct functions are delegated (Saltzer et al. 1984; Solum and Chung 2004). This decentralised architecture has allowed the Internet to maintain a high level of openness to new technologies, applications and devices. However, the increasing vertical integration between network operators and Content and Applications Providers (CAPs) may undermine such an open and decentralised structure, due to the substantive incentive that network operators may have to discriminate in favour of their commercial partners and against competitors (BEREC 2012; FCC 2015). Indeed, Internet traffic management has the potential to negatively impact end-users' capability to freely exchange information online, possibly jeopardising the full exercise of their fundamental rights as well as their possibility to "innovate without permission" (Belli and van Bergen 2013; Daigle 2014).

In the following sections we will provide a brief overview of the fundamental features of the Internet architecture, subsequently highlighting that the general aim of any net neutrality frameworks should be to preserve such features.

21.3.1   An Inherently Neutral Architecture

The original Internet structure was purposely designed to avoid centralisation, having an end-to-end design for efficiency and resilience purposes (Saltzer et al. 1984; Carpenter 1996). Such distributed architecture *de facto* delegated to end-users the possibility to decide how to use the network while keeping it interoperable, thus fostering the openness of the system and deflating barriers that may hinder user participation, communication and innovation. The basic assumption was that a network of heterogeneous networks, "however carefully designed, will be subject to failures of transmission at some statistically determined rate [and the] best way to cope with this is to accept it and give responsibility for the integrity of communication to the end system" (Carpenter 1996). To this end, information was fragmented into data packets to be transmitted independently of each other and independently from their content or application. The intelligence of the network was delegated to the application run by the end-users, responsible for reassembling data packets for various purposes. Indeed, specialised treatment of packets may have risked hindering interoperability of applications run by end-users in different networks while, on the contrary, non-discriminatory transmission of data packets represented a guarantee for interoperability. Particularly, the layered and end-to-end structure, determined a separation between transport functions, which were delegated to network operators, and application functions delegated to the end-points.

Therefore, the original configuration of the Internet was "organically neutral" (Weinberger 2014) because data packet transportation was grounded on a best-effort delivery that did not apply special treatment based on the content of the data packets or the type of application. Besides this organic feature of the original end-to-end network design, it is important to stress that, until the early 2000s, traffic management practices were not granular enough to allow application-or-content-specific discrimination while the small size and great number of local networks composing the Internet made discriminatory traffic management ineffective. Network operators were simply transporting data packets in a non-discriminatory fashion, therefore acting—and being legally defined—as "mere conduits".[7] Since its creation, openness and neutrality have been endogenous features of the Internet architecture: open Internet standards facilitate the development of new technologies and the provision of new services, while the non-discriminatory best-effort delivery of data-packets strengthens the free-flow of information and lowers barriers to entering the market of innovation. Conspicuously, such open and non-discriminatory structure empowers end-users allowing them to access and share innovation without interference, being able to freely "seek, receive and impart information and ideas of all kinds, regardless of frontiers" (ICCPR, art 19). It is therefore this endogenously neutral structure that enables end-users to be active participants to the Internet, capable of independently deciding how to use the network, by choosing—or even creating—any kind of applications, services and content, and by connecting any kind of device (Belli and van Bergen 2013).

However, as computer scientists know, technical change is continuous in the information technology industry and the principle of "constant change" is probably the only principle of the Internet able to survive indefinitely (Carpenter 1996). Indeed, over the past 20 years, the Internet ecosystem has been visibly changing. On the one hand, traditional media and communications systems have been converging onto the Internet environment and, simultaneously, the end-to-end nature of the Internet has been exploited for various malicious uses, such as the diffusion of

---

[7] See Digital Millennium Copyright Act ("DMCA") 1998, section 512; Directive on Certain Legal Aspects of Information Society Services, in particular Electronic Commerce, in the Internal Market (2000/31) also known as "the E-Commerce Directive", art. 12.

spam, vira, malware or DDoS attacks. What was a quintessentially open and decentralised environment has been gradually centralising due to the emergence of an increasing number of intermediaries, as well as the vertical integration of network operators with service providers. The Internet has been smoothly evolving from an end-to-end structure to a trust-to-trust one, where average users delegate to intermediaries the task of exercising the intelligence of the network, in order to provide a trustworthy and reliable Internet environment (Clark and Blumenthal 2011). As a result, the end-to-end structure has been complemented with trust-to-trust mechanisms, where network operators and other intermediaries act as trusted agents providing network integrity and security.

The evolution towards centralisation has been characterised by massive investments—by network operators—in the development and standardisation of technologies allowing controlling and efficiently managing Internet traffic conveyed through their networks. Although efficient traffic management can be considered as a meritorious goal, it must be noted that the vertical integration of network operators with CAPs offers a relevant incentive to shape Internet traffic discriminating against applications, services and content that are provided by competitors (BEREC 2012; FCC 2015). To this latter extent, the net neutrality debate has been focusing on discriminatory Internet traffic management practices that may be implemented by network operators in order to favour vertically integrated service providers or disfavour competing ones (Wu 2003; Clark 2007; Marsden 2010). In this regard, it must be noted that the need for net neutrality policies is due to the very evolution of the Internet environment where vertical integration can motivate abusive behaviours while technical advancements make them possible. Indeed, the originally open Internet environment was able to foster innovation by providing end-users with a general-purpose decentralised network in which data flows were treated on a non-discriminatory basis by default. In such an environment, net neutrality policies were obviously not needed because Internet players did not have the possibility to discriminate against each other's, thus self-regulating themselves in healthy fashion. On the contrary, the abovementioned evolution of the Internet ecosystem allows network operators to put in place discriminatory traffic management practices and may offer concrete incentives to limit openness (FCC 2015), thus putting end-users rights and capability to innovate in jeopardy. As Sir Tim Berners Lee famously pointed out, "[t]here have been suggestions that we don't need legislation because we haven't had it. These are nonsense because in fact we have had net neutrality in the past it is only recently that real explicit threats have occurred" (Berners Lee 2006).

This is the basic line of argument that has motivated the development of net neutrality frameworks around the world over the past 10 years. As we will argue in the next section, national approaches vary and involve a more or less ample spectrum of stakeholders in their definition and implementation, thus providing for different levels of flexibility as regards their concrete application. However, these different frameworks share many common elements that might be considered as best-practices and consolidated within an open policy-blueprint.

21.3.2   Towards Exogenous Neutrality

As we have previously argued the original Internet structure has been designed to be open and foster a non-discriminatory transmission of Internet traffic. Such endogenous non-discriminatory structure has been instrumental to unleash the creativity of Internet users, allowing them to shape the very evolution of the Internet. This design choice has been considered as beneficial both from an economics perspective (Economides and Tag 2012) and from a human rights perspective (Belli and De Filippi 2013; Belli and van Bergen 2013).

Particularly from an economics perspective, net neutrality aims at avoiding that network operators impose two-sided pricing on the Internet, charging—or exempting from—a fee specific content, applications or services. Such practice may indeed distort the market and potentially preclude access to those content and applications lacking a contractual relation with the operator (Economides and Tag 2012). Indeed, although traffic discrimination for commercial reasons might be lucrative for operators, it would determine a shift from a decentralised general-purpose communication system to a centralised system where the provision and fruition of applications, services and content is influenced—and potentially subject to—by the existence of a contractual relationship between the CAP and the network operator. From a human rights perspective, the aforementioned reasoning is echoed by prominent jurisprudence, according to which discriminatory traffic management can be seen as an interference with freedom of expression, which "applies not only to the content of information but also to the means of dissemination since any restriction imposed to the [means] necessarily interfere with the right to receive and impart information" (ECtHR 1990, 2012).

Hence, net neutrality policies should be seen as an exogenous effort to re-equilibrate a system that risks losing its general-purpose, due to some market players' temptation to redefine its architecture as a "controlled distribution medium like TV and radio" (Banisar et al. 2003). To this extent, net neutrality supporters argue that the net neutrality policies and regulations are instrumental to maintain an open Internet architecture and reduce incentives to discriminate Internet traffic based on commercial reasons, thus preserving the economic, social, cultural, and political potential of the Internet (Wu 2006; van Schewick 2010). However, it must be noted that, as freedom of expression, net neutrality should not be considered as an absolute principle and, accordingly, several approaches have been emerging over the past decade in order to appropriately frame net neutrality and define exceptions. In this regard, different national approaches have been experimented, based on market-driven self-regulation, multistakeholder co-regulation, or hard-law in the form of both legislation and administrative regulation.[8]

---

[8] For an overview of the existing regulatory approaches to net neutrality, see https://www.thisisnet-neutrality.org/beta/#map_wrap.

Since the elaboration of the first net neutrality approach, promoted by the FCC in 2005 through a Policy Statement, the core elements of net neutrality have been crystallising and further elements have been emerging as a consequence of the traffic management evolutions and the potential risks that such evolutions present. As originally argued by the FCC, net neutrality is grounded on the premise that Internet users are entitled to access any lawful content of their choice; run legal applications and use legal services of their choice; connect their choice of legal devices that do not harm the network; and enjoy competition (FCC 2005). The subsequent evolution of the net neutrality debate has been the recognition of the need for a transparent definition of the characteristics of the Internet connection contracted by the user. Notably, the 2009 Norwegian Guidelines for Internet Neutrality (Nkom 2009) considered this latter element as one of the fundamental pillars of its co-regulatory framework and transparency obligations were also enshrined within the EU Telecom Package reform of 2009.[9]

It should be noted that the Norwegian approach has shown to be particularly efficient, not only by reason of its flexibility, based on the co-operation of market players and consumers associations with the telecommunications regulator, but also for being particularly clear and forward-looking. Indeed, the Norwegian approach has for the first time recognised the essence of net neutrality as non-discriminatory treatment of Internet traffic while pioneering the issue of specialised services. Particularly, since 2009 the Norwegian Guidelines recognised the importance of providing clear information regarding the provision of "other services on the same physical connection" of Internet access. Such information is indeed essential for regulators and consumers associations in order to verify that the provision of innovative IP-based services with enhanced features, such as guaranteed quality of service or security (the "other services" also referred to as specialised services or managed services), does not impair the provision of Internet access for which the user has paid.

Moreover, transparency requirements have also been considered as essential by the FCC, since its 2010 Open Internet Order and have been subsequently confirmed by the 2015 FCC regulation, according to which operators "shall publicly disclose accurate information regarding the network management practices, performance, and commercial terms of [...] broadband Internet access services sufficient for consumers to make informed choices" (FCC 2010, 2015). Importantly, the 2015 FCC framework specifies the non-discriminatory nature of the traffic management, explicitly banning blocking and throttling practices as well as paid prioritisation, thus building strong safeguards against broadband providers' temptation to favour or disfavour specific Internet traffic for commercial reasons (FCC 2015).

Since 2010, the non-discriminatory treatment of Internet traffic has also been explicitly endorsed by several national laws, in countries such as Chile,[10] the

---

[9] See Directive 2009/136/EC, recital 23.

[10] See Ley N° 20.453 Consagra el principio de neutralidad en la red para los consumidores y usuarios de Internet http://www.leychile.cl/Navegar?idNorma=1016570.

Netherlands,[11] Slovenia[12] and Brazil,[13] which converge in the definition of exceptions to the general rule of non-discriminatory treatment. Indeed, discriminatory traffic management is usually allowed in order to enforce court orders or legal provisions; to guarantee the integrity and security of the networks, for instance to prevent or limit DDoS attacks; and to manage congestion at peak times. Moreover, the provision of specialised services—such as IPTV and e-health—is are also considered as an exception to the general non-discriminatory treatment although few regulators have clearly defined the characteristics of such services so far. In many jurisdictions, legislators have simply not addressed the issue yet, but despite rumours that specialized services are a threat to net neutrality, it has been mostly seen as a valid exception to the neutrality rule, as long as clear guarantees against their potential negative impact on Internet access are defined, such as in the Norwegian case.

Lastly, due to the extensive use of Deep Packet Inspection in order to manage Internet traffic, typically for blocking or throttling purposes (BEREC 2012), concerns have been growing with regard to the interference of such technique with regard to the privacy of end-users' communications. In this regard the European Data protection Supervisor has been particularly vocal, affirming that "risks to privacy, data protection and communication confidentiality are very high due to the high intrusive feature of DPI, which scans the whole content of the IP packets to find out specific patterns against pre-defined criteria established in inspection policies."[14]

Due to the widespread nature of the net neutrality debate and the shared need for effective policy solutions, it seems desirable to develop a common principle basis that would allow elaborating practicable and coherent national approaches. In the next section we provide some concrete net neutrality policy, which may be exploited for the development of legally interoperable net neutrality frameworks.

21.4   Conclusion: How to Make Net Neutrality Legally Interoperable

It is important to note that different juridical systems, as well as diverse markets, may require different solutions in order to establish efficient and sustainable net-neutrality frameworks. However, as it has been stressed above, national frameworks converge towards the protection of some basic elements deemed as

---

[11] See art.7.4a, Dutch Telecommunications Act https://www.bof.nl/2011/06/27/translations-of-key-dutch-internet-freedom-provisions/#nnexp.

[12] See art. 203, Slovenian Electronic Communications Act http://www.uradni-list.si/_pdf/2012/Ur/u2012109.pdf#!/u2012109-pdf.

[13] See art. 9, Lei N° 12.965, de 23 de abril de 2014, also known as Marco Civil da Internet no Brasil. http://www.planalto.gov.br/ccivil_03/_ato2011-2014/2014/lei/l12965.htm.

[14] See EDPS (2012), p. 3. See also EDPS (2011, 2013).

essential in order to guarantee the full enjoyment of end-users' rights while preserving the original openness and non-discriminatory nature of the Internet. To this end, it seems possible to distil some essential elements from the existing net neutrality frameworks, in order to define a common principle base on which interested policymakers or market actors can develop compatible net neutrality frameworks. Indeed, while the Internet is usually seen as an interconnection of electronic networks, it is important to stress that the online environment also determines an interconnection of juridical systems that may benefit from shared policies.

As highlighted above, existing approaches to net neutrality converge as regards some core elements. First, the necessity to foster a non-discriminatory Internet traffic management, specifically banning blocking, throttling and paid prioritisation. To this extent, it should also be noted that exceptions to the general non-discriminatory treatment are shared amongst existing frameworks as well as the necessity to transparently state how traffic will be managed. Secondly, increasing concerns due to the abuse of intrusive filtering techniques have led policymakers and regulators to foster the compatibility of traffic management techniques to privacy norms and regulations. Lastly, due to the users' near-impossibility to identify the negative effects of traffic management policies' the existing national approaches converge in allowing regulators to monitor the compliance of all stakeholders to the agreed (self-/co-)regulatory framework.

It is important to highlight that international efforts aimed at making net neutrality protection legally interoperable already exist. Since 2010, the 47 Council of Europe (CoE) members have prominently declared their "commitment to the principle of network neutrality" arguing that net neutrality should be "explored further within a Council of Europe framework with a view to providing guidance to member states and/or to facilitating the elaboration of guidelines with and for private sector actors in order to define more precisely acceptable management measures and minimum quality-of-service requirements."[15] Since then, the CoE Internet Governance Strategy has foreseen the development of "human rights policy principles on network neutrality",[16] while the participant to the CoE Multi-Stakeholder Dialogue on Network Neutrality and Human Rights stressed the need for the elaboration of CoE guidelines on net neutrality that could be recommended to CoE members (CDMSI 2013). The elements necessary for the elaboration of such guidelines have been provided to the CoE by the Model Framework on Network Neutrality, elaborated by the IGF Dynamic Coalition on Network Neutrality and offered to the CoE to be used as a working document for the elaboration of a recommendation on network neutrality (Belli and van Bergen 2013; CDMSI 2015).

---

[15] See CoE 2010, para 9.

[16] See CoE 2012 para I.8.e.

The elaboration process of the Model Framework by the DCNN has been based on the participatory process utilised by the working groups of the Internet Engineering Task Force (IETF), pioneering the transposition of such process within the Internet Governance Forum. Rather than elaborating an open technical standard to be voluntarily adopted by market players, as the IETF working groups do (Bradner 1996; Hoffman 2012), the DCNN aimed at the elaboration of an open net neutrality regulatory-standard (Belli and van Bergen 2013; Belli et al. 2015). The Model Framework has become a global reference for net neutrality protection, openly supported by a variety of civil society organisations.[17] However, it must be noted that, at the IETF level, once the working groups elaborate their "draft standards", the IETF process requires the organisation of a final consultation period, defined "Last Call", during which the entire IETF community has the possibility to present final remarks on the draft before its validation. Such last-call process does not exist at the IGF level, where the DCNN and other dynamic coalitions operate, and for this reason the 2014 IGF Chair's Summary explicitly stressed the "need to develop a process that allowed the entire IGF community to weigh in and validate the findings of the [DCNN]."[18] Such process has been initiated via a Request for Comments on a Net Neutrality Policy Statement, divulgated on the DCNN mailing-list as well as on several other specialised mailing-lists, and aimed at producing a draft policy statement that could be "validated by the entire IGF community." The initial draft—based on the Model Framework—has been refined via four consultation periods, open to all interested stakeholders, whose comments have been consolidated in a text, subsequently published on the IGF official website for a further comment period involving the entire IGF community.[19]

Importantly, the Statement contains policy indications that might be exploited in order to develop any kind of net neutrality framework, be it regulatory, co-regulatory or self-regulatory. The protection of net neutrality through such frameworks should be considered as an exogenous effort to restore and preserve the endogenous openness and non-discriminatory nature of the original Internet architecture, thanks to which the Internet has generated incredible economic, social, cultural, and political changes. As such, the use of an open policy standard may be instrumental to foster compatibility of national rules. As technical standards aim at offering the most efficient solution to solve a common problem in an interoperable fashion, the statement aims at offering a useful principle-based approach that can clarify the net neutrality debate and be exploited to develop legally interoperable frameworks, on a voluntary basis.

---

[17] See the website of the Global Coalition on Net Neutrality, a worldwide group of civil society activist, using the Model Framework as a "model rules" for the protection of net neutrality https://www.thisisnetneutrality.org/.

[18] See IGF (2014), p. 10.

[19] All information regarding the development process of the Net Neutrality Policy Statement can be found at http://www.networkneutrality.info/events.html.

21.5   Annex: Policy Statement on Network Neutrality[20]

21.5.1   Preamble

a) The Internet should be open, secure and accessible to all people.
b) Network Neutrality plays an instrumental role in preserving Internet openness; fostering the enjoyment of Internet users' human rights; promoting competition and equality of opportunity; safeguarding the generative peer-to-peer nature of the Internet; and spreading the benefits of the Internet to all people.
c) Managing Internet traffic in a transparent and non-discriminatory manner compatible with the Network Neutrality Principle serves the interests of the public by preserving a level playing field with minimal barriers to entry and by providing equal opportunity for the invention and development of new applications, services and business models.
d) Competition among broadband networks, technologies and all players of the Internet ecosystem is essential to ensure the openness of the Internet.
e) All individuals and stakeholders should have the possibility to participate in the elaboration of any Network Neutrality regulatory instrument.

Network Neutrality regulatory instruments should, at a minimum, provide the following safeguards.

21.5.1.1   Network Neutrality Principle

Network Neutrality is the principle according to which Internet traffic is treated without unreasonable discrimination, restriction or interference regardless of its sender, recipient, type or content.

21.5.1.2   Reasonable Traffic Management

Internet service providers should act in accordance with the Network Neutrality Principle. Any deviation from this principle may be considered as reasonable traffic management as long as it is necessary and proportionate to:

a) preserve network security and integrity;
b) mitigate the effects of temporary and exceptional congestion, primarily by means of protocol-agnostic measures or, when these measures do not prove practicable, by means of protocol-specific measures;
c) prioritise emergency services in the case of unforeseeable circumstances or force majeure.

---

[20] This Policy Statement is part of an Input Document on Network Neutrality, to be presented at the IGF 2015 Main Session on Dynamic Coalitions' Outcomes. The elaboration of this draft has been coordinated by Luca Belli and Michał Andrzej Woźniak, consolidating the comments received through several rounds of public consultation, organised by the IGF Dynamic Coalition on Network Neutrality from April to the end of September 2015.

21.5.1.3   Law Enforcement

None of the foregoing should prevent Internet service providers from giving force to a court order or a legal provision in accordance with human rights norms and international law.

21.5.1.4   Transparent Traffic Management

Internet service providers should publish meaningful and transparent information on characteristics and conditions of the Internet access services they offer, the connection speeds that are to be provided, and their traffic management practices, notably with regard to how Internet access services may be affected by simultaneous usage of other services provided by the Internet service provider.

21.5.1.5   Privacy

All players in the Internet value chain, including governments, shall provide robust and meaningful privacy protections for individuals' data in accordance with human rights norms and international law. In particular, any techniques to inspect or analyse Internet traffic shall be in accordance with privacy and data protection obligations and subject to clear legal protections.

21.5.1.6   Implementation

The competent national authorities should promote independent testing of Internet traffic management practices, ensure the availability of Internet access and evaluate the compatibility of Internet access policies with the Network Neutrality Principle as well as with the respect of human rights norms and international law. National authorities should publicly report their findings. Complaint procedures to address network neutrality violations should be available and violations should attract appropriate fines. All individuals and stakeholders should have the possibility to contribute to the detection, reporting and correction of violations of the Network Neutrality Principle.

References

Ansip, A. (2015). *Making the EU work for people: roaming and the open internet.* https://ec.europa.eu/commission/2014-2019/ansip/blog/making-eu-work-people-roaming-and-open-internet_en

Banisar, D., et al. (2003, September). Silenced: an international report on censorship and control of the Internet. Report by Privacy International and the GreenNet Educational Trust Supported by the Open Society Institute. http://silenced-an-international-report.blogspot.com.br/

Béland, D., & Orenstein, M. A. (2009). *How do transnational policy actors matter?* Annual Meeting of the Research Committee 19 of the International Sociological Association. Montreal.

Belli, L. (2015). *De la gouvernance à la régulation de l'Internet*. Paris: Berger-Levrault.

Belli, L., & De Filippi, P. (Eds.). (2013). *The Value of Network Neutrality for the Internet of Tomorrow. Report of the Dynamic Coalition on Network Neutrality*. Presented at the 8th United Nations Internet Governance Forum. Bali 2013.

Belli, L., & De Filippi, P. (Eds.). (2014). *Network Neutrality: An Ongoing Regulatory Debate. 2nd Report of the Dynamic Coalition on Network Neutrality*. Presented at the 9th United Nations Internet Governance Forum. Istanbul 2014.

Belli, L., van Bergan, M., & Michael, W. (2015). *A discourse principle approach to net neutrality policymaking: a model framework and its application. Net neutrality compendium*. Springer.

Belli, L., & Van Bergen, M. (2013). *Protecting Human Rights through Network Neutrality: Furthering Internet Users' Interest, Modernising Human Rights and Safeguarding the Open Internet*. Council of Europe. CDMSI(2013)misc19E.

BEREC. (2012). *A view of traffic management and other practices resulting in restrictions to the open Internet in Europe*. Findings from BEREC's and the European Commission's joint investigation. BoR (12) 30.

Berners Lee, T. (2006). *Net neutrality: this is serious*. http://dig.csail.mit.edu/breadcrumbs/node/144

Bradner, S. (1996). *The Internet Standards Process* – Revision 3, Request for Comments: 2026.

Carpenter, B. (1996). *Architectural Principles of the Internet, Request for Comments:* 1958 retrieved from https://www.ietf.org/rfc/rfc1958.txt

CDMSI. (2013). *Council of Europe Multi-Stakeholder Dialogue on Network Neutrality and Human Rights Strasbourg*, Outcome Paper prepared by Luca Belli. CDMSI(2013) misc18E.

CDMSI. (2015). *Draft Recommendation CM/Rec(2014)___of the Committee of Ministers to member States on protecting and promoting the right to freedom of expression and the right to private life with regard to network neutrality*. CDMSI(2014)005Rev10.

Cerf, V. (1987). *The Catenet Model for Internetworking*, DARPA/IPTO, retrieved from https://www.rfc-editor.org/ien/ien48.txt

Clark, D. (2007). Network neutrality: Words of power and 800-pound gorillas. *International Journal of Communication, 1*, 701–770.

Clark, D., & Blumenthal, M. (2011). The end-to-end argument and application design: The role of trust. *Federal Communications Law Journal, 63*(2), Article 3.

CoE. (2010). *Declaration of the Committee of Ministers on network neutrality*. Retrieved from https://wcd.coe.int/ViewDoc.jsp?id=1678287

CoE. (2012). *Internet Governance, Council of Europe Strategy 2012–2015*, CM (2011)175 final. Retrieved from https://wcd.coe.int/ViewDoc.jsp?id=1919461

Daigle, L. (2014). *Permissionless Innovation – Openness, not Anarchy*. Available at: http://www.internetsociety.org/blog/tech-matters/2014/04/permissionless-innovation-openness-not-anarchy

Economides, N., & Tåg, J. (2012). Network neutrality on the Internet: A two-sided market analysis. *Information Economics and Policy, 24*, 91–104.

ECtHR. (1990). *Autronic AG v. Switzerland*, 22 May 1990. Application no. 12726/87. http://hudoc.echr.coe.int/eng?i=001-57630

ECtHR. (2012). *Ahmet Yıldırım v. Turkey*. Application no. 3111/10. http://hudoc.echr.coe.int/fre?i=001-115705

EDPS. (2011). *Opinion of the European Data Protection Supervisor on net neutrality, traffic management and the protection of privacy and personal data*.

EDPS. (2012). *EDPS Comments on DC Connect's Public Consultation on "Specific Aspects of Transparency, Traffic Management and Switching in an Open Internet"*.

EDPS. (2013, November 14). *Opinion of the Europe an Data Protection Supervisor on the Proposal for a Regulation of the Europe an Parliament and of the Council laying down measures concerning the Europe an single market for electronic communications and to achieve a Connected Continent*.

FCC. (2005). *Policy Statement*. 20 FCC Rcd 14986, 14987–88. Retrieved from https://apps.fcc.gov/edocs_public/attachmatch/FCC-05-151A1.pdf

FCC. (2010). *Preserving the Open Internet*, GN Docket No. 09-191, WC Docket No. 07-52, Report and Order, 25 FCC Rcd 17905, 17911.

FCC. (2015). *Report and Order on Remand, Declaratory Ruling, and Order on the Matter of Protecting and Promoting the Open Internet*. GN Docket No. 14-28

Gasser, U., & Palfrey, J. (2007). *When and how ICT interoperability drives innovation*. The Berkman Center for Internet & Society, Harvard University.

Hoffman, P. (Ed.). (2012). *The Tao of IETF: A Novice's Guide to the Internet Engineering Task Force*. IETF Trust. Retrieved from http://www.ietf.org/tao.html

IGF Chair. (2014). *Connecting Continents for Enhanced Multistakeholder Internet Governance*. IGF 2014 Chair's Summary. Istanbul, Turkey.

ITU. (2015). *Interoperability in the digital ecosystem*. GSR discussion paper. Retrieved from http://www.itu.int/en/ITU-D/Conferences/GSR/Documents/GSR2015/Discussion_papers_ and_Presentations/Discussionpaper_interoperability.pdf

Jayadevan, P. K. (2015). *1.5 lakh mails and counting: India lodges one of its biggest online protests over net neutrality*. The Economic Times retrieved from http://articles.economictimes.indiatimes. com/2015-04-13/news/61103013_1_neutrality-data-charges-internet-service-providers

Jörgens, H. (2003). *Governance by Diffusion – Implementing Global Norms Through Cross-National Imitation and Learning*. Environmental Policy Research Centre of FFU-report. 07-2003.

Marsden, C. (2010). *Net neutrality: Towards a co-regulatory solution*. London: Bloomsbury Academic.

Nkom. (24 February 2009) *Network neutrality: Guidelines for Internet neutrality*. Version 1.0. http:// eng.nkom.no/technical/internet/net-neutrality/net-neutrality/_attachment/9222?_ts=1409aa375c1.

Palfrey J. & Gasser U. (2012). *Interop: The Promise and Perils of Highly Interconnected Systems*. New York, NY: Basic Books..

Saltzer, J. H., Reed, D. P., & Clark, D. D. (1984). End-to-end arguments in system design. *ACM Transactions on Computer Systems*, (2). http://web.mit.edu/saltzer/www/publications/endto-end/endtoend.pdf

Schultz, T. (2005). *Réguler le commerce électronique par la résolution des litiges en ligne: Une approche critique*. Bruxelles: Bruynat.

Senato della Repubblica. (2014). Disegno di legge Costituzionale d'Iniziativa del senatore Campanella comunicatio alla Presidenza il 10 luglio 2014. Introduzione dell'articolo 34-bis della Costituzione, recante disposizioni volte al riconoscimento del diritto di accesso ad internet. XVII LEGISLATURA N. 1561.

Solum, L., & Chung, M. (2004). The layer principle: Internet architecture and the law. *Notre Dame Law Review, 79*.

Sub-Commission on the Promotion and Protection of Human Rights. (2003). *Commentary on the norms on the responsibilities of transnational corporations and other business enterprises with regard to human rights*. U.N. Doc. E/CN.4/Sub.2/2003/38/Rev.2.

Tréguer, F. (2012). *Interoperability case study. The European Union as an institutional design for legal interoperability*. Berkman Center Research Publication No. 2012-18. SSRN:http://ssrn. com/abstract=2148543

Van Schewick, B. (2010). *Internet architecture and innovation*. Cambridge, MA: MIT Press.

Weber, R. (2014). *Legal interoperability as a tool for combatting fragmentation*. Global Commission on Internet Governance, Paper Series n°4. https://www.cigionline.org/sites/ default/files/gcig_paper_no4.pdf

Weinberger, D. (2014). *Organic net neutrality*. https://ting.com/blog/organic-net-neutrality/

White House. (2015). *The path to a free and open internet*. https://www.whitehouse.gov/ net-neutrality

Wu, T. (2006). *Testimony before the House Committee on the Judiciary*. Telecom & Antitrust Task Force on Network Neutrality: Competition, Innovation, and Nondiscriminatory Access. 109th Congress, 2nd Session.

Wu, T. (2003). Network neutrality, broadband discrimination. *Journal of Telecommunications and High Technology Law, 2*, 141–172.

Postface

Louis Pouzin

This Network Neutrality (NN) compendium covers a cornucopia of concepts and debates for further enrichment and understanding of the intrinsic complexity of the subject. There is no point in revisiting the contents, as thorough explanations have been produced by the editors.

Some aspects that were mentioned discreetly by some authors would merit longer developments, perhaps in a future compendium. Technically they do not create neutrality, but they facilitate the full enjoyment of users' rights and contribute to user's satisfaction and understanding. Below I highlight some essential points that should be considered for future debates.

- Users' behaviour and wishes

- It's customary to envision a handful of typical user classes, either in market surveys or in design blueprints. Actually users are distinct individuals with a large spectrum of feelings. They should be offered simple ways of making choices, observations and critiques, with concrete remedies to obtain a timely redress when they are negatively impacted by operators' traffic management practices or other service dysfunctions.
- Tariffs
- It's an essential component of the service. Communications cost money, and users need to correlate what they are charged with the service level. When appropriate, various tariffs could be offered for online tuning of the service (*e.g.* response time or bandwidth).
- Net diversity
- Internet is transnational, but not homogeneous. Crossing several operators networks applying different neutrality policies may not match user's expectations.
- Fragmentation
- Often used as a dirty word. Nonetheless internet is definitely fragmented in a multiplicity of rather incompatible services, Apple, Facebook, Google, etc. Internet fragmentation can be a consequence of conflicting national sovereignties but can also be a consequence of cyber-frontiers imposed by private actors.

© Springer International Publishing Switzerland 2016   299
L. Belli, P. De Filippi (eds.), *Net Neutrality Compendium*,
DOI 10.1007/978-3-319-26425-7

- Privacy, Security
- Lower layers (TCP) are insecure. Thus, security (if any) is implemented in upper layers in various ways. Security procedures should be non-discriminatory and explicitly documented.
- Mass Surveillance

- Introduced by the USA, and now being deployed by many governments. Trust is gone, with little prospect for returning soon. Intrusive traffic management techniques and stealthy collection of private data are common practice Encryption will be used, hopefully with moderation. Users will need training, and access to information will become more cumbersome.

Quite clearly the internet architecture as it stands today is showing its age. Created in the 70s as an experimental network, it still is. Overpatched and exceedingly complex, hence vulnerable, it is no longer a promising platform for developing long lasting innovations.

A more promising avenue is RINA (Recursive Inter-Network Architecture). http://irati.eu/i2cat-foundation/